Innovation Equity

Innovation Equity

Assessing and Managing the Monetary Value of New Products and Services

ELIE OFEK, EITAN MULLER, AND BARAK LIBAI

THE UNIVERSITY OF CHICAGO PRESS   CHICAGO AND LONDON

The University of Chicago Press, Chicago 60637
The University of Chicago Press, Ltd., London
© 2016 by The University of Chicago
All rights reserved. Published 2016.
Printed in the United States of America

25 24 23 22 21 20 19 18 17 16   1 2 3 4 5

ISBN-13: 978-0-226-61829-6 (cloth)
ISBN-13: 978-0-226-39414-5 (e-book)
DOI: 10.7208/chicago/9780226394145.001.0001

Library of Congress Cataloging-in-Publication Data

Names: Ofek, Elie, author. | Muller, Eitan, author. | Libai, Barak, author.
Title: Innovation equity : assessing and managing the monetary value of new
    products and services / Elie Ofek, Eitan Muller, and Barak Libai.
Description: Chicago : The University of Chicago Press, 2016. |
    Includes bibliographical references and index.
Identifiers: LCCN 2016009804 | ISBN 9780226618296 (cloth : alk. paper) |
    ISBN 9780226394145 (e-book)
Subjects: LCSH: Diffusion of innovations. | Diffusion of innovations—
    Econometric models. | Technological innovations—Economic aspects. |
    New products—Marketing. | New products—Prices.
Classification: LCC HC79.T4 O34 2016 | DDC 338/.064—dc23 LC record available at
    http://lccn.loc.gov/2016009804

♾ This paper meets the requirements of ANSI/NISO Z39.48-1992 (Permanence of Paper).

Contents

Introduction

There is something inherently captivating about innovations, something almost magical. When people hear about an innovation for the first time or see a demo of an early prototype, their ears perk up and their eyes open wide. People are often mesmerized by new products that use technologies seemingly taken straight from a sci-fi movie and are amazed by gadgets that reduce complex tasks to the push of a button or the stroke of a finger. Innovations hold the promise of connecting the surreal—what you never thought or dreamed possible—to real, actual products and services that can do things better or in new and more satisfying ways than anything preceding them.

Consider the following innovative concepts: driverless cars that can navigate traffic and zoom down highways by themselves while you sit back and relax; eyewear that can act as mobile computing devices, allowing you to surf the web, take pictures, and send messages while viewing everything on a tiny screen located an inch from your eye; a transportation system that can suck passengers at one end and relay them to their destination on the other end in a tenth of the time it would take the fastest train currently available (the "Hyperloop," as dubbed in the media); unmanned aerial vehicles, or drones, as they are often referred to, that deliver goods (even pizzas) ordered online to your home or office; sleek watches that not only act as advanced smartphones but can also measure vital signs, alert you of any impending health problem, and relay the information to health care providers for analysis; and the list goes on and on and on. These "outlandish" concepts are not figments of our imagination. All of them are, in fact, at some stage of development: early ideation, advanced testing, or nearing broad commercial launch. By the time you read this, some of them may in fact already be available at a brick-and-mortar store, e-store, or transportation depot near you. And, we should add, all of them are backed by for-profit companies.

While each of these innovations has that "shock and awe" factor that causes consumers to marvel at their very notion, all too quickly skepticism (or "realism," depending on how you choose to frame the critique) starts creeping in. It is not that difficult to shoot down an innovative concept, to come up with reasons a novel idea will never have strong enough legs to walk far beyond the R&D lab and fail to make strides with mainstream customers. And if you can't come up with these reasons yourself, rest assured that a host of detractors and naysayers will gladly lend you a hand. Innovations are therefore not only captivating but also typically polarizing.

Seeing Eye to Eye on the Value of Smart Glasses (And Time Will Tell the Commercial Fate of Smart Watches)

The aforementioned innovative concepts are no exception to the captivating-yet-polarizing rule of divergent opinions on the potential success of innovations. Take smart eyewear, for example: several notable companies, such as Sony, have initiated development efforts in this nascent area, yet Google has probably been the one that has garnered the most attention thus far with its Google Glass device. The first versions of the product featured a dedicated display smaller than a button, but the proximity to your eye provided the equivalent of looking at a twenty-five-inch monitor eight feet away. The Internet-connected Glass ran the Android operating system, and the combination of it being a head-mounted display and having voice recognition capabilities (you would say "OK Glass" to activate and "Take a picture" to snap a photo, for example) resulted in access to digital content and the ability to relay commands *hands free*. This quickly caught the eye (no pun intended) of many people looking for "the next big thing" after smartphones and tablets. *Time* hailed Google Glass as one of the best inventions of the year at the end of 2012, and in early 2013, *Fortune* suggested that "it's poised to possibly revolutionize computing." A prominent tech blogger, who amassed more than four million followers on Google+, went on record as saying, "I think this will be a product that will stand up for decades as the launch of a new genre."

But not everyone was kind to Glass. As soon as early prototypes became available, *Businessweek* cited critics who called it a "Segway for your face" (in reference to the personal transporter vehicle introduced with much fanfare in 2001 only to receive tepid, if not downright derogatory, subsequent reactions, with its owners ridiculed as they rode them; more on the Segway later in the book). The editor in chief of technology and entertainment site *The Verge* also questioned Glass's appeal, asking, "Who would want to wear this thing in public?" And, as if to add fuel to the skepticism fire, Jack Dorsey, cofounder of Twitter and recent founder of Square, said, "I think it's an amazing technology, but I just can't imagine my mom wearing them." Furthermore, many consumers and advocacy groups voiced serious concerns, suggesting that the device would violate basic privacies, such as being video recorded or photographed by someone wearing it without giving consent. Others raised safety fears, as a user would possibly be distracted when using the device, causing many to demand that drivers be banned from wearing them while operating a motor vehicle. In light of these issues, one individual, who was responding to a *New York Times* blog about Glass, emphatically commented, "I will never speak to anyone wearing these devices"; another wrote, "I predict Google Glass users upload a lot of close-up shots of incoming fists." These responses caused the blog's author, Nick Bilton, to riff off the old adage on innovation ("build it and they will come") to conclude his piece on Google Glass with the question "If they build it, will people wear it?"

Internal work on Glass didn't take place at Google's main campus in Mountain View, California. Rather, the initiative was housed at the company's newly established Google X facility, a research lab for what some might consider "moonshots," or highly risky projects based on unconventional ideas. Although Google does not release R&D figures for specific projects, its total R&D budget rose 79 percent to $6.8 billion in the two years following X's establishment, with Glass assumed to make up a nontrivial slice of that increase. But internal progress on Glass was only part of the story: instead of keeping all efforts under wraps until a final, polished, consumer-ready device was completed, Google decided to "test the waters" externally well ahead of a formal launch. In particular, after generating considerable buzz by unveiling the concept at prominent electronics and fashion shows (with skydivers and head-turning models sporting Glasses), the company made a preliminary version available to a select set of individuals, which it labeled "Explorers." The program's promotional material stated that Google was looking for "bold, creative individuals." The idea was to attract app developers, tech trendsetters, and prominent media figures and get them to wear and think of clever uses for Glass. Aside from more quickly building the "Glass ecosystem," this out-in-the-open approach was intended to provide the company first-hand market feedback to better understand how to adapt and modify the device. The approach would allow the company to cocreate the Glass experience with members of the Explorer community. Moreover, given the distinctive design of the Glass Explorer version (there was no way to mistake these gadgets for regular glasses), perhaps another reason for the move was to help evangelize the concept and prepare the market for when the device was ready for widespread public use. Being selected to "explore" didn't come with any freebies, mind you, as Explorers had to pay $1,500 to get their hands on Google's augmented reality prototype. About ten thousand individuals were screened, and many of them generated interesting ideas and applications. For example, one developer created a program he called "Winky," which let a Glass user take a photo with the wink of an eye. Now you have to admit, that sounds a little like magic!

The mantra of "fail fast to succeed sooner" appeared to ring true for Google's top brass, as the Explorer program was expanded in late 2013, and in May 2014 anyone willing to pay the steep $1,500 price tag could purchase a pair. But this wider release of what was clearly a beta version proved a bit too much: the shortcomings of a limited battery life, bugs (the system occasionally turned on or crashed unexpectedly), the lack of a "killer app," an awkward design, and the general public's reaction to people wearing smart eyewear resulted in a lot of negative sentiment. And the intense media attention that surrounded Glass since its unveiling but the lack of a clear positioning ("Is this an everyday smart device for the masses or a technology tool for professional applications?") wasn't helping. In early 2015, Google abruptly announced that it was ending its Explorer program and that January 19 would mark the last day the Glass prototype would be available for purchase.

But this was not the end of the story. Google appeared committed to Glass's future, declaring that what it had learned from the "exploration" phase prepared the project to be taken out of the X lab. The company would now put a dedicated team behind it, overseen by several technology heavyweights, including Tony Fadell, a former Apple exec credited with being the "father of the iPod" and founder of Nest Labs (which was acquired by Google). In contrast to the earlier out-in-the-open approach, development of future Glass versions would take place out of the public eye, and until the relaunch day, there would be "no peeking."

Assume for a moment that you are Google CEO and cofounder Larry

Page, and you've just given the green light to continue Glass's development. How do you assess how much a smart eyewear device is worth to the company going forward? After the debacle of the Explorer program, can you give shareholders a sense of the market opportunity here? Or if you were Sergei Brin, Google cofounder and director of its Special Projects Group,[1] would you feel confident that the yet-to-materialize financial returns on a Glass-type gadget will justify the resources now being committed?

Alternatively, say you're an occasional stock market investor intrigued by all the hoopla surrounding the emerging smartwear (or "wearables") industry. You learn that Sony is launching its own head-mounted device, currently named SmartEyeglass, initially to developers and at a relatively low price (about $860). You are also aware that other players are betting on wrist-mounted smart devices; indeed, the Apple Watch debuted just a few months after the Glass Explorer Edition had gone into stealth development mode. While you realize that the launch of a new consumer-oriented version of Glass is at least a year away, amid all the excitement accompanying wearables, you wonder if it will be a game changer for the company and if this is a good time to buy Google stock. Or you might be a partner at a venture capital firm willing to fund apps like Winky that take advantage of the "on-your-face" technologies coming out. How should you approach the many pitches you hear from software entrepreneurs? How much funding is wise to dole out?

For all these stakeholders—the Google executives, the private stock traders, and the institutional investors—an idea of the expected commercial performance of Glass would help. And rest assured that there is no shortage of predictions on the matter. Even as the prototype was being sold at top dollar, a host of analysts and technology "experts" were quick to look into their crystal balls and issue detailed forecasts. Indeed, the polarization in attitudes toward Glass was mirrored in these financial predictions that were, for lack of a better term, all over the place. The first thing these sources tended to disagree upon was the number of units that would sell each year. Several market intelligence firms issued forecasts that differed by a factor of nearly tenfold (940 percent, to be precise), with predictions ranging from only 1 million units sold roughly one year after the launch of a final version to 9.4 million total units in the same time frame.

Complicating matters, many of the forecasts had an "it depends" rider: *if* the price is low enough, *if* there are "killer apps," *if* the battery life is long enough, *if* there is a visible-to-others indicator that you are recording them—and the list of contingencies went on and on. If all these conditions are met, then the "it depends" analysts leaned toward a high estimate of unit sales; otherwise, they scaled back their assessments. For example, one firm predicted more than 21 million units of Glass sold in the third year postlaunch, up from 10.6 million units predicted to sell the year before, *if* many of the above conditions were resolved favorably. Otherwise, all bets are off, and its forecast took a nosedive.

A related issue is assessing the *monetary* opportunity at hand. One could simply multiply the unit forecast that the market intelligence analysts came up with by their best guess of the price Glass would be sold at, generating estimates that ranged from $200 million to more than $2 billion annually by the second year postlaunch. Indeed, many analysts sized the commercial opportunity of Glass this way. Others went a step beyond the device sales figures and predicted that Google would be able to generate considerable money from Glass in other ways, such as through advertising and apps, leading to estimates that the innovation could generate more than $3 billion a year.

Moreover, it is far from clear how to factor competition into these forecasts. For instance, does Apple Watch help expand the wearable category and thus benefit Glass or will this greatly anticipated smart timepiece result in a fight for the same potential customers and thus be a detriment to Google's ambitions? Or perhaps these innovations will behave like two distinct categories with very little interdependence. Mind you, on the eve of Watch's launch, analysts didn't disappoint in supplying views that were highly divergent: some predicted 2015 sales of eight million units while others suggested upwards of forty million. As you can imagine, the optimists—those assuming consumers would be wowed by Apple Watch's look, convenience, and advanced vibration technology—leaned toward the higher estimates, while those questioning the need for such a device to be constantly on one's wrist, critiquing the lack of useful functionality, bemoaning the limited screen size and interface, and balking at the price (the base model Watch retails at $349) advocated the lower forecast estimates.

Confusing? Well, some might argue that such wild variability in opinions and predictions is the hallmark of truly radical innovations. And that might be exactly what the Google scientists and Apple designers want to hear. But this certainly does not make the lives of company executives or investors any easier. What should they make of these forecasts? How should they size the commercial opportunity of an innovation? As Jack Dorsey bluntly put it, "What is the value of Glass?"

Turns Out We Know Something . . .

It is easy to forget that the vast majority of products and services we regularly use today were once considered *innovations*. Antibiotics, the washing machine, the personal computer, cable television, and even the Internet all enjoyed a period of "innovation grace" before being considered "old news" and classified as everyday products.

You might be wondering how that fairly obvious fact can help us think about the value of Glass to Google or Watch to Apple. That is where academia kicks in. The elaborate efforts of researchers from a host of fields to analyze the ins and outs of hundreds upon hundreds of past innovations have produced a body of knowledge on how new products and services tend to "behave" over time in the marketplace, particularly in terms of customer adoption patterns. How widely an innovation penetrates a market and how quickly it reaches that penetration level have been the focus of intense academic scrutiny. This research has produced illuminating frameworks and models that capture the primary forces governing the trajectory of innovation adoption, from the launch phase to the maturity ("everyday") phase to the phase where the innovation sees a decline in users who move on to newer things.

Alongside these efforts, scholars, particularly in marketing, have devoted a fair bit of attention to understanding how firms manage their customer base. They have come to recognize that this task is like orchestrating a "relationship concerto" that has three distinct "movements": first, the firm seeks to attract prospective individuals to become part of its customer base; second, it has to keep these customers satisfied so that the relationship is mutually beneficial—a healthy give and take; and lastly, it needs to prevent customers from leaving, either because they don't find the firm's offering worth their time and money or because a competitor's conducting baton has wooed them away. Firms effective at customer relationship management (CRM), so research has shown, are able to orchestrate these three movements profitably and on a sustained basis. This body of work has led to the formulation of highly useful models that view customers as long-term financial assets critical to the firm's well-being and prosperity.

Yet what we have only recently come to realize is that something quite powerful emerges when you bring these two avenues of research, on innovation adoption and customer relationship management, together under one roof. By capturing how many adopters an innovation can expect to garner over time, you're effectively getting a handle on the number of customers that will join the ranks of the firm that launches the innovation. Combining that with an analysis of how much all of these adopters are worth to the firm—in other words, how much of a financial asset they represent—in effect gives you the long-term monetary value of the innovation. With that, you have a framework for assessing the anticipated revenue growth and profitability evolution of a new product or a novel service, a way for gauging what we call *innovation equity*. The linking of the two research avenues is a match made in heaven, one that gives you a decent shot at providing an answer to questions like "What is the long-term value of smart watches?" or "What are the future profit implications of pricing smart eyewear at $500 versus $1,500 a pair?"

Why This Book?

As scholars specializing in the field of innovation and firm strategy, we (the three authors) have found it fascinating to study how some new products and services have transformed industries, created novel categories, and profoundly changed consumer behavior. It has been equally intriguing to us to analyze the travails and struggles that other innovations experienced as they strived to gain traction in the marketplace (often with little success).

We further have had the privilege to conduct research on and work closely with companies attempting to commercialize innovations. This allowed us to experience firsthand their need for more effective ways to assess the dynamics of new product performance in the marketplace. Increasingly, we came to realize that all stakeholders involved—from managers, to investors, to analysts, to public policy makers, and even to consumers—want to know not just how much adoption to expect but also how much of a return on investment to expect from innovations. In essence, they wanted guidance on how to put a dollar value on future earnings from an innovation.

But in the absence of a grounded and systematic approach for forecasting the profitability trajectory of new creations, what we frequently witnessed was that these stakeholders often resorted to simplistic, potentially misleading heuristics to perform this task. It therefore came as no surprise to us that survey after survey found senior managers—in industries ranging from consumer electronics to pharmaceuticals to telecommunications to enterprise software—expressing dissatisfaction when comparing their expected financial returns from R&D investments, based on the prelaunch forecasts they were given, with the actual returns they achieved on their innovations several years postlaunch. And with the National Science Foundation indicating that R&D spending globally has practically doubled over the past decade, growing at a faster pace than global gross domestic product (GDP), such dissatisfaction is truly unfortunate. These managers deserve better.

We have also taught a number of courses over the years at leading universities on the link between marketing and innovation and found business students hungry for compelling frameworks to understand and analyze the commercial performance of new products and services. These students struggle with how to connect the microlevel setting of a consumer considering whether to adopt an innovation, which they themselves have repeatedly faced, and the macrolevel penetration an innovation achieves in the general population over time. They crave ways that would enable them to assess how various business decisions and marketing actions can affect innovations' growth rates and long-term profitability. They welcome any light that can be cast on the topic of innovation monetization.

The immersion in scholarly research on the one hand and the multiple encounters with pedagogy and practice on the other hand have led us to the realization that there is a gap, and a wide one at that, between what academics *know* and what nonacademics—managers, analysts, students, and others involved with innovation initiatives—*want to know* about valuing the adoption trajectory of new products and services. Our goal in writing this book is to bridge this gap.

A key reason for this gap is that the body of knowledge that academic research has produced has largely remained within the confines of the proverbial ivory towers, disseminated mainly in academic outlets. Certainly, scholars have consulted on occasion and used parts of the accumulated wisdom in their applied recommendations, and certainly, a number of instructors have taught portions of the material to students in various formats and courses. But no one has written a book that, in one place, showcases the concepts, frameworks, and models in a way that is accessible to nonacademics. No one has assembled, for a business-minded audience, an intuitive view of the findings that connects the rich academic literature on innovation diffusion and that on customer relationship management. No one has provided a collection of concrete tools that allow making use of the findings in practical situations. Our book is in many ways an attempt to fill this void, an attempt to empower the innovation stakeholders out there: folks like the company executives and the private and institutional investors keen on assessing the commercial fate of innovations.

What's in This Book?

The book contains nine chapters that bridge the academic-practice divide on how to think about and obtain meaningful assessments of the commercial potential of innovations. Like a sound construction plan, the material is organized in a manner that first lays down the necessary foundations—in this case how innovations are expected to be adopted by the target population (the "innovation diffusion" model) and how the financial interaction between a firm and its customers evolves over time (the "customer lifetime value" model). After elucidating the primary forces relevant for understanding each of these models separately, the book provides a blueprint for assembling the main structure by showing how to combine these two bodies of knowledge into a unified framework for monetarily valuing new products and services—the quantity that we call *innovation equity*. All of this is captured in chapters 1 and 2.

The book proceeds from there to offer important embellishments to the main structure. In particular, it outlines how several additional factors, which have been shown to critically matter for the long-term commercial performance of new products and services, can be incorporated into the innovation equity framework. This includes the following topics:

- Marketing actions, such as advertising, pricing, seeding of product samples, and customer-to-customer referrals, that are intended to drive innovation adoption and generate more value from customers. These actions are examined in terms of their impact on customer acquisition, development, and retention (chapter 3).
- Differences among customer segments in their dispositions toward innovations and the implications of such heterogeneity for diffusion speed and customer management. Key phenomena that emerge as a result of these differences between customer segments, such as the "saddle" (a sales pattern that is first increasing, then decreasing, and then increasing again as time goes by) and the "chasm" (a near halt in sales because early adopters do not have much influence on mainstream adopters), are covered (chapters 4 and 5).
- Competition among firms whereby each launches its own version of the innovation in the same market space. Such competition can result in intricate diffusion effects—as the customers of one version can lead to future adoptions of either the very same version (a "within-brand" effect) or a rival's version (a "cross-brand" effect). The ramifications of competition for customer acquisi-

tion and attrition rates, and consequently for the market shares and profit dynamics of innovations, are addressed (chapter 6).

- Successive generations of new products and services within the same category, which can exhibit intricate demand interdependencies. In particular, while a next-generation innovation may expand the overall market potential for the category, it might also induce cannibalization because some consumers who would have bought the older generation in due course leapfrog to the new one. An approach for taking into account these intergenerational effects and their implications for adoption patterns is presented (chapter 7).

- Variations between countries in the market potential and pace of innovation diffusion as well as dissimilarities in the long-term profitability of customers in differing global locations. In this context, it is also important to consider cross-country effects, whereby the adoption pace in one country is affected by the timing and pace of adoption in another country. These issues, along with pointers to promising new sources of data on international adoption patterns, are discussed (chapter 8).

Each chapter develops a basic understanding and high-level set of intuitions on the topics it covers, with emphasis on explaining their relevance to the innovation equity framework. The treatment of these topics goes a step further by providing details on how to take the high-level intuitions and put them to use in actual business settings. As you will see, these how-to scenarios are presented in way that is pertinent both for those readers who wish to perform the analyses themselves and for those who primarily desire to glean strategic direction from what they can reveal. Examples from a variety of industries are sprinkled throughout to help bring the concepts and tools presented to life. Some examples, such as satellite radio and home video games, appear in several chapters to show how the various embellishments to the main framework can be meaningfully applied. At the end of each chapter, we provide key takeaways that highlight the central messages communicated.

The book concludes by circling back to review the themes covered in the first eight chapters with an eye toward highlighting aspects not previously addressed and providing implementation tips and caveats; a set of tangibles, including a summary checklist, for creating or critically reviewing innovation equity assessments in practice is presented. The emphasis in the closing chapter (chapter 9) is on conveying a concrete sense of how to take the material in the book and adapt it to various industry contexts.

We point out now (and will remind you when appropriate along the way) that the book's appendix contains key mathematical expressions that formalize the models and concepts described in the various chapters for interested readers. And in a companion website to this book (www .InnovationEquityBook.com), you'll find user-friendly spreadsheets that provide access to all the major analyses presented and offer several easy-to-use templates that you can configure to produce innovation equity assessments of your own.

When all is said and done, the down-to-earth manner in which we explain the state-of-the-art thinking on how innovations diffuse and how customers can be evaluated for profits, along with the numerous examples and toolkits to actually implement the ideas, should leave you empowered when it comes to placing a dollar value on an innovation.

*   *   *

It is difficult to escape the fact that "innovation" has been a hot topic for several years now—and not by chance or by virtue of sheer intellectual curiosity (though of course there is some of that too). Innovation has been touted as affecting the fames and fortunes of individuals, as making or breaking companies, and as an engine of growth for entire economies. Being able to understand and quantify the value that innovations can deliver is crucial for effectively managing these micro- and macrolevel processes. So whether you are a senior executive, a midlevel manager, a venture capitalist, a policy maker, a business student, or simply an avid consumer of novel technologies, this book will offer you new ways of thinking about innovation. We trust it will serve you as a source of insights, help frame your opinion, and give you pragmatic tools to responsibly drive the value of innovations forward. For us, consolidating what we have witnessed and learned through the years and putting the pieces together in one accessible place has been a remarkably rewarding journey. We believe that you will have a similar experience as you read the book. Enjoy the ride!

CHAPTER ONE

The Basic Diffusion Pattern of an Innovation

I wish developing great products was as easy as writing a check.—Steve Jobs

Imagine that you've just gotten back to your office from a long management meeting. The vice president of R&D took center stage, presenting a cool new technology that his scientists and engineers have been working on for the past two years. He informed the group that new products based on the breakthrough technology could be developed in a reasonable time frame—perhaps even a year from now—and asked for a green light and for green dollars to forge ahead with his development plans. The CEO seemed enthusiastic, exclaiming at one point that this may be the answer to the company's prayers. She is ready to "write the check" to fund development, yet being a prudent corporate leader, she has asked you, the vice president of marketing, to assess whether this new technology will succeed in the marketplace and to determine how long it would take to recoup the investment that the vice president of R&D asked for. Not one to shy away from a challenge, and quite impressed with the technology yourself, you promise a quick yet thorough analysis.

Eager to get started on the CEO's forecasting challenge, a few minutes later, you sit down at your desk, take another quick look at the demo video presented at the meeting, and go over your notes. And then it hits you: "If we launch an innovation based on this technology, is there any meaningful way, not just some wild speculation or overly naïve guess, to assess the return on investment (ROI) years down the road?" You're not quite sure where to begin. You might even start to panic a little as your report is due in less than two weeks.

Once you regain your composure, you recognize that you might want to break down the task in front of you into its fundamental components. To evaluate how well the proposed innovation will do in the marketplace—whether it's worth it for the CEO to write the check—it's useful to begin by studying how markets *generally* react to innovations and after that is understood, examining how *your* company's innovation might fare among consumers given its particular characteristics.

Innovations and the Marketplace: A Dynamic Relationship

One way to think about the market for an innovation is as the *collection of individuals who would consider adopting it at some point in time*. This simple definition entails several important notions relevant to constructing an effective commercial forecast for an innovation. First is the issue of *who* the individuals are that might find the innovation appealing; let's call that the *set of potential adopters*. Second is the issue of *when* an individual from the potential set will eventually adopt the innovation. Third is the issue of *why* an individual from that set would consider adopting it. As we will shortly see, answering these three questions—*who, when, why*—will create the foundation for constructing a powerful model that a company can use to project how demand for its innovations will likely evolve over time. This will help advance us in our quest to assess the commercial opportunity and expected ROI that an innovation presents.

It is instructive to begin by answering the last question—*why* a person adopts something new—and understand what causes individuals to bother with an innovation when they could simply stick to whatever it is they were doing before. Many sociologists, psychologists, marketing academics, behavioral economists, and practitioners have studied how individuals think about and react to novel concepts (a new product, a new service, a new social norm, an unfamiliar idea, etc.) and how they decide whether those concepts are worth embracing. In many respects, the findings from numerous studies conducted on the topic point to the fact that it is often more revealing to ask the question in the reverse—that is, "Why would a person *not* adopt something new?" It turns out that uncovering why people show a lack of interest in certain innovations or deem them unworthy of their time and money is critical to characterizing the manner in which we should expect the demand for an innovation to evolve over time. We examine these "barriers to adoption," as they are often called, and draw upon a classification schema proposed by esteemed innovation scholar Everett M. Rogers. The picture that will emerge from this examination is that of two main routes or forces that can lead to adoption.

Why do I need it? What's the relative advantage? Obviously, if the "new thing" under consideration is not perceived as delivering enough benefit or improvement over existing products and services to justify its cost, then consumers tend to pause, delay purchase, and even dismiss the innovation altogether. Take the Segway—or as it was officially called, the Segway Personal Transporter—as an example. This two-wheeled, self-balancing electric vehicle was introduced with much fanfare in December 2001 on the ABC News program *Good Morning America* by its inventor, Dean Kamen. Many notable industry pundits, including Steve Jobs and prominent venture capitalists, touted the Segway as a breakthrough that was "bigger than the Internet, and more important than the PC." They predicted that its rapid adoption would force the redesign of cities and make Segway Inc. the fastest company in history to reach $1 billion in sales. Obviously, these predictions did not come true, particularly the ones about how quickly it would be embraced by ordinary consumers. While this innovation is still with us, and its adoption figures are still on the rise (reports indicate that more than one hundred thousand Segways had been sold by the end of 2011, which marked the product's tenth anniversary), it was by no means an "instant success story." Although mainstream consumers marveled over the technology and were intrigued by its antics, very few rushed out to buy one.

What went wrong with the predictions? Given the widespread publicity that the Segway and its inventor enjoyed, including numerous appearances on television and radio and extensive print and online coverage, most consumers had heard about this new means of transportation and had seen video footage of it. So awareness per se does not seem to be the culprit. What is, then? One clue for why the pundits were so off target lies in how the innovation was described to consumers. When introducing the Segway, Kamen declared that it "will be to the car what the car was to the horse and buggy." Kamen, like many others at the time of the launch, seemed to believe that consumers would think of the Segway as a better and more useful means of transportation than the car. On a purely conceptual level, Kamen was right: consumers do tend to evaluate products and services (and just about anything else, for that matter) *relative* to something they are familiar with, which they can benchmark against. And this is particularly true in situations that involve considerable uncertainty for them, as is undoubtedly the case with most radical innovations. But with the Segway, a direct comparison to the car actually revealed many *relative disadvantages* for the average consumer: Kamen's Personal Transporter could be mounted by only one person at a time and delivered a top speed of merely twelve miles per hour and a riding range of ten miles between charges. These kinds of specs surely pale in comparison to even the cheapest of compact cars, which typically have room for four or five people, reach speeds of well above sixty miles per hour, deliver a range of several hundreds of miles between refueling stops, and in most cases have cargo space. Therefore, it was not clear to average consumers how they could possibly consider replacing their cars with the Segway. And with no compelling reason to add the Segway to the existing set of vehicles they owned (the national US average being about two vehicles per household), $5,000 seemed a bit too much to spend on a "wonder of technology" that didn't fulfill a perceived distinct need.

Contrast the Segway experience to that of Apple's iPad (as the harbinger of the tablet category). Three million devices were sold just eighty days after the official release date (in April 2010) and an additional 4.2 million units sold in the following quarter, far exceeding the predictions of many industry analysts. While prelaunch predictions were positive in disposition, most experts in this instance grossly underestimated the iPad's sales trajectory by well over 100 percent![1] As with the Segway, there was much fanfare in advance of the iPad's launch, with Steve Jobs declaring at the first unveiling that "this is a truly magical product." Hence most people knew about the iPad, were informed about its features, and had seen it on television and online. But in stark contrast to the Segway, many consumers were in a frenzy to get their hands on one, with long lines forming outside Apple stores when it became available.

What was the difference? Of course, the price tag on an iPad was lower than that of a Segway, yet many an electronic product under $1,000 has been launched only to collect dust on retailers' shelves. (Does anyone remember Sony's MiniDisc audio format or Samsung's YP-K5 portable MP3 player that could slide open to function as a boom box? Probably not.) To understand the difference in outcome, we must once again examine how the innovation was perceived by consumers and, specifically, *relative* to what other products its benefits were compared. While for decades the prospects of tablet devices like the iPad were viewed as "PC substitutes," Apple cleverly positioned its iPad primarily in relation to the iPhone, Apple's hugely popular smartphone device launched three years earlier. From a design standpoint, the iPad bore an unmistakable resemblance to its smartphone counterpart. Furthermore, the TV and print ads that Apple ran for the iPad highlighted the wide availability of applications, or "apps," virtually all of which were already available for the iPhone. The message in the these ads centered on the media and entertainment value proposition behind the device rather than on productivity or functional uses that one might typically associate with, say, a laptop—as Jobs said, it's about a "magical" experience, not a "practical" experience. Apple's intent was picked up by the marketplace as the initial reviews came back suggesting the iPad was "like a bigger iPhone."

All of this facilitated the iPad's rapid uptake in a number of ways. The iPhone had fascinated its users by allowing them to turn their cell phones into multimedia devices on the go: one could surf the web, play games, run a host of cool apps, and engage with social networking platforms anywhere, anytime. Moreover, the touch screen property of the iPhone enthralled consumers, proving to be a highly effective and intuitive user interface (innovation in user friendliness had been a long tradition at Apple). But when at home or sitting at the local Starbucks, the iPhone was somewhat inconvenient: its screen size was small (about 3.5 inches), it had good but not great visual resolution, and its limited ability to process and store data could be a drag. The iPad was positioned to fill that gap: it featured a screen nearly triple the size, enhanced picture resolution (a 9.7-inch display of 1024 · 768 pixels versus the iPhone's 320 · 480 at the time), and more processing power (an all-new 1 GHz chip compared to the iPhone's 600 MHz chip). Thus consumers could easily see how their endearing iPhone experience could become relevant for "off the go" settings with the iPad. In fact, many of the early iPad adopters, those who had lined up in front of stores for hours before they opened on April 10, 2010, were avid iPhone users.

Steve Jobs was rumored to have said, "[The iPad] will be the most important thing I have done," and he even admitted at one point that work on developing it actually started before any serious efforts were devoted to the iPhone. Yet he recognized that the iPad's success depended on setting the right *comparison anchor*: he realized that positioning the iPad as having advantages *relative to* the iPhone in certain contexts, and much less so relative to PCs, would likely facilitate market acceptance, but this meant that it was critical for consumers to first have adequate experience with the iPhone. Hence the timing for concluding development and launching each of these innovations was flipped. The significance of this framing strategy was explicitly brought to the fore when Apple launched its next-generation tablet, the iPad 2, in March 2011. Apple's CEO took a direct jab at competitors who, in his opinion, got the reference point for consumers all wrong: "A lot of folks in this tablet market are rushing in

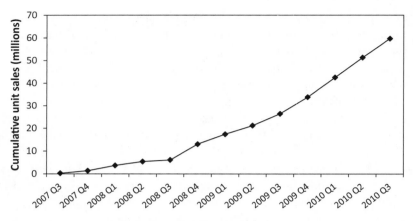

FIGURE 1.1. iPhone cumulative unit sales, Q3 2007–Q3 2010*

* 3G phones were introduced in late 2008, so some upgrading likely occurred during this period, an issue we pick up in chapter 7.

and they are thinking of this as the new PC. They're talking about speeds and feeds just like they did with PCs. Every bone in our bodies says this is not the right approach."

Figure 1.1 depicts the total number of iPhone units sold from the device's debut in fall 2007 and until shortly after the launch of the first iPad in spring 2010, each quarter adding the units sold in that quarter to all previous sales. Assuming that the majority of those purchasing an iPhone by Q2 2010 were first-time buyers—that is, they had not yet replaced their devices within this time frame—suggests that there was a base of more than fifty million users who could appreciate the iPad in relation to their iPhones.

What exactly is it? Why is it so complex? Can I try it first? The bottom line from the "Why do I need it?" barrier just discussed is that consumers' decision to adopt or not adopt an innovation is often based on whether they can perceive sufficient benefits from it relative to something they are familiar with and that they will compare it to. Yet a critical prelude to this step is whether they can even understand what the innovation does or how it works when it is presented to them.

Perhaps not surprisingly, the more difficult it is for consumers to understand the technology behind a new product or service and how one actually uses it, the less inclined they are to adopt it. Confusion breeds avoidance in the domain of innovations. In addition, the more opportunities a consumer has to physically "test drive" the innovation by experiencing it firsthand instead of just seeing it on television or on YouTube or reading about it on some tech site, the more he or she can gain an intuitive understanding of its operation and develop a sense of how it is used. These factors, which can greatly affect the willingness to adopt an innovation, have been termed the *complexity* and *trialability* of an innovation.

Once again, a comparison between the Segway and the iPad is revealing. In the case of the former, when it was launched, there was no convenient way for consumers to try the vehicle before deciding to purchase it. Segway Inc.'s management seemed to be convinced, perhaps fueled by the lofty prophecies of the notable industry pundits, that this was a mass-market product "out of the box." Consequently, it was initially distributed through Amazon.com. That's right: consumers were expected to purchase it online and had no practical way of trying it first. This was problematic given that for most people, it was not at all obvious how it worked or how easy or hard it would be to operate on a day-to-day basis. The Segway Personal Transporter boasted novel gyroscopic technology and advanced software, but what did all that mean to the lay consumer? How easy is it to maneuver a vehicle designed to react automatically to body posture? Is it safe? It has only two wheels, so why would it not fall over when it stops moving? How does it feel to ride a Segway at twelve miles per hour on the road? How about on the sidewalk? Can it go in reverse? What percentage of the time does it not do what it is supposed to? These were among the many questions consumers had, and it was difficult to get a true sense of the product without physically trying it out.

Moreover, the fact that it was all electric, which in 2001 was a very uncommon way for consumers to fuel their vehicles, further raised questions about convenience. There was a return policy in place, but that was clearly not enough for the vast majority of consumers to entertain spending $5,000. In subsequent years, Segway Inc. corrected many of these complexity and trialability issues, a point we will pick up in chapter 5, but at the outset, these barriers were present in spades.

The iPad was a totally different ball game in this respect. With more than three hundred Apple stores, located mainly in busy metropolitan areas where the bulk of its potential market resides and/or shops, consumers could walk in and play with the device extensively before deciding whether to buy it. Furthermore, because of extensive public familiarity with the iPhone, nothing seemed overly complex about the iPad. Consumers had gotten used to life with touch screens and had a good sense of how to conceptualize and take advantage of the new world of apps—two big draws for the iPad.

Should I care about what other people are doing or saying? Can I observe past adopters? Am I willing to be incompatible? As we have just seen, consumers consider adopting an innovation based on whether they "get it"—whether they understand how the purported benefits are relevant to them and how the innovation delivers superior value relative to existing options and whether they understand how it works and how it can be used. For the most part, we described a process that had a particular individual integrating information about the innovation—put forward either by the company responsible for the innovation in the form of ads, press releases, and online information or through exposure to media commentaries on the innovation. We also discussed the importance of personal, hands-on experience as part of the evaluation process. Yet the nature of these evaluations was largely independent of others who had confronted the very same adoption dilemma and the knowledge of what *they* chose to do: adopt, not adopt, or defer their decision.

But human beings are, for the most part, social creatures: we care about what other people do and say, particularly those we know at a more-than-casual level, and we believe that other people care about what we do and say. When the actions and opinions of our peers have the potential to change our own behavior (and vice versa), scholars typically call it "social contagion."

There are at least three mechanisms by which social contagion can have an effect on innovation adoption. First, as we have noted, the "newness" aspect of an innovation creates uncertainty about whether it is worth the hype that the firm has generated about it. And this uncertainty can be all the more difficult to endure when adoption involves substantial downsides. For example, on top of the price paid to purchase the innovation, consumers may need to spend time and money setting up the new product or service, exert effort to get rid of the old product they were using in order to make way for the new one, devote time to learning how to use the new product, and pay for expenses on complementary products (such as software and accessories) incurred in the process. And when you add to these practical costs the emotional costs of how it feels to get "burned"— frustration, regret, and perhaps even embarrassment at having to admit one has made a foolish decision—the downsides of adopting an innovation that "wasn't worth it" are compounded.

Due to these concerns, consumers typically feel much more comfortable adopting when they get assurances that the innovation does make sense for them and that any time, effort, and money they may have to incur will pay off. What better assurance than knowing that others, who faced the very same dilemma, have decided to adopt? And the more people who have adopted, the more confidence one can have that indeed the innovation is "worth it." The more adopters there are, the more likely it is that someone contemplating adoption will hear of and be able to ask others directly about the pros and cons of the innovation before committing to it. Incorporating adopters' experience-based impressions into one's own assessment is like an indirect form of "trialability," if you will. Furthermore, the larger the set of those that have already made the decision to adopt, the more likely it is that one can see the innovation in actual use. And for products that are more distinctly visible in public settings, or "observable," this confidence is reinforced even more. When seeing many people enjoying the innovation, a potential adopter likely thinks, "You can't fool so many people so much of the time, can you?" Conversely, of course, if one gets the sense that not many people have adopted the innovation, does not observe many active users, or finds no one to consult about it, the reverse is true, and an individual becomes much less inclined to adopt.

The second reason social aspects matter is that innovations can have an inherent "network-effect benefit"; that is to say, the benefits from using the product depend on how big the network of adopters is. Why might this be the case? Take the fax machine as an example. The technology presented a relative advantage over courier and even overnight mail services: faxes are faster, more convenient, and less costly to send. However, in order to derive any of these benefits, the party you're hoping to fax also has to have a fax machine. So the more businesses and individuals that owned or had access to fax machines—in other words, the larger the fax-connected network—the more value a given adopter could derive from his or her fax machine. Social networking platforms, like Facebook and Google+, embody the same characteristics: the more people one knows who are already on the platform, the more relevant it becomes to join.

Network-effect benefits can also be indirect. This situation arises when complementary products or services are involved. For example, the more individuals who adopt a video game console (such as Xbox One), the greater the incentive for game developers to create game titles for it. And the more game titles there are, the greater the benefit derived by consumers who own the game console. Or, for instance, the more people who adopt a pure electric vehicle (like the Nissan Leaf), the greater the incentive for infrastructure companies to install charging spots. And the more charging spots there are . . . well, you get the picture. This obviously brings up the so-called chicken-and-egg problem, whereby each of the complementary product makers would like its counterpart to sufficiently commit before it takes on a substantial investment. Such coordination issues have been known in some cases to delay investments and, in turn, adoption.

The third manner by which social influence arises is when publicly consuming certain products and brands has signaling implications—the power to confer status, imply identity, and convey group or clique membership. For example, most people would agree that a Volkswagen Beetle says something about its owner that is different from what a Porsche Roadster says about its owner—and the owners of both vehicles likely knew this very well when they made their purchase decision. (Drinking domestic versus imported beer in public is another example.) Social cues can be a factor when it comes to adopting innovations. The more an innovation differs from what was consumed beforehand and the more inconsistent it is with previous behavior in terms of how it looks or how it is used, the more the average person hesitates to be among the first to be seen with it. Such a lack of *compatibility* with prior practice makes an innovation seem like a foreign concept, something that just doesn't fit or belong, thus deterring adoption.

Incompatibility engenders fear of being ridiculed or scorned for violating the social norms, for breaking the mold. Not many people enjoy ridicule and scorn, nor do many people enjoy the feeling of being outcast from their social circles. Standing on the Segway makes you literally stand out (and not in a positive way), and as described in the introduction, wearing a smart eyewear device (like Google Glass) can cause you to look "weird" in others' eyes and appear to be violating social norms of privacy.

Of course, for trendsetters, those individuals who derive pleasure from being recognized as the first to embrace something new and breaking from the pack, the opposite is often true: incompatible innovations allow them to signal that they are different, nonconforming, and intrepid.

When such peer-signaling interactions are at work, an interesting social dynamic can emerge: the innovation becomes more socially acceptable (or less socially inacceptable) as more people adopt it. At some point, when a large enough proportion of the market has adopted, pressure begins to mount on the remaining population to embrace it as well. At this stage, the tables begin to turn; not adopting means running the risk of being perceived as a misfit or ridiculed as a laggard. Consider smartphones.

Not having one in early 2009 was not a big deal—chances were that most people around you didn't either (at that point, for example, only about thirteen million people had an iPhone; see figure 1.1). However, by late 2013, being smartphone-less could create awkward social situations and unpleasant peer reactions. A colleague or friend might expect you to immediately respond to an e-mail or search online for some information, even when you are not at your desk or at home with access to a computer. But if you were unable to do so, because all you had was a cell phone, it could result in being confronted with a pejorative response like "What? You don't have a smartphone?" or, worse yet, in people talking behind your back about how you are stuck in the past. Indeed, the greater the number of adopters, the more the norm shifts from what was acceptable preinnovation to what is de facto expected after the innovation became available.

Note that we have used the term "compatibility" in its social contagion, peer-effect context. However, it can also be used in a technological sense to indicate whether an innovation allows continued use of existing complementary products—for example, if a new video game console plays previous-generation games or if a new computer architecture smoothly runs software programmed for the previous version. Lack of compatibility in these cases means that one has to either give up one's existing stock of complements, simultaneously hold on to the old system, invest in emulators, or purchase new versions of the complementary products that are compatible with the innovation. Generally speaking, from a barriers-to-adoption standpoint, the more technologically incompatible a new system is, the less inclined consumers are to rush to adopt it.

So What Do All These Factors Boil down *Two*?

Now that we have gleaned some insights into what can facilitate or hinder consumer adoption of innovations and the factors that affect how the marketplace reacts to an innovation, we are in a better position to assist our vice president of marketing in thinking about the forecasting challenge. What would be helpful is a way to summarize the various factors we have just discussed into a small set of quantities or parameters that could be used for modeling the adoption process.

Figure 1.2 shows how one can map the various factors into two driving forces, corresponding to the two primary ways that lead to innovation

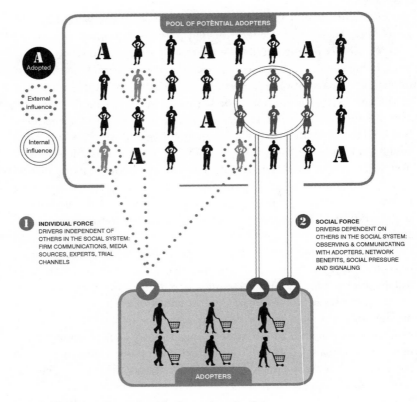

FIGURE I.2. The two forces that drive innovation adoption

adoption: the individual force and the social force. We now expand upon these adoption forces.

The *individual force* is at play when the decision to adopt the innovation is made regardless of others in the social system. This path to adoption reflects those cases where perceiving the innovation's benefits and costs does not depend on knowing the actions and behavior of others and where an individual forms a decision solely based on information gathered from sources that are outside his or her social circles. Such inputs can come from firm-initiated communications (advertising, press releases, online information, etc.), channels that provide access to try the innovation (demos at retailers or by salespeople, distribution of free samples, etc.), or the media (articles, interviews with company officials, etc.). The more explicit the need for the benefits provided by the innovation and the more easily consumers can be convinced by the information they receive about it from outside sources, the more robust the individually driven path to adoption is.

The *social force* is at play when the decision to adopt depends on the behavior of other individuals in the marketplace. That is to say, in this path to adoption, the driving forces depend on how many other people in the relevant social system have already adopted the innovation. The ability to know and see others' positive reactions to an innovation can reduce fears and concerns over costs and risks, intensify network benefits, or create social cues and pressures. And as more people are observed to have adopted, the more powerful the social influence is.

Because the drivers and sources of information in the individual path typically originate from "outside" the pool of potential adopters, whereas in the social path they come directly from "inside" the adopter pool, the former's effects on adoption have also been labeled *external influence* and the latter *internal influence*, as reflected in figure 1.2.

With the two adoption forces in mind, we can essentially express the likelihood that someone who has not yet adopted an innovation will do so in the current period through the following relationship:

EXPRESSION 1.1. The likelihood of a new adoption

Likelihood a person will adopt in the current period =
Individual force + Social force · Market penetration

In other words, the relationship in expression 1.1 says that to capture the probability that someone who has not yet adopted will do so at present, what is needed is a sense of how the decision will be governed by the relevant individual and social forces. Moreover, an important aspect of social influence is the degree the innovation has already penetrated in the relevant population. This last point summarizes the idea that as more people have adopted, providing more opportunities for current social interactions, the social route to adoption picks up momentum. We still have to define what a good measure of market penetration is, but the idea is that more widespread penetration renders the social forces more powerful.

Another way to think about the relationship in expression 1.1 is that it gives us the probability that a person who has not yet adopted will do so because of both forces, individual and social. If these forces are weak, the likelihood of adoption is low—that is to say, the barriers to adoption are quite formidable. We note though that because the social force is multiplied by a measure of the past adoption level (market penetration), if at some point, even years after the initial launch, this latter quantity becomes large enough, then the social path to adoption can become very robust—a point we will highlight later in this chapter.

The Missing Link and Completing the Basic Diffusion Model

At this point, we have a good handle on how to capture what drives someone to embrace an innovation. We have a snapshot, at any given point in time, of the likelihood that a person will adopt. But to get at how the demand for the innovation will evolve over time—what we call the *diffusion pattern of an innovation*—we seek to move from a single person to the total number of people likely to adopt in each time period following the new product's launch. In order to make this transition, we need to have a sense of how big the potential market is for the innovation—in other words, how many people in total belong to the set of potential adopters. In figure 1.2, for example, this would be the overall number of individuals in the top square from which possible adopters can come. If we are trying to capture the diffusion of an innovation in the United States, for instance, then for something like cell phones, this would be most of the population (say 90 percent of people over eighteen, 50 percent of those between the ages of ten and seventeen, and 25 percent of children ages five to nine); for high-definition televisions (HDTVs), this can be 80 percent of households that have an annual income level above some threshold; and for something like a new shaving razor, this could be a well-defined subset of men (those who don't have a beard, shave at least three times a week, etc.).

Now that we have all the necessary ingredients, we can adapt the relationship described in expression 1.1 to state the evolution of demand for an innovation over time. Simply put, what we are trying to do is characterize the total number of people that will adopt the innovation in each time period after the launch. Our aim in this chapter is to start with a basic model of innovation diffusion, to which we can add bells and whistles later. So assume for the time being that we can treat everyone in the target population the same way. That is to say, for every person, the same individual and social forces influence the decision to adopt. We separate the marketplace into those that have already adopted and those that have not—just like the two sets of people in figure 1.2 in the shaded rectangle at the bottom and the unshaded rectangle at the top, respectively. To obtain the number of new adoptions in the current time period, we multiply the set of people that have not yet adopted by the likelihood that each one of these people will adopt. And this likelihood is exactly what was captured in expression 1.1.

We are also in a position to define a measure for the "market penetration" term, which should reflect how widespread the adoption of the innovation has been thus far. Hence we define it as the ratio of the number of people who have already adopted to the long-run total number of potential adopters and call it the *proportion of past adoption*. This leads to the following model:

EXPRESSION 1.2. The basic diffusion model of an innovation
in the marketplace

Number of new adopters in this time period =
Number of people that have not yet adopted · [Individual force +
Social force · Proportion of past adoption]

It is quite straightforward to use the formulation in expression 1.2 to calculate the number of new adoptions in each subsequent period:

1. Subtract the number of new adopters in this period from the pool of remaining nonadopters at the start of the period. This yields the number of people who have not yet adopted to use for the next period calculation.
2. Add the number of new adopters in this period to the number of people who have already adopted in past periods. This yields the cumulative number of adopters by the end of the current period. Dividing this value by the total potential market of adopters (which is a fixed number reflecting the entire relevant market for the innovation) allows updating the proportion of past adoption to use for the next period calculation.
3. Plug the new quantities from steps 1 and 2 into the formula given in expression 1.2 to obtain the number of new adopters in the *next* time period.
4. Repeat steps 1 through 3 to get the number of new adopters two periods from now, and so on.

The basic diffusion model described in expression 1.2 was first proposed by marketing scholar Frank M. Bass in his seminal work on innovation diffusion; thus the model is often referred to as the Bass model. A formal version of the basic diffusion model is presented in math box 1 in the appendix.[2]

An Innovation's Diffusion Curve

Let's recap where we are with respect to modeling the market's reaction to an innovation once it is launched. We have laid out two primary forces that govern the adoption likelihood and connected these forces to the number of new adopters to expect in each time period from the long-run market potential pool. The result is the basic diffusion model.

To make things a bit more concrete, it is probably helpful to give a few numerical illustrations of how adoption is expected to unfold over time based on the basic diffusion model and to depict the pattern that emerges graphically. Subsequently, we will provide a real-life example using the case of satellite radio.

Table 1.1 provides a forecast for the diffusion of a hypothetical innovation over a thirty-year period. In this example, the total long-run potential market of adopters, which is typically denoted by the letter m, is fifty million (e.g., fifty million could be the number of US households that constitute the relevant population). The individual force, typically denoted by the letter p, equals 0.01, which means that there is a 1 percent chance every year that someone who has not yet adopted the innovation will do so independently of the influence of other consumers and only due to information conveyed by external entities. The social force, typically denoted by the letter q, equals 0.25, which means that every year, the proportion of consumers who have already adopted exerts a 25 percent influence on the adoption probability of the remaining pool of consumers; for example, if 10 percent of the market potential pool has adopted after five years, then in year 6, there is a 2.5 percent chance that someone will adopt the innovation as a result of the social force ($0.25 \cdot 0.1 = 0.025$, or 2.5 percent).

It should be quite straightforward to see how one transitions from year to year in table 1.1. For example, say we have the quantities of year 4 and we wish to calculate the quantities of year 5.

1. The total number of people that have not yet adopted by year 5 = (Long-run market potential – Total number of adopters by end of year 4) = 50m – 2.82m = 47.19m.
2. Dividing the total number of adopters by end of year 4 by the long-run market potential, we obtain

$$\text{Proportion of past adoption relevant for year } 5 =$$
$$2.82\text{m} / 50\text{m} = 5.64 \text{ percent.}$$

TABLE I.I **A numerical example of a basic diffusion model forecast**

Years since launch	Total number of adopters by end of current year (millions)	Proportion of past adoption (%)	Adoption due to individual force in current year (millions)	Adoption due to social force in current year (millions)	Number of new adopters in current year (millions)
1	0.50	1.00	0.500	0.000	0.500
2	1.12	2.24	0.495	0.124	0.619
3	1.88	3.76	0.489	0.273	0.762
4	2.82	5.64	0.481	0.453	0.934
5	3.95	7.90	0.472	0.664	1.136
6	5.32	10.64	0.460	0.910	1.370
7	6.96	13.91	0.447	1.189	1.635
8	8.88	17.77	0.430	1.497	1.928
9	11.12	22.24	0.411	1.826	2.237
10	13.67	27.34	0.389	2.162	2.551
11	16.52	33.04	0.363	2.483	2.847
12	19.62	39.24	0.335	2.765	3.100
13	22.90	45.81	0.304	2.980	3.284
14	26.28	52.55	0.271	3.103	3.374
15	29.63	59.26	0.237	3.117	3.354
16	32.85	65.71	0.204	3.018	3.221
17	35.84	71.68	0.171	2.817	2.988
18	38.52	77.04	0.142	2.537	2.679
19	40.85	81.69	0.115	2.211	2.326
20	42.81	85.61	0.092	1.870	1.961
21	44.41	88.84	0.072	1.540	1.612
22	45.71	91.43	0.056	1.240	1.295
23	46.74	93.47	0.043	0.980	1.023
24	47.53	95.06	0.033	0.763	0.795
25	48.14	96.29	0.025	0.587	0.611
26	48.61	97.22	0.019	0.447	0.466
27	48.96	97.92	0.014	0.338	0.352
28	49.23	98.45	0.010	0.254	0.265
29	49.42	98.85	0.008	0.191	0.198
30	49.57	99.14	0.006	0.142	0.148

Diffusion model parameters: $m = 50$ million, $p = 0.01$, $q = 0.25$.

3. Using the basic diffusion model given in expression 1.2,

Number of new adopters in year 5 =
Number of people who have not yet adopted by year 5 ·
[Individual force + Social force · Proportion of past adoption
relevant for year 5] = 47.19m · [0.01+0.25 · 0.0564] = 1.136m.

4. The total number of adopters by end of year 5 = (Total number of adopters by end of year 4 + Number of new adopters in year 5) = 3.95m.

5. Repeat steps 1–4 to see how the entire table was constructed (though you might want to use Microsoft Excel at some point, and a visit to the book's companion website, www.InnovationEquityBook.com, to obtain a sample worksheet may be well worth your time).

There are several interesting points to note from table 1.1. Initially, in the first year on the market, the table reflects the fact that those who embrace the innovation can be influenced by the individual force only (because in the first year, there simply aren't yet any past adopters that can exert a social force on others). These could be people who readily see why the innovation makes sense for them or those with a strong immediate need for its benefits because they have a burning problem it solves—they are willing to bet on the innovation even though no one they know has committed to it yet. But as time goes by, if we keep scrolling down past year 1, it is clear that things change: adoption as a result of the social force picks up steam, while adoption from the individual force dwindles. Indeed, starting from year 2, previous adopters begin exerting an influence on those that have not yet adopted. And because the former group grows from year to year, the social force's impact becomes more robust. The adoption pace (i.e., growth in the number of new adopters) keeps increasing until it reaches a maximum level (about thirteen to fourteen years postlaunch), after which it starts declining. The reason for this pattern is quite intuitive: as the number of adopters grows, the pool of remaining potential new adopters decreases; you are taking people from one bucket and moving them to the other bucket. Thus, even though more past adopters means more current social influence, there are fewer people left to influence. Eventually, by the end of year 30, there are hardly any "laggards" that could still adopt, as almost all the fifty million in the target group (99.14 percent of them, to be exact) have done so. If we plot the number of new adoptions each year from table 1.1 (the last column of the table) against time, we get the bell-shaped pattern shown in figure 1.3.

Another way to visualize how adoption progresses over time is to plot what is commonly referred to as the "cumulative diffusion curve." This means plotting against time the total number of adopters by the end of the current year (second column of table 1.1), which as explained in step 4, is obtained by iteratively adding current adopters to all past adopters. A variation of this plot uses the proportion of past adoption (the third column of table 1.1), which simply scales the cumulative numbers by the long-run market potential. Recall that this quantity can also be thought of as the

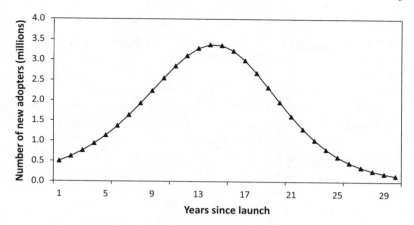

FIGURE 1.3. Number of new adopters in each year since the launch

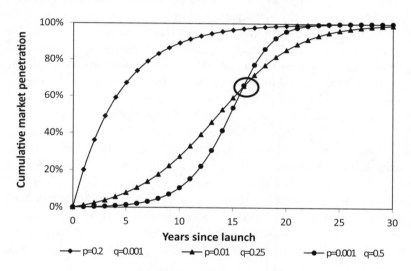

FIGURE 1.4. The basic diffusion model (cumulative penetration) with various levels of individual (p) and social (q) forces

market penetration level achieved every year. Figure 1.4 does just that. Focus for now on the triangle-symbol curve, which uses the values from the numerical example in table 1.1 (third column). What emerges is an S-shaped pattern: a slow start (a relatively flat line) followed by rapid growth (a steep upward-sloping line) and then a tapering off (a relatively flat line again). This diffusion pattern has been observed for many prominent innovations introduced over the past century, such as the telephone, television, microwave ovens, and cell phones. The basic diffusion model developed in this chapter is therefore capable of nicely generating this common evolution of adoption among members of the potential market for the innovation. Moreover, we have established a good understanding of why the curve might look this way and what main processes govern it.

Innovations can differ in terms of how strong the individual and social forces are at engendering adoption—in other words, by how much potential adopters can independently perceive the need for the innovation versus how much they are influenced by others' behavior. Put differently, innovations can vary in terms of p and q, even if the intended market, m, is the same. If we used different values for the individual and social forces in the basic diffusion model, what would be the implications for what the diffusion curve would look like? In figure 1.4, the cumulative diffusion curves for two other hypothetical innovations are also depicted (in all the curves, the total market potential is kept the same at m = 50 million). Compared to the triangle-symbol curve we just analyzed, the diamond-symbol curve is based on a much higher value for the individual force (p) and a much lower value for the social force (q). The reverse is true for the circle-symbol curve, which has a much lower p and a much higher q.

The diamond-symbol curve reveals that if the individual force is strong (p = 0.2), diffusion shoots up fairly quickly, and by year 10, approximately 90 percent of the potential population has adopted. By contrast, in the numerical example corresponding to the triangle-symbol curve, where p is only 0.01, by year 10, less than 30 percent penetration is reached. Rapid adoption, as in the diamond-symbol curve, would reflect situations where a strong explicit need for the innovation existed, such as when consumers were clamoring for the innovation even before it was launched or when the company's marketing efforts were very effective at persuading consumers to buy the new product or service.

On the other hand, when the individual force is meager (p = 0.001) yet the social force is strong (q = 0.5), as in the circle-symbol curve, adoption in the first few years will be very limited. The weak perceived value of the innovation, in conjunction with other possible barriers to adoption, results in very few people getting excited about it. The pace of purchases in the first few years postlaunch is thus very slow. Although the social force is quite high (double the level it was for the triangle-symbol curve), early on there are just not that many past adopters that can exert an influence (provide word-of-mouth recommendations, create network benefits, or exert social pressure). Hence we see a very shallow pattern until year 5. But once a critical mass of adopters is in place, the social force kicks in big time, and it becomes self-reinforcing: as more people adopt, the social impact on nonadopters grows. By year 10, the circle-symbol curve achieves a 10 percent penetration, smaller than for the other two curves, but that is enough to get the social snowball rolling, and by year 15 its penetration exceeds 50 percent. In fact, so strong is the social force in this case that even though the individual force is ten times smaller, the diffusion represented by the circle-symbol curve overtakes the one represented by the triangle-symbol curve at year 16 (when the two curves intersect) and reaches full penetration sooner.

The fact that diffusion curves can exhibit such striking differences in shape over time can have important implications for management. We will discuss several of these in connection with the satellite radio example we develop next.

The Basic Diffusion Model in Action: The Case of Satellite Radio

Satellite radio is by now an accepted reality in the United States. Most new car models today come equipped with satellite radio receivers, and several months of free service are typically provided for consumers to try the offering. Car rental companies regularly present satellite radio as an option to customers. The first such service was launched by XM Satellite Radio in fall 2001, followed shortly by Sirius in winter 2002.

The idea behind the innovative service was to place satellites in orbit that delivered more than a hundred radio channels nationally. There were supposedly numerous advantages over traditional radio (AM and FM): a wide range of content with multiple music channels featuring numerous genres and an array of talk shows and editorial picks; digital, high-quality transmission (all other radio broadcasts at the time of the launch were analog); continuous national coverage, which meant that channels would not fade out as one traveled long distances (as was the case with traditional, terrestrial-based radio that was limited in range and whose signal quality depended on one's proximity to the broadcasting station); and a digital display of song and artist information. Additionally, although traditional radio was provided free of charge, consumers "paid with their ears" by having to bear up to twenty minutes of advertising per hour. This was considered a big nuisance among many consumers and something that satellite radio promised to change. Indeed, satellite radio reduced advertising airtime considerably (and most music channels on both services were eventually commercial free).

But as the saying goes, there are no free lunches. To enjoy these benefits, a consumer would have to pay a monthly fee. Moreover, any existing car owner would have to buy and install a satellite radio receiver in the aftermarket.

As the new millennium approached and the launch date neared, the amount of prep work needed for each of the companies to successfully provide a satellite radio service was no small feat. An estimated $1 billion was required to develop the technology, build facilities, and put the satellites into orbit and time and effort had to be exerted in order to convince electronics companies to design appropriate receivers and to align car manufacturers and retailers to bring them to market. It was also critical to structure deals with various producers, artists, and talk show hosts to populate the content. Each of the stakeholders involved, from investors to senior management at partner companies, had to base their decision of whether and how to support satellite radio on the expected penetration level and ROI of the novel service. Consequently, the satellite radio firms quickly realized they had to develop reliable estimates for the potential market size of this nascent category and its rate of demand growth over time so that these would form the basis for funding discussions and fruitful collaboration talks. Otherwise, each of the parties would have to either formulate their own forecast, use some analyst-created prediction, or, worse yet, forgo partnership or funding because the whole "radio beamed from outer space" adventure seemed too fuzzy to base decisions on.

XM approached this task by turning to the basic diffusion model presented in this chapter. What did they do? Well, they first wanted to determine the potential market size for satellite radio as a new radio category (the parameter m in the model). To help accomplish this task, the company could use the findings from a national telephone survey it commissioned to identify target segments and estimate the potential market size at various price points for the service and receiver. More than six thousand surveys were completed. From the results, XM leaned toward a subscription fee of between $10 and $12, and strived to get receiver prices down to about $250 to $300 at retail. The number of survey participants that indicated they would potentially adopt the service at these prices corresponded to roughly twenty-five to thirty-one million consumers. For purposes of applying the basic diffusion model here as an example, the

TABLE 1.2 **A sample of basic diffusion model parameters for past innovations**

Product	p	q
Automobile radios	**0.016**	**0.410**
Calculators	0.143	0.520
Camcorders	0.001	0.143
Cable television	0.100	0.060
CD players	**0.055**	**0.378**
Cellular phones	**0.008**	**0.421**
Digital cameras	0.006	0.394
Home personal computers	0.121	0.281
Televisions, color	0.059	0.146
VCRs	0.025	0.603

midpoint of this range will serve us as the market potential: m = twenty-eight million. XM knew the market potential would not be achieved overnight and that it would take time for many of these would-be satellite radio customers to adopt—but how much time? At what point, for example, would 10 percent of this market potential likely be achieved? How about 50 percent of the potential? Well, that would be governed by the individual and social forces—the p and q parameters.

To come up with reasonable estimates for the two innovation adoption forces, XM resorted to a "How did comparable past innovations fare on these dimensions?" approach. This method takes advantage of the fact that once an innovation has sufficiently diffused, one can use the observed sales data to estimate the basic diffusion model parameters that best fit its actual adoption evolution over time. This has been done for numerous innovations, and table 1.2 provides a sample of parameter estimates for a number of prominent innovations that were available at the time. For satellite radio, it is plausible that innovations like the automobile radio (a previous innovation in the realm of radio hardware in the car), the cell phone (an innovation related to mobile access to information that also followed a subscription model), and the CD player (an audio innovation that transformed the consumption of music from analog to digital) provided a good set of benchmarks for assessing how individual and social forces might play out in this context. One could then take a simple average of the comparable-innovation parameters to arrive at plausible expected values for p and q for satellite radio. Alternatively, one could rate each of these past innovations on the degree of similarity to satellite radio—in terms of aspects that could influence market readiness and acceptance—and use these ratings as a basis for deciding how much weight to give to their parameters. For example, these aspects can be the factors identified earlier

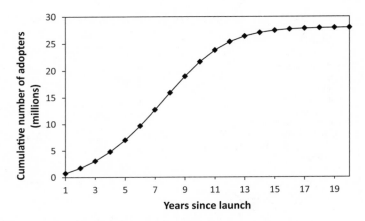

FIGURE 1.5. Cumulative diffusion curve for satellite radio

in this chapter as influencing adoption—relative advantage, complexity, trialability, compatibility, and social influences (which include observability, network benefits, and social pressure/cues). The rating task can be carried out by industry experts, company employees, or consumers (or a combination of these entities). Either way, the idea is to impute the desired (and as yet unknown) parameter values by way of analogy to pertinent innovations whose parameters are already known.

If one chooses the simplest approach of averaging across a number of analogous products that are deemed relevant, which we have taken to be automobile radios, cellular telephones, and CD players, one obtains the values $p = 0.026$ and $q = 0.403$.

Given what we learned from analyzing the diffusion curve examples in figure 1.4, these projected parameter values for satellite radio, particularly the ones based on automobile radios and cellular phones, would likely foretell the story of an innovation that will get off to a somewhat slow start in its first few years and then accelerate quite rapidly over the next few years. Constructing the cumulative diffusion curve for satellite radio as an innovation category based on a market potential of twenty-eight million, and adoption forces of $p = 0.026$ and $q = 0.403$, the curve would look like—what else?—an S-shaped pattern (see figure 1.5)!

How Good Is It?

What is the significance of using the basic diffusion model as the basis for crafting projections for satellite radio's uptake? The fact that it is based on

extensive academic research with respect to consumer adoption of innovations, has a nice mathematical and graphical representation, and seems
intuitive is one thing, but how well it works in practice is another. In other
words, did it do a good job at forecasting what years later was observed
to be the actual adoption pattern for satellite radio? Before answering
that question, one might first try to answer a different one: what were the
alternatives for predicting satellite radio adoption other than constructing a basic diffusion model? Figure 1.6 depicts the assessments of three
prominent analysts at the time for the first seven years that satellite radio
would be on the market.

Without exception, the analysts' models predicted far greater penetration in the first few years postlaunch than did the basic diffusion model
forecast we constructed here (per figure 1.5). Even the most conservative
of these alternative estimates, by analyst 1, predicted that satellite radio
would reach nearly fifteen million adopters by year 5, whereas figure 1.5
pegs adoption at only about seven million by that year—less than half!
A closer examination of how these analysts constructed their forecasts
reveals two things: First, because of the expectation that satellite radio
would appeal mostly to in-car listeners, adoption over time was modeled
as the percentage of penetration among US vehicles. For instance, according to one model, it was believed that satellite radio would reach
3 percent market penetration of US vehicles by the third year following
launch, 7.5 percent by the fifth year, and almost 15 percent by the seventh
year. Second, the growth rates predicted typically followed some preset

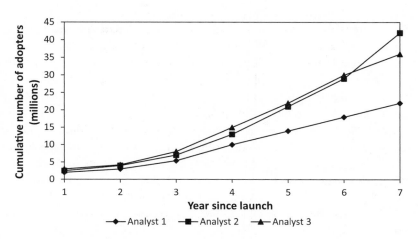

FIGURE 1.6. Prominent analyst predictions for satellite radio (prelaunch, end of 1999)

pattern, such as doubling every two to three years or exhibiting a constant growth rate. Some models we have seen try to fit specific financial targets and are constructed "in reverse"—for example, suggesting what the market penetration will be at some future year and then choosing growth rates that would achieve that mark. That is to say, such forecasts are not based on any explicit *behavioral process* by which potential customers consider innovations, nor do they differentiate between various *mechanisms* of adoption. Moreover, these approaches often do not offer a structured way to leverage information from the diffusion patterns of past innovations.

Consequently, what such predictions typically fail to pick up on is the possible need for a critical mass of adopters to initially form before rapid take-off can ensue. As we have seen, for example, with the circle-symbol curve in figure 1.4, if the social force is crucial for a particular innovation to diffuse—because there are network benefits, because consumers' uncertainty can be mitigated when knowing others have adopted, or because of the social pressure of being associated with the innovation—there will be a substantial period of critical mass buildup before rapid penetration takes place. Failure to account for this stage in the diffusion life cycle can lead to problems. Specifically, when an innovation is expected to have a strong social influence component, ignoring its effects may grossly *overestimate* adoption in the first few years. This overestimation can have a number of perilous managerial implications. First, the firm may invest heavily in production in the expectation of strong unit sales early on only to be confronted with overflowing warehouses and debt when the demand isn't there. A second, more acute problem is that management and investors might "freak out." The first few years after launch are an extremely anxious time. If sales don't materialize as quickly as hoped, if they are "way off" the projections presented on the eve of the introduction when the champagne bottles were uncorked, management may advocate for or be forced to take drastic measures, such as an increase in advertising spending, concessions to retailers, steep price cuts, or even pulling the plug on the new product or service. Furthermore, investors will be disappointed. They were told that the innovation would generate a certain sales level within just a few years. When that doesn't happen, often their conclusion is that either the innovation itself is a dud or the management team handling it is a dud—and further investments may be hard to come by.

However, as we have seen, it is quite possible that these conclusions are premature and that it is just a matter of time before takeoff occurs. The

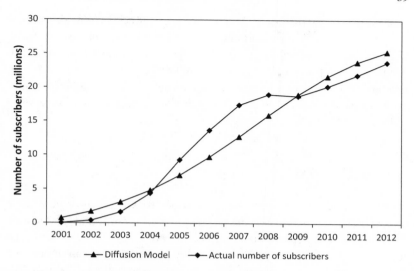

FIGURE I.7. Forecast versus actual diffusion curve of satellite radio*

* Total number of subscribers to XM and Sirius as reported by the companies.

critical mass needed to propel the snowball effect may be just around the corner. And in another twist, if indeed the social force is a major factor, then once sufficient adopters accumulate, a steep growth phase will occur. In this phase, analysts' roughly linear growth models will typically *under-estimate* sales. This will, of course, lead to the reverse issues—potential underproduction, not taking appropriate marketing actions, and not tapping into investor funds sufficiently in advance.

While highlighting the pros of the basic diffusion model compared to analyst prediction methods is insightful, the proof of the model's value ultimately needs to be "in the pudding." By the end of 2012, sufficient data were available to see how a basic diffusion model constructed prior to launch fared. Figure 1.7 plots the first twelve years of cumulative data for the diffusion of the satellite radio category as well as the basic diffusion model curve based on the parameters we derived from analogous innovations and prelaunch market research.

What can we say? Although the basic diffusion model forecast is a bit more conservative than the actual data for a number of years (2006–2008), and we discuss the possible reasons for this in more detail in chapter 6, it should be quite clear that both in terms of shape and in terms of relative fit, the basic diffusion model forecast comes fairly close to reality much of the time. In particular, in the first five years, the basic diffusion model forecast does a pretty good job of tracking actual adoption, as it does for the last four years. For example, as noted, by year 5, the basic diffusion model forecast predicts close to seven million people will have adopted a satellite radio service, while the actual data came in at about nine million. By contrast, the average of the three analyst predictions was about twenty million.

Are We There Yet?

Well, if that is the question, then you know the answer must be "We're *almost* there." Hopefully you are walking on much more solid ground now with respect to the forecasting task laid out at the beginning of the chapter. You conceptually understand the type of factors that can affect how likely consumers are to adopt an innovation. In particular, you realize that it is critical to get a handle on whether consumers are likely to be persuaded by firm and media communications or by previous adopters (or both). You have been exposed to a model that nicely and succinctly captures the two main processes that affect consumers' adoption timing and a way to think about how to select parameters for the model based on market research and information from previously launched innovations. But is that all that is needed to perform an ROI analysis to assess the advisability of the proposed innovation and get back to the CEO on whether to go ahead with writing the check? Well, not quite. The adoption pattern that has been described and modeled in this chapter is a critical first step in evaluating the market's reaction to an innovation, but it is by no means the final step. For many innovative technologies, like satellite radio, revenue from customers is generated each month postadoption because it entails delivering a recurring component (in this case a service). Furthermore, the cumulative adoption curves shown thus far depict scenarios in which new adopters are added to the existing customer base. Yet what if some customers, who were once new adopters, decide to terminate the relationship—that is to say, they decide the product or service is not for them anymore? There could also be cost implications in serving customers over time and revenue implications in trying to interest them in cross-selling opportunities. Therefore, we need to introduce concepts and tools that will allow us to model these long-run financial considerations of innovation adopters. That is the subject of the next chapter.

Key Takeaways

- Most innovations tend to exhibit a similar pattern of growth over time: a bell-shaped curve for the number of new adopters and an S-shaped curve for the cumulative number of adopters.
- The exact shape of these curves will depend on the specific characteristics of the innovation and its appeal versus barriers to potential adopters. Five factors — relative advantage, complexity, trialability, observability, and compatibility — are often used to understand differences in the speed of innovation adoption in a given population.
- Two primary forces drive the growth rate of innovation adoption: (1) the *individual force*, which reflects influences that are independent of others in the social system (e.g., firm-initiated communications), and (2) the *social force*, which reflects influences that are dependent on interaction with others in the social system (e.g., word of mouth).
- The basic diffusion model combines the individual and social forces, along with the anticipated total (long-run) market potential, and allows one to create an estimate of the number of new adopters over time (i.e., for generating the expected bell-shaped diffusion curve) for a new product or service. This model constitutes a key tool for managers to predict the future growth rate of the customer base for their specific innovation.

The Whole Is Bigger Than the Sum of Its (Diffusion and Customer Lifetime Value) Parts

The purpose of a business is to create a customer.—What Peter Drucker said in 1954

The purpose of a business is to create, manage, and retain many profitable customers for a long time.—What Peter Drucker might have said today

Three, two, one . . . blastoff! XM Satellite Radio's two satellites, aptly named "Rock" and "Roll," were launched into orbit in spring 2001 to the cheers of its ecstatic managers. The revolutionary radio service was set to begin broadcasting content in the fall of that year, but already certain sounds could be heard with crystal clarity. These were the voices of investors, asking whether the billions of dollars they had poured into the nascent venture would ever be recovered, and if so, when. They had good reason to be at least a bit nervous. Terrestrial radio (AM and FM) up to that point had been virtually free of charge to its listeners and, sooner or later, rival Sirius would launch its own service and pose a serious (no pun intended) competitive threat. Nevertheless, here was this yet-to-see-a-penny-in-revenues company claiming that it would convince consumers to spend hundreds of dollars on new radio receivers and pay a nontrivial monthly fee to listen in and that it could compete effectively in the satellite radio race that would soon heat up. For investors, it was undoubtedly not enough to see market research data suggesting that some consumers found the service potentially interesting. And while helpful, it was also probably not enough to be given a sense of how quickly these consumers might sign up. Investors most likely wanted XM management to give them a credible assessment of when they could see their precious money back and, ideally, a healthy return on it.

You might wonder what it would take to provide such a return on investment (ROI) forecast for an innovation. Stay tuned, as that is exactly what we aim to accomplish in this chapter.

Customers as Financial Assets

Famous management guru Peter Drucker once quipped that "the purpose of a business is to create a customer." Few in the business community would argue with that statement. But for many companies, creating customers is really only a starting point. The financial health of their enterprise often depends on holding onto those created customers and deriving direct or indirect earnings from them over time. These companies would probably want to adjust the quote to read, "The purpose of a business is to create a customer and have that customer generate profits for the business for a long time."

Examples of companies from a range of industries that see the world this way abound. A firm that specializes in shaving equipment is happy when a customer decides to buy its latest and greatest razor, but the bulk of its profits typically accrue over a long period, as the customer purchases new blades to replace the ones that wear out. In fact, a company like Gillette is often willing to sell its razor at minimal profit (sometimes even at a loss) in anticipation of future blade revenues. A firm that develops cool gaming apps might offer consumers its fun creations entirely for free. How will it make money? Well, if each consumer that downloads one of these apps keeps playing, and there are enough of them, then advertisers would likely be willing to pay for placing ads on the game. For Rovio Entertainment, the maker of *Angry Birds*, this model seems to have worked quite well. And most of us are probably familiar with how this "create the customer *now* and make money on them *later*" method works in the cable television arena. Companies like Comcast, Time Warner Cable, and Charter Communications sign you up with very appealing introductory offers (e.g., a ninety-day free trial) in the hopes that you stick around and pay monthly fees for years to come, potentially upgrading to premium packages along the way.

Given the prevalence of business models predicated on some form of recurring revenue that originates from customer engagement over time, a firm might as well view each customer as a financial asset that supplies it with periodic cash flows. Consequently, when the customer first buys a product, downloads an application, or signs up for a service, that customer is effectively associated with a long-term value to the firm that encompasses all expected future earnings from him or her.

But this "customer = financial asset" characterization seems like a cold, somewhat impersonal way to describe the nature of the interaction between a firm and its precious customers. Drucker might have disapproved. Perhaps it would be more agreeable to cast this interaction in a different light and think of it as an ongoing relationship between the firm and its customers, a relationship that is not just about "take" but also about "give": you provide value to customers by serving them and they return the favor by providing your company profits. A viable business thus means that you create a customer in the hopes of forming a mutually beneficial commitment. Viewed in this light, upon initiating the relationship, you might want to tell the customer, quoting Humphrey Bogart's famous line at the end of the classic film *Casablanca*, "I think this is the beginning of a beautiful friendship," and add to it, "one that hopefully lasts a lifetime."

A Lifetime of Value

Hopefully, the above discussion conveyed a sense that understanding the economics of the customer-firm relationship can advance us in our quest to provide a meaningful innovation-ROI forecast, specifically the "returns" part of the ROI acronym. What we are essentially after is a way to capture the "warm and fuzzy" aspects of the relationship while at the same time couching things in a "cold and hard" financial asset perspective.

Luckily, marketers have spent a considerable amount of time thinking through these very issues and developed a framework to address them. This framework is commonly referred to as the customer lifetime value model, or CLV model for short.

The major building blocks of the CLV model should come as no surprise to you given the description of what a healthy customer-firm connection entails. These building blocks include (1) the per-period profit margin, (2) the retention rate, (3) the discount factor, and (4) the acquisition cost. Each component allows quantifying a different critical element of the customer-firm relationship and, when appropriately combined, will be shown to yield the long-term value of each customer as assessed at any point in time—in particular, when he or she joins a service or buys a product for the first time. Figure 2.1 provides a simple schematic of the CLV model.

With that as a background, let's dive in and understand the different components of the CLV model better.

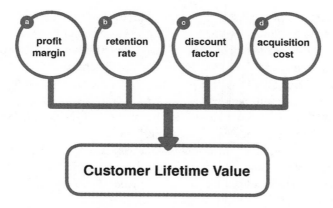

FIGURE 2.1. The customer lifetime value (CLV) model

The Per-Period Profit Margin: How Much Does the Firm Make on a Customer in Each Period?

We may not always be happy about it, but most of us have to pay bills on a fairly regular basis. Be it rent or mortgage payments, gym membership dues, cable television and Internet service fees, or wireless communication charges, somebody out there is giving us something we want, and we pay for it on a monthly or annual basis. And we may not realize it, but in many categories, even when there is no preset payment schedule and we are charged per specific item purchased or per specific use of the service, it is assumed that *on average,* we will exhibit some kind of repeat purchase frequency or payment regularity. For example, a typical man who shaves every day will buy a new pack of blades every other month; a person with an online brokerage account will make five stock trades a quarter; a tablet user will watch an on-demand movie once a week; an iPod owner will download two new songs a month from iTunes; and so on. These payments constitute the revenues that firms expect to earn from customers in each time period.

Of course, in order to provide customers with these products and services, firms typically incur some expenses, such as production, distribution, and personnel costs. For example, the blades need to be manufactured and shipped to stores, and the retailers need to be incentivized to stock them on shelves; the cellular phone grid needs to be maintained (or infrastructure leased at some cost per minute utilized), and customer support at retail locations and call centers must be staffed; content licensing fees need to be paid for each movie or song downloaded, and the IT infrastructure that supports this activity must be kept in working and up-to-date condition. It is often useful to express these expenses on a per-customer basis, and indeed many of them are directly linked to a particular customer transaction or activity. And one can translate expenses that are general and fixed in nature, like "maintaining the IT infrastructure," by dividing the expenditure by the total number of customers served.

Firms think of these expenses as the ongoing cost of doing business: applying Drucker's "business = customer" tenet, managers often attach a "cost-to-serve" number to each customer, which reflects all the expenses incurred in delivering value to the customer per period. With all this in mind, the definition of the *per-period profit margin* is now straightforward to express:

EXPRESSION 2.1. The per-period profit margin

Per-period profit margin = (Total revenues from the customer) –
(Cost to serve the customer)

So basically, you take all the revenues the customer generates in exchange for using or having access to the firm's products and services during the period, and you subtract from that the cost to serve that customer during the period. What you get is the net value the firm captures from the customer in each period.

Let's look at some concrete examples. A customer of a wireless service provider with a monthly bill that comes out to $50 per month on average typically has a cost-to-serve number of about $30. Therefore, the per-period profit margin of this customer would be $50 – $30 = $20 a month.

Consider an owner of a minitablet like the Kindle Fire, who buys five e-books and downloads three paid apps per quarter. At an average selling price of $10 per book and $3 per app, quarterly revenues from such a customer are $59 (or about $20 a month). Amazon, however, does not get to enjoy all these revenues, as it has to pay content licensing fees (about $7 per book) and only gets a cut from app sales (30 percent). Therefore, the per-period profit margin of such a customer would be about $17.70 per quarter (by subtracting $41.30 from $59).

Of course, per-period profit margins can differ across customers, may fluctuate over time, and exhibit an increasing or decreasing trend. In our wireless phone example, a heavy user may require more minutes each month and thus have a higher monthly bill relative to a light user; some consumers may talk more during the summer months than winter months (and vice versa for other consumers); and a person may at first use their wireless mobile phone only sparsely, as an "emergency" safety net for when they have no access to a landline, but later shift the majority of their phone calls to wireless. In the minitablet example, a consumer may at first only download a single book per quarter, but after getting used to the digital rather than print book format, he or she may read all books this way; a person may go from occasionally streaming a movie to doing so once a week; or an individual may slowly realize that it is more fun to play games on the device given its bigger screen than on a smartphone and after a while download many more gaming apps. All these consumption shifts would cause the per-period profit margin to change. That's fine; CLV can handle it.

Let's move on to the next building block of the model.

The Retention Rate: How Long Is the Customer Going to Stay with the Firm?

"Nothing lasts forever." Many musicians have used this line, or a variation of it, in their hit songs (Tears for Fears, Bryan Adams, Echo and the Bunnymen, to name a few). Unfortunately, many firms find themselves singing the very same lyric as far as the relationship with their customers is concerned. The "beautiful friendship" that began between the firm and its customers rarely lasts for more than several years, let alone forever. Customers may relocate, switch jobs, find a new partner, have kids, develop different needs as they age, be affected by economic or societal trends, receive better offers from other firms, or simply want to try something new. Any of these factors may cause customers to discontinue the relationship—cancel their subscription, stop buying refills, no longer download digital content, cease to actively use the service (causing advertisers to lose interest), and so on. In effect, they are no longer customers, at least not from a "generating returns" point of view. Thus while it might be tempting for a firm to just take the per-period profit margin it gets from a customer today and assume this earning will keep padding its bank account for the entire lifespan of the individual, it is more realistic to expect a shorter duration for the relationship. Firms must realize that they are always at risk of losing some of their customers and the associated profits that they yield.

The CLV model fully accommodates this reality. In particular, the tendency of customers to stay with the firm is captured by a measure called the "retention rate." When discussing the average or general retention rate of the customer base, it is common to define it as the ratio of those customers who are still with the firm at the end of the period to the total number of customers at the beginning of the period as in the following expression:

EXPRESSION 2.2. The retention rate

$$\text{Retention rate} = \frac{\text{Number of customer at the end of the period}}{\text{Number of customers at the beginning of the period}}$$

Note that the numerator of the ratio in this definition is based only on customers from the pool of those that started the period—that is, on customers that are part of the denominator set—and not on any new customers that joined in the interim (of course, those new customers would be relevant for calculating the retention rate in the next period).

In CLV terminology, the counterpart of the retention rate is called the "attrition" rate (sometimes referred to as the "churn" rate, though in chapter 6, we distinguish between the two terms). It is basically calculated as 1 − retention rate, and one can replace the 1 with *100 percent* when the retention rate is expressed as a percentage. For example, if we expect that, of a given group of customers at the beginning of the year, only 80 percent will stay on with the firm next year, then the yearly retention rate for this group is 0.8 and their attrition rate is 0.2. Another way to interpret a retention rate of 80 percent is that the probability of any given customer still being served by the firm in the next period is 0.8, while the probably that they will leave the firm is 0.2.

There are a few ways to assess the retention rate in practice. The first is to examine recent data on customers and estimate the attrition that took place in this time frame. Specifically, one can list the set of customers at the beginning of period A, take note of how many of them were still customers at the beginning of period B, use expression 2.2 to calculate the retention rate in period A, and then repeat this process for as many periods as desired or for which there are available data. The second way is to draw an analogy to the retention rate from other contexts. In some markets, such as wireless phone service and cable television, attrition rates are regularly recorded as part of financial reporting. If one is reasonably convinced that customers' tendency to stick with a product in one category is similar to that in another category, and the latter quantity can be obtained, then this "by-analogy" approach is plausible, at least as a proxy.

If at the end of each period a customer only has some probability of staying with the firm and starting the next period, what happens over time? Consider a case where the firm currently has 100 customers and the yearly retention rate is 0.9 (i.e., a 90 percent probability that someone who is a customer at the beginning of the current year will remain so the following year). Then if 100 customers started in year 1, we should expect 90 of them to open year 2. But once again, the 0.9 retention rate will kick in for those remaining customers, so we should expect only 81 of them to start year 3. If we keep following this "retention trail," we end up with only 73 customers starting year 4, 66 starting year 5, and so forth. What this tells us is that any initial group of customers the firm starts out with will gradually dwindle in numbers as we progress from period to period. And we can write this more formally as the following:

EXPRESSION 2.3. Retained customers

Number of customers at the beginning of period N =
(Initial number of customers) · (Retention rate)$^{N-1}$

Note from this expression that the probability that any one customer is still with the firm in period N in the future is (Retention rate)$^{N-1}$. This quantity will come in handy later.

It turns out that in the banking/financial sector, retention rates are the same order of magnitude as in this simple example. For instance, based on reported data, we know that Capital One (a US credit card company) has a yearly retention rate of about 0.85. Some industries exhibit lower retention rates. Such is the case in the wireless communication market, where nearly 2 percent of customers are lost each month. This means that the yearly attrition rate for wireless phone service providers is about 22 percent, which implies a retention rate of 78 percent (or 0.78). This kind of a retention rate implies that out of a group of 100 customers who start with the firm at the beginning of year 1, only about 37 customers will still be with the firm in year 5 ($100 \cdot 0.78^4$), or about half the number we found in the previous example when the retention rate was 0.9!

Figure 2.2 depicts the decline in a particular cohort of customers for a financial services firm (Capital One), a satellite radio company (XM), and a wireless communication provider (T-Mobile). As can be gleaned from the figure, it is clear that the number of customers from an initial cohort that stay with the firm decreases at a faster rate than what a straight line

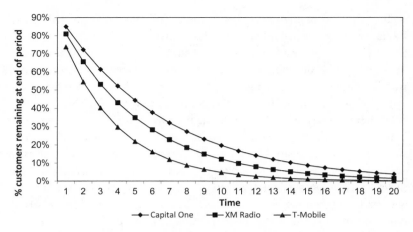

FIGURE 2.2. Decline in the number of customers of a given cohort for three select services

would exhibit, or as mathematicians would say, this number declines exponentially over time. Indeed, it may be disheartening for a firm to learn that even though it can retain about three-quarters of its customers each year, after just five years, it will lose nearly three-quarters of these customers.

The retention rate is a helpful metric that allows capturing the likelihood that a customer will stay with the firm at the end of each period, but how does it fit with the CLV model we are trying to build? It appears we need a more direct measure of how long we should expect a customer to be with the firm. In other words, what we are after is the expected duration or "lifetime" of the customer-firm relationship—the L part of the CLV model.

No worries. It is quite simple to use the retention rate we have been dealing with thus far to express the average number of periods a customer is expected to keep using the firm's products and/or services, or as marketers like to call it, the customer's "average stay":

EXPRESSION 2.4. The average stay of a customer

Average stay = 1 / (1 − Retention rate) = 1 / Attrition rate

Why does this relatively simple relationship hold? Let's get some intuition by way of plugging in numbers. If the retention rate is 0.8, as in an earlier example, then 20 percent of the initial cohort is expected to leave after one period, 16 percent of the initial cohort leaves after two periods (since of the 80 percent that remained after period 1, 20 percent are expected to leave in the next period, so $0.8 \cdot 0.2 = 0.16$), about 13 percent after three periods, and so on. If we compute the weighted average of the number of periods until each customer leaves, which is the same as the average stay, we get five periods. And this may not surprise you, as $5 \cdot 20$ percent $=$ 100 percent, or $1 / 0.2 = 5$.

The average stay of a Capital One cardholder, given a retention rate of 0.85, is $1 / 0.15 = 6.7$ years. The average stay of a T-Mobile subscriber, given a retention rate of 0.78, is $1 / 0.22 = 4.6$ years. One could also work in reverse. For example, analysts estimate that, on average, Kindle Fire users will hold on to their devices (before switching to a different one) for an average of three years. Since we can write attrition rate $= 1 /$ (average stay), this means that the Kindle Fire attrition rate is 0.33, and its retention rate is 0.67.

As these examples show, there is a positive relationship between the retention rate and the average stay—as one quantity goes up, so does the other. This relationship, however, is highly nonlinear, meaning that it cannot be depicted by a straight, linear line and that a small increase in the retention rate will have a relatively big effect on the average stay. Figure 2.3 demonstrates this nonlinear relationship for AT&T Wireless subscribers for the years 2004 through 2010. As can be derived from the figure, an increase of less than 20 percent in the annual retention rate (from

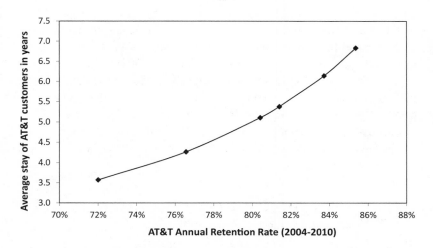

FIGURE 2.3. Average stay of AT&T subscribers as a function of the retention rate, 2004–10[*]

[*] The retention rate of AT&T customers indeed increased from 72 percent in 2004 to 85.4 percent in 2010.

72 percent to 85.4 percent) during this seven-year period resulted in an almost 90 percent increase of the time an average consumer remained an AT&T subscriber (from 3.6 to 6.8 years).

With the first two building blocks in hand—namely, the per-period profit margin and the retention rate as translated into an average stay—we can already get a rough sense of how the CLV model works. The former quantity is a measure of the value the firm hopes to capture from the customer in each period, and the latter is a measure of how many periods it expects the relationship to last. Multiplying these two quantities should give us an idea of what the customer's total value is to the firm over the anticipated lifetime of the relationship:

EXPRESSION 2.5. The nondiscounted customer lifetime value

$$\text{CLV}^{\text{nd}} = (\text{Per-period profit margin}) \cdot (\text{Average stay}) =$$
$$(\text{Per-period profit margin}) / (1 - \text{retention rate})$$

Let's see how this expression would play out for some of the examples we have been looking at in this chapter. For the wireless phone customer that generates per-period profit margins of $20 a month (= $240 a year) and has an average stay of 4.6 years, we get $\text{CLV}^{\text{nd}} = \$240 \cdot 4.6 = \$1{,}104$. For the minitablet customer with an expected average stay of 3 years and per-period profit margins of $17.7 a quarter (= $71 a year), we get $\text{CLV}^{\text{nd}} = \$71 \cdot 3 = \$212$.

Our quest for quantifying the value of the relationship between the customer and the firm is starting to come together. What is missing, you may ask? Well, you might have noticed that we put an "nd" superscript on the definition in expression 2.5. It stands for "nondiscounted," and it is there to signify that the definition is not entirely complete because we have not taken into account the time value of money. In other words, we haven't discounted earnings in future periods so that they are comparable to earnings in the current period. That is the essence of what the next building block of the model aims to do.

The Discount Factor: How Can the Firm Account for the Time Value of Future Customer Revenues?

Ask yourself this: "Is a dollar earned from the customer today the same as a dollar that will be earned from this customer five years from now?" Monetary experts would vehemently answer no, citing basic financial principles related to the opportunity cost of capital and arguing that the value of money in the future is lower than the value of the same nominal amount of money today. One way to think about why this may be so is that the firm can invest money it has in the current period and earn interest on it, so the one dollar invested today is expected to be worth more than one dollar five years from now. Another way to think about it is that if the firm borrows a dollar today, it will have to pay back more than a dollar five years from now, as the lender will expect some interest on the loan. Any way you choose to look at it, "time is money." Consequently, to properly quantify a customer's long-term value to the firm, we need to account for this common-sense monetary principle when we tally future earnings.

What we would like to do is put all the earnings on an equal footing by accommodating the discrepancy between the lower value of money in the future and the full value of money at present. In financial lingo, we need to properly *discount future cash flows* from the customer so that they are all in current dollar terms and thus comparable. But how?

In practice, when financial professionals are confronted with such a task, they use what's called a *discount factor*: they divide money expected to accrue at the end of this period by an appropriate discount factor, which allows adjusting the value of this money and expressing it in current, start-of-the-period terms. Money that is expected to be available only at the end of the next period is adjusted "twice": dividing this cash once makes it comparable to money earned at the end of this period, and dividing again makes it comparable to money earned today. Cash expected to be earned at the end of the third period needs to be adjusted three times, and so on. More generally, the present value of cash earned in a future period (assumed to accrue at the end of each period) is simply that cash divided by the discount factor taken to the power of the number of periods forward, which we again denote by N:

EXPRESSION 2.6. The present value of a future cash flow

$$\text{Present value} = \frac{\text{Cash flow}}{(\text{Discount factor})^N}$$

The customer lifetime value model has largely adopted this financial discounting approach and similarly looks at customers as investments or projects whose future per-period profit margins are worth less (in today's terms) as time proceeds. So simply replace "cash flow" with "per-period profit margin" in expression 2.6, and you're all set as far as CLV is concerned.

You might wonder what an appropriate discount factor looks like and where one would obtain it. A common approach in CLV modeling is to use the financial measure known as the weighted average cost of capital (WACC) for calculating the discount factor. Broadly, WACC takes the various types of capital a firm has (debt and equity), establishes their "cost" to the firm (based on the interest rate the firm faces), and weights these costs according to the proportion of each type of capital the firm has. WACC is an "effective interest rate" that firms often use to assess the ROI on various projects and initiatives they consider. The discount factor is taken as $(1 + WACC)$, or in plain English terms, $(1 + \text{effective interest rate})$.

Although WACC can differ by firm or even project, on average, at any given point in time, industries are associated with a typical WACC, reflecting the risks and ease of obtaining capital in each of them. A recent analysis (January 2013) by New York University researchers found that average WACCs ranged from a low of 3.13 percent in the electric utilities sector to a high of 10.97 percent in the private equity sector. Telecom services, like T-Mobile, had a WACC of 7.05 percent, which means that a reasonable discount factor for such companies would be $(1 + 0.0705) = 1.0705$. The WACC was determined to be 7.81 percent for the electronics industry and 7.66 percent for entertainment technology, which means that in our minitablet case, we could use something like 7.75 percent for WACC, with a corresponding discount factor of 1.0775. As economic and industry conditions change, so will the WACC values that are relevant to use for discounting cash flows to the current period (e.g., in January 2015 electronics and entertainment had WACC values of 7.37 percent and 7.61 percent, respectively).

With three of the model's building blocks now under our belt—the per-period profit margin, the retention rate, and the discount factor—we are ready to write an expression for CLV that does not have an "nd" (non-discounted) superscript attached to it. We need to modify CLV^{nd} so that each period into the future is discounted appropriately: one period out by the discount factor, two periods out by the discount factor squared, three periods out by the discount factor cubed, and so on. Because each period's cash flow needs to be discounted differently, it would be wise to form our customer lifetime value expression by looking at things on a period-by-period basis.

We just saw how to calculate the present value of a customer's cash flow earned in a given period in the future (by using the per-period profit margin and the discount rate, as in expression 2.6). Yet we also know that we cannot ignore the fact that across periods there is only some probability that the customer stays with the firm (given by the retention rate, as in expression 2.3) and generates these profit margins. Hence for each period, we can express the expected cash flow from the customer in present value terms,[1] which we will call the period-specific present value of a customer:

EXPRESSION 2.7. Present value of expected customer profits at any specific future period

$$\frac{\text{(Per-period profit margin)} \cdot \text{(Retention rate)}^{N-1}}{\text{(Discount factor)}^N}$$

Period-specific present value of a customer =

To obtain the expected financial value of a customer to the firm over N periods expressed in today's monetary terms, what remains is to sum up all the relevant period-specific present values of that customer. This leads to the following expression for CLV:

EXPRESSION 2.8. Customer lifetime value model (long version)

CLV = (Period 1 present value) + (Period 2 present value) + . . . + (Period N present value)

How many periods should we sum over? In other words, what should be the value of N in the CLV expression that we have just derived? In some instances, the firm might have reason to believe that after a predetermined number of periods, the relationship with the customer will end—for example, if there is a contract that is not expected to be renewed, if a next-generation product is planned that most customers will switch to, or if a patent will expire at a known date and imitators will critically disrupt the cash flow dynamics. Alternatively, the firm might have a particular horizon in mind for assessing the business results of its investments—for example, a three- or five-year span or the expected tenure of the current CEO. One could also advocate for using the average stay defined earlier as a benchmark for the number of periods to sum over.

However, in other instances, there may be no anticipated event that would impact the duration of the customer-firm relationship and no particular horizon over which the firm should assess cash flows from its customers. In theory, then, we could sum over a relatively long time, letting the retention rate take care of the possibility that the customer will leave the firm at any point in the future. It turns out that when the summation is over a long enough number of periods, the CLV expression can be very closely approximated by a simple formula (which happens to be the sum of an infinitely long geometric series). Specifically,

EXPRESSION 2.9. Customer lifetime value model (short version)

$$CLV = \frac{\text{Per-period profit margin}}{(\text{Discount factor}) - (\text{Retention rate})} = \frac{\text{Per-period profit margin}}{(1 + \text{Cost of capital}) - (\text{Retention rate})}$$

Notice the similarity with our earlier formula for customer lifetime value that did not incorporate discounting (expression 2.5). The only adjustment needed to account for discounting when the time horizon is "infinite" is to add the effective cost of capital to the denominator.[2]

Continuing with some of the examples examined earlier, a typical wireless phone subscriber who has recently joined the service has a CLV of ($20 · 12) / (1 + 0.0705 − 0.78) = $826, which is about $278 less than the previous value we calculated when we did not take discounting into account. And for a minitablet user, CLV is ($17.7 · 4) / (1 + 0.0775 − 0.67) = $174, which is smaller but more realistic than the $212 we would have obtained had we ignored the need to discount future customer cash flows.

At this point in our CLV journey, we seem to have a good way to quantify the value a customer generates for the firm throughout the relationship. So why is there a fourth building block in the CLV framework? Well, in our derivations so far, we assumed the customer-firm relationship had already formed, and our task was to evaluate the present value of all the future profit margin flows. But how does the relationship form? What if the firm has to exert effort and resources to get the customer to sign up in the first place? Surely we can't ignore these matters in the context of understanding the customer's profitability to the firm. That's why we need a fourth building block.

Acquisition Cost: What Does It Cost the Firm to Add a New Customer?

As you look back at figure 2.1, you might be a little puzzled as to why "acquisition costs" is depicted as the last block in the model and not the first one, since you need to acquire a customer before you can start making any kind of profits on him or her, don't you? Yes, that's true. However, the astute, forward-looking manager knows that unless you understand what someone is going to be worth to you once he or she joins your customer-base ranks, it makes very little sense to throw away money to try to acquire that customer in the first place. In other words, the output from analyzing the first three building blocks of the model, per the CLV expression we derived, is a benchmark against which the acquisition effort should be evaluated. That is why considering acquisition costs last may not be such a bad idea after all.

To acquire new customers, companies do a host of things. Some firms advertise on television, in print, or online. Others might offer free installation, free samples, or a free trial period. The use of rebates, "0 percent financing," and subsidies are additional ways firms try to entice would-be customers to buy in or sign up. These forms of marketing are largely intended to create awareness and persuade consumers to enter into the customer-firm relationship. All of these measures cost money—either in terms of the direct expenses involved or in terms of the personnel the company devotes to developing and executing them; often both types of expenses are incurred. In practice, there is rarely such a thing as a "free customer," and it is common to label all the expenses associated with attracting a customer as acquisition costs.

A wireless service provider, such as T-Mobile, might spend hundreds of millions a year on television advertising, require paying only 50 percent of the list price of the handset (thereby subsidizing the other 50 percent), and have an agreement to pay retailers like Best Buy a fee for every new subscriber they sign up at their stores. Similarly, in the case of the Kindle Fire, Amazon might decide to sell each device at a loss to encourage purchase as well as engage in television advertising. And a pharmaceutical company like Eli Lilly might spend millions of dollars compensating sales reps to visit physicians in hospitals and clinics, offer free samples, and engage in direct-to-consumer (DTC) advertising to have patients prescribed a new medication to treat a chronic condition like diabetes.

A more complete picture of the expected profitability of the customer-firm relationship should thus include what goes on in the "courting period." And as these costs are incurred upfront, it seems only logical to incorporate the expenses associated with this phase into the model by subtracting the acquisition costs from the present value of expected future earnings from the customer—that is, from CLV. Referring to the firm's activities during the acquisition phase, when it tries to attract new customers, as *prospecting* and to each individual who may (or may not) decide to become a customer as a *prospect* leads to the following definition for the prospective customer lifetime value (PCLV):

EXPRESSION 2.10. Prospective customer lifetime value

Prospective customer lifetime value =
Customer lifetime value – Acquisition costs

The distinction between a "customer" and a "prospective customer" is important. This is because it is rare for a company to achieve perfect success with its acquisition efforts. The conversion from being targeted to becoming a customer is typically far less than 100 percent (often less than 10 percent, in fact). Firms cast a marketing net, which can be quite wide initially, over a group of individuals that are candidates to be customers, but ultimately only a subset of those targeted actually sign on. This poses a question: how should we handle the costs associated with trying to acquire prospects that never become customers—that is, those who don't convert? Surely you would agree that it is reasonable to take these costs into account. What marketers customarily do is incorporate them into the acquisition costs of those prospects that were ultimately acquired. This is accomplished by taking all the costs expended in prospecting efforts and dividing by the number of customers actually acquired. Thus each customer's acquisition costs, which appear in expression 2.10, capture the fact that it was necessary to target a broader set of individuals in order to acquire just them.

Consider the following examples. Say that a free sample of a new razor, which costs the company $1 to make and distribute, was offered to one hundred thousand men at shopping malls on the east coast. If that effort resulted in ten thousand of these men switching to the new razor, the acquisition cost would be $10 (since $100,000 / 10,000 = $10). This is despite the fact that each of the men that converted to the new razor only received one sample that cost $1. In the wireless phone setting, if a company like T-Mobile spends $300 million on advertising in a year to reach a sizable portion of the population and ends up converting four million new subscribers to its service, the acquisition cost associated with the advertising portion alone is $75 ($300m / 4m), despite the fact that many people saw the ads (most of whom did not convert). To these types of prospecting expenses, we need to add costs that are incurred contingent on a specific customer acquisition, such as a handset subsidy of $150 and retail commissions of $100 per signed subscriber. Thus the fully loaded costs of acquiring a wireless service customer in this example would amount to $325. The prospective customer lifetime value of a cell phone subscriber is therefore $826 − $325 = $501.

As with other parameters of the CLV framework, one can sometimes use analogies from related product categories to assess acquisition costs. For instance, information on advertising and marketing spending, as well as the number of new customers acquired in a period, are often available from firms' financial reporting.

Taking Stock of Customer Lifetime Value

We have come a long way in our customer valuation journey. Before we move on, it is perhaps worthwhile to recap the primary stages and places we visited along the way. We started with providing a "quick and dirty" measure for CLV that took into account the profit margins from a customer in each future period and assumed we would earn those profit margins for the average amount of time the customer was expected to stay in the relationship (CLV^{nd}, per expression 2.5). We then realized that it would be more practical to scale future revenues by a discount factor so that profit margins earned in later periods are in present value terms, which gave us the expressions commonly used for quantifying CLV (per expressions 2.8 and 2.9). Finally, we noted that for the customer relationship to begin, the firm needs to attract potential customers through efforts that result in acquisition costs. Deducting these costs from CLV leads to the PCLV measure (per expression 2.10). The CLV expression is sufficient if one is interested in taking a snapshot of the current customer base and its value to the firm going forward, since these customers have already been acquired and their acquisition costs are already "sunk." Yet if the firm is at the phase of trying to acquire new customers, PCLV is the more appropriate measure.

You may have noticed that with each step of the way along the customer lifetime journey—from CLV^{nd} to CLV to PCLV—the overall value of the customer to the firm went down. While this might be viewed as unfortunate by the firm, it yields a more accurate assessment of a customer's worth. Figure 2.4 depicts this decreasing trend for the wireless phone service example we tracked throughout.

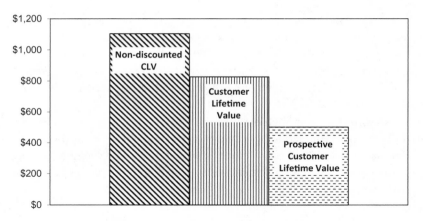

FIGURE 2.4. The various measures of lifetime value for wireless phone provision

Diffusion + Prospective Customer Lifetime Value = Innovation Equity

Recall Peter Drucker's powerful idea that the "purpose of a business is to create a customer." Note that Drucker talks about *a* customer. The CLV model we have developed and its PCLV extension indeed allow us to understand how firms can assess the long-run value to them of creating *a* customer. But no matter how much per-period profit margins we can squeeze out of *a* customer, and even if we can keep *a* customer for a relatively long time, for all practical purposes, one customer is not going to be enough. Firms typically need a lot of customers in order to be "in the black," and they can significantly boost their top line by growing the number of customers they serve. Upon further reflection then, and as suggested in the opening to this chapter, companies might want to amend Drucker's famous line to be, "The purpose of a business is to create, manage, and retain many profitable customers for a long time."

Let's try to understand the customer lifetime value implications of moving from a "single customer" perspective to a "multiple customers" perspective through the lens of a business that plans to launch an innovation into the marketplace, which, by the way, was the context in which Drucker made his famous line about customer creation. If all the customers for the innovation are acquired at the very same time, then summing up their respective PCLVs would yield the total value to the firm generated by the innovation. As firms often use average or typical quantities for each of the relevant customer lifetime value parameters, this would simply boil down to calculating PCLV once and multiplying by the entire set of customers acquired at launch.

But hold on. If the previous chapter taught us anything, it is that innovations tend to *diffuse* among members of the relevant population over time and that you rarely penetrate the full market potential, which we called *m*, in just one period. Moreover, because there are various factors that can drive adoption—both individual and social forces—adoption is seldom uniform: we may observe very few new adopters in some periods and many new adopters in other periods. So how can we continue to use customer lifetime value modeling to express the expected returns from introducing an innovation into the marketplace when new customers come on board at different times and at differing intensities? The answer, quite elegantly, is to combine the two models! Let the basic diffusion model and the CLV model work together and complement each other.

The idea of linking the two models is quite intuitive when you think about it. Recall that the basic diffusion model allows us to examine how the first-time adoption of an innovation takes place, what influences the process, and how it unfolds over time. The unit of analysis was the adopter, and we tracked the number of new adoptions in each time period. Customer lifetime value models, on the other hand, allow us to gauge the expected profits from acquiring each customer. And therein lies the connection: the timing of a new adoption can be thought of as the moment of customer acquisition! The basic diffusion model tells us how many customers we can expect to acquire in each period based on what we know about how innovations are adopted, and the customer lifetime value model tells us how much money we can expect to earn on each of these customers once acquired based on what we know about how customers act as financial assets to the firm.

Figure 2.5 provides a visualization of the proposed "marriage" between the two models. In the figure, the black dots along the diffusion curve represent the number of new adopters in each time period; the higher up a dot, the more new adopters in the period. Upon adoption, these individuals become acquired customers that have a lifetime value associated with them, and the vertical lines represent this value; the longer the line, the more lifetime value each acquired customer has.

There are a few things to note from figure 2.5. The first is that the diffusion of an innovation usually begins with a low number of new adopters, consistent with our understanding that early on, mainly the individual

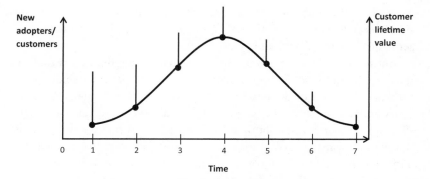

FIGURE 2.5. Innovation diffusion and customer lifetime value: Linking the two models

force is at work; it then picks up steam with a greater number of adopters, consistent with our understanding that the social force now has a snowball-like effect on adoption; and then tapers off as virtually all the relevant population has adopted. The second is that the customer lifetime value lines tend to get shorter and shorter over time. This is because CLV is assessed at the moment of acquisition. But if our vantage point is the time of launch (at t = 0 in the figure), that moment of acquisition can be several periods down the road depending on when adoption occurs. In order to assess all customer lifetime values in present dollar terms, it is only fair to apply standard discounting principles. Consequently, the farther out in time an adoption takes place, the more discounting needs to be incorporated, which lowers the lifetime value of the acquired customers. Of course, if future customers deliver greater profit margins or tend to have greater retention rates, that could mitigate the shrinking effect that discounting has. But if these factors stay roughly the same over time, then expect discounting to noticeably kick in and reduce the lifetime value of future adopters (as measured in present value terms).

To recap, combining the two models in order to value multiple customers that adopt an innovation over time entails following these steps:

1. Obtain the number of expected new customers in each period from the basic diffusion model.
2. Calculate the lifetime value of a customer acquired in each period; since we are in acquisition mode, use the PCLV model.
3. Multiply the number of expected new customers in a period by the PCLV of these customers; this yields the expected profits from all customers acquired in that period.

4. Discount expected profits for each future period using the appropriate term *(discount factor)$^{N-1}$.*

5. Sum up the discounted expected earnings from all periods within the relevant time horizon.

What do you get by following these five steps? You get the total expected profits from selling the innovation to customers in present dollar terms. You get an estimate of what the innovation is worth to the business summed across all future adopters and across time. You get innovation equity. That's right, folks: using the principles of how innovations diffuse through the marketplace, and merging them with the tenets of how to value customers over the lifetime of the relationship with the firm, produces an estimate of the return on an innovation. By comparing innovation equity to the efforts required—R&D, production facilities, and market readiness— you can generate a meaningful ROI forecast for an innovation. A formal representation of the steps involved in calculating innovation equity is given in math box 2 in the appendix.

The Innovation Equity of XM Satellite Radio: An ROI Forecasting Example

We now illustrate the innovation equity framework using the satellite radio example introduced in the previous chapter and, in so doing, close the loop with the questions that motivated this chapter—surely you remember those pesky XM investor queries on when they could expect to see a return on their investment?

As explained, there are five steps to follow, and we will walk through them one by one using relevant satellite radio inputs (available at the time of the launch). The output from each step is provided in table 2.1. Note that the analysis will be presented first at the category level, and we account for XM's share subsequently.

1. *The number of new customers in each time period* after the launch. This stuff we already know from the previous chapter. The three necessary ingredients of the basic diffusion model are the individual force, the social force, and the market potential, and for satellite radio we assessed those to be $p = 0.026$, $q = 0.403$, and $m = 28$ million, respectively (see the previous chapter if you need a refresher). Plugging these values into the model yields the number of new subscribers expected each year. This allows populating the second column in table 2.1.

TABLE 2.1 **Innovation equity for the satellite radio category**

Year	Number of new subscribers (000)	Lifetime value of a typical subscriber (PCLV)	Profits from customers acquired in period ($000)	Discounted profits ($000)
2001	728	$177	128,856	128,856
2002	995	177	176,115	161,130
2003	1,335	177	236,295	197,794
2004	1,746	177	309,042	236,678
2005	2,207	177	390,639	273,713
2006	2,664	177	471,528	302,278
2007	3,028	177	535,956	314,346
2008	3,195	177	565,515	303,461
2009	3,084	177	545,868	267,995
2010	2,698	177	477,546	214,503
2011	2,137	177	378,249	155,445
2012	1,543	177	273,111	102,687
2013	1,033	177	182,841	62,897
2014	653	177	115,581	36,377
2015	397	177	70,269	20,234

Innovation equity:

5 years = $1.0 billion
7 years = $1.6 billion
10 years = $2.4 billion
15 years = $2.8 billion

2. *The PCLV of each new subscriber.* To calculate this quantity, we need to know the four building blocks laid out in figure 2.1: the per-period profit margin, the retention rate, the discount factor, and the acquisition costs. We will use XM's anticipated values for these quantities as representative for both firms in the category.

a. *Per-period profit margin.* XM's prelaunch market research on the sensitivity of demand to satellite radio subscription prices suggested that a monthly charge of $10–$12 would maximize revenues. Conservatively, the company seriously considered a monthly fee of $9.99 to make the service more appealing at least early on. Analysts further posited that deals and discounts would be offered to customers willing to commit to long-term contracts. For purposes of forecasting, we choose to go with average subscription revenues of $11 per month. This yields annual revenues per subscriber of $132. From that number, we need to subtract the cost to serve each customer. Based on reported data in the satellite and cable television markets, in which the business model is a monthly subscription fee and the majority of ongoing expenses involve content royalties, programming, customer care, and billing issues, a cost-to-serve number of about $55 per customer a year is reasonable. This means that the profit margin for a typical satellite radio customer per year would be $132 – $55 = $77.

b. *Retention rate.* Once again, it is reasonable to assume that a service like satellite radio will have a retention rate comparable to that of cable television (83 percent) and mobile phone services (78 percent), where we obtained these rates from reported data. Taking the (rounded) average of the two yields a retention rate of 81 percent a year for an attrition rate of 19 percent. The average stay of a satellite radio customer is therefore expected to be just over five years.

c. *Discount factor.* Since this was a new venture (and category), one has to look for an industry from which to borrow the relevant WACC. An appropriate industry could be entertainment. Averaging WACC values for this industry in the three years prior to launch (9.37 percent, 9.38 percent, and 9.21 percent for the years 1998 to 2000) suggests using a value of 9.3 percent—that is, a discount factor of 1.093. Applying this discount factor, we can calculate each period's CLV as $77 / (1.093 – 0.81) = $272. From this number, we need to deduct acquisition costs to obtain PCLV.

d. *Acquisition cost.* This number can be difficult to assess prelaunch. The high acquisition costs wireless service providers incur (in the order of $325) reflects the hypercompetitiveness of this market. Acquisition costs for satellite radio would likely be in the form of a few months of free service (as a trial period), some advertising directed to attract new users, subsidies to various players in the value chain (radio manufacturers, distributors, retailers), and incentives to automakers to purchase and install receivers in new cars. The cost to XM of three to six months of free-trial service is about $20 per acquired customer (based on the cost-to-serve number we came up with), subsidies and commissions can range between $25 and $75 on each receiver produced and installed depending on how aggressive the company wishes to be, and planned advertising expenditures would likely be in the order of $20–$30 per new subscriber. According to these estimates, it would be reasonable to use an acquisition cost of about $95 per adopter, which takes into account firm prospecting efforts. Consequently, PCLV = $272 – $95 = $177.

3. For each period, multiply the number of new expected subscribers in that period by the PCLV estimate. This is where the two models, diffusion and (P)CLV, comingle—see the fourth column of table 2.1.

4. To express total expected profits from each period in present monetary terms, we need to apply the discount factor of 1.093 once more (since as you may recall, CLV is calculated from the vantage point of a given period going forward,

and we need to bring those profits "backward" to the current period). For example, to bring 2002 expected profits to 2001 terms, we divide these profits by 1.093; to bring 2003 expected profits to 2001 terms, we divide by 1.093^2, and so on. The last column of table 2.1 provides each period's discounted expected profits.

5. Now we're ready to put it all together. Adding all the discounted profits from each period over the desired horizon gives us the innovation equity for satellite radio for that time horizon. See the last four rows of table 2.1.

Recall that the basic diffusion model is meant to provide a forecast of the number of adopters at the category level—that is, not for a specific brand that markets its particular version of the innovation but rather for the adoption of all versions of the innovation in the marketplace. If only one company introduces the new product or service or is able to quickly dominate the market (e.g., due to patent protection or other barriers to entry), then the innovation equity calculated in table 2.1 is applicable to that specific company.

However, if other companies are expected to enter the market, one would need to assess the likely share of adopters that each competitor will attract. For example, long before XM Satellite Radio launched its service in fall 2001, its management knew the company would face a rival sooner or later, as the Federal Communication Commission (FCC) had granted another firm permission to launch a satellite radio service. The competitor, Sirius, was on track for commencing operations in early 2002. XM could not be entirely certain of the extent of competition it would face, as this would depend on Sirius's content, programing, subscription price, coverage quality, and marketing efforts, among other things. That said, based on the FCC's mandate to create a duopoly with the expectation that both players be viable in the long run, the similarity in preannounced radio content, and the extent of funding both firms received, there was no strong a priori reason to expect a nonsymmetric split in demand. And even if one were to argue that indirect network effects (e.g., as one service gained more subscribers, it could structure better deals with car makers or radio manufacturers) or scale effects (e.g., lower production costs or retailer support with more radios sold) could lead to a winner-take-all situation, it was not clear that either firm had the upper hand before the launch. Any way you played it out, a fifty-fifty split between the companies in adopters of the category seemed reasonable as a first-cut approximation in advance of the launch. Under this assumption, we can calculate the innovation equity of XM Satellite Radio, as a portion of the innovation

TABLE 2.2 **Innovation equity for XM Satellite Radio**
(assuming a 50 percent share of adopters in each period)

XM innovation equity:

5 years = $0.5 billion
7 years = $0.8 billion
10 years = $1.2 billion
15 years = $1.4 billion

equity of the satellite radio category, by taking half the values of the discounted profits column in table 2.1. This would result in the estimates
provided in table 2.2.

Assuming that to get XM's service up and running required funding
of about a billion dollars, the innovation equity analysis we've conducted
has revealed that, as seen at the time of the launch, this up-front investment would "pay itself off" in about ten years. For some investors, this
might be too long; for others, perhaps the ROI after fifteen years (of over
40 percent) is worth the wait; and some optimists might hope for a better-
than-equal market share relative to rival Sirius, resulting in a greater ROI.
At a minimum, what the combined framework developed in this chapter
has provided is a basis for evaluating the net present value of XM Satellite
Radio using an approach based on the solid fundamentals of how innovations get adopted in the marketplace and how customers produce returns
for the firm once they have adopted.

In chapter 6, we will more extensively cover the issue of gauging innovation diffusion and customer lifetime value at the brand level and discuss
ways to take customer switching between competitors into account. In
that chapter, we will also discuss the intense competitive dynamics that in
fact materialized in the satellite radio category and how such rivalry affected firms' innovation equity in ways that neither firm fully recognized
prelaunch. Yet for purposes of giving a preliminary assessment and responding to those who want to get a sense of the monetary returns on XM's
service prelaunch, a 50 percent share-of-adoptions approximation is probably a good start.

Some Final Innovation Equity Thoughts

Innovation equity is a powerful tool when you think about it. For a start-up
company, which is typically predicated on one main new product or service, it gives an idea of what the entire venture is worth. For a mature

company contemplating growth, it provides a way to assess the advisability of any proposed innovative project.

Innovation equity borrows from the rich research conducted over the last three decades on the diffusion of numerous innovations and on the intricacies of customer-firm relationships across a host of industries. It connects these two avenues by noting that "adoption," a focal aspect in the diffusion of innovations, can be treated as the point of "acquisition," a critical piece in assessing the lifetime value of the customer.

As might be suspected, in order to provide the first exposure to the combined framework, we made a number of reasonable assumptions, which allowed us to concentrate on the basics of what it takes to determine the equity of an innovation. The core recipe is now at your disposal. In the upcoming chapters, we will investigate a number of important business issues that are relevant to innovation and customer management and explain how they can be accommodated by modifying and expanding upon the basic diffusion model, the CLV model, and the innovation equity framework that brings the two together.

In concluding this chapter, we can't resist the temptation of stringing together a riddle to capture the essence of the material presented. Here it goes: "What do you get when you cross a diffusion model with a CLV model?" (Answer: see the title of this book!)

Key Takeaways

- For most innovations, each first-time adoption is the start of a customer-firm relationship in which the adopters generate profits for the firm over time.
- The financial value of the future stream of profits that a customer generates over time, properly discounted, is labeled the customer lifetime value (CLV). Thus each adoption can be likened to the acquisition of a new customer that is associated with a CLV.
- There are four components that drive CLV: the per-period profit margin (reflecting the revenue and cost of serving a customer in each period), the retention rate (reflecting the likelihood that a customer will stay with the firm at the end of the period), the discount factor (reflecting the time value of money and allows expressing revenues and costs in present value terms), and the acquisition cost (reflecting the expenses associated with acquiring a customer). When acquisition cost is subtracted from a customer's lifetime value, we denote this quantity as PCLV, thus incorporating the effect of prospecting efforts.

- Innovation equity is a financial assessment of the total future cash flows—across customers and across time—associated with the diffusion of a certain innovation. It is assessed by linking the number of new customers expected to arrive in each period (taken from the diffusion model discussed in the previous chapter) with the expected lifetime value of each new customer acquired (as discussed in this chapter). Properly discounting all future PCLVs and summing them over the desired time horizon yields the innovation equity of a new product or service.

CHAPTER THREE

Don't Just Stand There: Do Something!

Growing Innovation Equity through Marketing Actions

Innovation is like a plant that needs constant attention.—Florian Fichtl, World Bank

Consider the following conversation between two company employees, which we will refer to as *Person A* and *Person B*:

PERSON A: Should it be 250 megabytes?
PERSON B: I think 500 megabytes might work better.
PERSON A: OK. So what should be the capacity limit?
PERSON B: I'm thinking let's leave it at 8 gigabytes. Actually, you know what? I'm looking at some test results that just came in; better make that 16 gigabytes.

With all this technical talk about megabytes, gigabytes, and capacity limits, if you had to guess what these employees do at their company, you might be tempted to say "hardware engineering," or at the very least that the decisions they are trying to make are about the functionality and specs of the high-tech product they are designing. Those guesses would be wrong. This is the sort of conversation that likely took place between executives debating the best marketing approach for a recently launched digital service. To be more specific, it could be the type of conversation that Drew Houston, cofounder and CEO of Dropbox, might have had with another member of his management team about the referral incentive scheme to offer existing customers so that they hopefully bring in new customers after the innovative service had debuted.

If you are not familiar with it, Dropbox is a file-hosting application that allows its users to create special folders on each of their computers and mobile devices that are all synchronized, which means that, from the user's standpoint, each folder and its contents appear the same regardless of the computer/device used to access them or from which machine they were initially uploaded. Files placed in these folders are automatically backed up on remote servers the company manages, provided the devices used to do so are Internet connected. Furthermore, members can share files and entire folders with other Dropbox members, thereby creating a repository of common space: professionals can coordinate on work-related documents, students can pool information relevant for an assignment or team project, academics can collaborate on research files, and family members can share their favorite photos and videos.

The idea for Dropbox, so the story goes, came to Houston in late 2006 while waiting to take a bus from Boston to New York City. He planned to work on a programming project on his laptop during the four- to five-hour ride when he realized he'd forgotten his USB flash drive, with all the materials he needed stored on it, at home. So instead of working on the project, he began conceiving a more convenient and seamless solution to this storage problem. Eight and a half years later, the solution turned into a popular file-hosting service with more than three hundred million users. In between conception and commercial popularity came almost two years of start-up-style software development and testing and then years of efforts to generate strong demand and, ultimately, monetize it. Not an easy task, particularly in the first few years postlaunch when most consumers were likely wary of placing their precious documents up high on a "storage cloud" managed by a "no-name" start up.

Gardening Innovations for Growth

The opening quote to this chapter suggests a not-so-apparent parallel between innovations and plants. Yet this metaphor may not be all that crazy when you think about it: an innovation, like a plant, typically starts as a seed—a seed of a business idea, in this case. The idea is then worked on behind closed doors in the R&D facilities, much like the seed is planted in the dark soil, away from the public eye. Time and money is invested on product development efforts, much like time is invested watering the seed and infusing nutrients into the soil. And then, in due course, the innovation is completed and ready to be launched into the marketplace, much like the plant is ready to sprout out of the ground and greet the world.

However, as we all surely know, for a fledgling plant that has just budded to grow and blossom, more attention and care is needed. One must make sure the plant gets sufficient sunlight, consistently water it, and pluck any stray weeds trying to creep up and steal its sustenance and space. Is there an analogy on the innovation side of things for this stage of the plant's life?

To see whether the botanical metaphor extends beyond the R&D phase to the postlaunch phase, it's useful to recall the shape of the diffusion graphs that appeared in earlier chapters (e.g., figure 1.5). Successful innovations, those that do not "wilt" right out of the gate, do seem to have a substantial period of growth postlaunch, not growth in the literal sense but in the adoption sense—that is, these innovations experience customer growth. And, as we know, securing more customers, serving them over time, keeping them satisfied, and extracting revenues from them translate—or dare we say, bloom—into impressive innovation equity. So there is hope for our plant metaphor in the postlaunch phase after all. But as with a plant, just *standing there* and waiting for the flowers to bloom or for the fruits to ripen may not be the wisest course of action—you may want to *do something* to ensure the healthy growth of your innovation equity and to maximize the commercial opportunity. Much in the same spirit—from cultivating the seed of the idea that was planted in Houston's mind at the bus stop, to the intense R&D efforts needed to get the file-hosting concept to sprout, to the series of actions intended to facilitate the growth of the customer base, to bringing the company to revenue and profit fruition—the gardeners at Dropbox had their hands full.

In this chapter, we focus on the latter phases of such gardening stories and investigate the effect of taking various actions intended to facilitate the adoption and continued use of innovations. We further examine the key trade-offs involved in deciding which actions make sense financially and which ones do not. We will accomplish this by linking the postlaunch efforts to the diffusion and customer lifetime value models we have already seen so that the implications for innovation equity can be readily incorporated and appreciated. We will even explore how all this can be applied to Dropbox and the dilemmas it faced—including the one captured in the exchange between Person A and Person B about how much extra storage to offer customers who refer a friend and how much total free storage capacity to allow. In many ways, it will be a tale of evaluating marketing trade-offs.

Constant Attention: Affecting Customer Acquisition, Development, and Retention

Perceived value: this simple concept is at the heart of what separates successful from unsuccessful innovations. When customers *perceive* that they gain net *value* from an innovation, over and above other options in the marketplace and despite any barriers to embracing it, they will choose to adopt it. Perceived value is also what makes customers stick with an innovation and continue to use and pay for it. So the more the company behind the innovation can get people to appreciate the value it delivers and sustain this appreciation of superior value in the face of competition or changing economic conditions, the more likely the innovation will have enduring relevance in the eyes of customers. So how does one do that? How does one ensure that the perceived value of the innovation stays consistently high?

The short answer, perhaps not surprisingly, is *marketing*. And that short answer sounds like a promising one, except that the list of possible marketing actions one can engage in is long: advertising (on television, radio, magazines, billboards, online, etc.), public relations (PR) events, product placement (in movies, television shows, or online videos), giveaway samples, discounts, rebates, demos, road shows, social media content (Facebook, Twitter, YouTube), retailer incentives, sales force visits, and manufacturer subsidies. These are but a few of the marketing efforts firms might engage in to promote their offerings over the life cycle of the innovation. So tossing around the "*m* word" is not very helpful for a firm trying to select which marketing element(s) would best serve the goal of effectively convincing potential customers that it has something of value to offer them or, if they're already using the product, that they should not consider switching to a competitor. And since resources are typically not limitless, firms want to do this convincing as efficiently as possible.

The first step in figuring out whether to use a specific marketing tactic is to get a handle on what phase of the customer-innovation-firm relationship one is trying to have an impact on. At the risk of oversimplifying what is undoubtedly a complex set of interactions, it is useful to break this relationship into three main customer management stages: *acquisition*, *development*, and *retention*. The first stage, acquisition, refers to the phase of getting potential adopters to come on board; it is the transition from being a potential customer to becoming a customer. The second stage, development, refers to the phase of managing customers in the postadoption phase and capturing monetary value from them in exchange for the

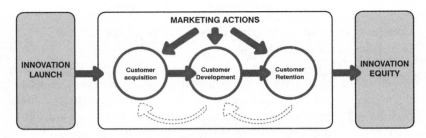

FIGURE 3.1. The impact of marketing actions: From innovation launch to innovation equity

benefits they are getting from the innovation and the firm's attention. Lastly, the third stage, retention, refers to the phase of hanging onto profitable customers and keeping them for as long as possible. As figure 3.1 depicts, these phases build upon each other—and each can be the focus of marketing actions.

Once an innovation has been unleashed to the world, effective marketing actions constitute the nutrients, the water, and the sunshine that will help the innovation deliver on its promise, allowing it to blossom and bear equity fruit. The right marketing actions will nudge customers across the various relationship stages in a way that delivers more equity for the firm. The good news is that all of these considerations will fit quite nicely into the diffusion and customer lifetime value (CLV) "planting pots."

Affecting Customer Acquisition

One cannot say enough about the acquisition stage of the customer-innovation-firm relationship. Without acquiring customers, you really have no one to serve, no one to retain, and essentially no one to bring on the innovation equity. This perhaps explains why so much attention is devoted to crafting marketing launch plans intended to create and grow the customer base.

As we explained in the previous chapter, the acquisition stage closely relates to the adoption side of the innovation equity story. Customer acquisition is what diffusion curves are "made of." We were further quite explicit in noting that firms often take actions to facilitate and prompt adoption and described how the expenses incurred can be accounted for as part of customer lifetime value analysis à la the acquisition cost component. And although we acknowledged the goal of these actions, we never really explained how to incorporate the presumed effects of marketing acquisition efforts into the adoption process. We showed how to incorporate the "negatives" (costs) but not the "positives" (impact on adoption).

To rectify this imbalance, recall that in developing the basic diffusion model, we boiled down an innovation's adoption trajectory into three key elements: the individual force, the social force, and the total (or long-run) market potential. Therefore, if a particular marketing action is implemented with the aim of bolstering customer acquisition, the question is, which of these three diffusion elements is impacted by the action and how?

An example might help illuminate the task at hand. When a company like Sony launches a new home video game console, like the PlayStation 3 (PS3) and more recently the PlayStation 4 (PS4), its production costs are typically quite high initially. In fact, back in 2006, given all the technological "goodies" that Sony packed into the PS3 console, such as a novel IBM processor (called the "Cell"), a Blu-ray player, and advanced wireless capabilities, industry analysts estimated that each PS3 cost more than $800 to make in early production batches. One might imagine that Sony would like to price the product at least that high so as to not lose money on each unit sold. But is that in its best interest? Would it be better to price it lower—that is, take a hit on the hardware (the console)—in order to make money on the software (game titles for which Sony gets royalties)? Moreover, without fail, pricing dilemmas arise again and again during the lifespan of a console. Production costs decline over time, reflecting experience that comes with volume and improvements in manufacturing processes, all of which cause component costs to decline dramatically and create opportunities for lowering the price. Indeed, industry analysts, with hindsight from six previous generations of video games, predicted that within three years of launch, the cost to make each PS3 console could drop by over 65 percent to something like $300 or less. This would allow Sony to cut its console price repeatedly and even be able to make a profit on each unit at some point. And with rivals Microsoft (Xbox 360) and Nintendo (Wii) enjoying similar economies of scale in production, as soon as one of these players lowers its price, it puts pressure on the others to respond in kind.

As Sony considered how many consoles it might hope to sell, which would translate into the number of customers it would acquire, how should it have thought about its pricing strategy for the PS3 console at launch? And thinking ahead, should it discount the price more aggressively than rivals as production costs decline?

In essence, what Sony needed to assess was whether short-term losses on the console due to price concessions could be compensated for by generating revenues from game titles and accessories in the medium and long terms. From a customer acquisition standpoint, there are several ways this can play out: one is if the price move spurs *more* adoption and another is if it spurs *faster* adoption. The basic diffusion model can handle both of these effects. "More adoption" in our world means a greater market potential (i.e., a greater value for the parameter m), while "faster adoption" means that the individual and/or social forces that drive adoption increase (i.e., greater values for the parameters p and/or q).

For instance, say that an initial assessment of the diffusion parameters for video game consoles in the United States, based on experience with previous console generations and adjustments for the generation in question, suggested values of $m = 110$ million as the market potential, $p = 0.02$ as the individual force, and $q = 0.3$ as the social force. Now suppose that a market research study reveals that at an $800 launch price, relative to an Xbox 360 priced at $400 and a Wii priced at $250, it would be reasonable to expect the PS3's market share to be about 10 percent of all units sold. The research further indicates that each $100 drop in introduction price, holding the actions of the other players constant, will likely allow Sony to increase the PS3's share of adopters in a given period by 5 percent. In addition, with manufacturing costs expected to come down, if all three players cut prices, the category's market potential will probably expand, as people who might not have considered consoles at all now become interested. Such a move could also accelerate adoption for those already interested in buying a console but who have to save money to afford one. A 10 percent price drop for all consoles would presumably lead to a 2.5 percent market expansion effect and a 10 percent acceleration effect.

For Sony, it should not be difficult at all to integrate such findings and assumptions into an evaluation of how many consoles it will likely be able to sell as prices change over time—in other words, to assess how many new customers it will acquire each period. It can use the basic diffusion model with the baseline parameters[1] ($m = 110$ million, $p = 0.02$, $q = 0.3$, and market share of 10 percent), letting the market potential increase by 2.5 percent each year and the individual force parameter increase by 10 percent each year (to reflect the impact of all players' expected price cuts). Then Sony can run a number of what-if analyses by plugging in various initial prices for its own console, say $700, $600, and $500, with corresponding market shares of 15 percent, 20 percent, and 25 percent, to see how the PS3's customer base is affected as a result. If Sony considers dropping the price by more than 10 percent in a given year, it can assume a proportional greater impact on its share of the market that year.[2]

While dropping the launch price is certainly an option for a console maker, Sony and its peers might consider other marketing actions, such as advertising during prime-time television shows like *The Big Bang Theory*[3] or a televised NFL football game. How might this kind of marketing action affect adoption?

DECISIONS, DECISIONS, DECISIONS.   Much research on customer behavior, particularly in the context of innovations, shows that adoption is rarely a spur-of-the-moment decision, particularly if we're talking about goods that cost more than a few dollars. Consumers typically go through several decision stages en route to purchasing a new product or subscribing to a new service. It usually starts with an *awareness* phase, where people first become cognizant that something new even exists. Then for there to be any hope of adoption, *interest* should ensue, whereby a level of curiosity or motivation to gather information and learn more is triggered. Then the individual, or organization in the context of possible adoption by a business entity, will likely go through a stage of careful *evaluation* to see if the innovation is worth the risks and costs associated with it relative to other options worth considering (and to whatever is currently being used to solve the problem or satisfy the need). If things are still on track, the potential customer might want to try the innovation, pilot it within the company, or visit a retail outlet to get a hands-on feel for it. If nothing derails the process up to this point and the trial goes well, the prospective buyer gains *confidence*, which leads to the final step of innovation *adoption*. A "funnel" structure applies to this decision-making process: starting with a wide set of all those aware of the innovation and dwindling at each decision stage until final adoption by those convinced that the innovation creates sufficient perceived net value for them.

Now let's go back to advertising a new console during a show like *The Big Bang Theory*, which is presumably of particular relevance to the target market for home video games. Depending on what it communicates, one can envision an ad during such a prime time show as having an effect on any of the five decision stages—from awareness to adoption. It can obviously generate awareness by informing viewers about the innovation ("The new console is here!"), or if the ad is engaging, it might generate interest to learn more among those already aware ("There are so many cool things you can do with the new console; look how much fun these gamers are having!"). One could imagine such effects increasing the market potential by bringing in people who would otherwise not consider purchasing. If the ad manages to convey the particulars of what the experience might be like to own the innovation and what makes the innovation's benefits unique ("gaming like never before, with astounding image and animation quality thanks to incredibly fast processing and a novel Blu-ray player"), it is likely to impact evaluation and desire to try out the device, which typically "speeds up" movement through the adoption funnel. Thus just like with price discounts, advertising can affect either the market potential m (broader awareness and interest in learning more) or the individual force p (already aware but prompted to try it out and give it serious consideration). Here we frame these diffusion effects in the context of the adoption funnel: when someone that would otherwise not enter the funnel is affected $\rightarrow$ the impact is on m; when someone who would have likely entered the funnel and reached the final stage anyway is influenced to move through the stages more quickly $\rightarrow$ the impact is on p; when someone who would have likely entered the funnel and moved through it at the same speed but is swayed to choose one brand's offering over another $\rightarrow$ the market share percentage is affected.

What about the social force, the parameter q in the basic diffusion model? Is there any way marketing actions can impact its effect on customer acquisition? Of course there is. After enough people have adopted, a firm might offer incentives for existing customers to refer new customers. A company can also foster usages that motivate customers to bring their friends along. For example, a console maker may create or promote video game titles that have social elements (such as multiplayer games). There are also various ways advertising can have a social impact. First, if the ad is "viral" in nature, in that its entertainment content is such that people want to talk about it with others or share it electronically, then the firm indirectly gets many more people to become aware of and engaged with its offering. Second, the ad can nudge someone to want to evaluate the innovation more diligently and gain more information by seeking the council of those that have already adopted. Third, a firm might publicize "aggregate" social outcomes to attest to the innovation's appeal—for example, by stating how many consumers have already adopted (as Pfizer did in the late 2000s with ads that told men with erectile dysfunction to "join the millions" who have already asked their physician about Viagra) or by presenting customer survey results (as Chevrolet did in 2013 in ads

TABLE 3.1 **The impact of marketing actions on customer acquisition: Total number of adopters in the home video games category (in millions)**

Year since launch	Base case	Market potential (m) up by 20 percent	Individual force (p) up by 20 percent	Social force (q) up by 20 percent
1	2.2	2.6	2.6	2.2
2	5.0	6.0	6.0	5.1
3	8.5	10.2	10.2	9.0
4	12.9	15.5	15.4	14.0
5	18.3	21.9	21.6	20.3
6	24.7	29.6	28.9	28.1
7	32.2	38.6	37.3	37.2
8	40.5	48.6	46.4	47.5
9	49.6	59.5	56.0	58.5
10	59.0	70.8	65.5	69.4

Baseline parameters: $m = 110$ million, $p = 0.02$, $q = 0.3$.

that touted its plug-in electric vehicle, the Volt, as receiving the highest customer satisfaction scores of any car by its owners).

It is actually important to distinguish between the various social effects that advertising can have. The first effect, people buzzing about and sharing the ad itself, is not necessarily linked to previous adoption, as nonadopters can be enamored by the ad and want others to see it without being interested in buying the featured product. Hence this kind of social effect is really about the ad reaching more people and garnering wider exposure than it otherwise would have (through passive viewership on television, for example), thus mostly impacting the market potential (m) element. The other effects—the network benefits from getting other people to embrace the innovation, the ad prompting nonadopters to seek advice from current users, and knowledge of customer base size and users' satisfaction levels—are linked to the number of previous adopters and, therefore, likely to impact the rate or speed of future adoption via the social force parameter (q).

A similar analysis to the one conducted on advertising can be applied to other forms of marketing aimed at acquisition—be they sales efforts, providing incentives for retailers to promote and demo a new product, direct mail, Facebook ads, and so on. The idea is to understand which decision stage in the adoption process is affected and which basic diffusion model aspect should be adjusted as a result of the marketing action.

Table 3.1 provides a sense of how customer acquisition at the category level would be impacted by a 20 percent change in each element of the basic diffusion model while holding the other two elements constant. As can be seen, ten years after launch, the impact translates into an increase in the number of customers acquired of about 11 percent for a greater individual force, 18 percent for a greater social force, and 20 percent for a greater market potential. It is interesting to note that increasing the individual force leads to faster acquisition early on, but the impact on the customer base size is overtaken by a greater social force in year 8—this is consistent with the idea that the social force, and any increase to it, is primarily felt when a critical mass of adopters has been established (which can take time).

In calculating the customers acquired in table 3.1, in each period, we assumed that either the marketing actions taken at launch have an enduring effect on the diffusion parameters or the marketing efforts are applied on a sustained basis. Otherwise, it may be more appropriate to change the relevant diffusion parameter for the duration of the campaign only and revert back to the previous levels at the campaign's conclusion.

It is also worth pointing out that when one examines the actual adoption data of an innovation that has been diffusing in the marketplace for quite some time, one is already "seeing" the effects of whatever marketing actions were undertaken since the launch. And if one uses such data to estimate the basic diffusion model parameters, the estimated values for m, p, and q will in essence embody the "average" levels of these parameters during the time frame studied, inclusive of any marketing actions that impacted their levels.

Growing the customer base is generally a good thing, no doubt about it. And you might look at the results by year 10 in table 3.1, assuming that is your time horizon, and conclude that if you had to choose which "up by 20 percent" you would support, then your ranking would be: market potential, social force, and lastly the individual force. But there are at least two issues that might give you pause. First, while the relative magnitude of the effect is assumed to be the same in all cases (i.e., a 20 percent bump in parameter value), we said nothing about the expenses that would need to be incurred to bring about the 20 percent change in each of the diffusion elements—in other words, what the associated acquisition costs are. Second, while the tally of customers acquired by year 10 supports the ranking, along the way there is a "crisscross" pattern in acquisition for the two adoption forces: initially the higher individual force dominates, but ultimately the greater social force prevails in terms of a larger customer base acquired. But this temporal component is important to dwell on. Money that is earned sooner can be more valuable than more money that is earned later.

The dilemma encountered in pricing home video game consoles is associated with similar caveats: you lose money when you discount the console, particularly on people that would have adopted at the higher price, but you gain more customers who generate a stream of revenues down the road through the purchase of game titles and accessories. Therefore, it is not enough to understand the positive effect of marketing interventions on customer acquisition/adoption, as there are other possibly negative profit-related considerations that must be thought through. And as with almost everything else in life, whether one marketing action makes more sense than another (or than doing nothing) comes down to understanding the trade-offs involved. You probably realize where we are headed with these arguments: in order to assess the advisability of various marketing actions, one needs to apply the innovation equity framework.

TRADE-OFFS, TRADE-OFFS, TRADE-OFFS. To examine the trade-offs just described more carefully, we turn again to the XM Satellite Radio example presented earlier (chapters 1 and 2). Say that in preparing for the long-anticipated debut of the service, XM's vice president of marketing suddenly has a "panic attack": he realizes that upon launch, very few vehicles will come preinstalled with receivers capable of decoding the satellite signals beamed from outer space. And even when some car models offer such radio receivers as a preinstalled option, one is essentially limited to the subset of people who are in the market for a new car. For all practical purposes, therefore, in the first few years postlaunch, most people who wish to sign up for the novel radio service will have to visit the "aftermarket"—that is, buy a receiver at an electronics or auto retail outlet and have it installed in a car they already own.

XM decided early on that it would not get involved in manufacturing radio receivers, focusing instead on the service: signal transmission (via satellites) and content. Electronics firms, like Alpine and Pioneer, would handle the receiver or hardware production aspect. The consumer electronics market is a margins-driven business, and each party in the value chain, primarily manufacturers and big-box retailers, expects a cut of its selling price, with 30–35 percent considered typical. So, for example, if it costs around $135 to make each receiver, then the manufacturer would sell it to retailers for about $200. In turn, retailers would charge consumers a price in the neighborhood of $300. Would that kind of a price tag put off consumers and dampen adoption of the service? Great reception quality and excellent content is fine and dandy, but would asking people to pay $300 upfront, on top of at least $10 in monthly fees for something that had been historically free, be a major deterrent? For a marketing manager tasked with getting customers to sign up quickly, this is definitely a source of anxiety.

XM management might not want to risk it, or at least try to mitigate the risk somewhat, by having consumers see a much lower price for XM-enabled receivers at retail. Indeed, market research revealed that a far greater number of consumers were willing to consider satellite radio when receivers were priced at $200 rather than at $300—over 25 percent more, in fact. There are various ways of lowering the "sticker price" consumers pay for a product. The most direct yet most costly approach would be to keep the retail price at $300 and offer consumers a $100 manufacturer's rebate. Such an action would result in a $100 acquisition cost for the company. An indirect though much cheaper way is to offer manufacturers a subsidy of about $45, which because of the way margins would be carried through the channel, would also result in lowering the final retail price by $100.[4] XM opted to consider the latter marketing approach.

While the expected positive effect of a radio receiver subsidy on expanding demand was grounded in market research, not to mention plain old Econ 101 logic, it is not clear whether the marketing tactic is justified from a return on investment (ROI) standpoint. A prudent CFO might very well raise doubts about such a move: "Aren't we just losing $45 on many customers who would have signed up and bought a receiver at the higher price, just to get a few more customers who are swayed by the discount?" The CFO seems to have a point. And assuming the expectation was already spend $40–$50 on acquisition efforts (such as on advertising and a ninety-day free trial), the financial executive may be more than a bit leery about authorizing yet another acquisition expense.

Clearly there is a trade-off here that needs to be assessed. To get at the positive side of the subsidy, the marketing vice president can run the basic diffusion model and incorporate a market potential of 31.5 million instead of 25 million based on the market research (to reflect a 25 percent impact, while keeping all other model parameters the same). Plotting out the cumulative diffusion curves with and without the subsidy, as in figure 3.2, helps visualize the impact on the acquisition of customers over time.

What is interesting to note from the figure is that the market potential increase takes time to fully materialize; you don't get the 6.5 million additional adopters overnight. In fact, at the beginning, the two graphs are close together and only gradually diverge. This should hopefully make sense. If the market potential is larger, then every single period there is a bigger pool of prospective customers that may be induced to adopt. At the

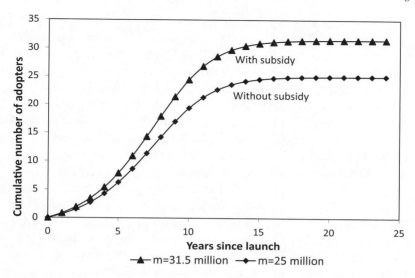

FIGURE 3.2. Impact of a $45 manufacturer subsidy on the diffusion of satellite radio

outset, however, since the individual force is relatively modest ($p = 0.026$), the presence of a greater market potential is moderate. But as adoptions pick up, the social force kicks in, and as it is multiplied by a greater market potential, the divergence between the graphs becomes more and more pronounced.

The significance of these dynamics, from a financial standpoint, cannot be overstated. The marketing action—namely, a subsidy that results in a lower retail price—allows XM to gradually acquire more customers as time goes by. But in assessing the monetary implications of this move in *today's* financial terms, how much sooner you attract those customers is critical. The CFO therefore has another reason to be uncertain about the whole subsidy idea. Luckily, the innovation equity framework can help arbitrate. It allows properly accounting for the time value of money (through the discount rate) depending on when more customers are acquired and incorporating the added acquisition cost. So what do we get if we mix all the ingredients together in this example? Following the steps outlined in chapter 2 for assessing innovation equity and using a twenty-year horizon, we get $1.5684 billion without the subsidy and $1.5756 billion with the subsidy: a difference of $7.2 million on the plus side.

So it is a close call whether to implement the subsidy. The net impact on innovation equity is surely nothing to write home about. For an innovation expected to have equity of more than a billion dollars, any marketing action that generates less than $10 million in incremental returns may be seen as a rounding error. That said, the higher diffusion curve sure looks a lot more attractive than the lower curve, and if it can be achieved without sacrificing the net present value of profits, it may make sense to go for it. And indeed XM implemented similar subsidies early on.

A few matters are worth highlighting with respect to our assessment of the radio receiver subsidy: First, we assumed that XM would continue all other marketing efforts as planned. However, if the subsidy can replace some of the other marketing efforts, such as reduce spending on television advertising, yet still deliver the increase in market potential, then the calculus is much more positive. For example, if the total acquisition cost is reduced to $85 with the subsidy (rather than the $95 we suggested in the previous chapter), the difference in innovation equity is close to $100 million, which is impressive. Second, to simplify the analysis, we implicitly assumed that rival Sirius would follow suit by lowering its receiver retail price to $200 so that we could continue to assume a fifty-fifty split between the two companies in the share of new adopters into the category. If this is not the case, XM would be increasing not only the pie (i.e., total category market potential) but most likely also its share of the increased pie.

Affecting Customer Development

Great news! You got some people to adopt your innovation. They are now firmly part of your diffusion curve. This is a sign that what you have introduced into the marketplace is perceived to be of sufficient value to at least some people and a sign that your acquisition efforts are working. Surely that is cause to celebrate and enjoy the moment.

What now? Well, if things go according to plan, then even as the customer base continues to grow, you should be able to capture some of the value you are creating back to your company—in other words, to cash in on the adopters. But is this the time to sit back and bask in the glow of customer acquisition success? You and your superiors or shareholders may wonder whether there is something that can be done to ensure—and perhaps increase—the profitability of the customers acquired.

The activities firms engage in to extract value from existing customers are typically referred to as *customer development efforts*. The idea is to devise ways to increase the share of customers' wallets—that is, get them to spend more postadoption. One way to do this is by creating additional products or services related to the innovation and convincing customers to pay for these add-ons. For example, a company might offer a basic service that most new customers sign up for, such as a cable television package that includes only a few general-interest channels, and a premium service that costs more and includes a number of high-quality options, like desirable movie and sports channel packages. By "upselling" customers the premium products and services, the company increases the profitability of each acquired customer.

Alternatively, when a company has a number of different offerings and can get an adopter of one innovation to also purchase one or more of the others, this represents another avenue for extracting additional profits. For example, if Apple gets a satisfied iPad customer to purchase a Mac instead of a PC, a profitable direct "cross-sell" has occurred; if Sony can get its console adopters to buy more games over the life cycle of the console, it benefits by collecting royalties, and an indirect cross-sell occurs.

Another way to develop customers is to do a better job of demonstrating and communicating the value that the innovation delivers. If done well, when the price goes up (or the introductory low price is no longer offered), customers are still willing to pay. For example, a medical device company that had been offering deep discounts to hospitals and clinics to encourage adoption could conduct additional studies that attest to the efficacy and long-term safety of its solution, allowing it to charge full price without sacrificing demand. In fact, head-to-head studies that compare the performance of a new drug or device to that of an existing drug or device in an effort to show superiority are becoming more commonplace in the medical industry. These studies often help justify charging higher prices than the competition and qualifying for reimbursement from health care payers.

It is also possible to make the most of acquired customers by reducing the cost of serving them while maintaining a healthy revenue stream. The wallet is unaffected in this case, but what it takes to open it is. For example, if a firm can cut back on the number of people it needs to staff its customer care center, send fewer sales reps to reinforce the use of a drug among physicians who have already prescribed it, or reduce retailer incentives to stock the item on shelves, then the firm can save a lot of money.

THE BUCK DOESN'T STOP AT ADOPTION. Our innovation equity framework feels right at home with the notion of customer development. How so? You may recall that one of the main building blocks of the customer lifetime value model was the per-period profit margin. This quantity is calculated by taking the total revenue from a customer in a period and subtracting from it the cost to serve that customer—that is, the cost incurred per period to generate the revenue, which includes any manufacturing-, service-, or marketing-related charges.

In some cases, the firm may not need to do much, and the per-period profit margin is expected to increase over time regardless. This can happen if production costs decline faster than the rate at which the firm lowers its price. In the home video game industry, hardware component costs typically decline so rapidly that a console maker breaks even or starts making money on the device by the third year postlaunch. Per-period customer profits may also increase if at the time of adoption, consumers sign up for cheaper, limited-use options, but later, as they better understand the value of the innovation to them through experience, they switch to more costly "heavy-use" plans. The cell phone industry in the United States is a prime example of this consumption dynamic. Many early adopters perceived the cell phone as an "in case of emergency" product—only to be used when there was an immediate need to be reached and a landline was unavailable or if they had to notify someone of a serious problem or accident. But consumers soon discovered that the ability to communicate with friends and family on the go, even just to shoot the breeze and gossip, was so gratifying that they subsequently switched to higher-cost plans with unlimited minutes.

Instances of increasing per-period profits from customers can also be found in business-to-business (B2B) settings. For example, many enterprise software solutions are based on the "software as a service" model (often abbreviated as SaaS), where the client does not buy the software itself but rather pays a recurring fee (monthly or annually) for the ability to use the system, which is often stored on remote servers. An adopting client might first have one business unit or a subset of employees use the new system and pay accordingly. If the software proves effective on the limited basis, the client may expand its use throughout the company.

More often than not, however, increasing the per-period profits from customers requires efforts, initiatives, or changes to the business model. Customers often need to be made aware of the upsell or cross-sell options, and even after becoming aware, a convincing nudge to buy them can't hurt. These actions can range from personalized efforts (through channels such as telemarketing and sales rep visits) to segment-level targeting based on demographics or past purchase behavior (via methods such as direct mail or text messaging) all the way to blanket coverage endeavors (using tactics such as an ad campaign during the Super Bowl).

Accommodating these customer development aspects into the innovation equity framework means adjusting the per-period profit margin. Specifically, it means assessing the expected impact on revenue and on the cost to serve per customer. That seems simple enough, but it may require handling with care, particularly the cost side of things. It matters if the expense the firm needs to incur is a one-time affair or a sustained expense that relates to each customer served. For example, in the case of an advertising blitz aimed at generating awareness for a cross-sell opportunity, one needs to include the expense only in the year it is incurred. In the case of a higher expenditure to manufacture or offer each upgraded version, it needs to be included as part of the ongoing per-period expenses. The reality is often a combination of both types of costs.

Without belaboring the point raised earlier in connection with customer acquisition, whether customer development efforts will grow innovation equity is again a matter of evaluating trade-offs. At a minimum, per-period profit margins should go up at some point. But if there are hefty costs that need to be incurred today and/or the rewards accrue too far into the future, a positive ROI may not be in the cards.

What makes things slightly more complicated—or interesting, depending on your point of view—is that firms are sometimes willing to engage in actions that entail taking a short-term hit on revenues from existing customers in the hopes of payback from future customers that might be acquired as a result. A *free* (*ware*) example might help shed light on this strategy as well as bring home many of the customer acquisition and development themes that have been introduced thus far.

CUSTOMER DEVELOPMENT IN A FREEWARE WORLD: THE CASE OF DROPBOX. One of the more fascinating developments in the business arena in recent years has been the dramatic increase of software available to customers for free—that's right: offerings that customers can access and enjoy at no cost whatsoever. Often labeled as *freeware*, the ubiquity of this phenomenon is nothing short of striking. Many of the most heavily used software-based products and services introduced over the last decade or so started out as free to consumers; names like Google, Skype, Facebook, YouTube, LinkedIn, and Angry Birds are just part of a long list that fall in this category. According to several research firms specializing in IT and digital industries, between 2012 and 2014 more than two-thirds of new smartphone apps available on the App Store and on Google Play were offered free.

While giving away things for free can be part of a noble social cause, few are the freeware enterprises that see pro bono activities as their mission in life. The overwhelming majority want to be profitable or demonstrate that they have the potential to be profitable so that some bigger company acquires them. And that is where the challenge lies for these budding companies: How do you impress investors or shareholders with your ability to make money when customers sign up for free? The answer lies in *customer development* post-sign-up. Here are a few of the common ways that freeware companies develop customers to generate revenues:

- *Freemium.* In this revenue model, the version the company allows you to sign up for at no cost is limited in its capabilities or is not "fully loaded" with all the available features or modules. The free version provides an opportunity to enjoy some of the benefits of the product, but the company also offers extra features or extended performance—a premium version, if you will. The company tries to steer as many customers as possible to upgrade or purchase the extras. For example, Skype lets you communicate with peers who are also Skype users, using voice or instant messaging, over an Internet connection. This basic service is free. But Skype also allows you to make calls from your Skype account to landlines and mobile phones. The latter service is paid for (in fact, you need to prepay to receive calling minutes).

- *Advertising.* In this revenue model, all the bells and whistles of the product or service are typically given to customers for free; there is no holding back on any goodies. Instead, advertisers are the ones who pay, and they are willing to do so in order to gain access to the attention of consumers. Thus any company that wishes to reach consumers of the free application must remit payment to the freeware provider to place an ad on its platform. While the ad-driven business model has been around for years—broadcast television clearly comes to mind—it has been embraced quite extensively in the digital world, and for good reason: the plethora of information that can be gathered on users in digital settings—which pages (and even products) they browsed or who else is in their circle of friends—has provided many more real-time, one-to-one targeting opportunities for advertisers. Often, the name of the game here is keeping customers "engaged" so that they desire to use the service extensively, stay on the website for long durations, or run the app repeatedly, thus increasing the opportunities for them to be targeted with ads. A good example of applying this model is the online social networking site Facebook. Anyone can join Facebook, never having to pay a single penny for unlimited use. And with close to one billion daily active users as of early 2015, spending hours and hours on the site per day, it's no wonder companies are eager to place ads that appear on members' Facebook pages.

- *Service provision.* Some freeware products are complicated. They embed features and capabilities that are not straightforward for all customers to take advantage of. In these cases, the freeware company may be able to generate revenues by charging for extra services that such customers desire. And this may be particularly true for products that generate interest among business users. Red Hat is an example. It develops open-source software, such as Red Hat Enterprise Linux, which is used by many individuals as well as businesses for free. A sufficient number of these businesses like the free aspect of the software and its constant updating by the community of developers but want some product customization or desire customer support so that they don't have to worry about running their mission-critical processes on the software. Red Hat readily offers these extra services—for a fee, of course.
- *In-app purchases.* In some cases, users of the freeware application wish to enhance their experience or want to express themselves within the virtual environment. A freeware company may provide opportunities to do so through digital "accessories" that are cleverly designed to augment the basic features and for which it charges money. These accessories can include special characters (or avatars), boost packs that give special capabilities within the virtual environment, unique ringtones, and so on. This practice has become quite common among online game and mobile app providers. In 2012, *Wired* reported that of the fifty highest-grossing apps in the games section of the iTunes App Store, only three did not support in-app purchases; in 2014 eMarketer indicated that 92 percent of free apps offered in-app purchase opportunities.

We have already surmised that lowering the price of an innovation is likely to positively affect the diffusion parameters. As the innovation gets cheaper, more people are undoubtedly willing to entertain purchase at some point and often the shorter the time it takes to go from awareness to adoption. Well, it doesn't get any cheaper than free. So on the one hand, the decision to pursue a freeware strategy makes sense: it allows you to boost customer acquisition, thus reinforcing what we said earlier. But what can you do to affect the other part of the innovation equity equation, the part where you need to make money on acquired customers? If you are one of these freeware companies, you quickly discover that you need to make a host of customer development marketing decisions.

One company for which this "acquire versus develop" dilemma has been quite salient is Dropbox, which we described at the beginning of this chapter. As we mentioned, Dropbox is a storage-hosting service that allows its users to back up files and synchronize them across computers and devices. Members also have the option of sharing files and folders with other users: family, friends, and colleagues. In fact, the three authors of this book shared all the documents related to *Innovation Equity* through Dropbox.

It is worth noting that the communal or collaborative aspect of Dropbox's value proposition — the ability to share files among users — generates a strong incentive for the company to encourage rapid adoption early. It is not just a matter of more past adopters bringing in more future adopters through word of mouth, though there is that of course. There is something more: the value created for each user potentially increases when a person he or she knows joins as well — what we called network-effect benefits in chapter 1. Dropbox delivers personal value, allowing a user to access and synchronize his or her files from any device and location, but it also delivers a *social value*: allowing a network of users to share digital content. However, if someone cannot bank on his or her friends and colleagues joining, then that network benefit is out the window.

The free sign-up Dropbox offers (on its consumer version)[5] helps remove adoption barriers and gets people to join with minimal hesitation — and the company expected quite a few barriers. Examples include concerns that important documents could be lost, corrupted, or compromised when stored remotely and relayed across the Internet by the "invisible hand" of a start-up; the requirement that consumers manage the software installation on each device by themselves (which was found to be a "high friction experience" for some); and overcoming the fact that for many people, the need to look for an alternative storage solution to replace the USB drive was not as readily apparent as it was for the company's founder.

What exactly do you get for the "zero down" at signup? Dropbox gives you an account with 2GB of storage. But "buyer" beware: every file counts toward that limit — files in folders that only you can view and manage, as well as those in all shared folders. What happens as you get hooked on the service, add a bunch of files to your personal folders, and accept invitations to share folders with friends? Well, you start bumping up against the limit; 2GB provides less storage freedom than you might have initially thought. If you are willing to sift through folders and delete files to make room, which can cause coordination problems when folders are shared (as you might want to check with your friends or collaborators beforehand), power to you. But if that course of action is too tedious or vexing, you might inquire about adding storage capacity. Normally, you would expect this to be the point where the freemium provider says, "You want more? No problem. Please sign up for the premium service and start paying." Indeed, Dropbox offers that option. Yet the company also gives you another way out of the capacity crunch: you can refer someone new to join the service[6] or, as Dropbox described once on its website, "spread the love to your friends, family, and coworkers." And for each new account referral, you get 500MB of additional storage—that's 25 percent more than what you started with: you get some of the premium for free as well.

Through its referral program, Dropbox, so it seems, is willing to further sacrifice revenues from existing customers in order to acquire more customers. The decision to allow free incremental upgrades in exchange for referrals in effect trades off enhanced innovation diffusion on the one hand, with reduced customer lifetime value on the other. Let's see how the innovation equity framework can help evaluate the financial advisability of this trade-off.

The fact that the basic service is deemed to have both personal and social value and is free means we can expect relatively high basic diffusion model parameters to begin with. For illustration purposes, assume that the long-run global market potential (m) for the entire category is about 2.5 billion users and that the diffusion rate parameters are 0.02 and 0.4 for the individual (p) and social (q) forces, respectively (these values are consistent with the diffusion parameters of related innovations, such as Internet access devices, which range from $p = 0.014$ to 0.03 and $q = 0.35$ to 0.6). Based on industry estimates, we will take Dropbox's share of the nascent category to be 24 percent of the global long-run potential user pool. Given the company's referral strategy, which differed from that of most other major players in the category who didn't offer such incentives, we will run a basic diffusion model for Dropbox as a separate entity with $m = 600$ million. We will also assume that the marketing referral scheme propels both of the base diffusion rate parameters by 25 percent for Dropbox. This seems reasonable: 500MB represents a 25 percent increase from the basic capacity granted upon signup, and a recent study found that 27 percent of Dropbox's users joined through referrals. The cumulative diffusion of acquired customers using these parameters reasonably tracks the actual number of Dropbox adopters known from published sources. The company had four million users in January 2010, and that increased to twenty-five million in April 2011, fifty million in May 2012, one hundred million in November 2012, two hundred million in November 2013, three hundred million in May 2014, and four hundred million by June 2015.

Turning to the CLV side of things, clearly Dropbox needs some users to go beyond free and pay for additional space. To that end, it limits the total amount of storage you can accumulate at no cost. Specifically, you can at most refer thirty-two friends and obtain an additional 16GB of storage, even if you are so popular that you could get a thousand people to sign up with the stroke of an e-mail. Recent data on freemium services show that roughly 20 percent of referrals are accepted, which means that on average, one would need to send out about 160 requests to max out on the free storage limit. Sure, 18GB (the initial 2GB plus the 16GB from referrals) sounds like a lot. However, there is another, more insidious aspect that needs to be considered here. The more friends, family, and coworkers you add, the more likely you will chew through storage space at a faster clip. Every additional referred person increases the chances that you will share more content with these new folks. As your network grows, so will the number of files added to shared folders. And your referred friends will likely invite their friends to join, and they might also add files to the folders you are sharing. So you'd better watch out: each extra 500MB of referral space might come with many files attached. Hence all that free referral space might not reduce your need to upgrade by as much as you'd initially thought.

As for stats on upgrading behavior, some estimates put the percentage of individuals who convert to become premium paying customers each year at about 1 percent on the conservative side and 1.5 percent on the more aggressive side—which does not sound like much of a spread, except that we are dealing with hundreds of millions of users, so each tenth of a percentage point can have huge ramifications. For our purposes, it might be reasonable to assume that without the referral incentive, if you were stuck with 2GB unless you upgraded, the conversion rate would be 1.25 percent, and that drops with the ability to increase capacity through referrals to 1 percent.[7] Dropbox's premium service for individuals (called Dropbox Pro) offers 1TB (1,000GB, which is up from the 100GB it offered until mid-2014) of extra space for $10 per month (actually "$9.99"). A year's commitment upfront gets you a 17 percent discount (you pay $99), and we will assume that roughly half of those that convert opt for the discount for an average of $110 of revenues from each paying customer annually. The cost to Dropbox of hosting an average paying customer is estimated to be between $20 and $30 a year;[8] thus its average per-period profit margin from a paying customer is $85. The retention rate of premium customers is taken to be 82.5 percent, which has been reported by other remote storage services. Lastly, a reasonable discount factor would be 7.5 percent, given the cost of capital in the relevant time period. Consequently, the lifetime value of a paying Dropbox customer can easily be calculated to be $340 (using expression 2.9 from chapter 2).

If you go down the checklist we laid out in chapter 2 for calculating innovation equity, then you will see that we have all the ingredients we need to assess the advisability of the referral incentive scheme. Using a ten-year time horizon from the launch, we get the following comparison: If Dropbox were to not offer the referral incentive, diffusion would be slower but conversion to premium more robust, and innovation equity comes out to be $4.48 billion. By offering the referral incentive, diffusion is faster and more robust, yet conversion to premium is more tepid, for an innovation equity of $4.94 billion—a 10 percent bump! Bottom line: Dropbox's strategy seems to be on the right track. In fact, one could make an argument for offering even more free space if the effect on diffusion continues to be strong and the conversion rates to premium hold up sufficiently.

What makes this analysis all the more compelling is that Dropbox initially invested heavily in other customer acquisition strategies, such as sponsored Google ads, that turned out to be quite costly relative to the number of new adoptions that materialized. Later, and somewhat counterintuitively for many industry observers, the company shifted to relying on referrals, which has now become its main acquisition channel. Drew Houston, Dropbox's founder and CEO, said, "It is hard to master freemium products unless you can build an organic customer acquisition engine. If you think of your free user cost as your marketing budget, then things begin to make more sense." Instead of traditional marketing tactics that entail up-front investment, Dropbox used its already acquired customers as an acquisition mechanism to sign up new customers. While there is a price to pay in terms of delayed customer development, the innovation equity analysis we conducted seems to bear the strategy out.

Indeed, if you go back to figure 3.1, the schematic we opened the chapter with to frame firm efforts postlaunch, Dropbox's strategy is what we had in mind by including a "backward-looping" arrow from customer development to customer acquisition. Although customer development is usually the stage in the relationship where you harvest the fruits of your past labor, it can also be an integral part of sowing the seeds for future crops.

Affecting Customer Retention

At this stage in the customer-innovation-firm relationship, things should be humming along: New customers continue to join, assuming the market potential has not yet been exhausted, while existing customers generate revenues *and* often help acquire new customers. As we've seen, the firm can do many things to facilitate and amplify these processes so that it gets the most equity out of the innovation. Trade-offs are sure to be encountered in evaluating which marketing options make the most sense, and navigating them profitably is the name of the game.

What can spoil the party, however, or at least put a damper on it, is if the customers a firm has worked so hard to acquire and has been nurturing meticulously for a steady stream of revenues decide to leave—in other words, they abandon the innovation. This shouldn't come as a total shock, as we have been taking this grim attrition eventuality into account in our analysis by including a retention rate—a number (less than one) that reflects the likelihood that a customer will continue to use the innovation in the next period. Yet in the spirit of the chapter's title, "Don't Just Stand There: Do Something!," you might ask what firms can do to affect this rate. Although it is rare for all customers to be "evergreens" who stick with an innovation throughout their entire life span, how can firms increase the retention rate and take measures to prevent customers from wilting away after a few short seasons?

To explore this issue in greater depth, it is helpful to first get a sense of what is at stake when a customer terminates the relationship and how the timing of a customer's departure matters.

THE POWER OF ONE.   In the XM Satellite Radio example we have been using, the retention rate was assumed to be 0.81, which means a 19 percent chance that a customer would terminate his or her subscription in the next period. Along with several other quantities (subscription revenues, cost to serve, and discount rate), we arrived at an average customer lifetime value of $272 for XM (see chapter 2 if you need a refresher on how we got to this figure).

A number of reasons might cause a subscriber to consider discontinuing the service. One reason could be related to changes in personal circumstances. For instance, take Doug, a hypothetical customer who signed up for satellite radio when he was living in the suburbs of Los Angeles in a big house with his wife and two kids. His job was smack-dab in the heart of the city, making his commute at least an hour, often longer, depending on traffic. Satellite radio was a godsend for Doug. On his way to work, he would listen to highly engaging talk shows, mixing in some eighties music (his favorite period) when he was in the mood and on occasion sprinkling in some heavy metal, a nostalgic reminder of the days he played electric guitar with a few buddies in college. On his way home, he would often catch a live broadcast of a Dodgers game or just take it easy with some classic rock. He just loved the ability to listen to what he wanted to when he wanted without commercials. After a few years, Doug's kids grew up and left home, so he and his wife decided to spend their empty-nest days closer to downtown. Doug was now within short cycling distance to work. He soon realized that he was barely listening to radio. As much as it pained him, he simply could not justify the expense and cancelled his XM subscription.

Other reasons for quitting an innovation could be related to low perceptions of derived value. When at any point in time the benefits from a new product or service are deemed insufficient to justify continued payment, the customer might head for the door. Consider Stacy, another hypothetical customer who lives in Manhattan. As a volunteer for several organizations, Stacy would spend many hours a week driving around the city delivering food to the needy, shuttling elderly folks to get medical treatment, and helping children from distressed homes with their schoolwork. Stacy was also a reggae junkie. None of the local free broadcast channels was exclusively devoted to this genre, let alone offering commentary and shows about trending bands. When news broke of a new radio service with more than a hundred channels, one of them devoted exclusively to Reggae, Stacy was among the very first adopters. However, there was one thing she didn't foresee: service quality issues. Satellite radio delivered exceptional sound quality and uninterrupted reception in open areas—where signal transmission was uninterrupted. But in high-density zones with narrow streets and exceedingly tall buildings ("urban canyons"), as in Manhattan, signal quality was uneven across town. Stacy would often hear background noises or have sound break up—disruptions she had definitely not signed up for. In such urban locations, ground-based transmitters, called terrestrial repeaters, are needed to receive satellite radio signals and rebroadcast them at higher power levels. At the time of the launch, XM had only set up eight hundred such repeaters in seventy-five cities across the United States—clearly not enough for Stacy. After a year, not sensing any real improvement in quality, Stacy cancelled her service.

While XM could not have done anything about the colossal changes in Doug's personal life and had to accept the fact that satellite radio has ceased to deliver sufficient value for him, XM might have been able to prevent Stacy from leaving. If the company had invested more efforts during the first few months of operations to get a better sense of the reception problems in urban canyons and installed more repeaters, perhaps Stacy would have been more satisfied with her experience. And as anyone in customer relationship management will tell you, satisfaction drives loyalty, which translates into retention and Stacy not cancelling her service.

Back to trade-offs: more terrestrial repeaters equals more costs, and XM in its first few years might want to invest in other areas, like signing up prominent show hosts, snagging exclusivity deals with major sports leagues, ensuring more car makers install XM radios as a standard feature, and so on. Any decision to invest directly in activities that will bolster the retention rate will therefore hinge on the ROI of keeping a customer on board for a longer duration. How can this be examined?

A different way to frame this question is in reverse: how much money does the firm *lose* when a customer is not retained? The answer to this question seems straightforward at first. If we remove an adopter from the customer base, we lose his or her stream of per-period profits from that point on. True. But a customer's value to the firm is not just contingent on the revenues derived directly from him or her. An existing customer can make another significant contribution to the company's innovation equity. Armed with our understanding of how diffusion "works," it should be quite clear that customers also contribute to equity because they exert a social force that can affect prospective adopters in the market potential pool. Acquired customers have an important role to play in accelerating diffusion. For example, each time someone uses XM Satellite Radio while driving with a friend or each time a subscriber talks about the service with others, he or she can potentially speed up adoption. But once subscription is terminated, so likely will the social influence he or she wielded, which may then slow the diffusion process—that is to say, some people might become XM customers later rather than sooner. And because of the discount rate (time equals money!), innovation equity is adversely affected by this delay. What could make matters even worse, of course, is if a former customer's dissatisfaction causes him or her to "bad mouth" satellite radio, which would result in a negative social force that slows diffusion even more or causes the market potential to contract.

Thus losing a customer has two negative financial consequences, or losses, for the firm: a "direct loss" stemming from the forfeiture of the customer's future per-period payments and an "indirect loss" resulting from the slower rate of future acquisition. The direct loss on innovation equity is assessed by taking the lifetime value of an already signed-up customer (i.e., CLV) at the period the customer leaves. The indirect loss incurred is calculated by computing the continued expected diffusion from the

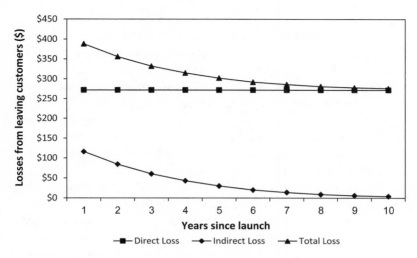

FIGURE 3.3. XM losses when a customer departs at different times*
* Measured as the change in innovation equity at the time of departure.

year the customer's departure takes place but decreasing the cumulative number of adopters by exactly one person, which then impacts the future adoption numbers through the basic diffusion model's social force. The decrease in innovation equity from having fewer customers in each ensuing period is then assessed using the framework presented in chapter 2.

Figure 3.3 depicts the two types of monetary losses XM would sustain from a single customer cancelling the service one year after launch, two years after launch, three years after launch, and so on—each point reflecting the corresponding change in innovation equity when evaluated at the time the departure takes place. As can be seen, the direct loss is not sensitive to the timing of customer attrition, but the indirect loss is. In particular, the latter type of loss decreases over time: early on it is as high as 41 percent of the direct loss yet dwindles down to about 2 percent of the direct loss by year 10.

Therefore, if our hypothetical customer Stacy leaves XM early on in the product life cycle, her social-force value will constitute a big part of what is at stake in letting her go. The total loss from not retaining her (the sum of the direct and indirect losses) at such a nascent stage is a tough blow for XM. If many like her are at risk of leaving due to disappointing quality and reception issues, then investing in more robust signal repeater coverage could well be worth it.

And by no means is this timing of customer departure problem unique to satellite radio. In fact, for some innovations, the indirect loss was found to be financially more costly in the first few years than the direct loss was. In other words, the firm may lose more money because nonretained customers no longer exert a social force that expedites future diffusion than because the payments they provide to the firm have ceased.

We would like to dwell for a moment on why the early periods postlaunch are so critical in terms of the social value each customer has. Recall that in this time frame, the bandwagon effect of innovation diffusion, where past adopters influence nonadopters to join their ranks, begins to emerge. After enough customers join, there is a takeoff in adoption, which is largely attributable to the social force that "feeds on itself." However, reaching the takeoff phase can take time, and because in the early periods there are relatively few customers that can help ignite the social process, each customer is important. A loss of even a few can delay the stream of income from future customers. This delay can cause a considerable loss of money because a nontrivial number of people will adopt later rather than sooner and hence their lifetime value contribution to equity will be discounted more heavily. In subsequent chapters, we explain how the basic diffusion model can be extended to explicitly account for the negative implications of customer attrition on social influence processes (particularly in chapters 6 and 9 and the associated math boxes).

DON'T DROP DROPBOX.   In the section on affecting customer acquisition, we mentioned that offering low introductory prices and consumer rebates can spur adoption. But the concessions firms make to increase the acquisition rate may solve one problem but create another. How? Say someone is not sure he or she really needs a new product or service. At a high price, he or she might opt to forgo purchasing, deeming the expense (which is certain) to the benefit (which is uncertain) as too risky. Yet at a much lower price, the mental calculus could easily flip, and the innovation becomes a gamble worth taking, even for people who are skeptical to begin with. Once adoption takes place and experience is gained, the uncertainty is resolved. For some, the innovation "fits like a glove," and continued usage and payment is a forgone conclusion. For others, however, the innovation proves to be much less relevant, and paying the regular price, or even continuing to pay the lower price, just doesn't make sense. They terminate use. Somewhat paradoxically, therefore, there can be situations where facilitating adoption on one end of the customer management rollercoaster leads to greater attrition on the other end. Whether the trade-off is worth it depends on the extent of the price discount given versus the duration of time that attracted customers, who are less loyal, stick with the firm.

A similar trade-off can occur between customer development efforts and retention. To see how this might happen, let's go back to the Dropbox example. When we explored this example earlier, we showed how to assess the advisability of offering referral incentives to existing customers. The trade-off was that the additional storage space potentially sped up the acquisition of new customers through a social force yet slowed the conversion of existing free customers to premium subscribers, thereby negatively affecting customer development.

Aside from the referral incentive, Dropbox can take other actions that bear on customer management. For instance, say the monthly fee for extra storage was lowered to $7.50 instead of $10; this would result in a CLV of $230 on average for each paying customer. And suppose the company conducted market research to conclude that the conversion rate from the free basic service to the premium paid service would rise as a result to 1.5 percent without much effect on the acquisition/diffusion rate parameters, as most of those who join don't consider the premium service initially. If the retention rate of paying customers stayed at 82.5 percent, the ten-year innovation equity with this pricing policy would be $4.14 billion—which is almost identical to the innovation equity at the higher monthly subscription price; the trade-off of lower profits from each paying customer roughly balances the greater conversion rate to the premium subscription. However, if the retention rate were to decrease because a substantial portion of those that converted later discovered that they don't really need that much more space and reverted back to being free users, such a pricing move will prove ill advised. Customer development and customer retention are also inextricably linked.

Closing the Metaphoric Loop

Whether it's to admire their beauty or enjoy their fruits, reaping the benefits from growing plants requires hard work and constant attention. Similarly, for innovations to deliver as much commercial performance as possible, one cannot stop at product development. One needs to continue to invest postlaunch in those actions that will most effectively impact the diffusion and lifetime value of customers. But as we have seen, trade-offs lurk. Navigating these trade-offs and understanding how the various phases of customer acquisition, development, and retention intertwine is the key to success.

Key Takeaways

- Marketing efforts can affect innovation equity by having an impact on the market potential, the speed of diffusion, and the customer lifetime value.
- The effects of marketing actions on customer lifetime value can occur at any of the three customer management phases: acquisition (adding new customers), development (increasing profits from existing customers), and retention (influencing existing customers to stay for a longer duration).
- Applying marketing actions often involves customer management trade-offs. For example, lowering the price can help expedite customer acquisition efforts yet have a negative effect on customer development. The innovation equity framework provides a way to analyze these trade-offs.
- The innovation equity framework also helps understand the multiple implications of losing a customer (attrition) on long-term profitability, particularly when attrition occurs early in the life cycle of a new product or service.

CHAPTER FOUR

Foreseeing Bumps and Potholes along the Diffusion Road

"I could tell you my adventures—beginning from this morning," said Alice a little timidly, "but it's no use going back to yesterday, because I was a different person then."
—From *Alice's Adventures in Wonderland* by Lewis Carroll

The term "electric drive vehicles" encompasses all car types that use electricity from on- or off-board electrical power sources. The electricity is stored in batteries and either serves as the primary fuel source, as with all-electric vehicles that require external recharging, or as a secondary fuel source to improve gas mileage efficiency, as with hybrid electric vehicles (HEVs) that recharge internally when the car brakes; some models balance multiple sources of energy and allow limited external recharging, as do plug-in hybrid electrics. By far the most popular electric drive vehicle throughout the 2000s was the HEV.

If you are a battery supplier for the electric drive category, you undoubtedly follow the diffusion pattern of these vehicles quite closely, as your fortunes literally rise and fall with their adoption level. The Panasonic EV Energy Company (later named Primearth EV Energy) was no exception. Primearth, which made high-voltage traction batteries for all of Toyota's hybrid cars as well as for several of Honda's and GM's hybrid models, had every reason to be optimistic heading into 2008. Up to that point, HEV sales in the United States had seen a dramatic rise since they were launched—from less than 10,000 units sold in 2000 to about 352,000 units sold in 2007.

But 2008 ended with disappointment: for the first time, unit sales were lower that year than in the preceding year. Perhaps this was just a fluke, a minor bump in an otherwise promising diffusion road. Alas, three years later, the situation looked even grimmer: HEV unit sales kept dropping in each consecutive year to a level of about 266,000 in 2011 (with all-electrics and plug-ins that year adding fewer than 17,500 units). Things seemed to be going in reverse. Heading into 2012, Primearth's management had every reason to be puzzled, perhaps even worried.

What could explain this decline in sales? First, it is true that the entire car industry suffered from soft sales during the time frame in question, largely due to the global economic recession. Yet the fraction electric drive vehicle sales represented out of total new car sales dropped by more than 30 percent between 2007 and 2011. Thus while the overall industry decline might account for some of the decrease, a big portion of the HEV decline remains unexplained. Second, gas prices fluctuated considerably during this period, reaching their highest and lowest levels in a decade within a span of less than six months. However, for most of 2008 to 2011, gas prices were well above the long-run average and trended upward, so it is difficult to argue that very low fuel costs deterred consumers from buying HEVs. Third, it is difficult to imagine that the electric drive vehicle market had already exhausted its entire adopter pool. With the annual number of new passenger vehicle sales in the United States averaging 12 million, the peak of 352,000 HEVs sold in 2007 does not seem anywhere near even half the sales potential these vehicles could achieve.

This last point is worth dwelling on. Recall that in chapter 1, we alluded to the fact that the adoption pace of an innovation tends to increase until it reaches about half the market potential, at which point the pace begins to slow down with fewer and fewer new adoptions in each subsequent period. Indeed, "pictures" of how prominent innovations diffused in the past, such as portable CD players depicted in figure 4.1, seem to support this pattern. The number of units sold climbed until it reached a peak in 2000, whereby growth was at its highest pace, and from there on, an unrelenting decline ensued. This diffusion progression gives rise to an S-shaped curve for the cumulative penetration level of an innovation over time, such as that observed in figure 4.2 for wireless phone service subscribers in Norway.

The logic for why unit sales grow steadily until reaching a peak level was given an intuitive explanation based on the nature of the diffusion process and how it unfolds. Simply put, more past adopters means more social influence and pressure on the nonadopters. And as the number of customers acquired increases from period to period, the social force becomes more powerful, leading to even more new adoptions. However, once half the market potential has been acquired, the group of nonadopt-

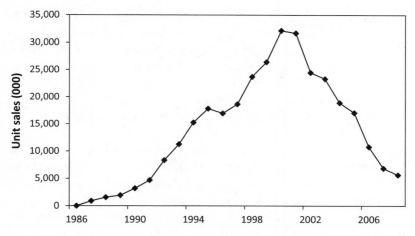

FIGURE 4.1. Unit sales over time of portable CD players in the United States (000)

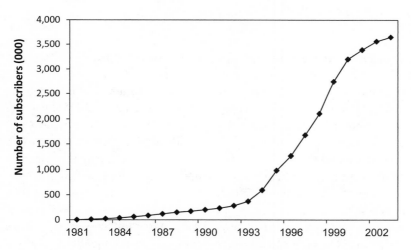

FIGURE 4.2. The cumulative number of wireless phone service subscribers in Norway

ers still waiting in the wings to embrace the innovation becomes smaller than the group of adopters. There are fewer people upon whom to exert influence, and consequently, the growth rate begins to decline. Continued sales, bounded by how many more people can be converted, advance toward the maximum penetration level at an ever decreasing pace.

This end-of-the-road fate is evident in the wireless phone service example of figure 4.2. By the late 1990s, once the penetration level crossed the 1.5 million subscriber mark, the pace of new adoptions slowed. And by 2003, with about 3.7 million subscribers acquired out of a total population size of 4.5 million, the untapped market potential was small; very few new adoptions took place thereafter. In the portable CD example of figure 4.1, by 2008 the number of units sold was less than 18 percent of that achieved at the peak eight years earlier. The market potential was close to depletion, just as a new generation of portable music devices (MP3 players) was gaining traction.

Given these curves and their relationship to the basic diffusion model, you start to wonder, is there something inherently "wrong" with HEVs and the electric drive vehicle category? If indeed their long-run market potential is much greater than 700,000 units—that is, the 352,000 peak observed in 2007 is not the midpoint of the relevant total adoption pool— why was there a continued drop in unit sales for four straight years? Will sales just continue to drop until they reach zero? The folks at Primearth EV Energy surely hoped not.

Two Peaks and a Prolonged Dip Make for a Diffusion Saddle

In chapter 1 we devoted quite a lot of time to explaining that by and large, new adoptions in each period are the result of two processes that become intertwined over time: Either someone "gets it" on his or her own and decides to adopt the innovation independently from others or someone "gets it" due to the influence of others—that is, social effects cause non-adopters to "see the light" and succumb to the innovation's allure. Now you may not have given much thought to it at the time, but when capturing these two adoption forces in our basic diffusion model (per expression 1.2), we assumed that all potential adopters—effectively everyone in the prospective pool of customers to acquire—were equally susceptible to these two forces. To be more precise, there was one parameter for the individual force (p) and one parameter for the social force (q).

The "single-parameter-per-adoption force" seems like a plausible modeling approach. It allows keeping things as simple as possible when attempting to forecast an innovation's diffusion in the face of considerable consumer uncertainty. It further reflects an average across the population in terms of the relevance of the various routes to adoption and should thus provide reasonable estimates. These conclusions probably hold true as long as using a basic diffusion model, constructed with a single param-

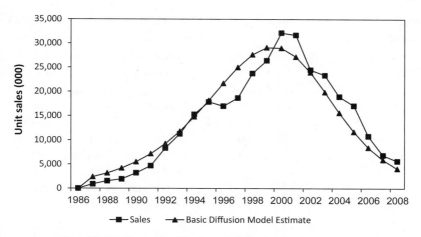

FIGURE 4.3. Portable CD players: Actual unit sales and basic diffusion model estimate

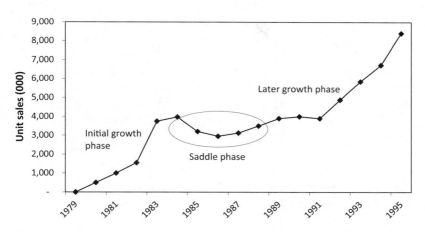

FIGURE 4.4. Unit sales of personal computers (PCs) in the United States (1979–95)

eter per adoption force, fits the actual data fairly well. Indeed, for CD players, word processors, cell phones, and many other innovations for that matter, we see a strong fit between curves based on the basic diffusion model and the actual data obtained years after the launch, as can be seen in figure 4.3 for CD players.

However, when taking a look at the sales pattern of yet another prominent innovation—the personal computer depicted in figure 4.4—we notice something strange about five years after the product's introduction into the marketplace. After a nice initial period of increasing sales between 1980 and 1984, where the annual growth rate of units sold was about 50 percent, the graph seems to take a nose dive for a few years. Subsequently, sales start growing again and, after about six years, surpass the initial 1984 peak and keep rising toward their "real" peak, which occurred in the early 2000s.

While it is true that there is a small "dip" in the diffusion data for portable CD players (per figure 4.4), note the difference in dips between the unit sales of CD players and PCs. In the former case, it's a one-year decline (in 1996) of less than 5 percent, a random fluctuation (or "noise") that we might expect to see in the sales of new products. In the case of PC sales, however, the decline is much more pronounced—greater than 25 percent at the lowest point—and lasted for multiple years.

PCs are not alone in exhibiting this saddlelike pattern. Color televisions, cordless phones, printers, and VCRs all exhibited a saddle diffusion pattern. Nor is the saddle phenomenon confined to the United States, as recent research has shown its emergence in several countries. For example, a study involving the diffusion pattern of prominent innovations in nineteen developed countries revealed the existence of a clear saddle pattern in about 45 percent of the innovation-country pairs examined. In these instances, on average, the decline in sales began after 30 percent of the long-run market potential had been penetrated and lasted for about eight years, and the depth of the drop was nearly 30 percent of the predecline peak.

Not All Adopters Are Created Equally, nor Do They Create New Adopters Equally

Why don't we see the familiar bell-shaped curves for the diffusion of so many innovations? Why are sales not monotonically growing until they reach a single, well-defined peak and decline from there on, as we have seen with other innovations? What should we make of the different pattern that looks more like a "peak-valley-peak"? How can it be explained?

To try to answer these questions, let's embark on a little thought experiment: Assume that an innovation is launched into the marketplace. The company behind it spends significant sums on promotion: running ads on prime-time television, providing incentives for retailers to properly merchandise and support the launch in stores, creating a dedicated website with tons of product information, and offering discounted prices. Who is most likely to purchase the innovation right away and generate early sales? We might naturally expect it to be those who are comfortable taking risks with new products and services and who have a strong desire to try novel things. Every category typically has these "innovation-forward" types who are on the lookout for cutting-edge technologies that can possibly fit their needs and address their problems better than existing solutions. They are undaunted, in fact even eager, to tinker with innovations, pore through manuals, and participate in online discussion forums to voice their opinions and comment on their experiences with technological advances. For them, novelty often equals coolness.

Continuing with our thought experiment, who do we believe is going to be next in the adoption line after the innovation forwards? Most likely it will be those who are much less of the "technology for the sake of technology" types and have a tendency to be risk averse when it comes to experimenting with "newfangled contraptions." Before they open their pocketbooks to buy, they want to be fully convinced that the new technology offers real benefits that are directly applicable to their usage and consumption patterns and to solving their problems. For these "innovation moderates," who are certainly more mainstream in what they look for, an innovation should not only be worth the price tag in terms of benefits but also not require too much time and effort to fit with other products they own and with their current work- or lifestyle. Compatibility is a big deal for these consumers.

These two segments seem to differ in several dimensions that are relevant for the adoption process. For the first segment, the innovation-forward consumers, we might expect the individual force (the parameter p of the basic diffusion model) to be a big factor. These individuals would likely pay attention to firms' communications and media coverage. They are usually able to tell, using their own judgment and past experiences, whether the innovation is a boon or a bust for them. They might listen to the opinions of others or take cue from what they observe others actually doing, but the social influences they are open to (the parameter q of the basic diffusion model) typically comes from like-minded technology enthusiasts or category experts: people with a proven track record of critically evaluating innovations as soon as they are made available and demonstrating their use and usefulness. Perceived expertise is key to the social influence process for the innovation forwards. Every category tends to have such a set of dedicated aficionados that exhibit this kind of behavior.

And given the time, effort, and money required to pursue their passion for innovations in the category and establish such expertise, we might expect the innovation-forward group to be relatively small in size (the parameter m in the basic diffusion model).

The second segment, the innovation moderates, are more passive in seeking information about new products and services and have a more cautious, even skeptical attitude to the hype firms try to create when touting their latest and greatest products. This attitude, along with the inclination to temper any excitement over possible rewards from new technologies with the risks and costs that often accompany them, suggests that the individual force will not have a strong impact on innovation moderates. With respect to their susceptibility to social influences, it seems plausible that innovation moderates would want to know that innovation forwards have taken a serious look at the innovation and have given it their stamp of approval. But is that enough? If moderates observe someone they deem a "techie" or a "gadget-friendly" geek using the novel product or service and talking effusively about it, will that prompt them to immediately adopt it themselves? Possibly not. It's not that the moderates look down on the innovation-forward population—often the contrary—but their belief is that what gets this group excited is not necessarily something that is relevant for them. Furthermore, they know that the innovation forwards are often tech savvy and have the motivation to invest effort in setting up and learning how to use novel products, characteristics that innovation moderates don't typically cultivate. In short, the innovation moderates believe that "*they* are different from *us*."

What might help moderates get over their "skepticism hump" is knowledge that pragmatic, risk-averse consumers like themselves have already taken the big step and adopted. Seeing other mainstream consumers use the new product successfully and hearing about their positive experiences would lead to a strong social force within this group. As far as the size of this segment is concerned, if our description represents what mainstream consumers are like, then it should be quite sizable. Indeed, the "main" in "mainstream" suggests that they constitute the majority of consumers.

At this point you might be wondering what this nice hypothetical narrative about various adopter groups and their distinct attitudes toward innovation has to do with the "bumpy" diffusion pattern seen in figure 4.4 and how it can explain the "pothole" that occurred several years after the launch of the PC. In essence, the narrative described how forwards and moderates exhibit dissimilar adoption behaviors that can be conceptually linked to the basic diffusion model, but how can this storyline help us think more systematically about the PC saddle?

First, it should be reassuring to know that the thought experiment we just went through is real and not just a hypothetical concoction. The general characteristics of the two adopter types have been corroborated by actual research. The logic has been borne out by numerous studies, practitioner accounts, and media reflections of how several past innovations diffused. The first-in-line adopters in those instances, generating the bulk of initial sales, have been found to represent a small fraction of the potential adoption pool—about 15–20 percent on average. These early market adopters have been shown to exhibit the traits described above in relation to their susceptibility to individual and social forces. More specifically, early market individuals are "more in touch" with new developments, are far more attentive to communications about new technologies in the press and in dedicated forums, and are primarily influenced by individuals within their peer group and typically not affected by others outside their group. The second segment, the innovation moderates or mainstream consumers, usually represent the lion's share of potential adopters, about 80–85 percent on average. They have been found to be less knowledgeable about new technological developments at the introduction stage yet are often malleable to social influences from either members of their own segment, the segment of innovation forwards, or both segments. Because members of the innovation-forward segment can exert an adoption force on anyone that has not yet adopted, while members of the mainstream segment primarily influence others in their own segment, some researchers have labeled the former group "influentials" and the latter group "imitators."

We next examine how these differences between segments can help us understand the PC saddle pattern observed between 1984 and 1991 (per figure 4.3). As the word "personal" in personal computer implies, the PC was intended from the get-go for individual ownership. The entire machine was at the disposal of the person who bought it or to which it was issued. This contrasted with mainframe computers that were installed in large organizations and overseen by IT staff. For the employees who utilized this shared computing resource, the actual bulky machines were out of sight; all they saw was a terminal. So who were the early buyers of PCs? Several media accounts from the late 1970s and early 1980s suggest that they were mainly "techies." These were consumers with a lot of fascination and interest in electronics and computing, many of whom had assembled their PC from kits and components and actively participated in various computer-related forums, such as the Homebrew Computer Club or the Boston Computer Society. Computing was a hobby of sorts for many of them, and they relished in the ability to click away in their spare time and the convenience of their own home. Some probably had experience with mainframe computing from work and were clamoring for a machine of their own that they could play with in their free time. Among those eager to get their hands on PCs were engineers, many of whom worked in IT departments, curious to learn how much technological power was really packed into these small boxes compared to the mainframes they were familiar with. In some instances, IT gurus even convinced their managers to purchase PCs as a way to increase productivity for certain business units that could highly benefit from them, even if at first only on a trial basis, in limited numbers, and with very specific applications in mind. They assured their superiors that they would take care of proper functionality and that they would be responsible for things working smoothly.

Such "PC hobbyists" as they were sometimes called were largely responsible for the remarkable growth between 1980 and 1984. These innovation forwards regarded the personal computer as a technological breakthrough, and based on early sales figures, the popular press hailed the transformative promise for everyday consumers. *Time* even named the PC as its Person of the Year for 1982, the first time in the history of the magazine that an inanimate object was bestowed the award.

Despite the strong endorsement of early market adopters and the declarations by the press, sales experienced a rough patch for seven long years. For a large portion of consumers—the average household—the impetus and conditions to adopt were just not ripe yet in those early PC years. For these folks, the notion of a computer in their home was somewhat foreign. Computers to them were those impersonal machines that large corporations employed to crunch data, not something they could easily envision as useful for private use. At home there was also no IT person to call with installation challenges or summon to help fix things, as was the case at work. And considering the nontrivial price and nonintuitive nature of interacting with commercially available computers—graphical user interfaces were not well integrated at the time and many operations were accomplished via a command-line screen—it was no wonder most consumers, for whom the expense was out of pocket, perceived insufficient benefits relative to the costs and efforts involved.

Furthermore, those that had adopted out of fascination with the technology were often perceived as niche technophiles. If anything, their adoption was "proof" that the PC may only be suited for computer buffs and *not* for the common consumer—at least not yet. As a result, after most PC innovation forwards had adopted, the diffusion rate slowed considerably. But as time progressed, little by little, average consumers began taking the PC plunge. After nearly a decade (i.e., by the early nineties), a sufficient critical mass of "ordinary Joes and Janes" had adopted and established for other average consumers that (1) it is not difficult to set up computers at home and master the technology and (2) there are various things you can do with a PC that are useful or entertaining. As adoption by mainstream consumers gained steam, more relevant software was developed to cater to them, and shopping for PCs got easier (more retail outlets stocked them, better-trained sales associates could explain their benefits and setup, etc.). Long story short: there appear to have been two separate diffusion processes going on—one for the computer enthusiasts and another for the average consumers. The former were very quick to show interest in PCs and influenced each other, while the latter showed lukewarm initial interest and were not overly inspired or convinced by the computer enthusiasts.

The moral of this story for our purposes is that when thinking about potential adopters for an innovation, we shouldn't necessarily treat everyone in the pool as being identical. Rather, when characterizing how the diffusion of an innovation might unfold, it is sometimes more realistic to regard the relevant population as comprising distinct groups in terms of what and who influences each of them to adopt. And although in essence there could exist numerous segments that differ along these lines, for most practical purposes, the population can be segmented into two groups: a set of innovation-forward consumers who tend to adopt soon after the launch and who constitute the early market and a set of innovation moderates who tend to adopt later and who constitute the mainstream market.

The Diffusion Model—*Take 2*

If indeed some innovations are expected to experience a "bumpy ride" along their diffusion path—an up-down-up-down trajectory in sales and new adoptions—is the basic diffusion model developed in chapter 1 still usable? Can we somehow "fix" or modify it so that it is flexible enough to reflect a single-peaked growth pattern, as we saw with cell phones and satellite radio, and, if necessary, a two-peaked saddle pattern, as we saw with the PC? The answer is a resounding yes! Here's how.

We know that the saddle pattern of growth can be explained by acknowledging the fact that potential adopters differ and that two segments can capture this heterogeneity fairly well. Furthermore, we discussed how the main components of the basic diffusion model can be linked to each segment's characteristics and adoption behavior. What remains is to move from the conceptual discussion of this link to something more concrete that will allow us to quantify the dynamics of the saddle formation process. Let's get started by taking a fresh look at figure 1.2 in chapter 1. Recall that it visually depicted how the diffusion of an innovation could be captured by three elements that are at the heart of the process: the individual force (the parameter p), the social force (the parameter q), and the long-run market potential (the parameter m).

It probably didn't strike you as noteworthy when you first looked at this figure, but in light of all that has been said in this chapter, you might now comment on the fact that everyone in the pool of consumers that have not yet adopted is featured in the same box, and aside from gender, they all look alike too! Furthermore, there is only one arrow per adoption force; hence the individual and social forces driving adoption are the same for each consumer. There are two processes that can push someone into the adopter camp—the individual process and the social process—but only one population type.

What if instead of one set of boxes, there were two—that is, two pools of have-not-yet-adopted consumers with separate arrows emanating from and flowing into each of their respective adopter boxes? What this expanded description suggests is that each segment of consumers has its own set of parameters for the long-run market potential and for the individual and social forces. Seems quite straightforward, but there is a twist: The twist is that members of the mainstream segment can be influenced by previous adopters from both segments, and we need to allow for the strength of the social force from each group of past adopters to differ. By contrast, the social force influencing the early market segment is "self-contained" within that group.

Taking this logic one step further, if we allow for *two* concurrent basic diffusion models instead of just one and look at the combined number of adoptions in each time period, we should be able to capture nonsmooth adoption patterns like saddles. And indeed, this is the case! To be more precise, expression 4.1 lays out the multisegment diffusion model that features two segments, each with its own set of diffusion parameters and with the flexibility to allow innovation-forward adopters to affect

innovation-moderate consumers. A formal description of the multisegment diffusion model is given in math box 4 in the appendix.

EXPRESSION 4.1. The multisegment diffusion model

Number of new adopters in this time period =
Sum of adopters from each segment:
Innovation-Forward Segment:
Consumers in segment that have not yet adopted · {Segment's individual force +
(Segment's social force · Segment's proportion of past adoption)}

+

Innovation-Moderate Segment:
Consumers in segment that have not yet adopted · {Segment's individual
force + (Segment's social force · Segment's proportion of past adoption) +
(Cross-segment social force · Innovation forwards' proportion of past adoption)}

Figure 4.5 provides an illustrative example of the multisegment diffusion
model just developed. It shows the total number of new adoptions over
time in a two-segment setting, with $p_1 = 0.1$, $q_1 = 0.5$, $m_1 = 10$ million, and
$p_2 = 0.0025$, $q_2 = 0.25$, $q_{21} = 0$, $m_2 = 50$ million. Note that a subscript 1
denotes the innovation-forward segment, and a subscript 2 denotes the
innovation-moderate segment; the 21 subscript denotes the social adoption force of group 1 members on group 2 members. From the fact that
$q_{21} = 0$, it should be clear that in this example there are no cross-segment
effects—that is, social forces only arise within segment. The two dashed
lines in figure 4.5 represent the adoptions arising from each segment respectively, and the solid line represents the total number of adoptions
(obtained by summing the number of new adoptions from each segment).
As expected, the separate basic diffusion model for each of the segments
has the familiar bell-shaped curve with a single peak, just as in figure 1.3
from chapter 1. The diffusion curve that belongs to the innovation forwards progresses quickly, reaching the peak of adoption in year 5 and
decreasing thereafter. By contrast, the diffusion curve that belongs to the
innovation moderates moves much more slowly, arriving at its peak of
adoption only in year 21. This asynchrony in diffusion speeds gives rise to
a period, between years 5 through 10, during which the decrease in adoptions from the first curve dominates the much slower growth in adoptions
from the second curve. Consequently, in year 10 we hit a diffusion trough
or valley. At that point, new adoptions from the second curve start gaining

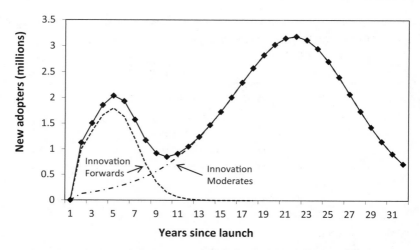

FIGURE 4.5. Producing a saddlelike pattern with the multisegment diffusion model

momentum, while the decline in adopters from the first segment is tapering off, and hence the total number of new adoptions begins climbing again.

Now that we have a modeling approach for producing a diffusion pattern that is saddle shaped, it is useful to take it to relevant real data and see how it performs. In 2001, the *Economist* listed seven consumer electronics innovations that had a profound commercial impact: "Apart from the personal computer (PC) and mobile telephone . . . five new product categories have achieved mass acceptance: the video recorder, videogame consoles, CD players, answering machines, and cordless phones."

We examined the diffusion rate of these seven major innovations and found that three of them displayed a distinct saddle pattern: PCs, VCRs, and cordless phones. In all these cases, there was an initial peak in sales, followed by a decline of over 10 percent from the peak, with sales surpassing the previous peak levels only three or more years later. We then estimated the multisegment diffusion model parameters for each of these three innovations; in all cases we were able to recover parameter values that, when plugged into this new model, exhibited close resemblance to the actual diffusion pattern. Averaging the parameters across the three innovations and plotting the corresponding "average" diffusion curve, one arrives at figure 4.6. We see that the average saddle period lasted almost four years, and the depth of the drop in adoptions, the saddle dip, is a little over 16 percent.

Hopefully, the reasons why a saddle diffusion pattern can emerge have become much clearer, as is how the basic diffusion model can be expanded to capture this phenomenon.

Allowing multiple segments to coexist and interact with each other, within the same model, enables capturing other types of diffusion-curve irregularities besides the saddle. Consider the multisegment diffusion model, but now let there be a significant cross-segment social effect between the early market innovation-forward and the mainstream innovation-moderate consumers (i.e., $q_{21} > 0$), with $p_1 = 0.1$, $q_1 = 0.5$, $m_1 = 10$ million, and $p_2 = 0.0025$, $q_2 = 0$, $q_{21} = 0.05$, $m_2 = 50$ million. Note that in this case there is no social force among mainstream adopters as $q_2 = 0$—that is, only innovation forwards create social adoption influence. A plot of how the overall diffusion of the innovation would progress with these values is presented in figure 4.7. We see a very steep initial rise in total adoptions, peaking at six years postlaunch at a much higher point than before (more than three million adoptions versus fewer than two million in figure 4.5), with the curve then very slowly decreasing from that level, with still more than 500,000 new adoptions after thirty years. It is not a saddle this time, as there is no initial peak, then a prolonged dip, and then another peak in the combined diffusion curve. Yet it also looks quite different from the classic bell-shaped diffusion curves we saw in previous chapters, which

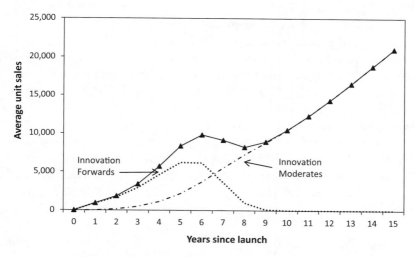

FIGURE 4.6. Average sales pattern of three consumer electronics products with a saddle[*]
[*] PC, VCR, and cordless phones.

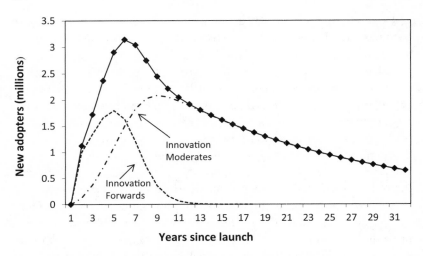

FIGURE 4.7. Multisegment diffusion model with a cross-segment social force

represent a homogeneous population and where the single peak is more symmetrically positioned: the curve's shape prior to the peak is similar to its shape after the peak, and the prepeak growth period takes about the same time as the postpeak decline period. The basic diffusion model is consistent with this characterization, as the peak it predicts occurs at exactly 50 percent penetration of the long-run market potential.

Armed with our multisegment diffusion model, we can better understand why the nonsymmetric pattern in figure 4.7 emerges. The early market segment of innovation forwards adopt very quickly, leading to a diffusion spike. However, the mainstream segment of innovation moderates have a modest individual force driving their adoption and are socially affected in this case only by the innovation forwards (who make up one-sixth of the total long-run population)—hence, their growth is very slow at first. Once the full set of innovation forwards has adopted (roughly at year 10), the social force they exert on the mainstream market achieves its maximum level and remains constant thereafter (in the example, since the cross-segment social force is $q_{21} = 0.05$, and at that point the proportion of past adoption for innovation forwards is 1, we have $0.05 \cdot 1 = 0.05$). Consequently, the self-reinforcing snowball effect that often emerges with the basic diffusion model is tempered for the innovation moderates and also results in a rather slow decline or "fat tail."

Taken together, the collection of examples depicted in figures 4.5–4.7 has revealed the flexibility of the multisegment diffusion model to capture a host of dynamic adoption situations, from cases where the early market has little impact on the main market to cases where the main market will only heed social influences exerted by the early market. In the former case, social contagion is effectively confined to members of the same segment: one only trusts the social force exerted by "in-group" peers. In the latter case, social contagion affecting the mainstream originates from "out-group" members, reflecting situations where key opinion leaders or market mavens have a disproportionately strong effect on the rest of the population. These influentials are the ones primarily responsible for driving the adoption of new trends and novel technologies, while the majority of consumers follow in their footsteps, taking their advice and copying their actions.

Assessing Innovation Equity in a Multisegment Population

Potential adopters can differ in terms of the forces that drive their behavior and, because of that, the overall diffusion curve may be "choppy" or "irregular." Very good to know, you might say, but how does this matter for assessing the value of an innovation to the firm? In other words, what impact might this have on the innovation equity framework?

To answer this question, as you might suspect, we have to link the multisegment diffusion model with the customer lifetime value (CLV) model—in essence, apply the principles introduced in the previous chapters while taking into account that two segments, rather than just one, are involved. The multisegment diffusion model should give us the number of new customers acquired from each segment in each period, and the CLV model should give us a way to assess how much money we can expect to make from each acquired customer.

If we believe that the main difference between the two segments (innovation forwards and moderates) is in their route-to-adoption characteristics—attitudes toward innovations, perceptions of risk and rewards, and susceptibility to adoption forces from various social groups—but not in their postadoption profitability, then it probably makes sense to use the same CLV parameters for all adopters. In other words, once a prospect becomes a customer, he or she behaves the same way regardless of which segment he or she originated from. Of course, this may not always be true. For example, innovation forwards may be inclined to stay on as loyal users of the new product or service for a longer duration, be more likely to buy upgrades and extras, and require less effort to serve over time, thus affecting their retention rate and per-period profit margin. But the opposite can also be true—for instance, if innovation moderates exhibit greater inertia, cling to basic versions and need much less ongoing support, or are willing to pay handsomely for accessories and enhancements. There is no well-established "rule" or conclusive research finding for how these customer segments differ postadoption, yet it is straightforward to incorporate any heterogeneity across the groups if there are particular reasons to believe differences exist and if one has a reasonable handle on their magnitude. For illustration purposes here, we will stick with the simple case whereby the CLV parameters are the same for all customers postadoption.

To see how the innovation equity framework can be applied with two consumer segments of distinct size and adoption force parameters, consider the following medical example. Assume that a pharmaceutical company is trying to forecast the return on investment (ROI) of a new drug for which it has just received FDA approval and which had cost $300 million to develop. The company has quite a lot of experience with the 250,000 relevant physicians from marketing its existing drug portfolio. It knows that some physicians in the target market are very proactive about new drugs and, in the interest of their patients, are willing to seriously consider them soon after they have been launched: gathering information from medical journals, looking closely at the trials submitted to the FDA, and meeting with company sales reps. A second set of physicians, on the other hand, are of the more wary type. These doctors typically worry that without long-term data on possible side effects and safety complications, it is too risky to try certain new drugs on their patients. Moreover, the clinical trials for the company's new drug were not done "head to head" against existing alternatives but only with respect to a placebo (the control condition where patients receive a sugar pill); hence, these wary physician types will likely question whether the new drug can deliver much of an efficacy improvement relative to the extant drugs that are far cheaper (some already available as generics). The skeptical doctors, who represent about 85 percent of the potential pool, are not very open to the flashy pitches made by pharmaceutical detailers and are far more impressed by knowing that other conservative doctors, whom they trust, have begun prescribing the new drug and are satisfied with the results.

Each physician, regardless of the segment from which he or she originates, treats about ten patients that have the chronic condition for which the drug is indicated. Once a physician is convinced of the merits of the new medication and overcomes any negative concerns, he or she is expected to prescribe it to all relevant patients under his or her care, as the existing drugs on the market are only modestly effective. An annual supply of the drug is priced at $360 and the profit margin is 80 percent (which includes production and marketing expenses). The company plans to spend heavily on converting physicians through targeted detailing efforts, ads in medical magazines, free samples, and booths at professional conferences. Acquisition costs are estimated at $1,000 per converted physician. Once a doctor adopts, there is a chance he or she will have a bad experience with the drug and completely stop prescribing it, which the company estimates at 10 percent every year (for a retention rate of 90 percent). The company has patent protection for eighteen years and uses a 12.5 percent annual cost of capital. The CLV parameters are thus all accounted for: per-period profit margin = $2,880 (10 patients @ $360 each @ 0.8 margins), retention rate = 0.9, discount factor = 1.125, acquisition cost = $1,000.

The company further assumes, after studying some diffusion curves of prominent drugs and medical devices launched in the past, that the multisegment diffusion model parameters should be similar to those that generated figure 4.5—that is, $p_I = 0.1$, $q_I = 0.5$, $p_2 = 0.0025$, $q_2 = 0.25$, and $q_{2I} = 0$, where segment 1 includes the innovation-forward physicians and segment 2 the innovation-moderate physicians. Adjusting the long-run market potential sizes to this case yields $m_I = 37,500$ and $m_2 = 212,500$. We are now ready to begin the analysis. We will use the finite version of innovation equity framework developed in chapter 2, which allows us to account for the fact that the drug has an eighteen-year window to generate strong profits before generics are introduced. Table 4.1 gives us everything we need in order to assess the equity of the new drug.

The way to read table 4.1 is as follows: The first column is the number of years since launch. The second and third columns show the number of innovation forward and innovation moderate physicians that adopt in each year. The fourth and fifth columns give the prospective customer lifetime values (PCLV) for each segment—that is, the monetary value to the firm of all new adopters from each segment in that year (taking into account acquisition costs). This is done by summing future profits stemming from all the new physicians who adopt in each year, up to year 18, and discounting the profits to that year. The last two columns discount these PCLV figures to the beginning of year 1 so they can be evaluated at the time of launch.

Several interesting conclusions emerge from the analysis presented in table 4.1. First, notice that by the time the patent expires, all innovation-forward physicians will have adopted the new drug, whereas fewer than half of the innovation moderates will have begun prescribing it. Another

TABLE 4.1 **Innovation equity for a newly approved drug**

Year since launch	Number of new physician adopters by end of year		Prospective customer lifetime value of new physician adopters in that year ($000)		Present value of new physician adopters ($000)	
	Innovation forwards	Innovation moderates	Innovation forwards	Innovation moderates	Innovation forwards	Innovation moderates
1	3,750	531	43,385	6,146	43,385	6,146
2	5,063	662	58,278	7,625	51,803	6,778
3	6,240	825	71,378	9,438	56,398	7,457
4	6,750	1,026	76,610	11,646	53,805	8,179
5	6,133	1,274	68,918	14,315	43,025	8,937
6	4,519	1,578	50,146	17,512	27,827	9,718
7	2,688	1,950	29,354	21,293	14,480	10,503
8	1,341	2,401	14,345	25,690	62,90	11,264
9	597	2,944	6,219	30,693	2,430	11,962
10	250	3,591	2,521	36,209	873	12,544
11	102	4,354	9,845	42,024	303	12,941
12	41	5,237	375	47,738	103	13,067
13	17	6,240	139	52,697	34	12,822
14	7	7,352	50	55,916	11	12,093
15	3	8,544	17	56,022	3	10,770
16	1	9,769	6	51,251	1	8,758
17	0	10,959	2	39,542	0	6,006
18	0	12,028	0	18,763	0	2,534
					Innovation equity	
Total:	37,500	94,140	422,728	544,518	300,765	172,481

aspect of the forecast is that, although they represent only about one-sixth of the potential market, the innovation-forward physicians create almost two-thirds of the total innovation equity—considerably more than the innovation-moderate physicians. Of course, these two points are related: because the bulk of innovation moderates take so long to come on board, they have fewer years to generate revenues for the company, and on top of that, later earned revenues suffer from a relatively high level of financial discounting. This is also evident from the fact that the present value of moderates is maximal for physicians acquired in year 12, even though the number of adopters is greater every year thereafter. Contrast that with the innovation forwards, whose rapid adoption results in maximal present value in year 3, which is very close to when their number of new adoptions is maximal (year 4).

You will also notice from table 4.1 that, for both segments, the present value contribution of new adopters to innovation equity initially increases and then decreases. The increasing phase is due to the fact that the number of new physician adopters grows in the first few years and discounting is limited. However, as time goes on, future cash flows from new adopters diminish, as both the number of years left until the patent expires gets smaller and discounting is more pronounced; for the innovation forwards the number of new adoptions decreases as well (once more than half of them have adopted).

Another conclusion is that the drug has a positive ROI: the total innovation equity is roughly $473 million relative to development costs of $300 million. Of course, any action by the firm that would induce innovation moderates to adopt at a faster pace (by increasing individual or social forces) or that would improve customer lifetime value (by increasing the retention rate or improving the profit margins) can have a big effect on profits. Importantly, now that the firm can analyze the implications for innovation equity of differentially applying more efforts to one group versus the other, smarter decisions can be made. For example, if the company makes a concerted effort to conduct trials that establish long-term safety and efficacy over existing drugs and assesses that this will increase the individual force for moderates from $p_2 = 0.0025$ to $p_{2new} = 0.005$, redoing the analysis reveals that this segment will now create $303 million worth of innovation equity—slightly *more* than the innovation-forward physicians! As long as these extra trials and the efforts to communicate the results cost less than $130 million (the bump in innovation equity from having the results of the trials), the firm should seriously consider this option. For companies in a race to beat the clock on patent expirations (or in categories where the entry of cheap knock-offs is a concern), a little boost to a slow starting segment can make a huge difference. The multisegment diffusion model, along with a corresponding expanded innovation equity analysis, paves the way to making informed decisions on this front.

The Road to Recovery

In closing, it is worthwhile to revisit the hybrid electric vehicle (HEV) predicament presented at the outset of this chapter. What should companies like Primearth EV Energy, the electric drive battery supplier, make of the dip in sales in the years following the 2007 peak of about 352,000 HEVs sold? From the vantage point of late 2011, whereby annual sales slowed to about 266,000 units, the depth of the dip was nearly 25 percent (20 percent if we include all-electric and plug-in hybrid vehicles), and the slump was already four years in duration. Based on what we now know about innovation diffusion in markets with multiple consumer segments, the question is whether the decline is the result of an adoption pace "mismatch" between the early market innovation forwards and the mainstream market innovation moderates. If so, we probably have a saddle on our hands and can expect sales to pick up soon; otherwise, it may be all downhill from here.

Looking at this issue through the rearview mirror of the Toyota Prius, the most popular HEV by far during this time frame (accounting for over 50 percent of all HEV units sold), is instructive. When the Prius was launched in the United States in 2000, the concept of hybrid cars was largely unfamiliar to the public. Borrowing from the typology of factors that impact adoption described in chapter 1, the innovation was somewhat *complex*, as consumers had to wrap their heads around a car that could charge its own battery when the brakes were applied, switch between gas and electric modes seamlessly, and get an average of forty-two miles per gallon in the city but only thirty miles per gallon on the highway (the opposite of pure gasoline-powered cars that achieve greater miles per gallon in highway driving). On top of that, the Prius was much more expensive relative to a comparable gasoline-fueled compact car.

By all accounts, "dark green" consumers, those who cared tremendously about the environment and who were not deterred by any of the barriers, were quick to adopt. As one prominent Northeast car dealer put it, "A small minority of consumers who were hyper-environmentalists strode into the dealerships right away to purchase the vehicle out of conviction." The car's distinctive, highly *observable* look was also a huge plus in terms of having social influence. Indeed, interviews conducted with early Prius owners revealed that they repeatedly referred to the hybrid car they purchased as being a "conversation maker," conveying "intelligence and distinctiveness," where in the latter description, it seems they were talking as much about how they perceived themselves as about how they perceived the car. All this implies that dark greens had a strong individual force as well as a high (within-segment) social force driving their adoption decision making.

But for the diffusion to sustain its momentum beyond dark greens, mainstream consumers, who are more practical and budget conscious, needed to come on board. Innovation moderates in this case likely cared somewhat about the environment, with public outcry more vocal in recent times over environmental issues like climate change, yet these consumers were at best "light green." The individual force driving their adoption was low, particularly with gasoline prices not high enough to make HEVs or other electric drive vehicles very appealing financially and despite the federal and state tax credits offered when purchasing many of the models. The social force exerted by the dark greens on the light greens was probably a mixed bag. On the one hand, as more dark greens adopted, there were greater reassurances that HEVs are safe and reliable, can be serviced with ease, and indeed cut down fuel emissions. But on the other hand, light greens may not have wanted to be labeled "tree huggers" and perhaps considered the dark greens impractical and naïve.

When integrating this information about the market reaction to the Prius with the ideas and models presented in this chapter about adoption by multiple segments, it perhaps comes as no surprise that the HEV diffusion pattern is "irregular." The decline in dark green adoption in the late 2000s was probably not compensated for quickly enough by light green consumer adoption, and the difficult economic climate during this time was a further deterrent for this group. Consequently, HEVs took a much greater hit than conventional internal combustion engine cars over the same time period.

So did the dip in HEV adoptions prove to be temporary or sustained? Good news! The decline is over: in 2012, sales of HEVs topped 430,000 units (487,000 if we include all other electric drive vehicles), thereby reversing course once again and resuming the progression en route to a much higher future diffusion peak. It is interesting to note that the saddle observed for electric drive vehicles—in terms of when it started post-launch, its depth, and its duration—corresponds remarkably well to the average saddle characteristics observed in other electronics-related categories. To verify this, just go back and take a look at figure 4.6.

As we have seen throughout this chapter, while the saddle phenomenon can be vexing when first encountered, it always has a happy ending: moderate, mainstream consumers eventually come into the picture to propel the diffusion curve upward. Are there cases that have a different ending, where the fact that the market is made up of multiple segments that differ in their adoption characteristics proves to be a bigger problem or one where deliberate firm intervention is needed to keep things on track? That is the topic of the next chapter.

Key Takeaways

- Some innovations exhibit a saddlelike diffusion pattern: in the midst of the growth stage, they experience a temporary decline in the number of new adopters per period; an increasing pace of new adoptions resumes after a few periods.

- The diffusion curve of an innovation that follows a saddlelike pattern features an early peak in units adopted followed by a trough and subsequent second peak. The time during which sales are below the early peak is on average about four years, and the maximal depth of the decline is above 15 percent.
- The saddle pattern can be attributed to the existence of two adopter segments:
  - Innovation forwards: early market consumers who typically have a strong individual force driving them to adopt new products and services
  - Innovation moderates: mainstream consumers who typically have a modest individual force driving them to adopt new products and services
- The innovation moderates often predominantly rely on social forces originating from within their own segment. Consequently, there can be a phase in which the innovation-forward segment has almost completely exhausted its market potential while very few in the moderate segment have adopted. The result is a temporary decline in the number of total adoptions until a social process is ignited within the innovation-moderate segment.
- A multisegment diffusion model is presented. The model allows capturing differences in the diffusion parameters for each of the two consumer types and is flexible enough to include the possibility of social effects between segments. This model can yield the saddlelike shape as well as other "nonstandard" diffusion patterns.
- The innovation equity framework can easily be adjusted to take multisegment diffusion into account, as shown in an analysis of a newly approved drug.

CHAPTER FIVE

Jumpstarting Stalled Adoption

Getting the Mainstream to Take the Plunge

It's like Gulliver and the Lilliputians. No one string was a big problem, but together they kept Gulliver down.—Geoffrey Moore

If you're like most people, then you absolutely adore penguins. The sight of a forty-inch-tall chubby creature waddling in the snow dressed in what looks like a tuxedo is a near guarantee to put a smile on anyone's face. Living mostly in the Southern Hemisphere, these flightless birds have been the subject of books, songs, and movies—from inspiring documentaries like *March of the Penguins* to endearing animated films like *Happy Feet*. And although they cannot fly, penguins sure can swim: Using their wings as paddles, penguins can stay underwater for almost fifteen minutes and reach speeds of ten to fifteen miles per hour. Swimming is vital for penguins, as the water is where they find their food: mainly small fish, krill, and squid.

So why talk about penguins in the context of markets for new products and services? What do penguins have to do with innovation diffusion or valuation? The connection is one of risk aversion to "taking the plunge." You see, although the ocean is where the penguin finds its food, it is also where its predators lurk. Leopard seals, sea lions, sharks, and killer whales all feast on penguins that dive into the water to feed. Unfortunately for the hungry penguins getting ready to jump in, there is hardly any way of knowing whether the spot they have chosen is predator free or predator infested. And as penguins are very social animals, they like doing everything, from traveling to feeding to breeding, in large groups; hence, they all want to dive in at the same time or else look for a different spot together. If only one or two brave penguins were to take the plunge and test the waters, so to speak, to signal that there is ample food on the one hand and no danger on the other—boy would that be reassuring to the rest of the colony. But absent such bravery, the penguin clan just huddles around close to the cliff edge and waits, and waits . . . and waits.

Some economists have called this phenomenon the "penguin effect" and suggested a metaphorical relationship between penguin behavior and that of mainstream consumers confronted with the prospects of embracing an uncertain innovation, or, to loosely borrow from Shakespeare, to dive in, or not to dive in? To adopt, or not to adopt? That is the question each of these parties faces.

The Adoption Dip Revisited

The dip in sales that innovations like the PC exhibited (see figure 4.4), though worrisome and probably unexpected at the time by the major computer makers, luckily was temporary. As explained in the previous chapter in the context of the multisegment diffusion model, mainstream innovation-moderate consumers had a lower individual force driving their adoption than did the early market innovation forwards, and social influence for members of the mainstream group came primarily from other mainstream adopters. That was why a steep initial uptick in PC adoptions was followed by a decline in sales. Yet after about five years from the start of the dip in new adoptions, enough "mainstreamers" had adopted to finally get the ball rolling, and a second, more robust peak in sales was in store for the PC.

But what if things are a bit more extreme? What if mainstream consumers, when presented with an innovation, are so concerned about the possible adoption challenges and so uncertain about the benefits that they don't readily see the value in adopting at all? They might feel it's too risky to adopt and decide to wait.

One thing that might sway them and help them overcome their adoption jitters is observing other mainstream consumers using the innovation and attesting to its value. Put differently, what if the only force they are willing to entertain en route to adoption is social? And not a social force from just any adopters: it has to be from other mainstream consumers, ordinary people similar to them. Linking this to the multisegment diffusion model, this narrative would correspond to having $p_2 = 0$ (i.e., no individual force prompting the mainstream segment to adopt), $q_2 > 0$ (i.e., a social force acting only among members of the mainstream segment), and $q_{21} = 0$ (i.e., no cross-segment social force).

Extreme adoption conditions like these create a bit of a problem, a chicken-and-egg predicament of sorts. As it stands, the innovation-forward segment will embrace the innovation early in the process and the segment's sales will peak soon after launch and begin to taper off. But these innovation forwards are "birds of a different feather" as far as members of the mainstream segment are concerned, not a relevant group to mimic. At the same time, the absence of an individual force for the mainstreamers means there won't be anyone among them interested enough or brave enough to take the plunge and adopt the innovation on his or her own. As a result, each mainstream consumer has no one he or she trusts to turn to, no one to be impressed by, no one to allay concerns, and no one to serve as a relevant point of reference for the innovation's value. In short, no social force will be applicable. A dip in sales will begin to form. Yet without any apparent adoption force at play for the innovation moderates—individual or social—it is not clear how this slide will reverse course. It isn't just a matter of "give it a little more time and it will work out by itself" as with the saddle. In effect, all we really have is the single diffusion curve of the innovation forwards. The mainstream innovation-moderate segment's market potential is untapped, as if it is not even part of the long-term adopter universe.

This state of events is not uncommon in high-tech markets, particularly ones that involve trying to convince businesses on the merits of adopting transformative new products or services. In these instances, mainstream customers take the form of pragmatic managers that fear making abrupt changes that could disrupt their company's workflow. For example, a new computer server that can supposedly run enterprise programs much faster sounds very appealing. But what if there is a risk that not all of your company's existing software applications will work properly on the new architecture? What if the improvement in speed is not 2 times more than your current system as hyped but closer to 1.1 times for the applications you care about most? What if a lot of IT personnel time will have to be dedicated to the new system makeover at the expense of supporting other mission-critical activities? If you are the CTO facing a decision on whether to switch to the new servers, with a CFO that constantly breathes down your neck to rein in expenses and a CEO that wants better bottom line results yesterday, are you going to push for the radical server shift? Are you willing to endure the barrage of business line managers' disgruntled e-mails about how they're mired in compatibility issues that are slowing them down rather than speeding them up? It's undoubtedly a tough call. Maybe you would feel more reassured if ten other CTOs, at corporations similar to yours in terms of organizational structure and how IT fits into the workflow of various business lines, had already adopted and could attest to the benefits they're enjoying and vouch for the fact that setting things up was not at all difficult. Armed with the experiences of these ten CTOs, you might feel more empowered to promote deployment of the new servers at your own company. But if the only "evidence" so far comes from a start-up whose nonconformist founder has authorized installing the new servers or from the CTO of a company that is completely outside your industry and who has only been piloting the novel servers for a niche application, you might not be sufficiently convinced and choose to watch from the sidelines, at least for the time being.

It is easy to see that if all the CTOs in the mainstream market have a similar attitude, adoption may never break out from the innovation-forward circle to the rest of the market. In effect, once the early market fully adopts, the diffusion process will get stuck. Recall that with the saddle phenomenon described in the previous chapter, things were not so extreme: the initial decline in sales gave rise to a transient dip in adoptions. The individual force for mainstream customers was not zero; hence, at some point a critical mass of them would adopt and pave the way to a recovery. But if no member of the mainstream market budges on his or her own, the diffusion pattern will look more like it's free-falling off a cliff into an abyss, or as some have called it, a *chasm*.

Climbing Back onto the Multisegment Diffusion Model Curve

In his pioneering work on the challenges of marketing high-tech innovations, Geoffrey Moore was one of the first to describe this adoption misfortune and highlight the importance of understanding the disconnect between the early market (the innovation-forward segment) and the mainstream market (the innovation-moderate segment). He used the term "chasm" to describe the steep decline in sales of an innovation when companies reach the transition point between these two market segments. Moore further gave prescriptive advice on how companies that reach this stage can, so to speak, "cross the chasm"—that is, successfully gain traction in the mainstream market and jumpstart the diffusion process that is stalled. What Moore proposes is a sequential effort that can be thought of as increasing the individual force (p) for a targeted subset of customers in the mainstream and, if those have been selected with forethought, subsequently relying on social forces (q) among members of the mainstream to do the rest.

To cross the chasm, therefore, you first need to find a specific subsegment of mainstream customers that appear to have a considerable amount to gain from whatever is novel about the innovation. In other words, they should have a compelling reason to want it. Importantly, members of the subsegment chosen should be highly amenable to social adoption forces, *and* after most of them have adopted, members of adjacent subsegments in the mainstream should be amenable to social forces from the originally targeted mainstream subsegment.

As should be clear, "targeting is king" in trying to escape the chasm. The first subsegment of mainstream customers targeted are typically called "beachheads," and the ability to use their adoption as evidence to convince others to adopt is often called their "referencability power." The idea is that if all goes well, the positive outcome achieved by a beachhead serves as a valid and powerful reference to impress others in the mainstream, as this customer is deemed similar to them and his or her adoption convincingly vouches for the innovation's value. Once a majority of customers in the first targeted subsegment have adopted, the firm introducing the innovation looks for customers in adjacent segments that share some characteristics with the first, with the hope that they will be open to taking the reference. As Moore metaphorically puts it, it's like bowling: send your best marketing effort to hit a pin that will knock down nearby pins, which will then hit pins adjacent to them, and so on. And if you selected that first pin well and hit it at just the right angle and force, then eventually all the pins will fall— a diffusion curve strike!

As the bowling metaphor suggests, choosing a good beachhead is critical for successful chasm crossing. Yet the question remains: how do you get that first customer to ease up and relax his or her apprehension and hesitation "muscles"? Since social adoption forces are out of the question, you have to ponder how to increase the individual adoption force. And one of the best ways to achieve that is through "massive customization," or what Moore calls the provision of the "whole product."

The "whole" in the "whole product" concept refers to providing the targeted customer with not just the essence of the innovation, the bare bones of what makes it novel, but any other element—such as additional features, services, or support functions—that from the customer's stand-point makes the innovation a plug-and-play solution to his or her prob-lem: a solution that is as compatible as possible with his or her existing be-havior and processes. The whole product allows the customer to achieve a compelling reason to buy "right out of the box." Thus while members of the early market segment were willing to live with just the core of the innovation—investing from their own money to purchase any add-ons that ensured they could properly use it, spending the time necessary to make it workable with their current systems and usage habits, and putting in the effort required to learn about how to install and troubleshoot—members of the mainstream market segment are not willing to engage in these actions. A core product is not enough for mainstream members. For them, such a product is associated with a diffusion model value for p that is simply too low. But if you provide them with a whole product, which bumps up the individual force sufficiently, their outlook might change dramatically. Because each subsegment in the mainstream might have slightly differing customizations that would have the most individual-force impact, it is dif-ficult to target many of them at the same time with a concerted effort, as you risk not serving any of them with a fully customized "whole" solution; the adage "something for everyone, everything for no one" comes to mind. Hence it is recommended to concentrate efforts narrowly at first and estab-lish a foothold in the mainstream for purposes of ultimately crossing the chasm in due course.

The electronic book industry is a good example of an innovation that was challenged by falling into a chasm. E-books first appeared in the mid-1990s and were hailed as a revolution that within a few years would sup-plant the centuries-old, ubiquitous paper book. A limited initial burst of e-book activity in the late 1990s, however, was followed by a dire lull of hardly any new downloads. A leading analyst in 2002 was quoted as say-ing, "We haven't issued forecasts for the industry in two years because the market is going nowhere. E-books were a dumb idea. I am very negative on this market."

But the gloomy outlook of such analysts turned out to be completely unwarranted, as we now know. The concept of e-books was simply "in-complete" at the beginning. But by the end of the decade, when devices became available that made reading from an electronic screen more com-fortable and less eye straining and, importantly, a critical mass of down-loadable titles became available, takeoff in the mainstream occurred. Pockets in the mainstream that initiated the process were libraries that began offering e-books to patrons (free is always a good way to initiate trialability and adoption) and professionals who traveled a lot and were burdened by lugging around print books and manuals needed for their job. The takeoff was further hastened into the rest of the mainstream when tablets like iPad and Kindle came to the fore in this period. As users began carrying their tablets around wherever they went, the value of having e-books on these devices became even more evident.

Electric Vehicles (EVs): A Tale of Two Chasms

The adoption of all-electric vehicles, which run solely on an electric battery, provides a good opportunity for examining the "core" versus "whole" product concept. Innovation forwards in this case comprised a mix of "dark green" environmentalists and consumers with strong political convictions. These groups were very quick to show their enthusiasm for cars that had zero emissions at the tailpipe, offered "infinite" miles per gallon (since they don't use gasoline at all), and held the promise of ridding the world of dependence on oil and the countries that produce it. Yet the vast majority of consumers were far less excited. When pure electric vehicles initially hit the automotive scene—for example, GM's EV1 concept launched in the mid-1990s or Ford's Th!nk City introduced in the early 2000s—they were at best a core product. The range these all-electric vehicles could be driven on a single charge was limited—about seventy to ninety miles, as compared to typical gasoline-powered vehicles, which get three hundred to three hundred fifty miles per tank. In addition, the time it took to fully charge the batteries was often more than four hours, and charging spots along driving routes were few and far between. On top of all that, since battery technology was still quite costly, so were the cars, even after government tax credits. The innovation forwards for this new vehicle class were content with the core product: they would remember to plug in every night, would meticulously calculate distances they planned to drive to make sure they would not run out of juice on the freeway, and were not overly bothered by the price tag. For them it was a small price to pay for ensuring a sustainable and politically viable future for the planet. Owning an electric car was much more a source of pride than a source of prudent cost savings. But most mainstream consumers were in a holding pattern for the whole product. If the range per charge was extended, if there was abundant infrastructure for quick charging, and if the economics worked out (at least to the point where the total cost of ownership was the same as for gas-powered cars or the payback period from saving on gas to cover the extra cost of the electric car was reasonable), then mainstream consumers would possibly be willing to entertain a switch.

Crossing the chasm with all-electric vehicles could take the form of focusing on a specific set of customers or submarkets, fixing the problems that they most care about, and tailoring cars to their specific needs. For example, one could start with companies or organizations that maintain a fleet of vehicles for their employees, where the cars can charge while parked in the company's parking lot. This also moves the onus of initial financing to the corporation's pocketbook rather than the consumer's wallet and could expedite adoption. Other options might be to start with cab companies or focus on countries where the limited car range is less of an acute issue due to the specific geography and urban layout.

An intriguing example is provided courtesy of Tesla Motors. In its efforts to engender adoption of EVs, Tesla "went the extra mile" and looked at both targeting and completing as much of the "whole product" as it possibly could. Its Model S, launched in 2012, has a very sleek exterior design (e.g., the door handles automatically retract flush into the door when not in use) and impressive performance numbers (zero to sixty miles per hour in under five seconds), which are sure draws for car lovers and luxury buyers. To control the car, the user interacts with a seventeen-inch high-resolution touch screen, thus replacing the decades-old dashboard in conventional cars. The computer powering the interface is connected to the Internet, providing access to apps, maps, and other useful information. These gadgets and features are attractors for consumers who are already well into their second- or third-generation smartphones and tablets. "Range anxiety" is greatly reduced with the Model S, as its battery allows for driving more than 200 miles (265 miles on the more advanced models) between charges. Moreover, Tesla took on the responsibility of setting up hundreds of Supercharger stations throughout the United States in strategically chosen locations that let drivers recharge their Model S for free in about twenty minutes. The company also piloted swap stations in California that had robots work for a mere ninety seconds under the car to replace a depleted battery with a fully charged one at a fee comparable to filling up a tank of gasoline. "Maintenance unease" in the case of a breakdown was pacified by having the option to request a "Tesla Ranger" dispatched to your locale, take your vehicle for repair, and leave a loaner until your original was delivered back fully fixed. "Future value" concerns were allayed by giving consumers the option of buying the car through Tesla's financing program, which guaranteed the owner could sell it back to the company at a price commensurate to what a comparable gas-powered BMW or Audi would fetch. Lastly, Tesla wanted consumers to get a feel for the car as part of their normal shopping routine. To do so, it opened its own stores in high-end malls and shopping centers. Hence, rather than having to make a dedicated trip to a remote dealership and walk around a parking lot crammed with dozens of cars, getting familiar with Tesla Motors and its Model S was more of an Apple Store–like experience. Although one cannot test-drive a Tesla in these places, consumers get to sit in the Model S; see the design firsthand; play with the onboard touch screen interface; and receive more information on financing, resale options, and maintenance and recharging infrastructure. In sum, consumers get the "whole" picture there.

Elon Musk, Tesla's founder and CEO, quipped after the Model S was launched, "There are people that take a lot of convincing." Musk did not settle for just talking his way into convincing people to adopt his electric vision. He took concrete steps to augment the core product so that it appealed to certain mainstream subsegments, beyond the "dark green" early adopters in this category. He removed "string after string" of barriers to adoption that could potentially "keep his innovation down," thereby avoiding Gulliver's predicament (per the chapter's opening quote).

The Model S turned many heads after its debut on June 22, 2012. It was the first electric car to win *Motor Trend*'s Car of the Year award and it received the highest car rating ever by *Consumer Reports*. As one prominent car review website, Edmunds, glowingly described, "Sleek, seductive, luxurious, powerful, and inspiring are all words you'd expect to hear about the latest European luxury sedan. But in this case, we're talking about one of America's latest homegrown electric vehicles, the 2013 Tesla Model S." From the perspective of the bowling metaphor, this clearly reflects a bull's-eye hit in terms of the intended target market, striking just the right pin to help knock down others.

Indeed, despite its $70,000-plus price tag, which could be lowered thanks to a federal tax credit of up to $7,500 and additional credits in some states, Model S sales during its first full year on the market far exceeded expectations, reaching a pace of almost 22,500 cars sold globally in 2013, with a trend toward accelerated production and sales in subsequent years (about 32,000 cars were sold globally in 2014). Tesla also announced future electric vehicles in the pipeline: the Model X—an all-electric cross-over due in late 2015—and a more affordable sedan down the road (expected to cost half the price of the Model S). Investors seemed to like what they were seeing with the Model S and what they were hearing about the future plans, as Tesla Motor's stock price climbed by more than 900 percent between August 1, 2012, and July 31, 2015. Time will tell whether Tesla's approach will be enough to provide a solid bridge to cross the EV chasm. In the meantime, it is instructive to compare Tesla's strategy to that of a different venture, Better Place, which did not fare so well.

The seeds of Better Place were sown at the 2006 World Economic Forum in Davos, Switzerland. As an invited Young Global Leader to the forum, Shai Agassi, a high-ranking SAP executive at the time, was asked to propose a way to make the world "a better place." Agassi certainly had good intentions when he suggested replacing gasoline-run cars with electric ones powered by renewable energy.

After being passed up for the CEO position at SAP, Agassi decided to pursue his visionary idea and find a way to facilitate the switch from gasoline- to electric-powered cars. He founded Better Place in October 2007 and firmly believed that one of the keys to success would be building the recharging infrastructure. In fact, Better Place preceded Tesla in devising the battery swap station concept as a way to provide drivers a quick range extension option when they were running out of juice on long trips. Agassi also believed that a major barrier to consumers buying EVs was their significantly higher price compared to gasoline-powered alternatives. The main culprit for the price differential, of course, was the high cost of the battery pack needed to power the vehicle. To overcome this disadvantage, Agassi proposed a novel idea: commercially decouple the car from the battery. Consumers would own the former, while Better Place would own the latter. To make it work financially, the consumer would pay a monthly service fee, based on driving miles, to have access to the battery, the infrastructure, and the costs associated with charging and swapping. The upfront electric vehicle's price tag would thus be more in line with, or even cheaper than, that of a conventional car. It made a lot of sense, given that the energy to power gasoline cars had always been a separate ongoing expense. So why force consumers to pay upfront for one of the main energy components, the battery? The business model Better Place proposed was equally novel for the car industry. Better Place would be the service provider for the ongoing operation of your vehicle, much like a wireless telecom service provider gives you a subsidized smartphone and signs you up to a multiyear contract based on minutes and data used per month.

By early 2008 Agassi had lined up $200 million in funding; obtained the commitment of a car maker, Renault-Nissan, to build a vehicle that would fit Better Place's recharging and swapping specs; garnered support from key Israeli politicians who would pass legislation exempting EVs from sales and import taxes (which in Israel could approach 100 percent); and assembled a talented management team. Agassi was considered a visionary with rock star status in many circles. He was invited to give speeches and make appearances at numerous functions and events. In 2009 he even made *Time*'s list of one hundred "people who most affect our world." Things seemed to be moving along very well: serious discussions with relevant bodies in Israel, Denmark, Australia, Japan, and Hawaii were under way to create conditions for setting up the vast infrastructure needed to support the Better Place model in each of these countries; Renault-Nissan was making progress on the new car; and swap station technology was becoming a reality. An impressive visitor center was built near Tel Aviv in 2010 to help explain the concept to consumers, let them drive a prototype of the car, and get hands-on experience with recharging technology. With each customer expected to have a positive lifetime value through the recurring service fee, and based on the rapid customer uptake it forecasted, Better Place could present promising projections of its worth to investors.

By early 2012, after raising hundreds of millions of dollars more in private financing and partially building the infrastructure in both Israel and Denmark, Better Place began delivering cars to consumers in these two countries while continuing its efforts in other markets. Many consumers visited the center but, unfortunately, very few bought a car and signed up for the service. Demand was extremely sluggish. Agassi's prediction of tens of thousands of adopters within the first year never materialized. Fewer than fifteen hundred cars were sold in total.

Better Place employed more than four hundred people in Israel alone and numerous personnel in other countries. Infrastructure commitments were costly. For example, it was estimated that each battery swap station cost roughly half a million dollars to build and deploy, and even a small country like Israel needed more than twenty of them for the network to provide adequate coverage. With expenses continuing to mount but with hardly any revenue, Better Place was driving at full speed down a dead-end road overlooking a dreadfully deep—you guessed it—chasm.

In October 2012, Agassi resigned as CEO of Better Place. His replacement, Evan Keitley, who had previously been in charge of Better Place Australia, was fired within months. The next CEO, Dan Cohen, didn't last more than a few months either, as the company filed for bankruptcy in May 2013.

What went wrong? How could an enterprise with so much positive buzz propelling it, with more than $800 million of investment backing it, and with a dynamic and highly regarded management team running it end up in the "worst place" a company could ever imagine? One can be sure that there was a lot of finger-pointing in the aftermath of Better Place's collapse. But fundamentally, one cannot ignore the lack of consumer enthusiasm when the "rubber met the road." The infrastructure was in place, the cars were waiting at the docks, and the service centers were up and running and ready to serve; it was all systems go. Yet consumers balked. With gasoline prices in Israel and Denmark topping $7.50 per gallon (almost $2 per liter) and internal combustion engine cars taxed at very high rates in both countries compared to electric vehicles, one can't help but wonder why the response from the market was so tepid.

Examining Better Place's approach through our multisegment diffusion model and Moore's chasm lenses provides a few clues. First, the car that Renault-Nissan developed for the venture was a rather "bland" offering (an electric version of the Renault Fluence), a typical four-door sedan with no special defining characteristics. In other words, it was not targeting any particular beachhead in the mainstream; it was as average as average can get for a car. This car was also the only model for sale, as Better Place could not convince any other automaker to commit to developing a car that would fit its charging and swapping standards. It had a rather modest range per charge—a little more than one hundred miles—and as only a handful of swap stations had been deployed, anxiety over running out of juice was likely still an obstacle. Lastly, although it sounds great in theory, the service commitment model, as a function of usage (in terms of miles driven), was highly incompatible with consumers' past experience. Pay as you go for refueling cars—that's how it had been and that is how it was most likely going to be for the time being, regardless of the energy source. The cell phone analogy, so it seems, was not quite relevant in this case. When cell phones came along, many people were accustomed to paying a base monthly fee for their landlines, and they could more or less predict their usage. Cars were a different story: consumers apparently weren't ready to give up the flexibility that comes with not committing to miles to be driven. Furthermore, with mobile phones, there was no issue with resale value, as most consumers don't expect to sell their used devices when they upgrade. But cars are a different category altogether: One has to consider the need to sell the car at some point, and this likely caused consumers to be somewhat wary of what would happen if they had to get out of a contract and whether not owning a central component, the battery, would complicate matters when time came to sell. In short, there was no strong individual force for any particular group in the mainstream to adopt, and there were too many unfamiliar strings attached. Making matters worse, the car's design didn't allow its drivers to stand out and signal their environmental commitment, in contrast to the Prius or Model S, which are easily recognizable. Taken together these barriers may have even hindered adoption among "dark green" innovation forwards.

Another issue that perhaps hurt Better Place is that instead of focusing geographically and catering to a particular market, through much of its existence the company actively pursued multiple markets simultaneously in an attempt to grow as fast as possible. Sadly, that never happened.

Will It Ever Cross?

Back in chapter 1, we noted that the Segway, the first personal transporter, was unveiled in late 2001 and came "equipped" with a host of barriers to adoption for mainstream consumers, from relative advantage issues in comparison to other means of transportation (too few of those) to compatibility issues in operating it daily given the existing infrastructure of roads and sidewalks (too many of those) to complexity issues in understanding how it works and how it might fit into one's lifestyle (too many of those as well).

The founder and his management team seemed to initially operate under the assumption that the Segway was a new product with mass-market appeal, an innovation that the average consumer could and would *readily* appreciate. It was deemed so intuitively superior to everything else available that the Segway would basically "sell itself." As a prime example of this mind-set, early on Segway distribution was exclusively through Amazon .com, and communications relied on media mentions and free public relations. But by going after mainstream consumers right off the bat, the company seemed to be putting the cart before the horse (or should we say the Segway in this case?). Ignoring the adoption process and the potential for saddles and chasms turned out to be misguided. No doubt there was a bunch of enthusiasts who could not wait to get their hands (and feet) on a Segway, a group that was won over within the first few years postlaunch. But that only led to a few tens of thousands of adoptions. The vast majority of consumers, however, remained underwhelmed. The Segway was on its way down into the depths of the chasm, high-tech stabilizing gyros and all.

Dean Kamen, the Segway's inventor, finally came to this inevitable realization, acknowledging that "although technology moves very quickly, people's mindset changes very slowly." The options for the company were to (1) wait, for what could be a long time and without any guarantees, until practical-minded consumers changed their mind-set or (2) try to build a bridge or erect a few ladders to cross the chasm and get the diffusion process moving in the upward direction again. Segway Inc. opted for the latter approach. Indeed, a shift to a targeted marketing strategy put the product back on a path of sales growth. In particular, the company primarily focused on two segments: the security market and the tourism market.

In the security and patrol market, Segway Inc. worked to generate interest among both for-profit companies, like those offering security services in shopping malls, and publicly funded organizations, like police departments. To appeal to this segment, the company created a version of the product especially tailored to the needs of police and security personnel and aptly named it the Segway Patroller. This "whole product" came with customized elements that were of particular value to the target market: increased visibility features (such as reflective shields), a lighting unit that would flash blue-and-red lights when on the chase, a special accessory bar for mounting equipment (such as additional lighting and audio devices), a cargo plate and bags to carry security and first-responder equipment, and a front bumper to protect the Segway in case it had to be "dumped" quickly when a fast dismount was necessary. A number of arguments can be made in support of targeting this segment to enable smooth crossing of the chasm: First, there are compelling use settings and economic benefits, particularly in areas where it is not practical to operate a car yet mobility is a considerable benefit. For example, using the Segway in parks can alleviate the need to maintain horses for patrol purposes (which is both expensive and inconvenient). At shopping malls, as one security company executive put it, there is a "multiplier effect": Segways enabled companies to hire fewer personnel to patrol the premises given the ease, speed, and effectiveness of getting around. Indeed, one manager calculated that each Segway results in annual savings of $50,000–$60,000 in personnel expenses (based on a ratio of 1 Segway allowing 1.5 fewer patrol personnel); with the Segway's price tag of about $5,000, that's a ten-fold return on investment in one year! Second, the security market has the potential to create a contagion effect in that demonstrating success in this market can spill over to influence adjacent markets that will presumably be willing to accept the "reference." For instance, proof of effectiveness and cost savings among police departments can serve as a strong reference for military and government customers. Emergency response units, such as paramedics who need to provide coverage during big events and navigate through crowds to treat people, are likely to find the robust use among security forces a source of confidence that Segways can help them perform their job better. Third, since many Segway-related security tasks are performed in public, average individuals are able to observe them in use and become more at ease with how simple they are to operate. While some may argue that it produces the exact opposite effect, whereby seeing uniformed personnel using the Segway as part of their job will deter the average consumer ("If it's for *them*, how can it be for *me*?"), the net effect of greater exposure in everyday settings could weigh in as positive.

To further cater to the security market, Segway developed a three-wheeled version of its personal transporter. It has enhanced traction and terrain capabilities, is weather resistant, is able to maneuver in reverse, and allows easy battery swaps. Having three wheels allows the vehicle to stay upright and stable after quick dismounts.

In the case of the tourism market, the company worked with firms and entrepreneurs who were willing to promote Segway-mounted tours, either as part of their existing sightseeing expeditions or as the only activity they offer tourists. From the standpoint of catering to these adopters, making the product "whole" entailed providing affordable leasing options (since a number of transporters would be needed to accommodate groups) and creating two versions of the product: a standard model (Segway i2) for urban areas and another for off-road touring (Segway x2). A host of accessories were developed that could be important for tourists: a handlebar bag (for carrying cameras, cell phones, etc.), reflectivity features for visibility, and parking stands to keep the Segway upright when not in use (e.g., when users wanted to dismount in public areas to get closer to an attraction). Arguments favoring crossing the chasm by targeting this segment are quite evident: First, there is a compelling economic incentive for operators to market Segway-based tours. The personal transporter allows one to cover more ground in a shorter duration; hence, tourists with a limited amount of time or for whom walking long distances is an issue would find the tours highly appealing and sign up for them. Second, sightseeing tours provide a low-cost option for many mainstream consumers to experience the Segway without having to commit thousands of dollars to buying one (most tours cost between $50–$100), and they can do so in the company of other consumers and with the reassuring presence of a guide. Third, there is potential for a contagion effect in that showing the success of Segway tours in popular sightseeing destinations (in cities like London or Rome) could lead to a desire to create similar experiences in other locations. And in true chasm-crossing fashion, many adjacent expansions have already materialized. For example, Segway tours have now become a common scene in adventure parks, zoos, universities, and more recently, ski resorts looking for activities to offer visitors during the off-season. Moreover, consumers that try the Segway on such tours may decide to purchase one. Indeed, Segway Inc. often lets tour operators act as dealers if they so desire, and several have reported Segway tourists converting to Segway buyers.

The attempts by Segway Inc. to bootstrap itself out of the chasm appear to have borne fruit and resulted in pockets of mainstream adopters that can sustain a healthy business and that have the potential to affect adjacent subsegments. To facilitate this process, the company also revamped its channel strategy: hundreds of dealerships and distribution points let interested individuals and parties test a Segway and consult with authorized experts. It is noteworthy that the segments Segway Inc. has chosen to help it cross the chasm are both set in a business-to-business (B2B) context, as opposed to a business-to-consumer (B2C) context. Oftentimes doing so makes crossing easier because of the nature of the marketing effort required (e.g., using a sales force to speak directly to people in relevant roles in an organization) and the ability to tout specific economic benefits (e.g., cost savings or additional revenue sources) and explain how the innovation can solve a well-identified "pain point."

Whether all these efforts will someday lead to widespread penetration of personal transporters among average households or whether Segway Inc.'s success will stay confined to very specific B2B segments has yet to unfold. A promising trend for the category as a whole is the commitment by several car manufacturers to develop vehicles that have been classified under the heading of "micromobility": small electric vehicles that can accommodate one or two passengers with limited range and speeds. A recent Frost & Sullivan report suggested that more than a hundred and fifty new models could be introduced by 2020. And some consider the recent influx of much cheaper "hoverboards"—self-balancing, two-wheeled, hands-free motorized gadgets—as another relevant development, perhaps even representing a natural consumer extension to Segways (though some early versions seem to have safety issues associated with them). The personal transporter category may benefit from the tailwinds of this influx of new vehicles. In the context of our multisegment diffusion model, this assessment would impact what we should take as the long-run potential of the mainstream segment (m_2).

It is perhaps somewhat ironic that, when asked about the Segway's prospects a few years after its launch, Geoffrey Moore expressed concern that there were so many uncertainties and barriers for common users that the Segway "is a product destined to live in the chasm forever." The metaphor he used for his assessment of the Segway's probable fate was taken from *Gulliver's Travels*, which describes how the mere six-inch-tall Lilliputians were able to overpower a six-foot human. Although they only had tiny ropes (the barriers) at their disposal, they tied so many of them that they managed to keep Gulliver (the Segway) down. In other words, the Segway in Moore's opinion came with too many barriers to adoption to be able to take off. Summit Strategic Investments, which acquired the company in 2013,[1] seems to disagree, announcing plans to grow and expand in the years to come.

Epi-nguin-logue

Conceptualizing the chasm phenomenon as a partial break in the diffusion pattern of an innovation and delineating ways to overcome it reinforce the main ideas introduced in the previous chapter. In particular, we sometimes need to treat the adoption of an innovation as composed of several separate diffusion processes, each having its own parameters of long-run market potential and individual and social forces. When there is at least some social force across segments, or if mainstream consumers have a sufficient individual adoption force, we should expect only a saddle to emerge: a dip in sales for a limited time frame that will ultimately recover. But if neither of these conditions holds, new adoptions will grind to a halt after the early market has completed its adoption, and a chasm between the early and mainstream markets is in the cards. A set of "surgical" chasm-crossing marketing actions may be needed to avert disaster and get back on the diffusion track.

To close our analogy from the beginning of this chapter as far as the hungry penguins are concerned, if none of them will dive into the water on its own, then someone has to give a few of them a little push. While in the wild the push might come from other penguins huddled together on the ice's edge, in the case of innovations, the firm typically has to give a few customers a "little push" in the form of a whole product to get them to take the plunge and adopt.

It goes without saying that everything that has been described in this chapter has innovation equity implications: adopter groups may differ in the timing of when they are expected to come on board as customers, in how costly it is to acquire them, in how much margin they generate per period, and in their tendency to drop out. Sometimes these differences are so extreme that a big divide can form in their adoption schedule. The targeted marketing efforts needed to overcome this divide, and the impact of such actions on the diffusion process, can be incorporated into innovation equity assessments.

Key Takeaways

- Markets that involve several segments, each with very different requirements from and attitudes toward an innovation, can create a halt in the diffusion pattern: One segment (sometimes called the "early market") fully adopts before the next segment (sometimes called the "mainstream market") even begins to consider doing so.
- At the heart of this phenomenon, also called the "chasm," is the lack of social influence between the segments, as well as a very low individual force driving adoption in the mainstream segment. Without intervention, it is unlikely that the mainstream's diffusion process will ever commence. Once it does, however, the social force within the mainstream segment can take over and drive adoption. These ideas can be captured in the multisegment diffusion model developed in the previous chapter.
- For the innovation to gain initial traction in the mainstream market, it is often necessary to supply a version of it that completely solves prospective mainstream customers' problems or fully satisfies a need that certain consumers have, and it should do so with minimal disruption to their existing behavior and with minimal uncertain investment on their part. This augmented solution is often called the "whole product."

- To engender adoption at this critical stage, it is sometimes recommended to have a narrow approach to target market selection, focusing on a select few customers or a subsegment of the mainstream population. This makes the task of supplying a whole product more manageable and likely to succeed. Once these targeted customers adopt, they can serve as a credible reference for other customers/subsegments that are part of the mainstream. The within-segment social adoption force kicks in from here on out.

Survival in the Presence of a Rival

Valuing Innovations at the Brand Level

Whether it's Google or Apple or free software, we've got some fantastic competitors and it keeps us on our toes.—Bill Gates

In spring 2001, XM Satellite Radio's two satellites ("Rock" and "Roll") went into orbit; on-ground signal enhancers were put into place; and XM, the first-ever satellite radio service, was formally launched to consumers in the fall of that year. A $100 million marketing campaign, which included ads featuring such artists as Snoop Dogg, B. B. King, and David Bowie "falling from the sky" into office buildings, barns, and hotel rooms, heralded the new radio service on movie theatre screens and television sets. And although the launch date, originally set for September 12, had to be pushed out by two weeks due to the tragic 9/11 terror attacks, XM was able to garner more than thirty thousand adopters within a few short months. This prompted its then-CEO, Hugh Panero, to declare at the 2002 Consumer Electronics Show, "Will people pay for radio? The answer is a resounding 'Yes.'"

At the time of the declaration, Panero was at the helm of the sole company offering satellite radio service. It was a good feeling to be the only game in town—in the entire country, for that matter. But that would soon change. On February 14, 2002, less than five months after XM's debut, Sirius began rolling out its own service, initially in four states and by the summer nationwide. To say that XM felt Sirius breathing down its neck from that day on would be an understatement.

For starters, although Panero was right that consumers *were* willing to pay for radio, for several years to come, *how much* they were asked to pay by each company was markedly different. XM launched with a subscription price of $9.99 per month, while rival Sirius priced its service at $12.95. Not to be undone by the higher price, Sirius boasted that all its music channels were commercial free. By contrast, two to four minutes of ads could be heard on many of XM's music channels (both services had limited advertising on nonmusic channels, such as talk shows and news). From the customer's perspective, was ridding oneself of ads when listening to music worth paying an extra $36 a year?

For some consumers, this was not a real or practical choice. With radio consumption most prevalent in cars, both companies worked tirelessly to secure exclusive deals with automakers to have only their respective receivers preinstalled in new vehicles; receivers were specific to the signal of each company and were not interchangeable. Within a few years, XM managed to reach exclusive distribution agreements with the likes of GM, Honda, Hyundai, and Toyota, while for its part, Sirius had exclusive arrangements with BMW, DaimlerChrysler, Ford, Mazda, and Mitsubishi. It was also common to offer three months of free service to new car buyers to get them to try, and hopefully continue with, a paid subscription after the trial period ended. In some sense, new car buyers that decided to adopt the technology were captive to either XM or Sirius.

Those who already owned a car and were interested in satellite radio had to buy and install a dedicated receiver. To prevent this from being too large of a barrier to adoption, the companies worked with consumer electronics manufacturers, such as Pioneer and Sony, to offer subsidies that lowered the end consumer price (you might remember that in chapter 3, we analyzed the merits of such subsidies).

XM's first mover advantage seemed to bear fruit as far as adoption in the first two years was concerned. It boasted 1.36 million subscribers by the end of 2003, while Sirius had only about 260,000 at the time. Heading into 2004, however, XM began worrying about losing its footing to rival Sirius in this nascent market. At retail, where a big portion of sales were taking place for the automotive aftermarket, Sirius's commercial-free music positioning seemed to resonate with consumers who were weary of the substantial airtime devoted to ads and the limited listening selections on FM and AM radio. In a move to eliminate this seeming disadvantage, XM announced in early 2004 that it too would cut all ads from its music channels.

Although the ad elimination move was good from a subscriber growth standpoint, as XM was able to add almost two million more customers in 2004, it made things difficult to manage from a customer profitability standpoint. Pricing the service at $9.99 a month, which amounted to $120 a year for a customer paying full price, was designed to be complemented by some ad revenues. However, as a new medium that had yet to prove its ad effectiveness and with a policy of no commercials on music channels, advertisers were not flocking to buy spots. XM's net ad revenues in 2004 totaled a "whopping" $8.5 million, which came out to a meager $0.33 per subscriber per month. With acquisition costs running at more than $100 per new subscriber on average and mounting operating expenses, the time horizon for each acquired customer to become profitable was looking very long. Not surprisingly, in spring 2005, XM raised its subscription price. Any guess on what the new price was? In true tit-for-tat competitive fashion, it was set to $12.95—exactly what Sirius had been charging all along!

With their music channel lineups similar, their approach to limiting the airing of ads the same, and their subscription prices identical, the two companies were left with basically one way to differentiate: securing exclusive, nonmusic content that appealed to consumers. That approach rapidly turned into an expensive arms race. Sports deals were a big part of it, with Sirius controlling transmission rights to the NBA and NFL, while XM locked down MLB and NASCAR. Entertainment celebrities were another part of it, with figures such as Bob Dylan and Oprah Winfrey contracted to host shows. And it was in this last category that Sirius dropped a bomb in fall 2004 when it announced that one of the biggest personalities in radio, Howard Stern, would be joining its ranks in January 2006.

Howard Stern was known as a "shock jock," earning that label for his outspoken and controversial style, which included salacious, sex-themed content and a mix of lewd jokes and macho politics. His popularity was undeniable at the time of the signing, as millions tuned in to his daily show, which was syndicated in numerous markets across North America. Stern's shift to satellite radio was described as a "watershed event" by Sirius's CEO at the time, Joseph Clayton. It was not, however, a cheap "event" by any means or measure: Sirius agreed to pay Stern $500 million over five years for producing and delivering the *Howard Stern Show* as well as stock incentives after he joined.

In the aftermath of the dramatic news, executives at each of the two satellite firms were faced with assessing the implications of the Howard Stern signing. Was the deal worth it for Sirius? How worried should XM be? With about four million total subscribers across both companies by the end of 2004, the satellite radio market had hardly reached 15 percent of its long-run expected penetration level. How would the battle for the remaining adopters shape up in light of Stern's move? Should Sirius expect to vastly outperform XM on new customer adoptions? Would existing XM customers switch to Sirius come January 2006, when Stern's show went live on Sirius? Would "getting Stern" prove to be a watershed event that drowns one or both of these bitter rivals, or could they stay afloat and ride its waves to greater profits?

Answers to these questions and much more will be discussed in this chapter.

Competing for Customers as Rival Innovations Diffuse

No doubt the first reaction to facing competition is that it is bad news. It often means fighting for the same customers and taking profit-lowering actions to preempt or counter rival moves. However, in the context of innovations that are still in the early phase of their life cycle, competitive forces may have more nuanced effects that are not all bad, at least not for all players.

An important thing to bear in mind with respect to similar innovations launched into the same market space is that all the "competing" is taking place while more and more new adopters enter the category. Consequently, as we explore the various ways competition can be accommodated within the innovation equity framework, it will prove beneficial to first handle the acquisition of new adopters and only subsequently capture the dynamics involved with the management and retention of customers. We will start with relatively simple approaches to incorporating competition and progress to more elaborate ones, which take into account a number of factors that come into play as a result of competitive interaction. This exposition will culminate in a comprehensive model of how the customer base of a firm that launches an innovation evolves in the face of rivalry.

As the category grows, each firm takes its "fair" share. We have certainly not ignored competitive pressures thus far in the book. One approach presented had the following formulation: Let the category as a whole follow a basic diffusion model process, with new adoptions (regardless of which firm is chosen by the customer) governed by category-level adoption forces (p and q); these adoptions originate from a single, long-run market potential pool (m). Then assume that each firm splits the pie of new adoptions, with each competitor getting a share. For example, in chapter 2 we calculated the innovation equity for XM in this way, assuming, for illustration purposes, that new adoptions for the satellite radio category are split evenly between XM and rival Sirius. Determining the split can be based on a host of considerations: the specific features of each firm's offering, the pricing model, the terms of the service, the effectiveness of marketing programs, and, if relevant, the brand names of the companies involved. Surveys of consumers and experts or other market research techniques (such as *conjoint analysis*, a method that allows measuring consumer preferences; see chapter 9 for more details) can be used to get a sense of the percentage of new adoptions that each brand is likely to garner. Of course, if the assessment is carried out shortly after the launch, then early data on how new adoptions are divided between rival innovations can be used as the basis for future predictions. One may decide to modify the share allocations over time depending on firm actions and consumer receptivity. For example, if one firm lowers price, fixes a problem with the product, augments the service, and so on, it may shift more share to itself at the expense of its rivals.

Each firm's innovation diffuses at a separate pace, drawing from a common pool of potential adopters. Another approach to modeling market evolution with multiple players is to let each competitor have its own basic diffusion model forces, reflecting its strengths and weaknesses in attracting new adopters, while still assuming a single, long-run market potential pool. This approach can be relevant when there are notable differences in the value proposition to consumers from each of the offerings or when the business models for generating revenues (ad driven, customer payment, freemium, etc.) are dissimilar.

Because the rate at which new customers are acquired from the common pool generally differs across companies in this approach, the market shares of the various competitors will organically change over time. In particular, a widening gap will form in favor of a company whose innovation has stronger diffusion forces. Figure 6.1 presents an example of how the market shares of two firms, one of which has diffusion parameters that exceed by 10 percent those of the second firm, would change over time. We see that the market shares of the two firms are initially about 5 percent apart and that gradually the gap increases to about a 10 percent market share difference after ten years.

A twist on this approach to incorporating competitive dynamics is to allow each firm to draw from a separate market potential pool, thereby

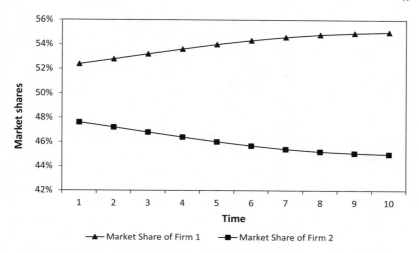

FIGURE 6.1. Market shares when diffusion parameters (p and q) of one firm are larger[*]

[*] The parameters are $p_1 = 0.029$; $p_2 = 0.026$; $q_1 = 0.44$; $q_2 = 0.40$.

allowing all basic diffusion model parameters to be firm or brand specific. However, the values chosen for each parameter, including the separate long-run market potential, should include some consideration of the anticipated competitive power (or weakness) of each firm relative to its rivals. This approach should not be entirely foreign: a version of it was employed in analyzing Dropbox's innovation equity in chapter 3. Although the cloud-based file-hosting market is crowded, Dropbox's rather unique business model, where customers could get more free storage space through referrals, suggested it has a differing set of adoption force parameters than the overall category. Based on early data, its market potential was taken to be a little over 20 percent of the expected long-run potential of the category as a whole.

Stepping Back for a Category- versus Brand-Level Diffusion Moment

The preceding discussion on the various approaches to analyzing innovation diffusion when consumers have multiple options to choose from highlights an important conceptual matter: should one think about adoption decisions as part of a two-stage or a one-stage process? In a two-stage process, potential adopters first make the "big" decision to adopt in the category, say smartphones or electric drive vehicles, and only after being convinced that they need or want something in the category do they choose the specific brand, say an Apple iPhone as opposed to a Samsung Galaxy or a Tesla Model S as opposed to a Nissan Leaf. Alternatively, in a one-stage process, consumers in effect simultaneously decide which brand they would like to own as they decide they want to enter the category.

It should be apparent that the first approach described to accommodate competition, whereby the category grows in new adoptions on its own and each competitor takes a share from this growth, is more consistent with the two-stage decision process. By contrast, the two other approaches, whereby each brand has its own adoption forces, are more consistent with the one-stage process, as new adopters are directly "funneled" to each brand. For the remainder of this chapter, we will follow the one-stage decision process to innovation adoption, with diffusion modeled at the brand level. Aside from reflecting many real-world situations, it allows much greater flexibility in capturing various phenomena vital to properly accounting for competitive interdependencies.

Another conceptual issue to consider in this category- versus brand-level debate relates to market potential. As already alluded to earlier, either the various brands draw from a common market potential pool or each draws from its own designated market potential. If one assumes the latter process, then competitive intensity is presumably low, as the brands do not compete for the attention and wallets of the same potential consumers; it is as if each brand appeals to its own segment with no overlap. The customary approach for studying markets where competition for acquiring innovation adopters is intense is to go with the common market pool assumption. We will follow this approach for the remainder of the chapter.

With these clarifications in mind, we now discuss how two important competitive issues, cross-brand communication and churn, can be fitted into one cohesive diffusion structure.

Caught in the Word of Mouth (WOM) Communication Crossfire

Consider the introduction of the iPhone by Apple in summer 2007, practically the first smartphone to have a multitouch screen and an ever-growing library of apps. Two key observations that followed this launch are noteworthy: First, there was considerable buzz about the new device, meaning there was a lot of excitement surrounding the iPhone accompanied by a lot of talk about it. Moreover, as the iPhone's sales grew and more people owned the device, so did its visibility—you could frequently spot one and notice adopters swiping their fingers over the phone's screen. Second, subsequent to Apple's iPhone launch, several leading handset manufacturers, such as Samsung and LG, introduced smartphones of their own with similar features and functionality (though based on Google's Android operating system and not Apple's iOS). Rather quickly, these rivals, particularly Samsung, gained adoption momentum.

When assessing the market's social communication dynamics in this case, one might wonder to what extent Apple's competitors were (and perhaps still are) benefiting from the buzz and visibility that the iPhone generated. On a more general level, the issue at hand is to what extent social forces exerted by owners of a particular brand influence others to adopt that specific brand. Apple would probably like to operate under the assumption that interpersonal communications from and the visibility of iPhone users primarily helps push its own product up the adoption ladder, in what is known as a "within-brand WOM" effect. However, it is entirely conceivable that other products in the category were benefiting from all the hoopla surrounding the iPhone, in what is called a "cross-brand WOM" effect. In fact, many in the industry believed that this latter effect was not to be dismissed. To quote a Verizon Wireless spokesperson from that period, "I would have to think that a rising tide lifts all ships," suggesting that the strong adoption level of the iPhone might very well indirectly help rival smartphone brands as well.

The existence of a within-brand WOM effect makes total sense: one might expect communication from customers of a given brand about their adoption experience to cause the recipients of these messages to mainly be aware of and consider that brand. Trusting the communication source is critical in overcoming innovation adoption jitters, so when a friend or good acquaintance advocates a specific brand, this typically serves as a powerful inducement to buy the same brand. Why might a cross-brand WOM effect exist? One primary reason is related to the decision-making process for innovations (outlined in chapter 3). Some consumers are indeed affected by the chatter, word of mouth, and visibility that the focal brand's customers generate. However, being diligent consumers, these potential adopters may want to examine what else is out there before committing to a specific brand. Or having heard about one brand of smartphones, they may be generally more attentive to ads about or price promotions for smartphones, possibly even those by a rival offering. And with consumers differing in their tastes, needs, and willingness to pay, the rising tide of iPhone adoptions may lead them to discover and settle on non-Apple phones that fit them better; thus lifting the fortunes of these other brands.

A similar dual WOM dynamic could very well be at play with respect to the tablet: when iPad customers tell or show their friends who have not yet purchased a tablet how their digital life has changed as a result of the new device, they might emphasize benefits unique to the iPad or they might broadly reflect on the wonders of having a touch-screen device that so deftly fills the gap between a smartphone and a laptop. If this communication results in the successful conversion of a nonadopter into an iPad customer, we would count the social force as having had a *within-brand* WOM effect. If, on the other hand, some of the attentive friends eventually buy a Samsung Galaxy Tab, the "pollination" that occurred would constitute a *cross-brand* WOM effect.

If your intuition suggests that the within-brand WOM effect should be more intense than the cross-brand influence, it would be correct. This issue was studied in the context of the mobile phone industry across a number of countries. Specifically, in sixteen West European countries, the impact of within-brand communication on generating new adoptions was found to be about twice, on average, that of cross-brand communications. That having been said, in many of these countries, several interesting competitive dynamics can be better understood and appreciated if one takes into account the dual WOM effects. To illustrate, we'll recount the story of how mobile phone rivalry shaped up in Sweden.

For a full decade, from 1982 to 1992, the Swedish mobile phone market was a monopoly with a single operator, TeliaSonera. In 1992, with the penetration level of mobile phones at about 10 percent of the adult population, the market was opened up to competition, and a new provider, Tele2, entered.[1] Tele2's entry coincided with the advent of GSM (Global System for Mobile), a new digital technology standard for mobile telephony. Tele2 grew very quickly: during its first four years in operation, it gained more than four hundred thousand subscribers. By comparison, TeliaSonera had toiled for nine years to achieve this number of subscribers. No wonder TeliaSonera executives began to feel the squeeze. The business press from that period reported that its management considered downsizing and layoffs. After all, it was reasonable to predict based on the early uptake that eventually, Tele2 would become the market leader and leave TeliaSonera in the dust.

These fears, however, turned out to be unfounded: Tele2's much shorter takeoff time to reach the first half million customers was not a sign of future dominance. As can be seen in figure 6.2, in the twelve years following its entry, and despite the fact that it continued to add subscribers at a

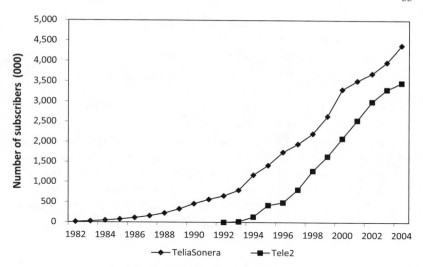

FIGURE 6.2. Wireless phone service market dynamics in Sweden

rapid pace, Tele2 never closed the gap with the incumbent. TeliaSonera kept adding subscribers and growing its sales. In fact, it grew faster than Tele2 for several years and was able to survive and do quite well.

Armed with our understanding that two types of WOM effects (within-brand and cross-brand) exist when multiple brands diffuse, let's unpack the competitive dynamics in the Swedish mobile phone market. When TeliaSonera launched its service back in the 1980s, it was all by itself. Hence by definition, the only type of WOM that could lead to adoption was of the within-brand type. On the other hand, when Tele2 launched, it could immediately tap into the cross-brand effect originating from the customer base of its rival, which by then had reached nearly seven hundred thousand subscribers, whose use of mobile phones and touting of the benefits likely led some nonadopters to explore participation in the category. And lo and behold, they discovered there was another brand to consider. This can help explain why Tele2 reached the half million milestone faster than TeliaSonera could a decade earlier when it had no cross-brand effect to leverage. However, these very same seven hundred thousand TeliaSonera customers who generated a cross-brand effect, which helped propel the social adoption of the entrant's service at a brisk pace, also generated a within-brand social force that benefited the incumbent. And given that the within-brand effect is typically stronger than the cross-brand effect, it enabled TeliaSonera to keep acquiring new customers rapidly, even as the entrant was growing its base.

This process can be self-reinforcing. As the firm with the initially larger customer base grows and adds more customers, so does the gap between it and its rival widen in terms of the within-brand WOM effect, which in turn induces the pool of those that have not yet adopted to be swayed more toward adopting the veteran firm. Thus, and as long as there are no big discrepancies in the technology or innovative features that the firms offer, the initial mass of customers that an incumbent firm has can form an increasing returns asset that leads to a widening of the customer base disparity. In many West European countries, this simultaneous pattern of relatively rapid takeoff by a mobile phone entrant accompanied by an even greater increase in subscriber growth for the incumbent was indeed observed.

You Win Some, You Lose Some: Churn and Disadoption Enter (and Exit) the Picture

Up to now we've focused on how the diffusion of innovations might play out in a competitive context in terms of the first-time adoption. In other words, we examined how the acquisition of customers by each firm, from the pool of those that have not yet adopted in the category, unfolds when multiple firms are vying for the business of these new customers. Yet what prevents the shrewd firm from pursuing customers *after* they have adopted a rival's offering? Companies rarely accept as a fait accompli, or a done deal, that once a customer attaches himself or herself to a competitor, he or she cannot be snatched away. A customer is a customer is a customer— whether that customer comes from the not-yet-adopted pool or from the competitor's already adopted pool.

Firms employ various mechanisms to poach customers from rivals: they can offer attractive deals and better pricing terms, they can run ads or send sales reps who point out deficiencies in a competitor's product or service relative to their own, or they can try to build a unique and enticing brand image, among other actions. Bear in mind also that with innovations, especially when the category itself is fairly nascent, customers might not know a priori whether the first brand they chose from the set of alternatives is indeed the best match for them; moreover, a new entrant can come along that was not initially available. This suggests that past adopters may very well be susceptible to switching brands, even though the long-run market potential is far from being exhausted—that is, the category itself is still diffusing.

Beware though that poaching is a two-way street: some of a company's customers might leave in favor of a rival at the same time that company is trying to steal its rivals' customers. Indeed, firms often evaluate their industry standing and ability to withstand the competition by measuring what portion of their customer base quit their service and signed up to a rival firm in each time period. This number is often called the *churn rate*. A high churn rate can be a sign that customers are unhappy with the firm's offering or with how it treats them or that they find a competitor's value proposition more appealing.

Aside from gaining customers from a rival by directly poaching them, there's also an indirect way this can occur. A customer that has adopted the offering of one of the firms in the category has three options at any point in time: stay with the current firm's offering, switch to a competitor's offering, or drop out of the market entirely. The last option is actually quite common with innovative categories. Consumers who are uncertain of the value proposition they can derive are willing to give one of the new products or services a try, especially if offered to them at a special intro-ductory price. But when the time comes to renew, repeat purchase, or continue to buy add-ons, they decide to abandon the category altogether. Among the reasons for dropping out of the category are high ex ante expectations that get dashed after use, finding shortcomings they hadn't anticipated, or being in a better position to make the cost-benefit trade-off after actually using the product. The ungratifying or uninspiring ex-perience with one brand may cast such strong doubt in some customers' minds that they choose to exit the category entirely rather than try a rival offering and be disappointed again. This behavior is common for new ser-vices such as satellite radio, novel lifestyle pharmaceuticals such as the erectile dysfunction category (which experienced a high drop-out rate for several years), and new consumer packaged goods such as a new type of dairy product.

The decision to discontinue partaking in a category is often referred to as *disadoption*, and the percentage of a firm's customers that make this decision in a given time period is thereby called the *disadoption rate*. We will shortly explain how a rival may be able to take advantage of a firm's customers that drop out of the category.

To recap, we have described two distinct processes that can result in a firm losing customers that it had already acquired: the churn rate refers

TABLE 6.1 **Annual churn, disadoption, and attrition for select categories**[*]

Focal firm	Competitor(s)	Data period		Customers (millions)	Churn (%)	Disadoption (%)	Attrition (%)
		From	To				
E*Trade (USA)	Ameritrade Charles Schwab	Dec. 1997	Mar. 2005	3.6	1	4	5
Mobistar (Belgium)	Belgacom BASE	Jan. 1996	Dec. 2004	2.8	16.1	6.9	23
SK Telecom (South Korea)	KT Group LG Telecom	Jan. 1984	Mar. 2005	19.0	18	9	27
XM Satellite Radio (USA)	Sirius	Sep. 2001	Dec. 2006	7.6	1.8	16.5	18.3

* Note that some firms use the term "churn" in their reports to refer to attrition; we follow the definition given in expression 6.1 and distinguish between churn and attrition.

to those customers that switch to competitors and the disadoption rate refers to those customers that discontinue using the category. The sum of these rates is typically called the *attrition rate*. So we can write by way of definition the following:

EXPRESSION 6.1. The rate of churn, disadoption, and attrition

Attrition rate = Churn rate + Disadoption rate

To get a sense of these three quantities in practice, table 6.1 provides a few examples. The metrics all refer to a focal firm. It is quite clear that these rates can differ wildly by firm and by industry. Some firms like to have a sense of their attrition rate and compare it with their acquisition rate so that the net addition of customers in a period can be assessed and reported to shareholders.

Churning customers go from one firm to a different one in the category. They are still customers . . . just someone else's. To account for churning customers, we need to take them off the books of the focal firm and place them on the books of competing firms and of course do the same for all firms so that the focal firm can benefit from rivals' churn. But what happens to the disadopters? How should we account for them? One eventuality is that they are *lost for good*. This reflects a case where customers that disadopt are never expected to reconsider purchasing any of the alternatives in the category. For all practical purposes, therefore, we write them off. This is the basic way marketers treat customer departures in typical customer lifetime value calculations and was implicitly the approach taken in our assessments in previous chapters, in the sense that when we assumed a customer left the firm—that is, was not retained—there was no way for the firm to bring him or her back. An obvious advantage of this approach is that it is simple and enables a relatively straightforward lifetime value analysis.

The alternative is that disadopting customers are merely "taking a break" from the category and might be back when product/service enhancements or price reductions by one or more firms take place. The rejoin-the-category case is common when early versions of an innovation do not supply sufficient utility or require extensive customer resources to take advantage of them. Improvements in quality, usability, and pricing, possibly coupled with mounting social pressure or a change in personal circumstances (e.g., marital status, education, employment, etc.), prompt a customer who had previously dropped the category to form favorable expectations about one or more of the offerings now available, and readoption becomes an option. For instance, one reason for the considerable efforts to improve online banking in the late 1990s was the realization that low perceived utility of the service in its initial form was driving widespread disadoption. When online banking became more user-friendly and functional, some of those who had tried it earlier and were disappointed eventually returned.

Aside from the fact that, in reality, we often observe customers weaving in and out of the category, the lost-for-good option is a problem for another reason: If there is a nonzero rate at which customers disadopt never to return again, then over time, no firm will have any customers left. The long-run market potential will deplete at some point, so there will be no place from which to attract new customers, and disadoption will dwindle each firm's existing customer base. While this eventuality could conceivably be a reflection of a category losing all relevance to consumers or may describe a fad that has passionate followers for a short period and then disappears into oblivion, it is not a desirable feature of a general model that encompasses innovations that do stick around. Hence we prefer to develop a framework that allows disadopters to reenter—and thus not doom—the category.

Allowing disadopters to reenter the category begs the question of which of the available brands they will choose and with what likelihood. On the one hand, it could be argued that their familiarity with the brand they used prior to disadopting makes that brand a prime candidate for them to pick. On the other hand, if the experience with the last brand consumed was disappointing and is what led them to disadopt, then that brand is perhaps the least likely to be chosen upon reentry. Getting into the nuances of each disadoption decision requires a lot of individual-level data, not to mention getting into the minds and hearts of these customers.

Since disadoption often occurs while the category is still diffusing—that is, the firms are still attracting new adopters from the long-run market potential pool according to their respective individual and social forces—one approach to handling disadopters is to assume that the same forces influence their reentry. This approach effectively treats those that have disadopted as being "blank slates": they may readopt any of the alternatives available pushed by the same forces via which new (first-time) adoptions take place. In some sense, this amounts to throwing disadopters back into the long-run market potential pool, where they become fair game for all competing firms to try to acquire. Indirectly, therefore, one company's loss due to disadoption could later become another company's gain upon readoption (and vice versa). While this approach obviously won't reflect the niceties of each and every disadopter's decision making, it has been shown on average to perform well in analyzing data in a number of competitive industries, such as the ones in table 6.1.

The bottom line is that as one tries to capture the growth of a particular brand's customer base from the common market potential pool of those that have yet to adopt, one also needs to account for customers switching to and from each of the competing brands, customers disadopting the category, and previous disadopters reentering. Metaphorically, the situation is akin to filling a leaky bucket: there is an inward flow of customers from a number of sources and an outward flow of departing customers to different locations.

Putting Together the Pieces: A Competitive Diffusion Model

As the above discussion revealed, competition among firms that launch innovations into the same market space introduces quite a few moving parts as far as customer dynamics are concerned. It's all good, though: we can build on the foundation of models already introduced—in particular, the basic diffusion model and the customer lifetime value model—and show how these moving parts can be accommodated in a fairly straightforward manner.

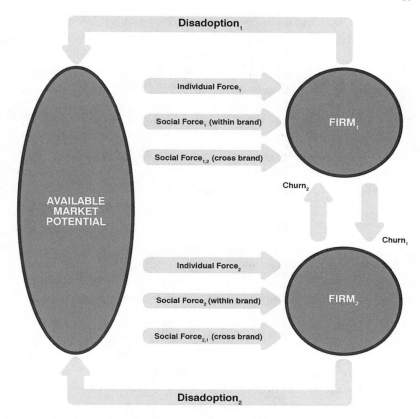

FIGURE 6.3. Customer dynamics in a competitive market

To understand the approach, it is helpful to visualize what a model that allows for competing brands should entail. Please turn your attention therefore to figure 6.3, where we see two firms going at it head to head, so to speak. Each firm keeps adding customers from the common market potential pool. This pool has been labeled "available market potential" to reflect the idea that customers who disadopt are also included in this group and may be acquired by either firm through individual or social forces (in similar fashion to those that have not yet adopted and that are part of this pool as well). The figure further separates the two types of social forces that can operate in a competitive context: the within-brand and the cross-brand WOM effects. The former behaves like the social force of the basic diffusion model, while the latter captures the fact that social influence from a firm's customers can ultimately result in acquisitions by a rival. Lastly, customers may decide to switch brands, resulting in churn to and from each firm. Note that since the firms may offer differing product/service profiles, possess differing marketing competencies in each customer management phase, and enjoy asymmetric brand power, the various quantities have a firm-specific subscript. The subscripts for the cross-brand social forces signify that they can differ from their respective within-brand social forces.

Figure 6.3 provides a clear-cut recipe for writing out an extension to the basic diffusion model to include competition. Expression 6.2 translates this recipe into our familiar formulation.

EXPRESSION 6.2. The competitive diffusion model

Net new customers acquired in this time period by firm_1 =
Available market potential · ($\text{Individual force}_1$ + Social force_1 · Proportion of adoption customer base_1 + $\text{Social force}_{1,2}$ · Proportion of adoption customer base_2) − Customer base_1 · Attrition_1 + Customer base_2 · Churn rate_2

A similar expression can be written for the competitor (firm_2). Notice that in expression 6.2, the social forces are generated by each firm's *current* customer base (as a proportion of the category's long-run market potential) and not by the entire cumulative past adoption, reflecting the assumption that past adopters that churned or disadopted are not relevant to these processes. A formal representation of the competitive diffusion model is given in math box 6 in the appendix. Next, we provide an example of how to apply this model as part of innovation equity assessments.

Putting Together the Pieces: A Price Discount Example

In chapter 3, we examined the impact of a hardware subsidy on XM's innovation equity (the purpose of the subsidy was to decrease the final retail price to consumers). We acknowledged competition from Sirius but followed the "category grows, each firm takes its fair share" approach described at the beginning of this chapter, whereby the category as a whole grows according to a basic diffusion model and each brand takes a share of new adopters according to an allocation rule. To simplify matters further, we assumed for illustration purposes that both XM and Sirius were

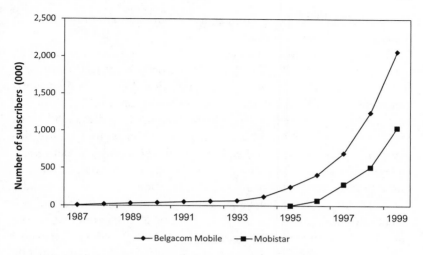

<small>FIGURE 6.4.</small> Early years of mobile telecommunication service in Belgium

expected to subsidize radio receivers and hence evenly split new adopters between them (fifty-fifty).

We would like once more to assess the advisability of a marketing action by a firm in the presence of a rival, this time using the more elaborate competitive model developed in this chapter (as summarized in figure 6.3 and expression 6.2). The competitive diffusion model is well suited to evaluating the profit implications of the asymmetric situation in which one firm takes a marketing action—say a price discount—that is not matched by its rival.

For this purpose, the Belgian mobile telecommunication market will serve as our setting: Belgacom Mobile (a.k.a. Proximus) was the first entrant into the market in 1987, followed by Mobistar in 1996. Similar to what we saw in the Swedish mobile telecommunication market, the initial growth of Mobistar was faster than that of the incumbent: it took Belgacom more than ten years to reach one million subscribers, while it took the newcomer less than four years to reach that same number (see figure 6.4).

Suppose that in considering how to combat the new entrant's rapid growth, Belgacom entertained the idea of instituting a permanent 10 percent price cut across all the wireless service packages it offered. Presuming it would be difficult for newcomer Mobistar to match this 10 percent price break, what would be the effect of the proposed asymmetric price reduction on the market shares of the two firms and on Belgacom's profitability? From an innovation equity standpoint, should Belgacom in hindsight have gone ahead with such a move?

As emphasized throughout, in order to properly quantify the effect of a marketing action such as the proposed Belgacom price reduction, we need to consider its effect on two aspects: innovation diffusion and customer management. Recall that in the customer lifetime value (CLV) model we have used thus far, we explicitly took into account the possibility that customers may leave the firm—having incorporated an attrition rate (which equals 1 – retention rate)—at which point the firm ceases to derive revenues from the departing customers. We did not separate out the attrition rate into its components—churn and disadoption—nor did we consider the possibility that customers may reenter the market in the future. The competitive diffusion model, however, does take into account where departing customers go and allows the firm to "reunite" with lost customers in the future—a richer model, no doubt. Yet to be consistent, the attrition rates in the two models, CLV and competitive diffusion, should converge when they're part of an innovation equity assessment.

The parameter values needed for analyzing the Belgian mobile telecom market are known or can be estimated from publicly available data. To quantify the impact of a price reduction on these parameters, it is useful to know the price elasticity of demand in the relevant market—that is, how demand for the service will change in response to a 1 percent change in price. Although we don't have data specific to the Belgian market, we rely on an external evaluation of the mobile telecommunication market, which found the price elasticity to be –0.5. This means that a 1 percent decrease in price would bring a corresponding 0.5 percent increase in demand. A 10 percent decrease in price would result in approximately a 5 percent increase in demand. For simplicity, we assume in our example that the response to a 10 percent price change by Belgacom affects all its customer-related parameters in a similar fashion—that is, churn and disadoption decrease by 5 percent each to reflect the fact that existing customers find the service more appealing at the lower price and hence are less likely to leave Belgacom, while the diffusion parameters (p and q) increase by 5 percent each to reflect greater appeal to new adopters. The trade-off of the price cut from Belgacom's perspective, of course, is that the per-period revenues from each customer, also called the average revenue per user (ARPU), will go down. If one assumes that customers would use the service in exactly the same manner after the price change, then Belgacom's ARPU would go down by 10 percent. However, one could reasonably expect the price elasticity effect to apply to each customer's

TABLE 6.2 **Belgacom customer lifetime value model parameters and analysis with and without price cut***

	No price cut	10 percent price cut
Churn rate (%)	16	15.2
Disadoption rate (%)	7	6.7
Attrition rate (%)	23	21.9
Retention rate (%)	77	78.2
ARPU (annual; $)	686	651
Average costs per user (annual; $)	250	250
Subscriber lifetime value ($)	1,321	1,258

* Financial discount rate taken to be 10 percent.

usage level as well, which would go up, and hence only a 5 percent net decrease in ARPU would result. We will take this latter approach. The per-period profit margin is then obtained by deducting the average cost to serve a customer from the ARPU.

Table 6.2 presents the changes in the CLV model parameters resulting from the 10 percent price decrease. As can be seen, despite the fact that retention has gone up, the decline in the ARPU reduces the CLV of a subscriber from $1,321 to $1,258. The question now is whether this decrease will be offset by an increase in the adoption forces (p and q), which affect the way demand evolves for Belgacom's service.

To estimate the various parameters of the competitive diffusion model, as depicted in expression 6.2, we used actual data on the evolution of subscribers over time for both competitors with no price cut. We find that for Belgacom, $p_1 = 0.0013$ and $q_1 = 0.999$; for Mobistar, $p_2 = 0.005$ and $q_2 = 0.698$, and the cross-brand social force, which was taken to be the same in both directions, is $q_{21} = q_{12} = 0.12$ (though as explained, given the initial installed base of Belgacom that multiplies this parameter, its resulting cross-brand effect on Mobistar adoptions is much stronger).

Table 6.3 summarizes the customer base growth of the two firms, as well as the profits derived from subscribers for the first five years following Mobistar's entry. The second and third columns show the number of Belgacom and Mobistar subscribers if no discount is given, while the fifth and sixth columns show these quantities with diffusion parameters up 5 percent for Belgacom as a result of the price discount. We see that the total number of Belgacom subscribers increases by almost 400,000 during the five-year span following the price cut (from 3.3 million to 3.7 million), while Mobistar's subscriber base decreases slightly because of facing a cheaper rival. In terms of market share, Belgacom gains 2.5 percent over the case where no price discount is given. Although this might not sound like a dramatic

TABLE 6.3 **The effects of a 10 percent price discount by Belgacom at the entry time of Mobistar**

	Belgacom subscribers acquired (000)	Mobistar subscribers acquired (000)	Belgacom profits from customers acquired ($000)	Belgacom subscribers acquired (000)	Mobistar subscribers acquired (000)	Belgacom profits from customers acquired ($000)
	No discount			10 percent discount		
1996	196	113	258,523	211	111	265,720
1997	357	212	471,023	394	211	496,403
1998	614	377	811,824	693	379	872,451
1999	949	609	1,254,111	1,079	613	1,357,819
2000	1,186	824	1,566,848	1,319	817	1,660,004

increase, it is enough to trump the loss in CLV seen in table 6.2: the innovation equity change in Belgacom's favor, as evaluated from the vantage point of 1996 (when the price cut is proposed to have been implemented), is calculated by taking the net present value of columns 4 and 7 in table 6.3 (using a 10 percent cost of capital discount rate). This calculation reveals an overall improvement in innovation equity of about $200 million (from $3.06 to $3.27 billion), suggesting the price cut would have been worth pursuing: Belgacom could have been more aggressive.

Linking Advanced Rivalry Topics to the Competitive Diffusion Model

A competitive marketplace requires firms to think strategically about customer management. Beyond the marketing tactics each firm can engage in as it contends with rivals for the business of potential customers, a host of additional intriguing issues can arise once one opens the competition floodgates. And this is all the more true when innovations are involved. In the next few subsections, we explore a number of these issues, with an eye toward connecting them to the concepts and modeling approaches covered thus far.

Standards Wars and Stealthy Tactics

Every so often, the combination of innovation and competition entails more than just a few firms jockeying for market shares with products or services that are by and large interchangeable. Sometimes this combination involves much higher stakes that can result in dramatic lopsided outcomes. The situation in the videocassette recording (VCR) market, from the mid-1970s throughout the 1980s, is one such example.

Although a number of firms developed their own cassette technology for video recording and playback (that allowed taping television shows for later viewing, buying or renting recorded movies, etc.), Sony and JVC were the main rivals in the space. Sony called its format Betamax, while JVC dubbed its version VHS (Video Home System). The two formats were "incompatible," which means that video recorded in the Betamax format could not be later viewed with a device intended for the VHS format and vice versa. Sony's format was presumably of higher quality (superior resolution, sound, and image stability) but in the first few years had only one hour of recording time per cassette. VHS, on the other hand, provided a two-hour recording window. Although Sony firmly believed that its format was superior, within a few years, the adoption balance was tilting in JVC's favor, and once it started tilting, there was no going back. While Sony had launched products using its standard more than a year ahead of JVC, and thus Betamax initially held a 100 percent share of the VCR market, by the late 1980s fortunes had reversed as VHS's market share in the United States climbed to about 90 percent. In 1988, despite marketing efforts and multiple product enhancements, Sony practically conceded defeat when it brought to market its own VHS devices.

What went so horribly wrong for Sony in the "Betamax–VHS format war" is tightly linked to the economic notion of increasing returns to scale: once a particular standard, format, or protocol gets sufficiently ahead of others in the pack in terms of adoption, there is a tendency for it to get even further ahead. Increasing returns to scale have the power to turn a small advantage into an insurmountable one. JVC played its cards right and put itself in a great position to benefit from both supply- and demand-side increasing returns to scale, while Sony did not. First, JVC let other electronics companies license the VHS format (in exchange for royalties), while Sony initially kept its format proprietary. Consequently, other electronics firms had an incentive to push the VHS format, and competition among them resulted in lower device prices. At the same time, it turned out that the better Betamax quality was not sufficient to justify the higher price for consumers, and the drawback of a shorter playback time (imagine the inconvenience of getting two cassettes for most movies and having to change them midway through, not to mention the hassle of storing that many more cassettes).

As more consumers began adopting VHS, a vicious cycle began: On the supply side, greater production meant spreading a lot of fixed costs onto more units and also getting more efficient at the production process, all of which led to lower manufacturing costs that in turn allowed price to come down even further. This resulted in Sony's devices getting *relatively* more expensive. On the demand side, network effects were a big factor. Recall that network effects are customer benefits that depend on the number of people that use a particular product or service. With video recording, it's not difficult to see how network effects arose: a consumer benefits when more friends and family use the same format because he or she can then swap videos with them, bring over a video to show at a friend's house without having to worry about whether it will play, ask a friend to record a show for him or her without agonizing about the format, and so on. Indirect network effects also arise in this case: as more consumers use a format, there is more incentive for studios to create video content for that format and for retailers to carry them. And as the user network of a particular format grows, so do these direct and indirect benefits. Thus even though Sony modified its strategy in the mid-1980s and allowed other companies to license Betamax and increased the recording duration, it was too late. By then VHS was already too entrenched in production efficiencies and delivering network benefits to be dislodged from its reigning throne.

After losing the VCR format war by not properly tapping into increasing returns to scale, Sony was determined not to lose future video-recording format wars. Luckily, the entire industry was able to coordinate on a single standard that succeeded videocassette technology, as the DVD (digital videodisk) format was embraced "peacefully" by all players in the mid-1990s. However, the ensuing generation of video storage technology, high-definition optical discs, which began in 2006, was again characterized by unbridled rivalry. In this go-around, the main contenders were Toshiba, with its HD-DVD format, and Sony, with its Blu-ray format. Sony knew that to win this war, it had to garner the bulk of early adoption and tilt the scales in its favor. Thus aside from intense marketing efforts that accompanied the launch, it pursued a Trojan horse tactic: it decided to incorporate a Blu-ray player into its new gaming platform, the PlayStation 3 (PS3), which was launched in November 2006. Instantly, any PS3 customer became a "Blu-ray adopter in disguise."

So determined was Sony to succeed in getting Blu-rays into the hands of PS3 console buyers and having them serve as a "sleeper" captive market for its video format that it was willing to take a profit hit. The inclusion of the Blu-ray player raised manufacturing costs considerably and meant that Sony was initially losing money on each PS3 unit sold. But consider this: a PS3, which on top of doubling as a Blu-ray video player could also play games, music, and connect to the Internet, was in many cases cheaper (at a price of $499 or $599 depending on the amount of memory) than many stand-alone Blu-ray or HD DVD models (priced at $700–$1,000); even the most basic stand-alone Blu-ray models cost upwards of $400 at the time.

The approach worked. The huge installed base of PS3s (more than 7.5 million consoles sold by the end of 2007, much more than sales of stand-alone Blu-ray players) meant that many consumers were equipped to watch movies produced in that format at no additional cost. As strong network effects began kicking in, several major movie studios announced that they would support the Blu-ray format only. Toshiba for its part tried to counter by allowing its HD-DVD to connect as a separate device to Microsoft's successful Xbox 360. But in this case the consumer had to make a conscious decision to shell out an extra $200 for the high-definition player, when Xbox 360 games played just fine in the DVD format (which came standard with the console) without the HD-DVD attachment. Once Warner Bros., the only major studio that was still releasing movies in both formats, declared that it would support Blu-ray only, many prominent US retailers such as Wal-Mart and Best Buy dropped HD-DVDs from their shelves. Soon after this action, in February 2008, Toshiba waved the white flag, announcing it would no longer manufacture HD DVD devices. HD DVD's life was brief: less than two years from birth to burial.

When only one firm's standard remains standing following a format or platform battle, the situation is typically called a "winner-takes-all" market. The video storage/recording industry clearly exhibited this type of outcome. That said, not all standards wars end with a single winner; some end up with a few incompatible platforms that survive. Smartphone operating systems are one such case, with Apple's iOS and Google's Android platforms both alive and kicking in the smartphone market. (At the time of writing, the two standards held more than 90 percent share.) And while Android-based devices were becoming more ubiquitous, profit-wise, iPhones were generating well-above-average profits. The ability of multiple formats to remain viable, despite the existence of network and other increasing returns effects, often depends on heterogeneity in consumer tastes and the ability of the various formats to cater to these tastes. Brand image can play a role as well, allowing one player to maintain a strong following for its format even as more functionality-oriented or price-conscious consumers gravitate to formats supported by other players. The ability of third-party software producers to simultaneously cater to these differing formats—such as apps in the case of smartphones—is also a major factor influencing the long-term survival of two or more rival platforms.

Regarding the modeling of customer adoption in markets where winner-takes-all or winner-takes-most outcomes occur, a number of adjustments can be made to the competitive diffusion model. For example, in the event that one format can attract adopters from a particular segment that the rival does not have much access to, as was the case for Blu-ray with gamers, one can imagine allowing that format to draw adopters both from the common pool of potential adopters and exclusively from a separate "captive" pool. Second, note that the social force of the basic diffusion model already embodies the idea that a firm with a larger base of customers has an advantage in converting potential adopters into customers. One could further let the churn and disadoption rates be a function of the size of a firm's customer base to reflect the fact that as a firm's customer base increases, its customers are less likely to leave. Incorporating these factors into the model will likely lead to one firm growing at a much faster pace than a rival. There could also be a threshold level below which, if a firm's share dips, that firm is expected to drop out. These kinds of modifications and embellishments enable creating innovation equity projections for analyzing such markets.

Sowing the Seeds of Increasing Returns to Scale

As we have seen, due to the powerful implications of increasing returns to scale, any advantage in the customer base size early on can quickly escalate into a decisive blow to a competitor that doesn't manage to keep up; a disadvantage in network effects and in production costs can act like merciless quicksand. Consequently, aside from trying to be first to launch, firms often try to engage in marketing efforts to secure a cadre of adopters as early as possible.

One approach to meeting this challenge is to espouse a "go big or go home" mentality—that is, try to go all out with a media blitz and offer low prices to all consumers in an attempt to cast as wide a net as possible. While this approach certainly has some face validity as a way to pique the interest of a broad set of consumers, it may be extremely costly to implement, and success is by no means guaranteed: a firm may find itself going big but packing up to go home with a huge hole in its bank account. This is especially true if all firms are guided by this mentality: consumers end up being bombarded with messages from all competitors that at best they ignore and at worst confuse and annoy them and put them off buying any product.

The flip approach is to cast a narrow net; perhaps only a few fishing lines is the better metaphor here. The idea is to "go small" but do so effectively by employing a seeding campaign. Such campaigns target a very specific set of individuals and get them to try the new product or service. The hope is to win them over and that their subsequent advocacy propels rapid adoption among many other consumers who listen to them. The initial set of targeted customers, so to speak, forms the seed for the ensuing growth spurt. Here are a few examples of seeding campaigns that prominent firms employed to achieve these objectives:

- *Microsoft.* Preceding the formal launch of its Windows 95 operating system, the company gave away copies of the software to 450,000 opinion-leading PC users in the United States (an estimated 5 percent of the United States market potential). The record-breaking speed of the software's sales in the postlaunch period was attributed in part to this giveaway. More recently, Microsoft hosted thousands of "parties" in fourteen countries to help introduce Windows 7. Microsoft estimated that seven million people were likely eventually reached by communications stemming from those parties.
- *Hewlett-Packard.* In 2008, HP provided thirty-one leading US bloggers with the company's new Dragon HDX laptop and asked them to create online competitions for which the Dragon laptop was the prize. According to HP, the results of their "31 Days of the Dragon" campaign were exceptional: in addition to a huge lift in online searches for the Dragon, HP observed an immediate 85 percent bump in Dragon sales and a 15 percent increase in traffic to its site.
- *Ford Motor Company.* In 2009, Ford gave one hundred influencers a new Ford Fiesta with the aim of these bloggers helping to promote the new car model, which was set to reach US dealers in early 2010. These new Fiesta owners completed monthly challenges and posted videos and blogged about their experiences. The campaign gained 6.2 million YouTube views, 750,000 Flickr views, and 40 million Twitter impressions. In addition, 132,000 drivers signed up for updates on the new Fiesta, and more than 6,000 preordered the car.

An important question when considering a seeding campaign is what characteristics one should look for in the individuals that will be seeded with the innovation. Naturally firms would like to target seeds that have as much influence on others as possible. Thus particular attention has been given to the identification of what are known as "opinion leaders"—people that presumably have a disproportionate effect on others. Often, two kinds of such influential individuals are considered: *hubs* and *experts*. Hubs are people with relatively many connections and a large number of social network ties. In today's digitally connected society, many firms believe they can identify hubs via information they gather from online social media services such as Facebook and Twitter. The working assumption is that if a hub adopts early, he or she will communicate with or will be seen by many others compared to the average customer who has far fewer connections (e.g., fewer friends on Facebook or followers on Twitter). In the case of experts, the influence comes not from the sheer number of connections but the effectiveness of each communication to a connected individual. Experts are people whose word of mouth is relatively impactful within their social network, largely because they are considered highly knowledgeable in the specific field. Of course, a person may be both a hub and an expert—for example, a very popular tech blogger.

Caution is warranted, though, as many connections listed in online social networking sites may not represent actual influence. Many people have "phantom" connections or acquaintances who accepted their friendship invitation but who don't pay attention to anything they post. Consequently, the information gathered from such sources may not always provide a reliable reflection of actual consumption-relevant interactions among customers. Furthermore, market reports by firms such as the Keller Fay Group suggest that the majority of consumption-relevant social influence still occurs offline, mostly face to face. These types of connections and interactions are much more difficult to track.

A different seeding approach tries to focus not on opinion leaders with many or strong connections but on "revenue leaders." These are individuals that are likely to be lavish spenders. There are two advantages in targeting revenue leaders: First, their adoption generates much more profit than that of average-spending customers. Second, their word of mouth often creates more innovation equity. The reason for this is the tendency of people to be in a social network with others who are similar to them—what is known as *homophily*. Several studies have shown a positive correlation between the revenue one person generates and the revenue generated by others in that person's close social network. Therefore, revenue leaders create equity not because they affect a multitude of consumers but because they affect the right consumers from a CLV standpoint. The strategy of targeting revenue leaders rather than opinion leaders is considered beneficial when the profit dispersion among customers is large and when some segments feel comfortable adopting an innovation that is deemed niche (perhaps initially even somewhat exclusive) rather than mass market: they're comfortable not being part of the herd. Identifying these types often requires knowing individuals' purchasing habits in several categories and drawing an inference on their likely willingness to spend on the firm's innovation.

The discussion on implementing seeding programs to win over a specific set of customers, who in turn influence other potential adopters, should hopefully trigger memories of the multisegment diffusion model described in detail in chapter 4. In effect, the opinion leaders that firms try to convert are what we called innovation forwards, or "influentials," and have a strong impact on those we referred to as innovation moderates, or "imitators." The twist introduced here is that you may need to consider the multisegment framework in light of competition, as a rival may "attack" the influentials' segment as well for purposes of seeding. Combining both multisegment and competitive considerations undoubtedly leads to a complex modeling task. Simplifications are strongly recommended, for example by assuming similarity in some parameters across rivals to make things manageable. At a minimum, we hope that understanding the forces and processes at play when multiple segments and multiple firms are involved provides a lens through which to assess any forecast put forward when these issues are expected to play a role.

Pirates on the High Seas of Adoption: Friends or Foes?

Offering physical goods requires procuring materials, assembling parts, packaging and shipping the finished product, and securing retail channels to reach customers. These steps make physical product counterfeiting a nontrivial task, especially in countries where authorities are aware of the problem and try to combat it. Product knock-offs are certainly not impossible to bring to market, but do involve manufacturing and logistical challenges. And regardless of the imitation's final quality, which is often lower, they are still costly. Digital products, on the other hand, are unburdened by many of these challenges and costs: all the stages involved in duplication and distribution are accomplished digitally and pretty much for free. Moreover, while an entity producing a physical copycat product will likely charge something for it to recoup production and distribution costs and to make a profit, in many cases digital products, especially entertainment content like games, movies, television shows, and music, are often supplied at no charge for altruistic or social reasons. New technologies, like peer-to-peer file-sharing services that allow transferring very large files by breaking them up into smaller downloads (such as BitTorrent), have simplified the reproduction process and improved the experience tremendously. Copyright laws are typically the only barrier to digital counterfeiting, and in many parts of the world, such laws are weak or enforced halfheartedly. Not surprisingly then, piracy, which is the accepted term for the illegal distribution of software protected under intellectual property laws, has become rampant, as more people around the globe have access to the Internet and to digital devices.

At first glance, piracy seems like a terrible thing for the original producer of the content: it invests all this money in things like development and design, hiring artists, and marketing effort to generate demand, and then some unscrupulous party comes along and smugly free-rides on all this investment. The authentic content may be more readily accessible, as it can be found on several mainstream websites and available at approved venues (such as with movies that can be viewed in theatres or streamed legally on demand from cable company feeds, available for digital purchase at Amazon Prime, or rented through Netflix or Redbox). However, with social networking rampant and web-savvy consumers on the prowl, free pirated content is not difficult to stumble upon. And rest assured that no matter what the content, there will virtually always be some pirate willing to supply it. If instead of paying for the genuine digital good, a consumer downloads or streams the pirated version, the original producer loses revenue and profits.

This problem is compounded by the fact that for many people, the perception is that anything they can access online is (or should be) public domain. Indeed a recent survey revealed that 70 percent of consumers "find nothing wrong with online piracy." So widespread is the problem that various organizations publish top-ten lists of the most pirated forms of digital content. For example, the ten movies that made the 2014 list were downloaded illegally more than 270 million times, with *The Wolf of Wall Street* and *Frozen* leading the way at about 30 million downloads apiece. The growth in piracy is noteworthy, as the top ten movies that made the list the year before only reached about 75 million illegal downloads.

Piracy is undeniably a form of competition, typically not from a legitimate company that has offices, management, employees, and shareholders, but from a myriad of private individuals that can be anywhere and strike anytime, day or night. As with any competitor, the firm producing the original content faces the dilemma of how to fight back. It can place watchdogs that scour the Internet and remove pirated content from sites, or it can take legal actions against a few individuals and try to publicize these cases in an effort to deter others. While it is questionable how effective these measures are at combating the piracy phenomenon, perhaps the more important question is whether the firm should be combating piracy at all. Is piracy really a pernicious enemy that needs to be eradicated at all costs?

The first issue at hand is evaluating the premise that every pirated copy that is consumed displaces a legitimate, original copy sale that would have otherwise taken place. It is entirely conceivable that the majority of those who download a free version of a particular movie or game would not have otherwise considered paying for it to begin with. If that is the case, then the existence of piracy effectively expands the pool of potential adopters beyond the size that would have been relevant if there were no illegal copies. No harm, no foul.

The second issue is what happens once someone consumes a pirated good. If that person talks to friends, posts a review of the content, or sends a link to others, suddenly his or her involvement goes beyond personal consumption and enters the realm of social contagion. If the social contagion prompts individuals who would not have considered purchasing the authentic good to consume the pirated version, again, no harm no foul. However, if such social influence has some hand in engendering future paid adoption for the original good, then not only should the brand manager of this good not call foul, but he or she should actually be pleased about it. The director of HBO's *Game of Thrones,* David Petrarca, seems to share that mind-set. In commenting on the fact that his smash series was the most popular free-streamed television show of 2012 (with more than four million illegal downloads for a single episode), he surprised reporters by indicating that he considers such piracy a good thing. It's not that he condones illegal behavior, but rather, in his view, shows like *Game of Thrones* "thrive on the cultural buzz" created when more people watch the show. He went as far as saying, "That's how they survive." In a similar vein, at the 2012 Midem conference in Cannes (one of the largest trade fairs of the music industry), the CEO of Rovio, publisher of *Angry Birds*, remarked, "Piracy may not be a bad thing. . . . It can get us more business at the end of the day."

Essentially, what is going on here should not be unfamiliar to you. Benefiting from the social impact of a rival, in this case the pirated version, is exactly what the cross-brand WOM effect discussed earlier in this chapter is all about. It is therefore quite straightforward to capture the possible negative, neutral, and positive implications of facing copycats within the competitive diffusion model. It makes sense to allow the pirated version to draw from a separate pool of potential adopters as well as from the common available pool, reflecting the fact that some consumers would never consider paying for the genuine good, while others would. Then in addition to within-brand WOM effects for both the legal and pirated versions, one can include a cross-brand WOM effect that allows potential adopters from the common available pool to be influenced to buy the legal version by those that have consumed the counterfeit/illegal good.

Having delved much deeper into how competitive dynamics affect the innovation equity playbook and having covered possible avenues to model the various pertinent effects, we are ready to return to the satellite radio saga of the rivalry between XM and Sirius that was heating up toward the end of 2004.

Welcome Back to *The Howard Stern Show*! Now You Can Listen to It Live on . . . SiriusXM

Writing the names of the two satellite radio companies together as one, *SiriusXM*, in the title of this subsection is not a typo; it reflects a single commercial entity spelled as an eight-letter name. But we're getting ahead of ourselves.

Let's go back to the luring of Howard Stern by Sirius in October 2004. Why did the popular shock jock agree to leave traditional radio in the first place? It was a risky move for the self-proclaimed "King of All Media": his show was broadcast on scores of radio stations nationwide and at its peak had a total listenership of some twenty million, with more than six million listeners on any given day. In fall 2004, when the deal with him was being finalized, Sirius had a meager six hundred thousand subscribers—a far cry from what Stern was used to.

A big part of Stern's willingness to move was undoubtedly related to financial incentives—Sirius was offering him an attractive package worth much more than his salary at Infinity Broadcasting, Stern's employer at the time. Yet another big part of his willingness to jump the terrestrial radio ship was the rapidly changing climate with respect to what the public deemed appropriate to air on broadcast radio and television. This prompted the Federal Communications Commission (FCC), which regulated this industry, to take a stricter stance on what it deemed indecent content.

Many believe the trigger for this change was Super Bowl XXXVIII in February 2004, in which the New England Patriots beat the Carolina Panthers 32 to 29. But the heroics of projected Hall of Fame quarterback Tom Brady and clutch kicker Adam Vinateri in the dramatic last-minute win had nothing to do with what ignited the wrath of the FCC. Rather, it was attributable to a brief moment during the halftime show when artists Justin Timberlake and Janet Jackson were performing a duet together. As Timberlake sang the final line, "I'm gonna have you naked by the end of this song," he pulled off part of Jackson's costume and revealed her right breast. CBS, the television network broadcasting the game, claimed that the incident was not intentional and insisted that Ms. Jackson's nipple was not technically exposed as it was covered by a "nipple shield." Despite these pleas, the FCC ended up fining Viacom, the media conglomerate that owns CBS, to the tune of $550,000 for indecent exposure. The fine was only the tip of the iceberg. The so-called wardrobe malfunction seen by 144 million viewers sparked a public outcry over what should be allowed on the airwaves. Repercussions followed: several class action lawsuits were filed against Timberlake, Jackson, and CBS and congressional leaders weighed whether to impose tighter controls on content and increase by as much as tenfold the fines that the FCC could levy on offending broadcasters. More to our point, there was mounting pressure on media company executives to reign in obscene, salacious, sex-oriented content or face scrutiny and serious fines. Unfortunately, this was exactly the type of content that Stern's show thrived on. It didn't take long for Clear Channel Communications, the leading US radio operator, to pull *The Howard Stern Show*, which it syndicated from Viacom, from all its stations. "The Super Bowl did us in," remarked Stern in reference to the stifling environment he began sensing within Viacom, adding that it made him feel "dead inside" creatively. Satellite radio, on the other hand, because it was subscription based and not broadcast, was largely unregulated and exempt from this type of FCC oversight. Stern decided that it was time to pack up and leave. He was obligated by contract to continue producing the show at Infinity Broadcasting until the end of 2005, but he already had one foot out the door when he negotiated the deal with Sirius in late October 2004.

Stern's five-year deal with Sirius had two main components. The first was an annual budget of $100 million for production and staff, most of which went toward Stern's personal compensation (estimates put his cut

of the annual budget at $80 million). The second was a set of stock in-
centives based on the number of subscribers Sirius would acquire in the
future. More specifically, Stern would receive Sirius stocks contingent on
the number of subscribers exceeding forecasted targets (which were calculated in 2004 before the signing). In a sense, Stern would get a "bonus"
if Sirius was able to acquire more subscribers than it projected it would
get without him.

Evaluating the "Stern Effect"

While the deal was apparently right for Stern, was its cost right for Sirius?
In other words, would the expense of including Stern in its lineup result
in a positive return on investment (ROI)? Adding a famous celebrity who
produces content in high demand is much like improving the quality of a
product or incorporating a new feature into it. To some extent, it is also a
marketing communication tool given the popularity the celebrity enjoys.
Hence, in assessing the ROI question within the context of a new service
that is still penetrating the market, we need to look at the implications
the Stern deal could have on two things: the prospective lifetime value of
customers and the innovation diffusion parameters.

The impact on customers' lifetime value can be examined by studying
the data in table 6.4, which were obtained from the annual reports of Sirius and XM (10-K forms) for the two years before and two years after the
debut of *The Howard Stern Show* on Sirius. For starters, we could have
anticipated a decrease in the attrition rate after Stern began his tenure
at Sirius. This failed to materialize. A bit to the contrary, in the ensuing years, the attrition rate slightly increased. We can thus reasonably
conclude that signing up Howard Stern had no discernible effect on the
retention of Sirius customers. The monthly ARPU increased by about
7 percent to $11 in 2006 yet decreased the following year to roughly the
pre-Stern level. We can conclude that the signing of Howard Stern had no
meaningful effect on average customer revenues. Therefore, and assuming the cost of serving a customer per month roughly stayed the same, the
per-period profits per customer acquired didn't change by much for Sirius.

As for XM, the rise in ARPU in 2005, continuing into 2006–2007, is
almost certainly the result of the price hike in early 2005 that put XM's
subscription fee on par with Sirius's; not surprisingly, by 2007 both had a
very similar ARPU. By the way, if you're wondering why the average revenue per subscriber is lower for both firms than the $12.95 a month official

TABLE 6.4 **Customer lifetime value data for Sirius and XM, 2004–7**

Monthly attrition (%)	2004	2005	2006	2007
Sirius	1.6	1.5	1.9	2.2
XM	1.2	1.5	1.8	1.8
Monthly ARPU ($)				
Sirius	10.2	10.3	11.0	10.5
XM	8.7	9.5	10.1	10.8
Subscriber acquisition costs (SAC; $)				
Sirius	177	139	114	101
XM	62	65	65	75
Marketing expenses (000s for year; $)				
Sirius (as reported under "marketing and sales")	202,848	197,675	203,682	173,572
XM (as reported under "advertising and marketing")	88,076	182,438	164,379	178,743

or "list" rate, that has to do with promotions both companies ran to attract and retain customers.

The only CLV-related metrics that do seem to have been impacted by Stern's defection to Sirius are the acquisition costs. The table reports two measures associated with acquisition expenses. The first are the subscriber acquisition costs (SAC) per new subscriber added, which typically include subsidies and distribution expenses (including any payments to auto dealers and retailers to promote the service to sign up new customers). The second are marketing-related expenses associated with acquisition efforts, such as advertising, media, promotional events, and so on. In the case of XM, the marketing expenses listed in the table are directly tied to acquisition efforts; hence, the company also reported a cost per gross acquisition (CPGA) figure that includes both the SAC and the advertising and marketing expenses (the latter are divided by gross subscriber additions in the year, so they are on a per-acquisition basis). CPGA for XM comes out to $100, $109, $108, and $121 from 2004 to 2007, respectively. For Sirius, the marketing and sales expenses reported reflect several types of customer management efforts, including a portion for retention; hence, they cannot be easily translated into acquisition efforts. Nonetheless, it does seem that starting in 2005, as momentum was building for Howard Stern's big switch, Sirius was spending less on SAC, while other marketing-related expenses didn't materially increase (in 2007 they were actually lower than in 2004). By contrast, it is clear that XM ratcheted up advertising and marketing expenses quite heavily in light of its rival's move, thus seeing its CPGA climb by more than 20 percent over a three-year span.

These trends make sense if one considers how heavily Howard Stern publicized his upcoming move during the fourteen months between the signing of the deal and his departure from Infinity Broadcasting. Not only was Stern giving television interviews to propagate the message that satellite radio was "the next big thing," but on his daily show, he ranted relentlessly about broadcast radio's stifling environment and talked up his enthusiasm about switching to Sirius. The situation got so bad that Infinity Broadcasting even suspended him for a day, apparently because he was blabbing too much about Sirius. For many of his loyal fans, there was no need for incentives or any extra marketing effort: where Stern went, they went. This surely brought down acquisition costs for Sirius. XM, on the other hand, felt like it was in a tug-of-war over new adopters who became more familiar with the Sirius name because of all the free advertising that Stern and the media were supplying. XM had to counter with more advertising and marketing to pull in new customers.

Turning now to the diffusion side of things—that is, how the subscriber bases grew in the pre–/post–Howard Stern satellite radio era—an interesting pattern emerges. Figure 6.5 plots two diffusion curves for the category as a whole (the sum of XM and Sirius subscribers) from 2001 to 2008. The diamond-symbol curve is the forecasted growth based on our estimates for the model parameters prelaunch (as derived in chapter 1). The square-symbol curve is the actual number of total subscribers as reported by the companies in their quarterly financial statements. It is not difficult to see that while the "actual" slightly trailed the "forecast" up until Q3 of 2004, the situation began an impressive reversal following the signing of Howard Stern in that quarter. It seems undeniable that Stern catapulted the satellite radio category to new adoption heights. The big question is, who stood to gain from this?

Industry analysts, looking at the growth in subscribers during this period, indicated their belief that at least part of the growth for *both* firms was indeed attributable to the "Stern effect," as they called it. Sirius had to concede as much when the King of All Media came by to collect his stock option bonuses—as the realized growth in subscribers exceeded the targets set in the contract based on Sirius's pre-Stern forecasts (the shares granted to him in 2006 and 2007 were roughly worth $300 million).

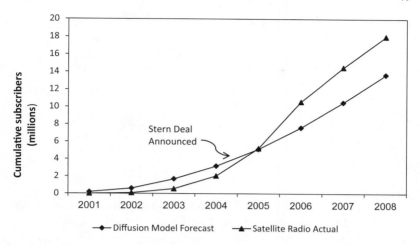

FIGURE 6.5. Forecasted and actual cumulative subscribers for satellite radio category

Hugh Panero, XM's CEO at the time, also concurred with the analysts' assessments, declaring that "Howard Stern has raised awareness of the entire satellite category." The sentiment was consistent with the familiar principle, described earlier in the chapter, of a rising tide lifting all ships. Can we corroborate these qualitative sentiments and verify that both firms benefited in terms of subscriber additions? Can we provide a rough assessment of whether Sirius achieved a positive ROI as a result of the whole Stern affair?

To shed light on these matters, we need to go a level deeper than that of the category and compare each company's forecasted number of subscribers in the absence of Stern with its actual number of subscribers that materialized. For the forecasted subscriber figures, we turn to the competitive diffusion model, which accounts for churn and disadoption, and use our prelaunch estimates for the common long-run market potential and the adoption forces (as derived in chapter 1). We note that the companies would have had to formulate these forecasts in fall 2004—that is, only three years after XM launched (and less than that for Sirius); hence, there is not enough data to empirically estimate the diffusion parameters.

Having run the competitive model, you will be pleased to know that the parameters we have been using thus far appear to have face validity. For example, the model predicts 3.1 million XM subscribers at the end of 2004, while the actual number was 3.2 million. For Sirius, the model's forecast leading up to the Stern announcement is a bit off compared to

TABLE 6.5 **XM and Sirius subscribers (at the end of calendar year)**

	Actual subscribers		Forecasted subscribers		Difference (actual − forecast)		Stern-generated new subscribers in period	
	XM	Sirius	XM	Sirius	XM	Sirius	XM	Sirius
2005	5,932,805	3,316,560	4,134,045	2,256,000	1,798,760	1,060,560	1,798,760	1,060,560
2006	7,627,873	6,024,000	5,089,177	3,707,000	2,538,696	2,317,000	739,936	1,256,440
2007	9,100,000	8,321,785	5,950,552	5,291,000	3,149,448	3,030,785	610,752	713,785
2008	9,850,741	9,153,115	6,687,692	7,192,000	3,163,049	1,961,115	13,601	0

the actual data, suggesting that Sirius had lower adoption forces than XM early on. Many analysts indicated that Sirius was aggressive in getting Stern for exactly that reason. Notably, Sirius's own forecast of subscribers beyond 2004 but without Stern, which they had to specify as part of the contract, shows reasonable accord with the competitive diffusion model forecast. For example, the company predicted 3.7 and 5.3 million subscribers by the ends of 2006 and 2007, respectively, compared to 4.1 million and 5 million for these years using the modeling approach proposed here. Although we do not have information on how Sirius generated its numbers, the fact that our forecasts and theirs are in the same ballpark is encouraging.

Table 6.5 integrates all these elements. The second and third columns of the table give the total number of subscribers each firm actually achieved in the four years following the announcement of the Stern deal, as per their annual reports. The next two columns are the forecasted subscriber numbers—for XM based on the competitive diffusion model and for Sirius based on the company's predictions (we present these for Sirius as they are the ones relevant for Stern's bonus triggers and thus important for assessing the deal). The subsequent two columns give us the difference between the actual and forecasted number of subscribers, and the last pair of columns calculate the net positive change (if any) in additional subscribers from the previous year for each company. Put differently, the last two columns capture by how much the gap between the actual and forecasted number of subscribers further positively widened each year, representing the "Stern-generated" new subscribers in the period. What we see is quite intriguing: while Sirius surely gained more subscribers than it otherwise would have for three consecutive years, XM also seems to have fared well during this period, and much of the jump in subscriptions took place during 2005, the year Stern heavily promoted his upcoming move to satellite radio. It further seems that by 2008, Stern was not responsible for adding new Sirius subscribers, and 2008 is a year that should be treated with extra caution anyway, as we will explain in a bit.

Combining tables 6.4 and 6.5, we can evaluate by how much Sirius's innovation equity increased as a result of the Stern effect. Applying the principles of CLV analysis from chapter 2, we get that each new Sirius subscriber was worth $234 (for 2005), $263 (for 2006), and $242 (for 2007). If we assume that Sirius incurred minimal acquisition costs on Stern-generated customers, we can multiply the net additional subscribers (last column of table 6.5) by the corresponding year's CLV (discounted properly so that everything is in 2005 dollar terms) and sum up. The result is a net innovation equity increase of close to $700 million ($692 million, to be exact).[2] Taking the net present value of all the payouts Sirius would need to incur for honoring the five-year deal (including the stock options that were granted) yields an expenditure of a little more than $650 million ($654 million, to be exact). All in all, the deal seems to be pretty much "on the money." And while a $38 million return on a $654 million investment (in net present value terms) may not be cause for widespread celebration, we must not forget that Sirius was in a dire situation relative to XM prior to the deal's announcement; convincing Stern to set up his media kingdom at Sirius's studios undoubtedly helped Sirius turn that around.

If You Can't Beat 'Em, Join 'Em

Judging by the acceleration of innovation diffusion witnessed during the 2005–2007 time frame, one might conclude that Stern coming on board the Sirius ship was indeed a "watershed event," as proclaimed by Sirius's CEO shortly after the signing. But that would ignore the competitive ripple effects that accompanied the whole Stern affair. First, as mentioned before, XM intensified its marketing activity considerably in order not to lose the battle over new adopters. From Sirius's vantage point, it was only a matter of time before the pool of devout Stern followers would be exhausted, and his impact on wooing other consumers was waning quickly by 2008. Sooner or later Sirius would have to pump more money into marketing as well. Second, and quite importantly, keeping customers satisfied and attracting new ones depended heavily on lining up desirable programming portfolios, beyond music and beyond Stern. However, with both firms vying to secure exclusive deals with the same entities, and with

Stern's contract serving as a benchmark, those deals got ever more expensive. The artists, personalities, and sports league executives realized they could play the two satellite radio firms to see which of them would bid the most for their services or for transmission rights. At XM, programming and content costs skyrocketed from under $33 million in 2004 to well above $180 million in 2007 (e.g., the Major League Baseball deal cost XM nearly $60 million annually, and Oprah Winfrey's show cost close to $20 million a year). At Sirius the situation was not much better, especially with Stern's contract on the books. Programming costs escalated from roughly $63 million in 2004 to $236 million in 2007, and 2006 was an especially rough year with Stern's stock option payouts causing the programming costs to exceed the $520 million mark.

Neither firm had anticipated that competitive dynamics would drive up programming costs so precipitously. If anything, these costs were supposed to have stabilized after a few years and then be spread over the growing customer base. Furthermore, in 2007 it seemed as though both companies were locked in at the $12.95 per month price point, each reluctant to raise subscription fees unilaterally for fear of losing the acquisition battle or ceding the retention battle to churn and disadoption. As the companies had other major expenses, such as planned satellite maintenance and replacement, hefty net losses became unavoidable. At XM, for four straight years, net losses exceeded $640 million, while at Sirius net losses were well above $550 million each year (almost double that in 2006 alone). The future looked bleak. The intense rivalry between the two firms was driving their satellite services into the ground (pun intended). To investors and company officials, there seemed to be only one way out: merge!

In 2007, details began surfacing of what a proposed "merger of equals" between the two companies would look like. Mel Karmazin, Sirius's CEO at the time, would be the CEO of the merged company, while Gary Parsons from XM would serve as chairman of the board. Many industry analysts were skeptical the merger would be approved. There were two daunting hurdles to clear: the FCC and the Justice Department. When the FCC issued the satellite radio licenses back in 1997, it stipulated that "one licensee will not be permitted to acquire control of the other remaining one." Obviously this was intended to avoid a monopoly from forming. So for the merger to go through, the FCC would effectively have to repeal its own rule. Concerns over monopolistic practices that could hurt consumers fell under the purview of the Justice Department, which would have to be convinced that the deal did not violate antitrust laws. In their defense, Sirius and XM managers argued that the relevant competitive landscape was far broader than just the two of them and that it had greatly evolved over the decade since the licenses were granted. Aside from free traditional AM-FM radio, Karmazin and his XM counterpart argued that they were now also facing competition from other forms of digital and mobile entertainment, including iPods, smartphones, tablets, and streaming Internet services—categories predicted to explode going forward. The companies further argued that by merging, they would actually offer customers better value, since the content on both services would become readily available with only one subscription.[3] Implicitly, merging would also allow them to obtain content at more reasonable costs and perhaps pass on the savings to customers. At any rate, if the dire business situation they faced caused one of the firms to go under, the end result would be a single satellite radio service.

After a lengthy, fifty-seven-week review process, the Justice Department bought these arguments and approved the merger. The FCC took another seventeen weeks beyond that and, in a historic three-to-two vote, approved the merger under a few conditions, the most notable of which was a three-year freeze on subscription prices. With the hurdles cleared, XM stock ceased trading on July 28, 2008, and SiriusXM became the name of the new company.[4] Programming was merged in November of that year, and the first receivers to play both Sirius and XM audio became available for purchase within a few months.

Postmerger Postscript

The merger in mid-2008 came just as a rough patch in the US economy was setting in. The global economic recession caused many consumers to tighten their spending belts, and satellite radio was seen as an expendable luxury for some. Moreover, the automobile sector was hit especially hard over the next year, which was bad news for SiriusXM, as much of its customer acquisition was tied to new vehicle sales. Indeed, net new subscriptions took a nosedive in 2009. Nonetheless, the enormous savings effected by the merger seemed to be doing the trick. Analysts estimated, for instance, that after the merger, any original content deals were negotiated at much lower rates than before, on the order of 50 percent lower. Acquisition costs per subscriber declined to $64 that year, and marketing expenses for the company were certainly lower than the combined total for the two firms prior to the merger. SiriusXM managed to finish 2009 with the first-ever net profit in the satellite radio category! Still, the company needed more cash to continue its operations. Liberty Media Corporation, noting positive fundamentals of the now-solo player, stepped in with the necessary funds.

Liberty Media's bet paid off. The economy, and particularly car sales, began rebounding in 2010, and along with them, new subscriptions. That same year, SiriusXM and Howard Stern negotiated a five-year extension that would last into 2015. Although the company had to pay top dollar to retain the services of the prized show host, who was still regarded the most popular figure in radio, the terms were more favorable: $80 million annually and no stocks. In an interesting twist, and with his contract extension settled, Stern made no bones about expressing his belief that he was owed money on the previous contract. His claim was that his popularity played an integral role in helping Sirius merge with XM. Therefore, according to his logic, the XM customers that became part of the company should be counted toward his stock bonus for exceeding subscriber targets. SiriusXM saw things differently, arguing that the bonus triggers were "only relevant for Sirius subscribers." Stern filed a $300+ million lawsuit over the matter. The judge sided with SiriusXM and dismissed the claim.[5] Stern appealed and lost again in 2013. The legal ruling seemed to suggest that linking the roughly ten million XM subscribers who became SiriusXM customers overnight in July 2008 to Stern's pull was a stretch. However, as we have seen in table 6.5, it does appear at least somewhat plausible that Stern's dramatic move to satellite radio and the buzz that surrounded it lifted the diffusion ship of XM prior to the merger (even taking into account XM's increased marketing budget). Stern might have a case that he helped XM bring in customers that it would otherwise not have obtained, and hence when XM joined forces with Sirius, he should be rewarded for those additional adopters. You be the judge of that!

In mid-2011, when the freeze on subscription fees expired, SiriusXM quickly exercised its right and increased the monthly fee to $14.49, roughly $18 more per year per subscriber. The company predicted there would be no noticeable effect on attrition or acquisition costs, as the value of the service justified the new price.[6] And it was right: attrition continued to hover around 1.8–1.9 percent a month, and subscriber acquisition costs continued to steadily drop to $50 by 2013. Another modest price increase ($0.50 a month) was implemented in early 2014.

We're confident the SiriusXM saga will continue to generate juicy stories well past 2014: more potential price hikes loom, and in December 2015 Stern's contract was renewed for an additional five years (and who knows what else might happen). It is worth bearing in mind that it would be entirely feasible to use the innovation equity framework at any of these business junctures to evaluate the financial implications. One would have to take the existing customer base as already acquired, play out adoption dynamics according to the diffusion model,[7] and apply the CLV model (with parameters that are now well-grounded in past data).

Key Takeaways

- Often, more than one firm launches a version of an innovation into the category. This introduces a set of competitive and customer dynamics that affect the process by which the innovation diffuses and bear on each firm's innovation equity.

- There are a number of simple ways to capture the implications of having multiple firms vying for the business of new adopters. One approach assumes a single diffusion process occurring at the category level, with each firm receiving a share of new adoptions based on its relative appeal. Another approach assumes separate diffusion processes for each firm yet has them compete for new customers from a common pool of potential adopters.

- With competition there can be two types of social forces: within brand and cross brand. In the within-brand case, the influence of existing customers of a particular brand results in potential adopters purchasing that same brand (much like in the basic diffusion model). In the cross-brand case, the influence of existing customers of a particular brand results in potential adopters purchasing a competing brand.

- Under competition, it can be important to account for what happens if a customer leaves the firm and is not retained. When a departing customer switches from one brand to a rival brand, this is called churn; when a departing customer no longer participates in the category, this is called disadoption. The rate at which the firm loses customers in each period to both churn and disadoption is called the *attrition rate*. This rate should correspond to the attrition rate used in the customer lifetime value model (and which is the complement of the retention rate).

- The competitive diffusion model presented in this chapter allows taking into account the effects of the various social forces, and those of churn and disadoption, on the evolution of a firm's customer base when it faces rivalry in the same innovation category.

- The competitive diffusion model can be connected to a host of market phenomena involving rivalry: the faster initial growth rates that entrants exhibit
relative to what incumbents experienced; the effectiveness of building a sizable
customer base early through seeding programs; and how piracy, the supplying
of illegal and free versions of an innovation or new content, can benefit the
original producing firm.

Leaping Ahead to Valuing the Next Generation

Forecasting is very difficult, especially about the future. —Mark Twain

"**M**usic makes the world go 'round." That saying has been true for centuries if not millennia. Human beings' passion for listening, singing, and dancing to music has resulted in a plethora of musical genres and instruments that vary across cultures and that have evolved over time.

Most people today take for granted that until quite recently, music could only be enjoyed live. One or more artists, professional or amateur, had to be playing or singing in the moment and in person in order for the audience to experience the pleasures of music. Only in the last 140 years has this fundamental live aspect of music changed. The advent of the phonograph in 1877, which allowed recording actual sounds and then playing them back at a later time, marked the birth of an entirely new category: recorded music (and recorded sound, more generally, of course).

Yet as the second millennium came to a close, hardly anyone was still listening to music played on phonographs. Recorded music wasn't dead by any means—it was alive and healthy—but it had gone through multiple metamorphoses, or technological *generations*, as we like to call them in the world of innovations. For example, by 1998, several generations later, chances are that most people were listening to compact discs, or CDs, on their CD players.

Why single out that year? Because that was the year another metamorphosis was making its debut: the first MP3 players were launched into the marketplace. MP3 was a digital music coding format that was touted as enabling the next generation of players in the recorded music category.

Consider a consultant to Diamond Multimedia, a company that in 1998 was about to introduce one of the first portable MP3 players, the Rio

PMP300, who was tasked with predicting sales of this new device. As a starting point, the consultant might focus on trying to forecast the growth trajectory of the entire class of portable MP3 players, recognizing that more companies were bound to launch devices that used the new format to play music. How should the consultant go about accomplishing this forecasting task? "Use the diffusion parameters of past innovations," you might suggest—and indeed that sounds like sensible advice, to which the consultant might quickly reply, "Which ones?" The CD player comes to mind, no doubt. After all, it belongs to the same product category. But two issues might give the consultant pause upon contemplating the use of that innovation to help forecast the growth trajectory of MP3 players. First, CD players were launched back in the early 1980s—so almost two decades had gone by—and the question is whether the adoption forces and market potential were still relevant. Second, it was far from clear that CD players had stopped diffusing by 1998; on the contrary, the consultant takes a look at CD player sales and notices that they are still going strong. The consultant seeks help on whether applying portable CD player diffusion information to the MP3 context is "legit" and how to handle the fact that there would be a period of a few years where the two music player generations were concurrently on the market.

A Trip Down Memory Lane: Generation after Generation of Portable Music Innovation

The need for a device that would play recorded music, especially a portable one, existed well before the first Walkman appeared in Japan in 1979—an innovation that apparently owes its genesis to pressure from Sony's chairman at the time, who wanted to hear his favorite operas during frequent plane trips. In fact, as early as the 1920s, gramophones were used not only in homes but also at picnics and other outdoor activities. In the classic film *Out of Africa*, set around World War I, when Karen Blixen (played by Meryl Streep) hears prerecorded music for the first time on her farm, she discovers Denys Finch Hatton (played by Robert Redford) operating a gramophone: "Look, they finally made a machine that's really useful!" he says.

As we noted already, the first practical device that could play recorded music was the phonograph, which was invented in 1877 by Thomas Edison and used a metal spinning cylinder. The recording phonograph had a mouthpiece, and when one would speak or sing into it, the sound vibrations were indented onto a metal cylinder by the recording needle. A playback needle could then trace the grooves made on the cylinder as it spun and re-create the previously recorded sounds. Edison was beside himself when he was able to record and then listen to his voice singing "Mary Had a Little Lamb." His invention ushered in a new industry for the sale of sound recordings, and the cylinder was the main format used for about twenty-five to thirty years. The gramophone, mentioned in connection with Meryl Streep's movie scene, was introduced in the late 1880s and used a disc apparatus instead of a cylinder. An early "standards war" between the two modes erupted. Making matters even more unsettled, there was no universally accepted speed for the turntable to spin at (measured in number of revolutions per minute, or RPMs). In the end, and despite Edison's considerable reputation and aggressive push, by the mid-1910s, the gramophone disc (at 78 RPM) won the war.

Gramophones satisfied consumers' portable music needs to a certain extent: they reproduced music and were manually operated; one had to turn a crank for the apparatus to start revolving, so no additional power source was required. However, the device was rather large, the sound was metallic, and the scratchy noises that often accompanied playback as the needle passed through the disc's grooves was not a welcome feature. (Much later, DJs popularized the practice of scratching vinyl records in club settings, but as an added sound effect and not as part of the main playback.)

An electric version of the gramophone, which did not require physical effort, was introduced in the 1940s, and advances in recording technology brought mono and stereo music systems with better sound quality. Yet as far as portable devices that could produce recorded music were concerned, there was no real alternative to mechanical gramophones until the late 1950s, when battery-operated transistor radios appeared on the scene, which were small and light enough to carry around. Things took a dramatic turn when cassette players, which used a magnetic strip, were introduced in the mid-1960s and served as precursors to Sony's legendary Walkman—the first personal version of compact cassette players introduced in the 1970s. Then came the digital technologies: portable CD players in the early 1980s and MP3 players, like the Rio PMP300, in the late 1990s.

We should obviously point out that while all of these innovations are linked to the "portable music" category, they are by no means perfect substitutes for one another. That is to say, there was no fixed set of attributes that each subsequent innovation improved upon. Often a successive generation delivered additional benefits not found before, thereby complementing its predecessors on certain dimensions. In other cases, a new generation product was actually lacking in a few characteristics, and that required making trade-offs, or caused consumers to hold on to multiple generations. For example, radio could play music (prerecorded as well as captured live) but not "on demand," as the broadcast station decided what and when to air content. On the other hand, radio provided news and other forms of entertainment. Even seemingly closer substitutes, such as cassette players and CD players, differed on some important attributes: while CDs delivered better quality sound and were typically more durable than tapes, it was not as easy to copy music from disc to disc as it was to do so with cassettes.

The historical perspective we have provided on the recorded music industry at large and the portable aspects of it in particular is by no means exhaustive. Admittedly, we've omitted many twists and turns that transpired, and our sincere apologies go out to anyone and for any phase that we neglected to mention. Our modest aim was to provide a sense that MP3 players came on the heels of previous music player innovations, each of which enjoyed its "golden era" of commercial success. Inevitably, though, a newer generation came along and supplanted the previous one. What remains unanswered is just how quickly the transition across successive generations occurred and whether or not there was any regularity to it from generation to generation.

To address this matter, it is instructive to roll ahead the calendar by a decade and examine the unit sales patterns of portable CD and MP3 players. It is apparent from figure 7.1a that when MP3 players were first introduced in the late 1990s, CD player sales had not yet peaked; this peak occurred a few years later, in 2000–2001, after which portable CD player sales began declining rather rapidly. Concomitantly, MP3 player sales began to climb, but only in 2004 did they start to take off and exhibit rapid growth. Note that as the changing of the guard from CD to MP3 was taking place, the category as a whole, which is the summation of CD and MP3 player sales, grew rather nicely through 2008, as seen in figure 7.1b.

These observations bring up an important set of points worth highlighting. Two processes are at play here: the continued diffusion of the category as a whole—in our case, the growth of portable music players as depicted in figure 7.1b—and the *substitution pattern* between successive

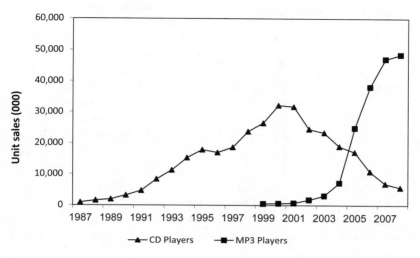

FIGURE 7.1A. Sales of two successive generations of portable music players (CD and MP3)

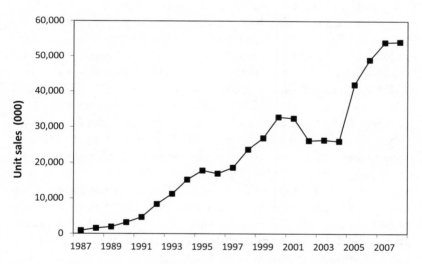

FIGURE 7.1B. Total category sales of portable music players (sum of CD and MP3 player sales)

generations within the same category, portable CD players and portable MP3 players, as depicted in figure 7.1a. It is frequently the case that the category itself will grow following the introduction of a next-generation innovation, with the previous generation initially continuing to grow and then declining rather rapidly as the newer generation overtakes it.

Another point worth noting is that there is sometimes a temporary flattening or even a drop in total category sales for a short period—in this case, occurring between 2002 and 2004. The culprit is oftentimes a customer wait-and-see stance, which results in a delay in making purchase decisions. Five to six years after they began selling, the majority of consumers were already aware of MP3 players yet were hesitant to buy them because they were waiting to see if the new format would catch on. Furthermore, most had amassed large libraries of CDs—at no small cost, mind you—which would have to be replaced to take advantage of the new technology. However, many were beginning to sense the winds of change, realizing that the CD might be a dying technology and hence were not purchasing CD players. This wait-and-see stance led to a drop in category sales across those three years from the 2001 level. Yet by 2008, as consumer uncertainty resolved and MP3 player sales eventually took off, category sales reached new heights.

Upon further review, figure 7.1b might trigger memories of a similar sales trajectory encountered earlier in this book—namely, the "saddle." The phenomenon here, however, is different in nature from the one discussed in chapter 4. There, the dip in sales emerged because a single innovation was diffusing at differing speeds across two relatively distinct segments of the population—early market adopters ("innovation forwards") and mainstream adopters ("innovation moderates"). Here, MP3 player sales in isolation do not exhibit a saddle pattern between 2001 and 2005. Rather, it is the category as a whole—the sum of portable CD and MP3 player sales—that exhibits this property. To reiterate why the phenomenon occurs, note that in the case of two successive generations that have overlapping periods of diffusion, the rapid decline in sales of the former generation (CD players) is due to the fact that consumers are cognizant that the aging technology is likely on its way out and hesitate to invest in it (and this generation might have already passed its peak of adoptions anyway) while at the same time delaying purchase of the next generation (MP3 players) that has yet to prove itself.

What Gets Passed on from Generation to Generation

Common wisdom among many industry experts, particularly in high-tech markets, is that a new generation diffuses in the market much faster than its predecessors in the category did. It is not uncommon to hear public

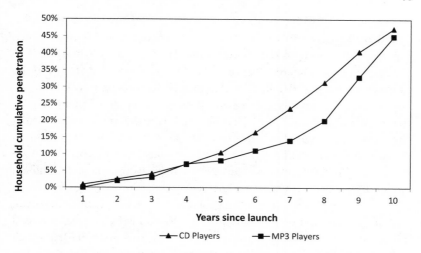

FIGURE 7.2. Household cumulative penetration levels of CD and MP3 players

remarks to this effect, such as the following statement by a UK analyst on the sales of DVD (digital video disc) players several years after their appearance: "This level has been achieved in eight years, substantially quicker than the 20 years it took VCRs to reach this point." On its face, this statement appears to have validity not only for successive generations in the video recording and playback category but for others as well. Indeed, if you look back at figure 7.1a, it appears that portable MP3 player sales took off faster than CD player sales. It took about twelve years for CD players to reach sales of twenty-five million units, while MP3 players reached that same level of unit sales after only six years.

A different picture emerges, however, if you look at *penetration* levels instead of sales levels. Let us elaborate what we mean by that. The penetration level of an innovation refers to the share or percentage of the total relevant population that adopts it at a certain time. In our basic diffusion model terminology, it is the number of new adopters of the innovation in a given time period divided by the innovation's long-run market potential. The *cumulative penetration level* would then refer to the percentage of the total market potential that has already adopted by a certain point in time. Figure 7.2 shows the US household *cumulative penetration* figures for the portable music players we have been studying—that is, the percentage of all US households that had at least one CD player or one MP3 player (by any member of the family) after a given number of years postlaunch. To be able to compare the penetration trajectories of the two generations, note that the horizontal axis in figure 7.2 refers to the first ten years each generation has been on the market—namely, from 1987 to 1997 for CD players and from 1998 to 2008 for MP3 players. From the patterns in the figure, it is evident, and quite remarkable, that there is relatively little variation in the growth pattern of the two products. If at all, CD players penetrated at a slightly faster clip. Thus while it is true that more portable MP3 players sold (per figure 7.1a when comparing corresponding periods), there was also growth in the number of US households (e.g., in 1990 there were about 90 million households, but by 2005 there were almost 110 million households; an increase of over 20 percent).

Another striking point that can be gleaned from this figure is that even for highly successful innovations such as CD and MP3 players, it took a full decade before roughly 50 percent of the long-run target market, which in both generations was taken as the total number of US households, bought into the innovation and adopted the product.

The fact that there is little or no acceleration in penetration levels when comparing successive technology generations was reported in several academic studies on the subject and across a diverse set of industries. As yet another example of this phenomenon, consider the home video games category, which has been mentioned in several places in this book. There are now eight distinct video game console generations, beginning with the Atari 2600, which literally created the category back in 1977, all the way to the PlayStation 4 (PS4), Xbox One, and Wii U, which make up the eighth generation launched in the 2012–2013 time frame. Figure 7.3 depicts the unit sales of three successive generations of video games consoles (all brands) in the United States over a fifteen-year period (between 1989 and 2004). These generations fall somewhere in the middle of the spectrum, representing the fourth, fifth, and sixth installments in the sequence. The "bit" nomenclature in the labels refers to the computer processor (known as the CPU) technology used in the consoles of each respective generation. Thus, for example, a sixteen-bit CPU handles instructions that are sixteen bits in size each. Presumably, the greater the instruction size, the more powerful the processor is and correspondingly the game console using it.

Eyeballing the unit sales graphs, it is quite clear that the growth patterns for the various generations are almost identical, despite each of them achieving a different, and sequentially greater, market potential. In fact, even in the ensuing seventh generation, which began in 2005 and included

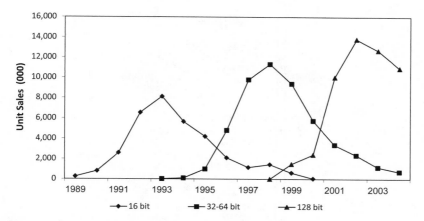

FIGURE 7.3. Unit sales of three successive generations of video game consoles in the United States

the Xbox 360, the PlayStation 3 (PS3), and the Wii, the total market potential was greater than all previous ones, reaching about 110 million units sold by the end of 2013 (and up slightly to 113 million by mid-2015).

Back to music: when revisiting the consultant's challenge of constructing a forecast for MP3 player sales, we will want to use these two insights about successive technology generations in a category: (1) the similarity they can exhibit in the speed of diffusion and (2) the possibility of differences in market potential. But before that, it will prove useful to examine a bit more closely what goes on "under the hood" of these successive-generation diffusion curves as far as customer adoption is concerned.

The Sources of Demand for Successive Innovation Generations: Newcomers, Leapfroggers, and Upgraders

When a breakthrough innovation creates an entirely new category—the first device to play recorded music, the first video game console, the first mainframe computer—we essentially have a "blank slate" as far as demand is concerned. Every adopter comes from a single pool—the pool of "new to the category" consumers. However, when a subsequent innovation follows in the category creator's footsteps (i.e., it is a next-generation iteration), things get more complex. Not one, not two, but actually three adopter "pools" form and need to be accounted for. To understand where

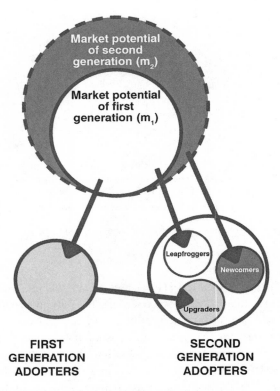

FIGURE 7.4. Sources of demand for successive innovation generations

these three adopter types originate from, please take a look at figure 7.4 and focus on the two upper circles.

The inner white circle represents the potential adopter pool relevant to the first-generation innovation that created the category—the single pool from which that innovation can draw customers. Members of this group that decide to embrace the innovation are siphoned off to the grey shaded circle of "first-generation adopters." When the second generation comes along, due to the fact that it typically introduces significant enhancements and new features—and possibly as a result of changes in the population's demographics—the set of relevant consumers typically increases beyond those that were willing to consider adopting the first generation. Hence the outer (dashed-line) shaded circle, which represents the total market potential for the second generation, is larger. Notice that the first-generation market potential circle is "embedded" in that of the second-generation circle and that a separate circle captures adopters of the first generation, and this helps visualize the three sources of demand for a next generation, also known as *newcomers, leapfroggers,* and *upgraders.*

Newcomers are those adopters that get added into the mix as a result of the category expansion effect that the second generation engenders. Not only did these consumers not adopt the first generation, but if the second generation hadn't come along, they were unlikely to ever participate in the category. In figure 7.4, newcomers originate from the area between the dashed-line and solid-line upper circles—that is, the area between the two market potentials.

Leapfroggers are those adopters who originate from a group that falls within the market potential of the first generation but who in essence "skip" that generation and go directly to the next one. In innovation-world jargon, they "leapfrog a generation." In figure 7.4, they emanate from the white, solid-line market potential circle but, importantly, have not moved to the lower-left circle of first generation adopters.

Upgraders are those adopters who actually embraced the first-generation innovation yet are swayed to switch to the next generation. In figure 7.4, they originate from the lower-left circle of first generation adopters (and were formerly part of the first generation's market potential circle).

Upgrading and leapfrogging can introduce *cannibalization* into the next-generation picture. In the case of a product or service that generates one-time revenues upon acquisition, such as the purchase of a durable good, upgrading typically results in a positive outcome for the firm, as it gets to earn profits twice on the same customer. In the case of a product or service that yields recurring revenues to the firm, such as a repeat-purchase consumer packaged good or a financial service, when a customer upgrades, he or she ceases buying the old generation and starts paying for the new one; the next-generation thus cuts into the previous generation's revenue stream. Whether this is profitable depends in large part on the per-period profit margins the new generation attains from each customer; if those are higher than before, cannibalization is beneficial to the firm.

With leapfrogging, the customer forgoes the first generation altogether, so in the case of a one-time purchase good, the first generation is fully cannibalized in a certain sense, and the firm gets to earn only once across the generations. And as you might suspect, the sooner the next generation is launched, the less opportunity the first generation will have to capitalize on its long-run market potential: More folks will consider forgoing the first generation in favor of the newer one. In the case of recurring purchase products or services, leapfrogging is beneficial as long as customer per-period profit margins are not compromised relative to the previous generation.

When a third generation appears, things can get a bit complicated, as leapfrogging can encompass multiple groups: those in the market potential of the first or the second generation who have not yet adopted any product and move directly to the third generation and those who adopted the first generation but who skip the second generation and find themselves upgrading directly to the third. Similar patterns arise with each subsequent generation launched, although at some point past generations die out completely; they are no longer sold or supported.

It further turns out that leapfrogging is highly dependent on the technology and category in question. For example, mobile telephony, particularly in Europe, is a market where limited leapfrogging occurred. The likely reason is the nontrivial time lag across mobile technology generations—about ten years between the introduction of the first and second generations and likewise between the second and third generations. For instance, in Denmark, the first mobile telephony generation, which was analog, was introduced in 1982; the second generation, which was digital, commenced in 1992; and the third generation, digital as well, was introduced in 2003. Analog handsets were considered museum pieces by 2003, as the very last Danish subscribers (all eighteen thousand of them) who were still clinging desperately to their analog phones had upgraded to digital by 2002 (prior to the third-generation launch). Thus treating leapfrogging as minimal in mobile telephony is a good working assumption. Put differently, ten or more years for mobile phones in Europe was a sufficient period such that all those in the market potential for each generation had already adopted it by the time the next generation came along.

By contrast, when the time lag between successive generations is fairly short, expect leapfrogging to play a big role. Microsoft operating systems are a prime—and often ridiculed—example of this. Take the company's Vista operating system, which was released globally to much fanfare in early 2007, five years after the previous generation, Windows XP, was introduced. Vista was somewhat poorly received by the market, achieving disappointing sales numbers. Microsoft released its ensuing operating system, Windows 7, less than three years later in 2009 (denying that its release date had been sped up). The leapfrogging that materialized upon the introduction of Windows 7 had two manifestations, both of which are consistent with our above description of this behavior. First, most PC manufacturers continued to sell their products with the Microsoft XP operating system more than two years into the introduction of Vista, which meant that many end users still had Windows XP when Windows 7 was released. Second, when Windows 7 was publicly preannounced over a year before its launch, some of the potential Vista adopters decided to wait and not upgrade to it, thus prolonging their use of XP. To make a long story short, many consumers found themselves in a position to skip from Windows XP directly to Windows 7 and forgo the Vista generation altogether. Indeed, by April 2010, six months into its launch, Windows 7 had sold more than one hundred million copies.

At the time of writing, it appears that a similar pattern may be occurring with Windows 8, the successor to Windows 7, which was launched in late 2012. Amid mixed reactions to its appeal, a big chunk of the market seems to be willing to leapfrog over Windows 8 to the next generation. The successor, by the way, is called Windows 10 and not 9, a "name skipping" strategy that perhaps reflects Microsoft's desire to signal a big or fundamental change over the previous generation in order to attract more customers.

A Next-Generation Diffusion Model and Applications

Armed with an understanding of the demand sources for successive innovation generations, we're ready to give things a bit more structure. It's relatively straightforward to build upon the basic diffusion model presented in chapter 1, which accommodated the single innovation case, to model the case of two generations diffusing concurrently in the marketplace. We aptly call these successive generations: generation 1 (G_1) and generation 2 (G_2). A few things to pay attention to: First, the long-run market potential should be allowed to differ across generations to capture scenarios like the market expansion effect of the next generation or demographic changes in the population. Second, we probably don't want to a priori preclude the possibility that successive generations have varied rates of diffusion; hence, each generation should be allowed to have its own adoption-force parameters. Third, in setting up the social force, we have to make sure that only the relevant set of past adopters influences potential future adopters for each generation. In particular, G_1 adopters that have not yet upgraded (i.e., they're still current G_1 users) can impact the remaining G_1 potential adopters, and G_2 adopters can impact all remaining G_2 potential adopters.

With those guidelines in mind, and in accordance with figure 7.4, expression 7.1 provides a simple way to think about how to model the number of new adoptions for each generation.

EXPRESSION 7.1. The next-generation diffusion model

Generation 1: Number of new G_1 adopters in this time period =
G_1 potential customers who have not yet adopted · [Individual force G_1 +
Social force G_1 · Proportion of adoption G_1]

Generation 2: Number of new G_2 adopters in this time period =
G_2 potential customers who have not yet adopted ·
[Individual force G_2 + Social force G_2 · Proportion of adoption G_2]

Integrating these expressions with our conceptual discussion on the sources of demand, a few things are worth pointing out. "G_1 potential customers who have not yet adopted" corresponds to the remaining set of people in the upper white circle of figure 7.4 who have not yet moved out of this circle (to either generation 1 or generation 2), while "G_2 potential customers who have not yet adopted" corresponds to people in any of the three circles (the two upper and the lower left) in figure 7.4 from which an arrow leads into the "second-generation adopters" circle. Note also that the specific term for generation 1 accounts for those who decide to adopt G_1 in the period. However, as we know, there will also be a subset of past G_1 adopters who decide to upgrade to G_2. Therefore, if we want to express the *net* number of new G_1 adopters in the period (i.e., the change in the size of G_1's customer base), we need to subtract the upgraders from the generation 1 expression. The net number of new G_1 adopters, which may be negative, can then be used to calculate the "Proportion of adoption G_1," which takes into account that not everyone that adopted G_1 in the past is still relevant for generating social influence for G_1 adoption in the future (as some have upgraded to G_2). Math box 7 in the appendix formalizes these ideas and also shows how to break down G_2 adopters into the various demand sources.

One implication of the next-generation diffusion model is that it can be used in conjunction with historical data to compare the adoption forces—the p and q parameters—across successive generations to see whether they are similar or different. For example, one could first estimate the diffusion rate parameters for G_1, multiply them by a constant parameter, and plug into the diffusion expression for G_2. Then, using historical data on the diffusion of G_2, one would estimate this constant parameter (while not constraining the long-run market potential parameter m—that is, letting it be a free parameter to be estimated from the data). If the estimated constant is different than 1, it implies that the adoption forces changed from one generation to the next; otherwise, if the constant is not statistically different than 1, it implies that the rate of diffusion is similar across generations.

Such an analysis was conducted for the twelve categories featured in table 7.1. In eleven of them, encompassing thirty-seven out of the thirty-nine generations studied, the answer to the question "Was there any diffusion acceleration across successive generations?" was an emphatic "No!" Only in one product category, steel making, were the adoption-force parameters statistically greater across generations—that is, there was accelerated diffusion with each successive generation.

Table 7.1 also specifies the number of years that elapsed between the launch of each successive generation in the categories studied—also referred to as the *intergeneration time*. A commonly held belief is that intergeneration times decrease with each subsequent generation in a category. From this comprehensive study at least, such a pattern is not found on a consistent basis. Intergeneration times actually increase in five product categories (television, video game console, personal computer, rigid disk drive, and steel making). In two other categories (IBM GP computer and tire cord), there is no clear and consistent pattern across generations. For the other five categories (audio system, flexible disk drive, home entertainment, oil cracking, optical disk drive), there are data on only two generations, and thus the change in intergeneration times was not possible to ascertain at the time the study was conducted.

The steelmaking category, in which later generations did diffuse more rapidly, is also one in which several decades passed between the introduction of each successive innovation: thirty-seven years between open-hearth and electric-furnace technologies and forty-nine years between the latter and the basic oxygen method. What this seems to suggest is that if the time between two successive generations is not too long, the diffusion rate parameters (i.e., the adoption forces p and q) are likely to be fairly similar.

However, if the time lag between generations is long, then indeed one needs to exercise caution in relying on past-generation diffusion parameters for the current generation, as they may differ. This makes sense, as

TABLE 7.1 **Examining diffusion acceleration across generations in twelve product categories**

Category	Geographic scope	Generation	Year introduced	Intergeneration time	Diffusion acceleration
Audio system	US	Tape deck	1953		
	US	CD player	1983	30	No
Flexible disk drive	Global	5.25″	1976		
	Global	3.5″	1981	5	No
Home entertainment	US	VCR	1972		
	US	DVD	1997	25	No
IBM GP computer	US	650, 701–709	1955		
	US	1620, 140x, 70xx	1959	4	No
	US	360, 1130, 1800	1965	6	No
	US	370, system 3, system 7	1970	5	No
Oil cracking	US	Catalytic cracking	1938		
	US	Hydro cracking	1962	24	No
Optical disk drive	Global	CD-ROM	1985		
	Global	DVD-ROM	1996	11	No
Personal computer	US	Desktop PC kits	1975		
	US	Manufactured PC	1977	2	No
	US	App. software PC	1979	2	No
	US	IBM PC compatible	1982	3	No
	US	Hard drive home PC	1984	2	No
	US	32-bit desktop PC	1987	3	No
	US	Windows PC	1990	3	No
	US	Multimedia PC	1993	3	No
	US	Internet PC	1997	4	No
Rigid disk drive	Global	5.25″	1980		
	Global	3.5″	1983	3	No
	Global	2.5″	1988	5	No
Steel making	US	Open hearth	1868		
	US	Electric furnace	1905	37	Yes
	US	Basic oxygen	1954	49	Yes
Television	US	Electronic black and white	1939		
	US	Electronic color	1954	15	No
	US	Digital	1998	44	No
Tire cord	US	Cotton	1910		
	US	Rayon	1938	28	No
	US	Nylon	1947	9	No
	US	Polyester	1962	15	No
Video game console	US	16-bit machines	1989		
	US	32–64-bit machines	1993	4	No
	US	128-bit machines	1999	6	No

the longer the time gap between each successive generation, the more contextual factors may have evolved in the interim: new ways to communicate (for both firms with consumers and consumers among themselves, such as digital social media), changes in socioeconomic factors in a country (greater or lower gross domestic product, or higher or lower per-capita disposable income levels), regulatory changes, cultural taste shifts in the population, and so on, all of which can have an impact on the adoption forces. The more time that elapses, the less "stable" the parameters across generations may be, which is why only making comparisons between two *successive* generations (one that comes on the heels of the other) is recommended. Further, there seems to be some "macrolevel" evidence that entirely new technology classes—in effect, the first generation of a category—that were launched in the latter part of the twentieth century (such as the Internet and PC) are diffusing more rapidly than entirely new technologies launched at the beginning of the twentieth century did (such as the automobile); one hundred years is a long time indeed.

An additional aspect of the study summarized in table 7.1 is that it encompassed both US-only data and, in three instances, global data, so the conclusions seem quite universal. To examine global robustness at a more granular, country-by-country level, let's revisit the mobile phone category mentioned earlier in connection with leapfrogging behavior (and the lack thereof in Europe).

Table 7.2 presents information on twenty-eight countries with respect to two generations of mobile telephony technologies. Applying a similar empirical analysis to that described in connection with table 7.1 reveals that for all twenty-eight countries, there is no statistically significant acceleration. The diffusion rate adoption forces remained relatively unchanged across the two successive mobile generations in North America, South America, Europe, the Middle East, and all the way to the Far East. What makes this finding even more remarkable is that the long-run market potentials estimated from the data were found to differ widely across generations in all the countries studied (compare columns 3 and 5 in table 7.2). While digital mobile phone technology certainly expanded the market, it diffused at the same pace as its analog counterpart in the previous generation.

It is important to stress that because the long-run market potentials expanded so dramatically from one generation to the next in all countries while the adoption force parameters remained fairly unchanged, we would expect to see many more unit sales in the next generation relative

TABLE 7.2 **Two generations of mobile telephony in selected countries**

Country	G1 (analog) year of introduction	G1 market potential in millions of subscribers	G2 (digital) year of introduction	G2 market potential in millions of subscribers
Australia	1987	2.36	1993	23.1
Austria	1990	0.33	1994	8.3
Belgium	1987	0.05	1994	8.3
Chile	1991	0.38	1997	15.8
Denmark	1982	0.30	1992	5.4
Finland	1982	0.70	1992	5.1
France	1985	0.40	1992	44.3
Germany	1985	0.77	1992	67.3
Hungary	1990	0.11	1994	8.5
Indonesia	1988	0.12	1994	79.9
Ireland	1986	0.19	1993	4.0
Israel	1987	1.10	1994	7.5
Italy	1990	4.90	1993	66.1
Korea	1984	1.80	1996	38.7
Malaysia	1985	0.84	1994	30.0
Netherlands	1985	0.27	1994	14.7
New Zealand	1987	0.91	1993	4.7
Norway	1981	0.53	1993	4.6
Philippines	1990	1.10	1994	36.4
Poland	1992	0.12	1996	40.0
Portugal	1989	0.02	1992	10.4
Puerto Rico	1986	0.64	1995	2.1
Saudi Arabia	1985	0.02	1996	29.9
Singapore	1988	0.14	1994	5.7
Spain	1990	1.20	1995	39.2
Sweden	1982	0.98	1992	9.8
Switzerland	1988	0.26	1993	6.2
UK	1985	3.10	1992	63.5
Average	1987	0.84	1994	24.3

to its predecessor when comparing corresponding year-by-year data post-launch. However, the cumulative penetration levels (percentage of the long-term potential that adopts) will exhibit a fairly close resemblance, as will the general shape of the penetration diffusion curves.

Music to a Forecaster's Ears

As Mark Twain eloquently put it—per his quote that opens this chapter—forecasting is difficult. The nuance in his statement, and why it undoubtedly raises a chuckle or at least a smile, is that he reinforces just how challenging forecasting is by adding "especially about the future," as if suggesting that somehow there is such a thing as forecasting the present or the past. Smiles and chuckles aside, in some sense, there *is* such a thing as "forecasting the past": the concepts, models, analysis, and robust evidence presented in this chapter point to the fact that "forecasting" the past—in other words, studying past innovations carefully and quantifying their diffusion patterns—can certainly help in forecasting the future. And this is particularly true in the context of successive generations within the same category. Estimating the adoption force parameters of a previous generation should be considered highly relevant to predicting the diffusion trajectory of the next generation. The part that is a bit more difficult, and the evidence bears Twain out on this, is that the long-run market potential (m) may not be tightly linked to the previous generation's market potential. More often than not, there is a newcomer expansion effect— due not only to demographics (population changes) but also to the inclusion of people who were around but weren't part of the target market for the previous generation, possibly because the next generation is a considerable improvement over the previous generation in performance, added benefits, or convenience and ease of use.

These conclusions should be music to the ears of the consultant trying to forecast the sales of portable MP3 players from the late 1990s onwards. Of course, he or she did not have the data we showed earlier on the first decade of MP3 player unit sales (figure 7.2) at his or her disposal (the whole point of forecasting the future); however, the guidelines for the approach to take are well grounded. There appears to be ample support for creating a forecast of MP3 player penetration using the historical data that were available in 1998 on the penetration of the previous generation in the category. Specifically, the consultant can take the estimated portable CD player p and q basic diffusion model parameters and apply them to the MP3 player case. As for the long-run market potential (m), the consultant can take the portable CD player value as a starting point but is strongly advised, especially for a category that has general consumer appeal, to check for changes in demographics and to conduct further market research to examine whether there will be a sizable market expansion effect—for example, by showing early prototypes of MP3 players to consumers and understanding how likely they would be to consider adopting them. In addition, optimistic and pessimistic scenarios for the market potential may be crafted based on how the main barriers to adoption are expected to get resolved. For example, at the time there was a big debate on how widely digital music content would be made available by copyright holders and at what price. The optimistic scenario would assume all songs would be made available at relatively low prices; the reverse would be true for the pessimistic case.

Customer (after) Lifetime Values

At this point you may be wondering about all the other aspects of the innovation equity framework—namely, the customer management part of the story. Are there are any regularities or patterns with respect to the customer lifetime value (CLV) parameters in the context of successive generations? Unfortunately, we are not aware of any meaningful study that has shed conclusive light on this question. Clearly, if the successive innovation is in a one-time purchase category, where each customer buys the new generation in question at the point of adoption and there are no ensuing revenue streams, then assessing how the price of the good will evolve over time and having a handle on the discount rate will go a long way toward projecting innovation equity. In these cases, attrition rate is less critical to understand, as customers pay all their dues upon acquisition. In other scenarios—for example, services that entail recurring monthly fees—firms may look at metrics from past generations, such as the attrition rate, per-period revenues or margins, and so on, to have a starting point and adjust from there.

   As an example, in the home video game market, attrition is not a big issue given the typical intergeneration times of five to eight years (and most gamers hang on to and use their consoles during this time frame, so disadoption until the next generation arrives is not a prevalent phenomenon). However, the business model of a console maker is largely predicated on the margins or royalties earned from the sale of game titles over time. A common metric used to gauge how successful a firm is at generating revenues from an acquired customer in this industry is the *tie ratio*. This quantity is the number of game titles sold for the console system divided by the total number of systems sold up until that point. In other words, it captures how many games, on average, each gamer buys for his or her console. The number typically grows during the generation's lifespan, as most gamers keep adding new games to their collection. Table 7.3 provides tie ratios for two recent console generations, the sixth and seventh, spanning the 2000 through the mid-2015 time frame.

   As can be seen, the tie ratios are quite similar across these two generations for each of the console makers, both in the United States and globally,

TABLE 7.3 **Tie ratios for two console generations (as of July 2015)***

Generation 6			Generation 7		
	North America	Global		North America	Global
Xbox (Microsoft)	12.16	11.01	Xbox 360 (Microsoft)	11.87	11.28
PS2 (Sony)	12.27	10.54	PS3 (Sony)	12.76	10.63
GameCube (Nintendo)	10.76	9.60	Wii (Nintendo)	10.97	9.33

* Tie ratio = the number of software game titles sold per console.

suggesting that once a customer is acquired in the sense that he or she purchases a console of a given brand, he or she is likely to buy the same number of games over the time span that he or she keeps playing with the system. And although in mid-2015, generation 7 (G7) was still "alive," as owners of that generation's consoles could still buy games for their machines and decide to delay or not upgrade to generation 8 (G8) consoles that were all launched by late 2013, it is hard to imagine the tie ratios for G7 going up by much. Very few new games were being released for G7 consoles, and the vast majority of new hardware sales were of the G8 kind. Indeed, by mid-2015, software sales for the Xbox One, PS4, and Wii U were outpacing sales of the corresponding previous-generation consoles. Looking specifically at the Wii probably gives a good indication that tie ratios for G7 had stabilized, as its successor, the Wii U, was the first G8 game console to be introduced in late 2012. Industry data show that between March 2014 and July 2015, the Wii's tie ratio changed by less than 3 percent.

Pulling all this information together, for someone in early 2014 interested in assessing the innovation equity of a G8 console, a possible approach could be as follows: (1) For the diffusion modeling aspects, use the adoption force parameters (p and q) from G7. Take the long-run market potential achieved in G7 for the category and incorporate any demographic changes as well as run a survey to assess the possibility of a market expansion effect (for m). Plug G7 and G8 parameters into the next-generation diffusion model (expression 7.1). (2) For the per-period profit metrics, on the hardware side, use the price of the console in question at launch and the previous generation's pricing dynamics, along with analyst estimates of production costs; on the software side, use the G7 game titles-to-consoles tie ratio (data are available yearly, or one can just assume a linear growth rate for the tie ratio over the expected course of the generation), and combine that with the typical per-game royalty (about 15 percent for games costing around $50–$60). A reasonable discount rate to use would be 7.67 percent (based on public sources for the entertainment technology sector), and the average intergeneration time is about seven years.

The only tricky part in forming this G8 innovation equity assessment, which lies somewhere between steps 1 and 2, is to predict the share of adopters that would land in the customer base of each console brand. One would probably need to supplement the known benchmark market shares achieved for G7 with information on how the new generation consoles differ from one another and how customers value these differences. A host of market research tools exist to perform this task, and we discuss several of them in chapter 9.

Timing Is Everything: When Should IBM Have Introduced Its Next Mainframe System?

As an illustration of how one might use the accumulated wisdom on next-generation innovations to improve financial performance, consider the following scenario: A company has a product in the market that is selling quite well and generating sizable revenues. The company realizes, however, that at some point, it will want to introduce the next generation of the product currently on the market—to benefit from upgrading and market expansion as well as to ward off potential competitors from considering entry. What is the "right time" to launch the sequel?

The release timing of a next-generation product or service is no trivial matter, especially for technology-driven firms, and has many ramifications. In particular, R&D programs are risky and costly, so if a firm has a particular introduction date in mind, it needs to make sure the development resources (personnel, equipment, funding, management, etc.) are in place to be able to meet the expected launch date. Expediting the development time typically requires more intense, and hence costly, outlays. In addition, production has to be secured and marketing programs need to be created and ready to roll, again requiring forward planning and resources. Although much of this is true for any innovative effort, what complicates matters for selecting the introduction time of a next generation is its *interaction with the current generation*: On the one hand, you don't want to wait too long to introduce, as you could enjoy a market expansion effect and get many of the current generation adopters to upgrade sooner rather

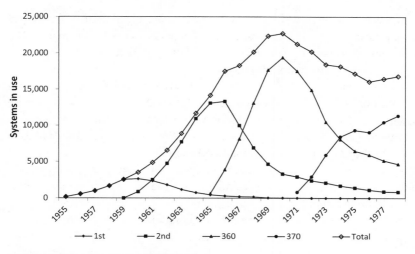

FIGURE 7.5. Four generations of IBM mainframes

than later. This incentive is all the more pronounced if the next generation yields greater customer per-period profit margins. On the other hand, you don't want to introduce the next installment too soon, as then you risk encouraging leapfrogging behavior and thereby missing out on the opportunity of making two sales to the same individual (or client in a business-to-business context).

We will demonstrate these timing considerations, and how to integrate our observations on next-generation innovations from the chapter, using the example of IBM general-purpose computers (also known as "mainframes"). Figure 7.5 depicts four IBM mainframe generations that were marketed over a twenty-five-year span in which the company enjoyed a near monopoly in the category.

We begin by briefly describing these generations, introduced at intervals of roughly every four to six years. The first generation was based on the then-state-of-the-art technology of vacuum tubes; the second was based on transistors; the third, dubbed the "360 family," included integrated circuits; the fourth, called the "370 family," was based on silicon chips. We observe in figure 7.5 both the diffusion of the category (IBM mainframes) as a whole with the top triangle-symbol curve as well as the substitution patterns among the four successive generations.

A quick note on the unit of analysis in the figure: the number of "systems in use" for a given generation is equal to the number of customers that are currently using it. This number is not the same as everyone that has ever adopted the particular generation because some of these past adopters may have upgraded to the next generation or disadopted the category. The systems-in-use number provides a good measure, therefore, at any point in time of how many people are the actual customers of each generation.

For purposes of illustration, we concentrate on two successive generations out of the four—the second and third—during the years they were diffusing (from 1965 until 1972, one year after the fourth generation was launched and began garnering demand). We will evaluate the timing at which the 360 series was released and examine the profit implications of moving the release date back by one year. Granted, this is a retrospective examination, but it will illuminate how the concepts and models presented in this chapter can come to life.

We use the next-generation diffusion model presented earlier (expression 7.1) to estimate from the data the various adoption-related parameters. For example, we find that the long-run market potential for the 360 series is roughly double what it was for the second generation (26,996 versus 13,383 clients). So the third generation in the sequence enjoyed a clear market expansion effect, enabling it to attract many newcomers. The model also allows us to separate 360 series adopters into the three sources: newcomers, upgraders from the previous generation, and leapfroggers—those in the market potential for the second generation who jumped on the third generation's bandwagon without having adopted the second.

Whether the demand for the next generation is made up of mainly newcomers, upgraders, or leapfroggers has implications with respect to its innovation equity. Newcomers represent extra demand that is not relevant for the previous generation, so the firm has an incentive to "book" these adopters as soon as possible. Upgraders and leapfroggers, on the other hand, may come with cannibalization "baggage": they were or would have been users of the old generation but instead either shift or skip to the new generation. In evaluating the net innovation equity gain from expediting the introduction of the new generation, therefore, we have to subtract revenues that would have gone to the old generation from these types. These "lost" revenues represent the opportunity cost of not delaying the introduction of the new generation.[1]

The actual introduction year of the 360 family of mainframes was 1965. What would the financial consequences have been had IBM introduced this family a year earlier, in 1964? To address this question, we use the parameters estimated from the data of the actual diffusion of the two generations and then move the starting time of the third generation a year

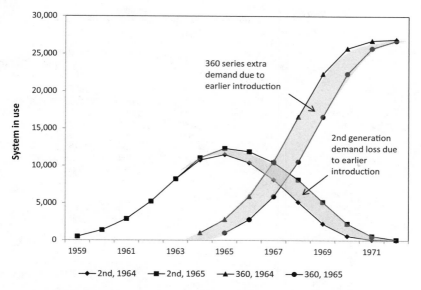

FIGURE 7.6. IBM systems-in-use with two introduction times for the 360 family*

* "2nd, 1964" denotes the growth of the second generation if the 360 series is introduced in 1964
and similarly for the rest.

back and see how this affects the innovation equity. Figure 7.6 nicely
captures the countervailing effects of this early introduction on the two
generations by allowing a comparison of the actual (1965 introduction)
and counterfactual (1964 introduction) diffusion of systems in use. The
360 family enjoys extra demand from the earlier introduction date. This
demand is depicted as the shaded area between the two curves of the 360
family. The second generation, however, achieves lower use rates because
of losing the demand it would have gotten from customers who choose
the next generation instead (leapfroggers and upgraders). This is represented by the shaded area in between the two diffusion curves of the second generation.

Tables 7.4a and b provide the numerical values upon which the diffusion curves of figure 7.6 are based. Specifically, the second column of table 7.4a details the diffusion of the 360 family if the introduction year was
1965 (original), while the third column gives the associated values if the
introduction year had been 1964. Similarly the second and third columns
of table 7.4b provide the diffusion of the second generation under the two
timing scenarios.

TABLE 7.4A **Gains from the early introduction of the 360: Impact on the 360 series**

	360 introduced in 1965	360 introduced in 1964	Difference	Gross profits per system	Value of difference
		Systems in use		USD	USD (000)
1964	–	1,026	1,026	51,240	52,564
1965	1,026	2,842	1,816	53,568	97,271
1966	2,842	5,895	3,054	55,800	170,392
1967	5,895	10,568	4,672	60,180	281,189
1968	10,568	16,594	6,026	61,248	369,097
1969	16,594	22,360	5,766	76,860	443,189
1970	22,360	25,762	3,402	92,988	316,302
1971	25,762	26,798	1,036	91,512	94,832
1972	26,798	26,971	173	80,520	13,898

TABLE 7.4B **Losses from the early introduction of the 360: Impact on the second generation**

	360 introduced in 1965	360 introduced in 1964	Difference	Gross profits per system	Value of difference
		Systems in use		USD	USD (000)
1964	11,085	10,772	313	32,940	10,297
1965	12,350	11,520	830	33,480	27,775
1966	11,913	10,409	1,504	49,104	73,830
1967	10,455	8,140	2,315	45,878	106,226
1968	8,144	5,156	2,987	43,152	128,911
1969	5,157	2,298	2,859	45,384	129,731
1970	2,298	612	1,686	46,872	79,039
1971	612	98	514	46,128	23,697
1972	98	13	86	27,084	2,318

The 360 family was a well-received addition in the marketplace. While it was higher priced, customers, which were businesses, were willing to pay for it. This is reflected in the fourth column in each table that gives the gross profit margin that IBM earned for each unit in use per year. These figures suggest that indeed IBM would have liked to get customers onto the 360 family earlier, as the gross margin on these systems is higher than for the second generation. What remains unanswered is just how much rolling back the introduction time would have been worth. The last columns in the tables help provide the answer.

Applying a relevant cost of capital (discount factor) of 15 percent to bring all the annual figures to 1964 terms, we find that the net present value

(NPV) of the total loss incurred to the second generation due to the earlier introduction of the 360 series is about $298 million, while the total gain to the 360 series is about $920 million. The difference, of about $620 million, is therefore the "innovation equity" gain that IBM would have garnered had the introduction of the 360 family been brought backward one year. To put this potential net gain into perspective, we can calculate the total value of the 360 family using the actual adoption numbers of all its systems in use (from 1965 to 1972) along with the annual gross profits per unit from table 7.4a. The resultant NPV comes out to be roughly $3 billion. Thus IBM could have earned another 21 percent in profits from the 360 family had it introduced that family a year earlier.

Although this assessment suggests that IBM could have benefited considerably from expediting the release of the 360 family, it of course does not take into account the R&D, production, and marketing challenges and expenses that would have been required to make the product ready and available for introduction sooner. In addition, the calculations assume that the annual gross profits would have stayed the same despite the earlier release, though some might argue that IBM would have had to go to market more aggressively if the introduction time had been shifted. Nonetheless, the assessment yields a fairly useful benchmark for evaluating whether to speed up or slow down the development and launch date of a next-generation product.

Listening to Twain . . . Again

History doesn't repeat itself, but it does rhyme.—Mark Twain

You should certainly not walk away from this chapter thinking that each new generation will exactly mirror its predecessor in terms of the diffusion and CLV numbers; it's a virtual certainty that it will not. The total relevant market will probably differ, often expanding from generation to generation, and the mix of demand sources (newcomers, upgraders, and leapfroggers) may change as well. Furthermore, per-period revenues, or the costs required to maintain them, and the discount factor often do not remain constant. And the more time that transpires between generations, the more it becomes conceivable that modes of communication and environmental conditions (social, economic, or political) will have changed in ways that impact innovation uptake.

Having said all that, there is evidence to support a number of generational regularities. Adoption forces, both individual and social, do tend to exhibit a likeness across successive generations, and some aspects of the business model can be fairly similar. At a minimum, the previous-generation characteristics, aside from the long-run market potential, provide a good starting point for a forecast. For those factors that are expected to change, one can conduct a market survey to modify previous-generation estimates, apply knowledge from analogous categories that recently exhibited successive generation introductions to get a sense of the adjustments needed, and complement these efforts with secondary information on demographic and socioeconomic changes. When uncertainty remains, create optimistic and conservative scenarios anchored around the previous-generation values.

Forecasting is very difficult, as Mark Twain reminded us. But he also offered a piece of advice worth listening to: it's useful to look back at history—in our case the previous generation—as some aspects do "rhyme" and are relevant for forecasting the next generation.

Key Takeaways

- Once a new category is created, over time, it is typical to observe the introduction of successive innovation generations in the category.
- While it is common wisdom that newer generations diffuse faster than older ones, research in this area suggests that often the difference between generations reflects growth in the long-run market potential rather than a fundamental change in the diffusion speed. Looking at penetration levels rather than at absolute adoption can help in comparing successive generations.
- There is typically a timing overlap between successive generations, with the previous generation still diffusing as the next generation begins garnering customers.
- A next-generation innovation can attract adopters from three demand sources: those who adopted the previous generation and are switching or adding the new one ("upgraders"), those who are part of the market potential of the previous generation but forgo it and skip directly to the next generation ("leapfroggers"), and those who are part of a new set of potential adopters in the category resulting from a market expansion effect of the next generation ("newcomers").
- The next-generation diffusion model presented in this chapter allows capturing the dynamics of multiple generations diffusing simultaneously and accounting for the various types of customer adoption behavior.

- By combining assessments of customer lifetime value and long-run market potential parameters for the next generation with knowledge of the diffusion rate (i.e., adoption force) parameters of the previous generation, the proposed model can be used to formulate innovation equity projections for successive generations.

CHAPTER EIGHT

Innovation Equity Makes the World Go 'Round

It has been said that arguing against globalization is like arguing against the laws of gravity.
—Kofi Annan (former UN secretary)

Smartphones have come up more than once in this book. We talked about their basic diffusion process, about marketing factors that could affect their commercial success, and about competitive dynamics in the category. For the most part, even if not explicitly stated, we had one market in mind—the US market. This was true for several other innovations presented as well. To be fair, we have sprinkled in other countries' cases here and there, such as in our analysis of mobile telephony in Europe. But even then, we looked at each country as a separate context when examining such issues as competition among firms and next-generation predictions. We have also on occasion presented aggregated worldwide data for innovations, as with home video games, disregarding the makeup of these data by country. Yet virtually all major innovations we can think of seem to cross borders over time, and the firms introducing them invariably seek to grow beyond their new product's initial breeding ground. Hence a single-country analysis seems a tad shortsighted and a completely aggregated outlook perhaps overly farsighted.

It is probably no big revelation, for instance, that Apple had global aspirations for its prized smartphone innovation, the iPhone. From its conception, the device was meant to be an international hit. What is less clear is how the company should have thought about, and attempted to facilitate, adoption and profitability in each of the countries the device eventually entered. The first-generation iPhone, which debuted in June 2007, was released in only a handful of countries—six, to be precise. In contrast, the second-generation iPhone 3G, which first came out in July 2008, ultimately reached more than eighty countries, by most counts. Aside from the number of countries targeted in each iPhone generation, there is a question of *why* Apple chose the specific countries it did in each instance. Moreover, regardless of which countries were selected, there is the question of *how* the rollout should have unfolded. Was it in Apple's best interest to pursue all the selected countries simultaneously and with the same marketing intensity, or was a staggered approach warranted for maximizing the business opportunity? If staggered, what should have been the order of countries or regions targeted at different times?

To be able to answer these questions, it turns out that we need to dive into a long-standing debate—one might say a debate of global proportions.

The Globalization Debate

As early as 1983, renowned Harvard Business School professor Theodore Levitt wrote a seminal paper in which he coined the term "globalization," arguing that firms should look at the world not as composed of many individual markets but rather as one big market. He posited that technology was impacting travel and communications in such a way that the world would soon be heading toward commonality among nations rather than distinctiveness. This view has certainly gained momentum over the years among academics, corporate managers, and journalists, all of whom espouse the view that the world is "converging," or becoming one flat playing field. If true, this trend toward commonality would seem to imply that companies like Apple need not differentiate among various countries when it comes to analyzing or predicting business outcomes. In particular, the commercial performance of an innovation in one country should largely mirror that of other countries.

Others, however, question the notion that the world is rapidly converging, noting that in the second decade of the twenty-first century, undistinguishable similarity still seems to be the exception rather than the rule when comparing various regions around the globe. Countries differ, often significantly, in the wealth of their populations, the average education level, the degree of competition, the infrastructure (roads, electricity, broadband, etc.), government structure, and laws and their enforcement. History and culture have a hand in creating additional dissimilarities among peoples and nations that persist to this day.

The possibility that considerable heterogeneity will manifest itself when comparing countries to one another suggests that Apple, or any company launching an innovation for that matter, needs to take these differences into account when assessing the prospects of going global. To the extent that these differences impact the diffusion pace of innovations and the effectiveness of customer management efforts, we might expect the innovation equity arising from each global location to vary as well, even after controlling for the size of the population in each country. Not one but multiple diffusion and customer lifetime value (CLV) profiles may need to be constructed. This seems like a daunting task. Where does one begin? Pack your bags, put on your hiking boots, and get ready to embark on a trip around the world to unravel the intricacies of *global* innovation equity.

Taking Innovation Equity Global

The path we will follow in our quest to provide more clarity on valuing innovations in a global context will be rather straightforward and linked directly to the main themes presented throughout the book, though we certainly hope to provide some interesting "sightseeing" of new phenomena and concepts along the way.

To be more specific, we will look at the various elements of the basic diffusion and CLV models and strive to cover two primary aspects. First, we will delve into what we know from various studies about how the parameters of these two models differ across international locations and present what seem to be useful generalizations regarding how country characteristics can help predict variations. We will explain how one can adjust the basic diffusion model to account for some of the relevant issues. Second, we will provide some practical guidance, through an illustrative example, on how to go about applying what we know to a scenario wherein an innovation moves from its home base launch pad to other countries.

Diffusion Profiles on the Global Stage

VARIABILITY IN SCALE.   We begin by examining whether to expect the long-run market potential for a given innovation (the by-now familiar parameter m), sometimes referred to as the *scale of diffusion*, to differ by country. Obviously, one immediately has to take into account the fact that, in absolute number terms, the market potential will likely be affected by a country's population size. The more interesting question, then, is whether, for a given population size, different countries will have differing long-run market potentials, and if so, what the differences can be attributed to. One might expect, for example, the average income of the population to affect the market potential, particularly for innovations that are pricey. Another issue relates to the infrastructure in place in a country or the adoption level of complementary goods and services, which are often prerequisites for consumers to be able to fully benefit from innovations. For example, the cumulative penetration level of personal computers in a country can serve as an upper limit for the number of software products and computer accessories that can be sold. In other cases, the cumulative penetration level of an enabling standard defines the market potential for a new product or service: the market potential for an Android versus iPhone application could vary depending on how well received each of these platforms is in various countries.

As noted, population sizes are typically dissimilar across countries, which is why researchers often find it more meaningful to examine the percentage of a population that is expected to ever adopt the innovation when studying innovation diffusion at the international level rather than the absolute number of long-term potential adopters. Specifically, to facilitate comparison across countries, it is common to use a "penetration ceiling" parameter, which represents the fraction of the population relevant to the innovation in question. The decision of what a priori penetration ceiling to use for a country naturally depends on the specific product or service but also on certain characteristics of the country. Research from the late 1990s that examined the growth of mobile services around the world, for example, used the following criteria in setting the penetration ceiling in each country: the percentage of the population that is literate, resides in an urban area, and has sufficient income to afford basic telephone services. Based on these criteria, the ceiling for the adoption of mobile services in countries such as the United States, the United Kingdom, and Germany was determined to be above 50 percent, while in many developing countries, it was below 10 percent. For an innovation in the telephony space launched today, almost two decades later, these ceilings would probably be different as the infrastructure and wealth of the average citizen in each of the countries in question have changed considerably. Generally speaking, research seems to indicate that the level of a country's economic development correlates strongly with the expected penetration ceiling. For instance, in a study looking at the diffusion of a number of consumer electronics (such as VCR players, CD players, fax machines, microwave ovens, and camcorders) across multiple countries, the average penetration ceiling was 52 percent for developed countries and 17 percent for developing countries. Furthermore, the study showed that a 1 percent change in a country's international trade or urbanization level is likely to increase the market penetration ceiling by about 0.5 percent and 0.2 percent, respectively.

Although having a sense of what factors can affect the penetration ceiling is helpful, and provided one knows the value of these factors in various countries it is then possible to adjust the ceiling of one country relative to another's; there's nothing like getting direct measures based on actual diffusion data. Analyzing such information can further illuminate whether globalization is indeed leading to convergence in adoption patterns or whether different locales still exhibit marked distinctness. A case in point is a study that examined the diffusion of broadband connectivity among European Organization for Economic Co-operation and Development (OECD) member countries between 2001 and 2010. The definition of broadband included technologies such as DSL, cable, fiber optics, and other wired technologies with a download speed of at least 256 kbits. Take a look at table 8.1 and focus your attention for now only on the first and last columns (we will get to the two middle columns in a bit). The study used published data on subscriptions and applied the basic diffusion model. The penetration ceiling is expressed as the number of "subscriptions per 100 inhabitants," effectively the same metric as we defined above.

One could conjecture that since all the countries in the study are in one geographic region (Europe) and members of the same economic forum, we will see little variation across them. Based on the data and its analysis, that conjecture seems off—way off. It is easy to see that while the average for these twenty countries is about twenty-seven broadband subscriptions per one hundred inhabitants, the values range from a low of fewer than twelve in Poland to a high of more than thirty-eight in the Netherlands— more than a threefold difference. It is also instructive to put these numbers into a household-level perspective, assuming each household has one broadband subscription. The average number of people in a household in the sampled countries is 2.44, so when full long-run penetration is reached, roughly 65 percent of households in these countries will have a subscription. In the Netherlands, where the average family size is only 2.1, achieving full long-run penetration would imply that 80 percent of households have adopted.

VARIABILITY IN SPEED.   How quickly innovations tend to diffuse in various countries has been a favorite topic among marketing and innovation

TABLE 8.1 **Broadband diffusion parameters for European Organization for Economic Co-operation and Development member countries**

Country	Individual force (p)	Social force (q)	Market potential (subscriptions per 100 inhabitants)
Austria	0.09	0.42	24.6
Belgium	0.13	0.18	35.4
Czech Republic	0.03	0.66	14.7
Denmark	0.05	0.83	37.5
Finland	0.04	1.20	28.5
France	0.07	0.46	34.8
Germany	0.03	0.71	33.2
Greece	0.003	1.04	20.1
Hungary	0.03	0.66	20.5
Ireland	0.02	0.82	21.3
Italy	0.08	0.49	22.7
Luxembourg	0.05	0.63	35.5
Netherlands	0.10	0.64	38.3
Norway	0.07	0.77	34.5
Poland	0.01	1.05	11.7
Portugal	0.11	0.20	23.1
Slovakia	0.01	0.84	13.0
Spain	0.07	0.51	23.8
Sweden	0.04	0.89	32.2
United Kingdom	0.06	0.66	31.3
Average	0.05	0.68	26.8

scholars. We thus have the benefit of numerous studies that allow us to compare the adoption forces, which in turn impact the speed of diffusion, by country. So as not to keep you in suspense, we will come right out and say that most of these studies reveal extensive differences. Referring again to table 8.1, concentrating this time on the second and third columns of the table, we observe one such example of this. Eyeballing the numbers in the table, it is not difficult to see that the values for the individual force (p) exhibit considerable variance between these European countries: while the average is 0.05, the values range from less than 0.01 in countries such as Greece, Poland, and Slovakia to levels greater than 0.1 in Belgium, the Netherlands, and Portugal—more than a tenfold difference! Similar heterogeneity in values can be detected when comparing the social force of adoption.

It is common to classify the factors that help explain these variances in adoption forces into three "buckets": an economic bucket, a cultural bucket, and a cross-country effect bucket. It is not difficult to envisage why economic factors can affect diffusion speed. If disposable income is low, for example, potential adopters may need more time to save up prior to purchasing or may decide to wait for prices to come down.

The set of cultural aspects that can affect diffusion speed are closely linked to how information tends to spread within a country. In particular, the extent to which people have a propensity to rely on others, through word of mouth or observation, in making consumption decisions looms large. For example, in a recent study, 19 percent of US respondents and 14 percent of German respondents indicated "friends or family" as the primary source of information on products, while for respondents in Brazil (4 percent), China (8 percent), and Italy (6 percent), this source was found to be less prominent. A few noteworthy generalizations regarding diffusion speed, which have emerged from research in this area, are discussed.

Similar to the penetration ceiling and its relation to the economic wealth of a country's citizens, higher per capita gross domestic product (GDP) is correlated with greater diffusion speed. The effect here is typically on the individual adoption force (p). Intuitively, a lower per capita wealth level makes potential adopters see less of a benefit for the relatively high price they would incur (as a percentage of their annual income), and this is compounded if there are complementary goods or services that are needed in order to take advantage of the innovation (e.g., you need to buy software or game titles on top of having to purchase the computer or game console). Lower-income populations also often have less exposure to new products (as less communication effort is expended and fewer retail access points are available for such populations).

Although culture is a multifaceted construct, many elements of which are difficult to measure and quantify, it clearly matters. For example, several studies suggest that in *collectivist* and in highly *homophilous* cultures, diffusion speed is greater. A collectivist culture refers to societies that stress interdependence among members who seek the welfare and survival of the group above that of the individual. Collectivist cultures are characterized by a preference for conformity and cooperation in relationships. In homophilous cultures, individuals tend to associate and bond with others who they see as similar to themselves.

Conversely, diffusion is typically slower in countries where the population is more individualistic. An individualistic culture is defined as oriented around the self instead of identifying with a group mentality and one where people see each other as only loosely linked, value personal goals above those of the group, and emphasize personal achievements. Slower diffusion is also expected in cultures that are more heterogeneous—that is, where people perceive more differences than similarities between themselves and others in the society. These relationships make intuitive sense, particularly as they pertain to the social force (the parameter q), because each previous adopter is more likely to affect a nonadopter the greater there is a tendency toward conformity and the more each citizen of the country perceives himself or herself as similar to others, thus increasing the propensity to imitate past adopters, which, as you may recall, is exactly what the social force captures. Researchers have developed scales for measuring these cultural characteristics and classified countries based on them. For example, Japan is rated as more collectivist and less individualistic, whereas the United States is the opposite.

The factors affecting diffusion speed that are associated with the last bucket, the cross-country effects bucket, deserve a bit more elaboration, so we will discuss them in a separate subsection.

CROSS-COUNTRY EFFECTS: CLOUT, SUSCEPTIBILITY, AND TAKEOFF. So far, proponents of the "nonconverging" view appear to be winning the globalization debate, at least as far as innovation diffusion is concerned. We have presented evidence that different countries, even ones in the same continent, still exhibit a fair amount of variance in their basic diffusion model profiles. Tapping into the rich academic research on the topic, we were further able to link these scale and speed differences to a number of characteristics: demographic, economic, and cultural. Presumably, the more any two countries differ along these characteristics, the more likely their diffusion scales and speeds, for the very same innovation, will differ. But does it matter who these two countries are or where they are located with respect to each other? Are there particular interactions between countries that we should pay attention to?

Research into these very questions suggests that, as you might have intuitively guessed, geographic proximity matters. There are two things to consider. The first is that countries that are physically closer to each other tend to be more similar with respect to economic development and culture than countries that are distant from one another; hence, their response to innovations can be expected to be similar. There are exceptions, of course, but geographically adjacent Denmark and Sweden are a prime example of this "closeness rule" (check out how similar their basic diffusion model parameters are in table 8.1). The second issue to consider deals with influence. The closer two countries are to each other physically and the closer they are to each other on various economic and cultural dimensions, the more we might expect the people in one country to be affected by the adopters of the other. If, for example, two countries see frequent cross-border travel by their inhabitants, for work or pleasure, it might not be unreasonable to expect their populations to influence each other. The existence of borders on the map won't stop the social force of adoption from doing its thing. And while such cross-country social influences, whereby the past adopters of one country influence the nonadopters of another country, tend to be weaker than within-country social influences, they have been detected in several studies. Barring political circumstances that do come into play on occasion, borders blur as far as the diffusion of innovations is concerned. And it should be emphasized that although being neighbors can often increase the chances of social influence, two countries need not be physically contiguous for there to be an effect; as long as there is some level of relatedness between the two populations, it can exist. This "blurring of the lines" aspect of cross-country effects suggests that not all hope is lost for the claim that some degree of global convergence is taking place. While the world is far from being one big global market, perhaps with the breakneck pace that digital media are enhancing connectivity, we will see a bit more interdependence among countries, at least as far as innovation diffusion is concerned.

Interestingly, cross-country social influence has been linked to another phenomenon in the context of international diffusion: expediting a "lagging" country's diffusion process. Specifically, if an innovation begins its adoption cycle in a certain country after several other countries have already begun embracing it, the diffusion in the lagging country can be faster than what it would have otherwise been. Armed with the cross-country effect, it is not difficult to envision why such timing can matter: When the lagging country finally enters the picture in terms of innovation adoption, it enjoys a social effect from all the adopters of the leading countries—that is, those countries that began their adoption cycle much earlier. The leading countries, on the other hand, had no (or negligible) installed bases of customers from other countries to induce their citizens to adopt more rapidly. It is a bit like the cross-brand word of mouth (WOM) effect we discussed in chapter 6 in conjunction with the order of entry of competitors, where a later entrant benefited from adoption tailwinds originating from the incumbent's installed base (except that here, rivalry issues and churn across countries are not relevant).

The cross-country social effect is a plausible explanation for the "lead–lag" phenomenon whereby later countries have quicker diffusion processes. However, there are possible alternative reasons why this phenomenon may be observed or, at a minimum, other factors that can reinforce faster adoption in addition to cross-country effects. Most notably, the tendency of innovations to go down in price over time can cause the diffusion curve of a lagging country to reach milestone penetration levels in less time than the diffusion curves of leading countries, where adoption began at higher price points, reached these milestones. Similarly, the fact that innovations tend to improve or become more reliable and bug free over time, after the leading countries served as guinea pigs, can result in faster adoption by laggard countries.

From a managerial standpoint, the fact that diffusion in one country can affect the diffusion speed in another country has important strategic implications. In particular, what if the cross-country effects are asymmetric? In other words, what if adoption of an innovation in country A has a strong effect on the pool of potential adopters in country B, but the reverse effect, B's cross-country effect on A, is weak? In that case, the innovating firm may wish to initially market more heavily (or even exclusively) to consumers in country A than to those in country B.

Given the importance of this issue for firms' international rollout plans, like Apple's simultaneous versus staggered iPhone 3G dilemma alluded to earlier, it's no wonder it has been investigated by a number of scholars. Several of these studies employed a measure called *time-to-takeoff* to facilitate quantifying the degree of interdependence between countries. The time-to-takeoff is defined as the duration of time that elapses from the launch of an innovation until the moment its sales growth rate surpasses some threshold. The hockey stick metaphor comes to mind: the time-to-takeoff is the flat part of the stick, from the left edge of the horizontal part to the point where the stick begins to shoot up nearly vertically.

One such study examined more than fifty countries and measured the extent by which a focal country's time-to-takeoff is influenced by other countries' adoptions and, in turn, how much influence the focal country has on the time-to-takeoff of other countries. The study involved eight consumer electronics products (CD players, PCs, video cameras, digital cameras, mobile phones, Internet access, the ISDN digital communication standard, and DVD players) with data that spanned nearly three decades (1977–2004). Each country was given a "foreign clout" score, capturing its tendency to impact the time-to-takeoff of other countries, and "foreign susceptibility" score, capturing the extent its time-to-takeoff is impacted by that of other countries.

TABLE 8.2 **Top twenty countries in terms of foreign susceptibility and clout**

Country	Foreign susceptibility rank	Country	Foreign clout rank
Singapore	1	Belgium	1
Vietnam	2	Hong Kong	2
India	3	Germany	3
Pakistan	4	Taiwan	4
China	5	Netherlands	5
Indonesia	6	France	6
Philippines	7	Singapore	7
Morocco	8	Japan	8
Hungary	9	Italy	9
Romania	10	Canada	10
Peru	11	Russia	11
Colombia	12	Czech Republic	12
Thailand	13	United States	13
Ecuador	14	United Kingdom	14
Turkey	15	Malaysia	15
Bulgaria	16	South Korea	16
Poland	17	Ireland	17
Russia	18	Switzerland	18
Croatia	19	Spain	19
Brazil	20	Mexico	20

Table 8.2 presents the main findings from the study. The two rightmost columns list the top twenty countries in terms of foreign clout, while the two leftmost columns list the top twenty countries in terms of foreign susceptibility. This dual ranking suggests that indeed influence is asymmetric in many cases: some countries have strong influence on how quickly takeoff occurs in other countries, and conversely, some countries are highly "impressionable"; when diffusion picks up in other countries, they are strongly affected. Countries thus seem to differ in the degree to which cross-country effects play a role for them, and this should be taken into account when orchestrating international rollouts. Much like targeting key opinion leaders or influential segments, these findings suggest that much can be gained by strategically choosing the order of countries to enter.

The study also largely confirmed our previous assertion that cross-country spillover effects are stronger the closer/more similar countries are to one another, both geographically and economically (but not always culturally).

In closing this subsection on cross-country influence, it is worth pointing out that it is not at all difficult to incorporate these effects into our innovation equity framework by enriching the basic diffusion model. The expanded modeling here is similar to how we expressed (in chapter 4) the scenario whereby multiple segments exist in a given market, with added terms to reflect the social effects across segments. In the case of modeling global diffusion, each expression is for a different country, and the additional influence terms reflect cross-country forces. We should allow each country's population to have a "social force" that influences adoption in other countries and, in turn, include social force terms that allow each country to be affected by the adoption level of the other countries (recall that in the multisegment diffusion model, we allowed for the possibility of a one-directional effect from the influential, innovation-forward segment to the imitator, innovation-moderate segment). The cross-country adoption forces—that is, the respective q parameters—need not be equal, allowing for asymmetric clout and susceptibility. We could also allow one country to start its diffusion process sooner so that when a second country begins its process, there is already an installed base of customers that has accumulated in the first country that exerts a cross-country adoption force. As always, formal details of this global diffusion model appear in the appendix (math box 8). It is useful to note that if you expect a country's adoption to be significantly impacted by one or more of the other countries, then a forecast using only the basic diffusion model will likely underestimate the growth pace of an innovation in that country. By the same token, if you have the diffusion data and are retrospectively trying to estimate parameters, assuming a basic diffusion model will lead you to overestimate their value, as some of the growth in adoptions should be attributed to foreign country influence rather than to domestic adoption forces.

Customer Lifetime Value Profiles on the Global Stage

Similar to the variance we observed in diffusion parameters, the CLV profiles may not be identical across countries. You may recall that there are three primary variables to consider here: the per-period profit margin, the retention rate, and the acquisition cost. We make a few global observations regarding each of these CLV components, which again point to divergence rather than convergence across countries and cultures.

DIFFERENCES IN PER-PERIOD CUSTOMER PROFIT MARGINS.   The per-period profitability of customers in various locales around the world will likely be affected by a number of factors. On the revenue side, willingness and ability to pay for the innovation (which may be subject to import taxes), preference for foreign versus domestic brands, and the intensity of local competition can differ by country. On the cost side, issues such as labor costs, shipping expenses, the need to adapt the product to local standards, and the cost of meeting local regulations can have consequences and create variation across countries.

Given the many factors that can affect per-period profit margins, it is no wonder that the prices of popular consumer products, even those that have been around for years, are found to vary considerably around the world. A well-known demonstration of this fact is the Big Mac Index, published by the *Economist*, which compares the price of a McDonald's Big Mac across major cities. As the index shows, the nominal price and the number of work hours needed (given average salaries in each location) to buy a Big Mac differ considerably across the globe: the Big Mac was found to cost 63 percent more (in USD currency) in the United States than in China, for example. Large variations have also been found for the iPod Nano in nominal as well as salary-adjusted prices. While differences in the prices of new products and services would probably affect demand evolution (through the diffusion model parameters), they will clearly have a direct impact on the per-period profit margins of a customer and hence on the CLV model.

In addition to the price paid upon adoption for the innovation, it is important to remember that per-period profit margins will often originate from service-related or add-on-related revenues that follow the initial purchase. These subsequent revenues may vary across countries and cultures. For example, with smartphones, subscribers in European countries such as the United Kingdom, Germany, France, Spain, and Italy were reported to have used fewer services on their smartphones than did consumers in the United States, China, Brazil, and Japan. In particular, consumers in the United States were found to be the most likely to use seven or more add-on services (61 percent of all US smartphone users) followed closely by those in China (56 percent) and Brazil (53 percent).

DIFFERENCES IN THE RETENTION RATE.   There are also indications that attrition and retention rates can differ quite widely globally. As you may recall, the attrition rate is composed of the churn rate (switching to competitors) and the disadoption rate (leaving the category, possibly temporarily). Consequently, differences in the intensity of competition and the availability of viable alternatives may play a considerable role in creating variability in retention rates among countries. For example, research conducted on the global mobile phone industry by Nokia looked specifically at customers' loyalty to their service provider. It was generally found that customer retention is high in emerging markets yet much lower in mature and developed markets. The intensity of competition and the ability to switch between networks probably played a significant part in this finding. In this respect, low switching costs—for example, the ease of changing suppliers and minimal termination penalties—result in high attrition and disloyalty.

Variability in retention rates can also stem from cross-cultural differences. For example, different perceptions of fairness and responsibility affect how consumers in diverse cultures assess firms' service recovery and customer care efforts; these can impact dissatisfaction levels and hence the tendency to leave providers.

DIFFERENCES IN CUSTOMER ACQUISITION COSTS.   Finally, customer acquisition costs can vary dramatically between countries. Some of the difference will be related to the expected variance in the price promotions required to entice customers and the ultimate response to them. For example, if a wireless service provider considers subsidizing a handset to acquire more customers, the level of subsidy needed to achieve a certain impact on demand will be related to consumers' willingness to pay for the handset and their subsequent willingness to pay for services (if the latter is high, a greater subsidy can be given). Other issues include advertising effectiveness that may vary among countries and how fierce competition is over new adopters. Cross-country transfer of information can also play a role. When the iPhone arrived in later-adopting countries, people there already knew about it and did not need much convincing. Because awareness and anticipation were so high, it lowered the need to advertise relative to the marketing efforts undertaken in the leading countries, such as the United States.

Taking Innovation Equity Global: An Example

You might be wondering how the abundance of accumulated knowledge about multinational diffusion processes and customer lifetime value can be used to assess innovation equity in various countries. This sort of analysis could be helpful in determining not only the order of entering into each country or the level of marketing effort to exert in each of them and at what times but if entry is advisable at all. In what follows, we provide an illustration for how one can go about performing this sort of analysis by turning to our familiar satellite radio context and examining whether there is room to consider offering such a service outside of North America.

The satellite radio services of Sirius and XM were extended in late 2005 to Canada and could also be received by US subscribers in parts of Mexico. In 2011, the FCC (Federal Communications Commission) allowed SiriusXM (by that point, the two companies had merged and even combined their names, as described at the end of chapter 6) to set up repeaters in Hawaii and Alaska to allow transmission there as well. However, there had been no attempt by the two firms to expand into markets outside of North America.

To what extent are international markets attractive for launching a satellite radio service similar to that of SiriusXM? In thinking about this question, bear in mind that such a launch would involve large investments in infrastructure (satellites in orbit and terrestrial repeaters in dense urban areas), obtaining radio licenses in the specific countries, negotiating royalty deals for carrying local content or producing it, dealing with automakers and retailers to ensure that prospective customers can get satellite radio hardware in a convenient way, and running marketing campaigns to generate demand. Consequently, the results need to be promising in terms of the number of subscribers and the revenues that can be earned from them so as to recoup these costs and efforts in a reasonable time frame.

The lackluster experiences of several companies that tried to introduce satellite radio services outside the United States give room for pause. The tale of one such company, WorldSpace, is worth telling. WorldSpace was a Washington, DC–based firm founded by an Ethiopian-born lawyer who sought to provide satellite radio programming primarily in developing countries. WorldSpace began transmitting signals in October 1999 in Africa, thus beating both XM and Sirius in commencing satellite radio operations. Soon thereafter, WorldSpace offered services in Asia, with the Indian market accounting for the majority of its subscribers. The company went public in mid-2005 on the NASDAQ, and entry into European markets was on the horizon, with plans to commence service in Italy in late 2009 and later expand into Germany and Switzerland. But those European plans never materialized. While the stock closed on its first day of trading back in 2005 at a price of $22.36, by October 2008 each share was trading at a lowly $0.18. WorldSpace had to file for bankruptcy.

What went wrong? As we already know, satellites are costly (WorldSpace had two of them in orbit, AfriStar and AsiaStar), and programming is not cheap (each location required its own lineup of local content, which had to be either licensed or produced by WorldSpace). But one of the major problems had to do with the fact that in low-GDP-per-capita countries such as Kenya and India, the adoption of innovations is expected to be slow, and in this case, compared to the US it was considerably slower. A related problem was that per-period profit margins tend to be modest in low-GDP-per-capita countries, and in this case they were considerably lower. To be more specific, despite broadcasting for almost eight years, the total number of subscribers WorldSpace had amassed when it filed for bankruptcy was fewer than two hundred thousand. Revenues were another sore issue: given the very low willingness to pay in places like India, the basic subscription was priced at less than the equivalent of $3 per month. The radio receivers had to be heavily subsidized, and along with other marketing expenses to entice consumers to sign up, acquisition costs were high (by some estimates around $175 per subscriber—higher than those for XM). It is estimated that investment and funding of more than $2.5 billion had poured into WorldSpace—which changed its name to 1WorldSpace as its demise loomed nearer—very little of which was ever recovered.

It is a grim tale, but one has to ponder whether the suboptimal choice of initial countries to enter was the culprit. Perhaps had the European plans been implemented sooner, prior to any attempt to enter Africa or Asia, WorldSpace's fate would have been different. Indeed there is room to speculate, based on the preceding sections of this chapter, that for certain countries in Europe, where disposable incomes are high and there is similarity to the United States inasmuch as entertainment consumption is concerned, robust demand exists for a dedicated satellite radio service. The diffusion and CLV metrics for the service could have been promising enough to justify entry. Moreover, there could be cross-country effects between the United States and several western European countries that would expedite adoption. We are left with the open question of whether satellite radio can succeed in Europe, particularly Western Europe. Can another company pick up where WorldSpace left off? SiriusXM is one such company that might want to consider the move, but others may wish to evaluate the opportunity as well. For example, Solaris Mobile, a Dublin-based operator that provides access to satellite and terrestrial network infrastructure for mobile communications across Europe, suggested in 2013 that their technology could be used to provide a pan-European digital radio platform. Should EchoStar Mobile, a publicly traded company based in Colorado that recently acquired Solaris Mobile, push forward with the idea of a pan-European satellite radio service? Answering these questions boils down to assessing whether there is enough innovation equity across a number of European countries to cover the nontrivial costs that would be involved.

Next, we present some concrete thoughts on how such an analysis can be conducted for an illustrative sample of six European countries: Austria, Belgium, Denmark, France, Italy, and the Netherlands.

Bridging the Atlantic Divide: Connecting US and European Innovation Equity Parameters

If you've been paying attention to the globalization debate throughout this chapter, then you realize we shouldn't blindly apply the satellite radio diffusion and CLV model parameters from the United States to the six European countries of interest. To assume that these parameters will be exactly the same as those used for Sirius and XM is asking for trouble and is inconsistent with evidence that these parameters do differ by country. To establish reasonable customized values for each of the European countries, we essentially have two options. The first would be to conduct a large-scale market research program in each of them. Aside from the nontrivial logistics and costs involved with this approach, it could prove challenging to get meaningful responses from consumers that most likely have not had any experience with satellite radio and to convert the responses to relevant quantities for use in a forecast. The second approach is to somehow rely on information from past innovations and adapt that information to the case of satellite radio outside the United States. We opt here for the latter approach and explain how it might work.

We start with characterizing the basic diffusion model profiles in each country. The idea is to find a benchmark innovation (or several of them) for which we know the long-run market potential and adoption forces in each of the countries and for which we believe that the relationship among corresponding parameters across countries is representative for our purposes. That is, while we recognize that the absolute value of the parameters from a previous innovation won't always carry over exactly to the satellite radio case, there is room to believe that the relative magnitudes across the countries will. For example, if one country's individual adoption force (p) is 35 percent greater than that of another country's for a previous benchmark innovation, we can assume that this relationship will hold up between their individual adoption forces for satellite radio. Then all we need are esti-

TABLE 8.3 **Diffusion parameters for wireless mobile service in countries of interest**

Country	Individual-force parameter p	Social-force parameter q	Penetration ceiling c	Population size (000)	Market potential m (000)
Austria	0.0005	0.144	0.459	7,666	3,519
Belgium	0.0012	0.184	0.417	9,922	4,137
Denmark	0.0018	0.167	0.702	5,133	3,603
France	0.0001	0.353	0.537	56,596	30,392
Italy	0.0001	0.295	0.405	57,772	23,398
Netherlands	0.0007	0.304	0.576	15,022	8,653
US	0.0005	0.437	0.74	252,502	186,851

mates for the satellite radio parameters of one of the countries, and we can solve for the remaining countries by applying the relationships found for the benchmark innovation. This may sound complicated, but in fact it is quite simple and will hopefully become clearer as we go.

The previous innovation we will use is wireless mobile service. Table 8.3 presents the basic diffusion model parameters for the countries of interest to us based on an academic study that used actual adoption data in a host of countries (up to 1998).

What we need now is a country for which we have an estimate of the basic diffusion model parameters for satellite radio. That country would, of course, be the United States. Then since we have the United States values for wireless service diffusion parameters as well, we will be able to "build a bridge" between the two innovations for all six European countries. Specifically, consider the parameters of individual force (p) and social force (q). The values we have used throughout the book for satellite radio in the United States are 0.026 and 0.403, respectively (if the analysis is conducted well after satellite radio has diffused in the United States, then one can update these values by estimating them from the data). Dividing the US parameter values for satellite radio by those of wireless services yields the following ratios for the individual and social forces, respectively: 0.026 / 0.0005 = 52 and 0.403 / 0.437 = 0.92. Assuming that these ratios are good approximations for the other countries, we can use them to convert the wireless service values to satellite radio values. For example, for Belgium, the value of the individual force (p) would be 0.0012 · 52 = 0.06, while the social force value (q) would be 0.184 · 0.92 = 0.16.

A similar approach can be used for calculating the expected penetration ceilings. Recall that the long-run market potential for satellite radio in the United States was assessed at 28 million adopters out of the US population of 285 million at the launch. The penetration ceiling for satellite radio in the United States is therefore 28 million / 285 million = 0.098—that is, about 10 percent of the US population in the long run is expected to adopt satellite radio. For mobile wireless service, the ceiling at the time was assessed at 0.74 (i.e., 74 percent of the population will adopt a cell phone service). The ratio of penetration ceilings for the two innovations is 0.098 / 0.74 = 0.132, reflecting the fact that satellite radio targets a much smaller portion of the population than does mobile telephony. Once again, this ratio can be used to update the penetration ceilings of the different countries. Continuing with the example of Belgium, we would thus compute its penetration ceiling to be 0.417 · 0.132 = 0.055.

Following the approach outlined above, and using the US information on both innovations as the connecting bridge, we can create a set of parameters for the expected diffusion of satellite radio in the six European countries as shown in table 8.4.

A procedure similar in spirit to the one used for establishing the basic diffusion model parameters can be performed for the CLV parameters. Unfortunately, the academic studies we cited on mobile phone services did not provide CLV information. So we need to find other sources that will help us create a bridge between the satellite radio estimates we have for the United States and those projected for the European countries. One option is to use data from respectable published sources, such as the OECD. The OECD releases statistics on comparative price levels in various member countries for a common basket of final consumption goods, allowing one to evaluate the purchasing power of, say, one dollar between any two countries. A comparison of European purchasing power levels to those of the United States can give us some indication of the relative variability to

TABLE 8.4 **Diffusion model parameter assessments for satellite radio for the countries of interest**

Country	Individual-force parameter p	Social-force parameter q	Penetration ceiling c	Population size (thousands)	Market potential m (thousands)
Austria	0.026	0.133	0.061	8,653	527
Belgium	0.0624	0.170	0.055	11,199	620
Denmark	0.0936	0.154	0.093	5,794	540
France	0.0052	0.326	0.071	63,880	4,554
Italy	0.0052	0.272	0.054	65,207	3,506
Netherlands	0.0364	0.280	0.076	16,955	1,297
US	0.026	0.403	0.098	285,000	28,000

TABLE 8.5 **Customer lifetime value model parameter assessments for satellite radio for the countries of interest**

Country	Estimated retention, wireless	Estimated retention, satellite	Multiplication ratio for revenues and costs	Estimated per-period profit, satellite ($)	Estimated acquisition costs, satellite ($)
Austria	0.82	0.89	1.14	88	108
Belgium	0.54	0.60	1.19	92	113
Denmark	0.78	0.85	1.51	116	143
France	0.78	0.85	1.16	89	110
Italy	0.85	0.93	1.12	86	106
Netherlands	0.79	0.86	1.17	90	111
United States	0.74	0.81	1.00	77	95

be expected between the United States and the other countries as far as customer profitability is concerned. In particular, these ratios can be used to adjust the per-period customer profit margins and acquisition costs of the US satellite radio CLV model to each of the six European countries.[1] For example, price levels in Denmark are reported to be 51 percent higher than in the United States. Hence we would apply a factor of 1.51 to adjust the US satellite radio per-period profit margins ($77) and acquisition costs ($95) to obtain values of $116 and $143, respectively, for Denmark.

As for retention rates, the relative price levels across countries are not necessarily the most indicative of how likely customers are to stay with a product or service before they disadopt or churn. Here, we can use direct information from publicly available market research reports on the average mobile wireless service retention rates for the pertinent countries, and again we make the assumption that the ratios between countries with respect to retention rates in that benchmark industry are similar to those for satellite radio. For the United States, the retention rate in the wireless phone service category was estimated to be 74 percent (on an annualized basis). As the retention rate for satellite radio in the United States was 81 percent, the ratio is 0.81 / 0.74 = 1.09. As with the diffusion parameters, we can now multiply the known retention rates for the wireless phone category in each country by this ratio to obtain estimates for satellite radio. Table 8.5 presents the results for all CLV model parameters derived by applying the procedures and information described above.

Now that we have the basic diffusion model and the CLV model parameters for the six countries of interest for satellite radio, we can construct innovation equity assessments. The CLV and innovation equity per country

TABLE 8.6 **Satellite radio innovation equity for the countries of interest**

Country	Customer lifetime value ($)	Innovation equity (10 years, $ in millions)
Austria	442	43.6
Belgium	185	22.1
Denmark	480	108.3
France	374	151.5
Italy	526	150.4
Netherlands	394	28.0
United States	272	2,400

over a ten-year span are presented in table 8.6. For simplicity, we applied a single cost of capital of 9.3 percent, consistent with the discount rate used in chapter 2 (though it would be prudent to adjust this rate depending on when and where in the world a company secures its funding and resources).

Adding up the numbers, one gets an innovation equity assessment of a little more than $500 million for the six European countries that we have used as an illustrative sample. This can be compared to the expected costs of getting the service up and running and the annual operating costs during the ten-year horizon (properly discounted) to make the case for or against entering Europe. Given that these anticipated costs could differ depending on the capabilities of the firm considering the move, the conclusion might differ as well. Furthermore, one could imagine that other European countries would be considered for the initial launch or added over time, such as the United Kingdom and Germany (as the satellites would likely be able to cover them as well, though terrestrial repeaters would still be needed), which would increase the innovation equity of the endeavor.

It's useful to put the analysis we conducted into perspective: we had to work with readily available data and make several assumptions along the way. One could definitely expand on the analysis in a number of ways to gain more confidence in the results. For example, another industry aside from (or in addition to) wireless phone service can be used as the analogy from which to extrapolate to satellite radio. Market research can be conducted to either assess the parameters for each country outright or examine how similar European consumers are relative to US consumers regarding both desire and willingness to pay for satellite radio. For example, one could conduct the same type of market research in Europe as XM did in the United States and adjust some of the tables in this chapter. In addition, note that we have not incorporated any cross-country effects that might occur. If we add those into the picture, the innovation equity figures will likely go up (as diffusion speed should increase). One way to do that is to use information from extant studies, such as the one reported in connection with table 8.2, along with the global diffusion model, which takes such effects into account (see math box 8 in the appendix). Nonetheless, conceptually, the simple analysis performed here can serve as a guidepost for how to examine the innovation equity that may accrue when entering new markets in the global arena.

In Search of Trending Information in Search Data

As we have seen, obtaining data for assessing the financial value from launching an innovation in target countries can be a complex task. Broadly, two types of information are commonly used: (1) information from other countries for the very same innovation (assuming it has begun to diffuse in the other countries or that market research was conducted to generate estimates in these countries) and (2) information from previous innovations in the target country that are likely to be indicative of how the innovation at hand will perform. One then needs to adapt these values to the innovation in question for the target country.

There are several sources that can be tapped into for obtaining this sort of information. Academic articles that examined the global diffusion of innovations are one option. Industry associations and market research companies that publish studies on new product growth and customer profitability metrics by country are an additional outlet. Market reports, often published by industry interest groups, in which several key performance indicators of a company are compared to competitors' performance (or the industry average) in various international markets, can also be an excellent source of inputs.

The above "conventional" information sources represent what has been available—and in fact used for several years—and it is important to seek out these sources when conducting global innovation assessments of the kind we have been discussing here. We would be remiss, however, if we did not at least mention some promising new resources for obtaining information relevant to international innovation analyses: sites such as Google Trends and Google Global Market Finder. These sites enable users to examine with high granularity the patterns of online searches being conducted for any word or phrase. As search presumably correlates strongly with interest, these sites provide an unprecedented opportunity to explore the diffusion of "interest level" in any concept or product and to do so by country and over time.

On Google Trends, for example, the horizontal axis of the graph created in the main tool (in its current form) represents time and the vertical axis represents how frequently a given term is searched for, relative to the maximum number of searches ever conducted for that term (the maximum search level gets a score of "100" and all other levels are given numbers between 0 and 100). Google Trends offers a set of additional tools that enable fine-tuning inquiries. With *regional interest*, for example, one can compare search volume patterns across specific countries and cities. With *related searches*, one can examine which keywords those searching for the primary term were also frequently conducting searches for.

Although a notable limitation of Google Trends is that searches for a particular word or phrase are presented in relative and not absolute terms (i.e., the total number of searches is not given) and data are available only since 2004, it has the potential to be an effective aid for gaining information on new product and service diffusion patterns. In order for that to be true, however, search patterns need to be reflective or predictive of actual behavior, such as adoption of and willingness to pay for innovations. There are some indications that Google Trends data can be used with a reasonable degree of confidence to track phenomena such as the spread of an illness in a population or the unemployment rates in various countries. In terms of new product growth, some evidence points to a high degree of correlation between searching for terms associated with an innovation and its actual sales.

Global Market Finder uses data from online searches around the world to show the number of times people searched for specific keywords in fifty-six languages. Combined with Google's AdWords, the tool provides estimates of competitive bids for each keyword by market and language. This enables managers to assess the degree of competitiveness in a given country/region, the popularity of specific keywords/products in various areas around the world, and advertising costs in various locales. This information can help with several aspects of assessing global innovation equity, such as the expected market potential and customer acquisition costs in various countries.

To see how one might use these promising new resources in the context of innovation spread, we proceed with an example from the realm of social media. Specifically, we will show how Google Trends can be used in connection with the diffusion pattern of Facebook around the world.

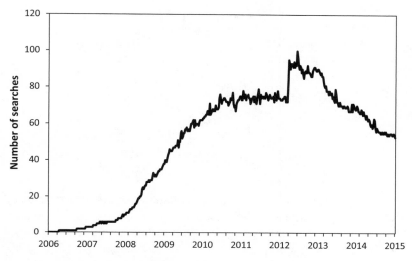

Worldwide searches for the term "Facebook"

Searching for Global Trends: The Case of Facebook

Figure 8.1 shows how Google searches for the popular social media application Facebook evolved over time from the start of 2007 until mid-2015. What is notable about the worldwide pattern of searches conducted is that, consistent with the diffusion curve for many innovations we have seen throughout this book, they seem to exhibit a slow start followed by a takeoff period (around the beginning of 2008), a leveling-off phase, and a decline that starts in 2013.[2] Such decline is consistent with reports on a decrease in the global active use of Facebook at that time period and may be related to the increased active use of other social media platforms and networking applications such as Snapchat, especially among teenagers.

However, breaking down search data by country reveals striking diversity in search levels. A 2015 snapshot of Google Trend's regional interest tool suggests, for example, that the relative intensity of searches is especially high in Turkey and Tunisia, as can be seen in table 8.7. By contrast, when inspecting the full list, one can see that in countries where other social media applications dominate, such as parts of the former Soviet Union, search intensity for Facebook is especially low.

Online tools such as Google Trends thus provide scholars and practitioners with a useful means to assess the spread of interest in new products and services across the globe. Of course, caution should be applied. Not in all cases will information on searches be a good proxy for adoption intent.

TABLE 8.7 **Relative intensity of Facebook searches across select countries, 2015**

1	Turkey	100
2	Tunisia	86
3	Venezuela	84
4	Algeria	77
5	Peru	76
6	Ecuador	75
7	Columbia	75
8	Nicaragua	69
9	El Salvador	68
10	Mexico	67

Nonetheless, we can reasonably speculate that these tools will continue to evolve, and new features will be added to existing ones, which will enable a much better understanding of global diffusion and global customer management components in future years. It will be interesting to see how robustly and quickly these new tools are themselves adopted and to what extent they replace conventional sources of information. Your forecast is as good as ours.

How Far and How Fast Did the Apple (iPhone) Fall from the (US) Tree?

In closing, we would like to return to Apple's global iPhone strategy between June 2007 and September 2009. What is clear in retrospect is that Apple followed a "staggered" approach. For example, the first-generation iPhone was first released in the United States, and it then took more than four months before consumers in the United Kingdom, Germany, and France could get their hands on the device, followed by Austria and Ireland some four months later. Those were the "lucky six," and one could say the rollout occurred in three sequential "waves." Based on what we have seen in this chapter, it probably made some sense to start with the United States, given the size of the country, its high GDP per capita, and the strong cultural fascination with the Apple brand. But note that, with the exception of Austria, all the remaining countries targeted are on the top twenty list of foreign clout (per table 8.2). The clout measure seems relevant for the next-generation iPhone 3G, which arrived a year later, as well. Apple followed a similar rollout approach of staggered introduction waves, though for the 3G model, each wave was typically much wider in terms of the number of countries included. The waves were also more far reaching, as not only the US and western European countries were included. The first wave also saw releases in Asian and Latin American countries as well as Australia and New Zealand. Shortly after that, Eastern European countries and India got their turn. Middle Eastern countries like Saudi Arabia and Southeast Asian countries such as Indonesia had to wait until early 2009 to get their hands on it. And while Hong Kong was part of the first 3G wave in July 2008, China, the world's second-largest economy and most populous nation, was only welcomed into the iPhone family late in 2009 (after the 3GS was launched). Many of the countries that were added later, not surprisingly, were high on the foreign susceptibility measure. To summarize, judging by how things played out, it appears that Steve Jobs and his management team had a good understanding of cross-country effects as well as how to navigate the characteristics of what made some countries more conducive to generating high innovation equity. By design, Apple iPhones did ultimately fall far from the US tree—just not all at once.

It should also be pointed out that Apple did not follow a uniform marketing approach in each country. One of the main differences was the types of agreements it had with wireless service carriers. In some countries, there was an exclusive agreement, as was the case in the United States with AT&T (the only iPhone service provider until early 2011). Despite consumer resentment over the lack of carrier choice, Apple typically benefited handsomely from granting such arrangements. For example, AT&T had to fork over roughly $10 a month from every iPhone customer's bill. Apple thus not only earned immediate profit from the sale of the device but also had recurring per-period profits from each user. The subsidy consumers received on the device from the service providers, in return for a period of service lock-in, also varied by country. Apple was quite active in affecting this subsidy level when possible, which in turn seemed to affect the rate of adoptions and expected customer profitability. In countries where subsidies were not provided, like India, the iPhone 3G's $700+ price tag was prohibitive for most consumers. And although there was near universal "buzz" over the iPhone, and it enjoyed extensive media coverage, with some hailing the device as "the Jesus phone," Apple still ran marketing campaigns. Here, too, there seemed to be significant variance in expenditure by region. Apple was estimated to have spent nearly $650 million on advertising the iPhone in the United States between 2007 and 2011, much more than in any other region, let alone country. This fact is a testament to two things: (1) how susceptible US consumers are to marketing communications compared to consumers in other countries and (2) how competitive the US market was, or was expected to become, which Apple felt merited a sustained advertising effort to preempt and prevent churn.

Speaking of apples falling from a tree, which is considered the inspiration for Sir Isaac Newton's famous discovery of the law of universal gravitation, and in reference to the opening quote by former UN secretary Kofi Annan, if by "globalization" we mean that all countries are becoming virtually indistinguishable in terms of how business is conducted in them and in how consumers behave and react to firm efforts, it would seem that the components of innovation equity are, for now, "defying the laws of gravity."

Key Takeaways

- Innovation equity assessments may differ across countries (even after controlling for population sizes) because the diffusion model and the customer lifetime value model parameters are typically not the same.
- An innovation's diffusion scale and speed (i.e., its long-run market potential and adoption forces, respectively) are affected by country-specific factors. These factors can include the country's economic environment, such as GDP and the cost of doing business, and its cultural orientation, such as how people interact with each other and how they perceive their roles within the society.
- When comparing long-run market potentials across countries, it is often meaningful to consider the share of the population relevant to the innovation's adoption, a quantity called the "penetration ceiling." In practice, this quantity is often determined by evaluating the percentage of a country's population that meets certain criteria (e.g., lives in urban areas, has annual income or education above some level, etc.).
- Cross-cultural differences in the degree of collectivism, defined as a society's tendency to place the group's interests above those of the individual, and the degree of homophily, defined as the tendency in a society for individuals to bond with others who are similar to them, are particularly relevant to understanding variations in the within-country social adoption force.
- Adoption in some countries can affect adoption in other countries through social forces. Proximity, both geographically and culturally, and the influence (or clout) that certain countries historically have on others determine the strength of such cross-country social forces. A global diffusion model can be constructed

to account for these effects and, in conjunction with knowledge of how a benchmark innovation diffused in certain countries, can be used to create a diffusion forecast for the innovation at hand in these countries.

- Differences across countries in customer per-period profit margins tend to be related to per-capita income, domestic competition intensity, the regulatory/tax environment, and distribution and labor costs. Differences in retention rates tend to be related to the ease of switching between brands and cultural perceptions of service responsibility. Differences in the acquisition costs tend to be related to the effectiveness of marketing programs, income levels, and how quickly information travels across countries.

- Emerging online data sources, such as Google Trends, can help managers better understand the commercial prospects of new products and services in various countries and obtain proxy inputs for performing innovation equity assessments.

CHAPTER NINE

Making the Framework "Work" for You

[Enter Quote Here]—You

B y now we hope you're convinced that the task of assessing an innovation's value doesn't have to be left to random guesswork. We hope you agree that there can be some method to the seeming madness of forecasting an innovation's unit sales growth and assessing the monetary returns from customers adopting it. We hope the innovation equity framework has inspired you to look at the commercial prospects of new products and services with different eyes. And last but not least, we hope you feel sufficiently empowered by the insights, models, and examples that have been presented throughout, to the point where you are ready to make use of them for your own purposes.

This concluding chapter will revolve around this very theme, making sure you have what you need to apply the innovation equity framework to your context. It will offer guidance on the steps to take when implementing the various models in practice, outline issues you should pay attention to when adapting the concepts to your situation, and point you toward useful resources . . . all in an effort to get you well on your way to becoming an innovation equity pro.

In thinking about how best to organize this chapter, we decided to have a sort of pseudodialogue with you, the reader, by using a "frequently asked questions" (FAQ) format. This allows us to frame the various implementation tidbits as issues you may be wondering about now or may encounter in the future. The specific questions included herein are representative of the inquiries and comments we have typically received from other scholars, practitioners, and students over the years. In several instances, we link the response to a question back to a chapter in the book, so on occasion, the presentation will serve the purpose of a review or a reminder of pertinent material that was covered. And for the hands-on oriented among you, we will be referring throughout the chapter to spreadsheets that are available on the book's companion website (http://www.InnovationEquityBook.com). These will allow you to have at your fingertips tools to conduct the key analyses described while customizing them to your own innovation scenario. In the references and recommended reading section, we point to material that may be of relevance to those of you seeking additional information or more advanced treatment of the responses to the FAQs.

In perfect harmony with the flow of the book, we will separate the FAQs and the answers to them into those that pertain to innovation diffusion, those that pertain to customer lifetime value, and those that pertain to the framework that combines these two topics. The various "specialty" topics we examined using the combined framework—marketing mix activity, the existence of multiple segments, competition, next generations, and global launches—will be sprinkled throughout the answers provided. We end the chapter with an innovation equity checklist—a practical summary of the key steps and points you should have in mind when implementing the framework or applying the material to your setting—and with a few final words to wrap things up.

Whether you need to create a monetary forecast for upper management, instruct others on how to construct a forecast, review and critique a projection by a third party, or simply desire a clearer vantage point from which to gauge the commercial prospects of an upcoming new product launch, for any and all these purposes, we trust you will find this chapter helpful. Use it in the way that is most beneficial to you: read the entire set of FAQs in one go or zoom in on those particular issues that you care about at present and are of burning importance and then come back at a later time for other issues as needed.

FAQs on Diffusion of Innovations Topics

The various diffusion models presented in the book give us a way to forecast the acquisition phase of the customer-firm relationship. They aim to capture the innovation's adoption process over time. Fundamental issues regarding the basic diffusion model (upon which all other models were built) were explored in depth in chapter 1. Many embellishments and advanced aspects were covered throughout the book. Below you will find some common questions that arise with the diffusion side of the innovation equity framework.

Can I use the various diffusion models covered in the book for any type of innovation?

The term "innovation" is indeed very broad; hence, there could certainly be a question whether diffusion modeling is relevant in every single instance. You will be pleased to know that the short answer is yes. Any innovation, which by definition embodies some newness in it and aims to garner adoption from a target population, can be a good candidate for the innovation diffusion models presented in this book.

The long answer to the question qualifies this statement in that some innovations are "better candidates" than others. For example, if we classify innovations on an incremental-to-radical scale, then the less incremental an innovation, the more meaningful it becomes to use the models in this book. This is because incremental innovations tend to be minor improvements over existing products or services in the marketplace and consequently involve much less uncertainty on the part of would-be adopters. Individuals' consideration of whether to embrace such innovations tends to have little interdependence on the decisions or views of others. Hence the social adoption force typically plays a limited role. And although firms' marketing efforts may be highly relevant, the impact of these efforts on adoption is fairly predictable. We can extrapolate from what is known about the elasticity of demand for the existing alternatives or from running a set of test market studies on the new product.

Radical, or breakthrough, innovations, on the other hand, presumably offer substantially greater or novel benefits and often open up entirely new categories. Naturally, they tend to involve much greater uncertainty on the part of potential customers who may feel they are taking on considerable risk by adopting. For these kinds of innovations, the impact of marketing actions on the individual force or the long-run market potential is less obvious. And social adoption forces, like hearing the opinions of past adopters about the innovation, seeing others use it, and the role of distinct segments in the diffusion process (such as "influentials" and "imitators"; see chapter 4 for more details on these groups), are often critical to understanding and foreseeing the dynamics of adoption.

On top of the incremental-radical classification, scholars tend to agree that innovations that are complex to understand, that involve substantial learning and switching costs on the part of customers, or that bear on one's social status tend to be well suited to applying the basic diffusion model and the various extensions to it. We note, however, that there does not appear to be a hard and fast rule regarding which industries are more amenable to the models presented here. One might suspect, for example, that repeat-purchase supermarket items, also referred to as fast-moving consumer goods (FMCG), would not fit the models presented here particularly well. While that is probably true for a new variant of an existing product, say a new yogurt flavor, this may not hold for an entirely new type of FMCG, say the emergence of the Greek yogurt class.

Many of the examples presented throughout the book involved innovations that are consumer-facing — that is, business-to-consumer (B2C). If my innovation is of the industrial or business-to-business (B2B) kind, are the frameworks still relevant?

There is absolutely no denying that a big chunk of the economy in general, and business activity in particular, revolves around products and services that are sold from one company to another company or organization — rather than from a company to individual consumers — and much of this business activity involves innovations. The commercial success of a new enterprise software application, for example, would entail its parent company attempting to get other firms to adopt and integrate it as part of their IT platform. A medical company may rely on hospitals and clinics to adopt a new device (e.g., a heart stent). Moreover, many innovations predominantly involve a B2B sale even when the final user of the product is a private consumer. For instance, the maker of an innovative hardware component (e.g., Intel, AMD, or Nvidia, which design processors and graphics cards) may need to convince companies that make computers (e.g., Dell or HP) to incorporate its novel chip into new machines, even though end consumers ultimately buy the computers with the innovative chips "inside."

You'll be glad to know that the innovation diffusion models and related concepts are largely applicable when businesses are the adopting unit. In fact, several studies have used diffusion modeling in various B2B contexts. (The IBM mainframe example presented in chapter 7 is based on one such study.) If this seems curious to you, then perhaps it has to do with better understanding how the social adoption force can be relevant here. In some sense, the term "social" implies being part of some group or segment of the population and relates to how members of these groups may interact with one another. But that would be a narrow definition as far as innovations and their diffusion are concerned. Recall that what the social adoption force is essentially intended to capture is any kind of effect that previous adopters have on the remaining potential adopters. Therefore, the relevance of a social adoption force in B2B settings boils down to examining whether past adoption by businesses or organizations influences the future adoption of businesses that have not yet adopted. The unit of analysis likewise changes from a consumer to a company or institutional entity.

In explaining the mechanisms through which social adoption forces operate, we highlighted things like "word of mouth" (WOM) and "observing" others. WOM, or information transfer between firms more generally, can certainly exist in industrial contexts as well. For example, decision makers within a firm considering the adoption of a new technology may wish to talk to decision makers in firms that have already adopted it to understand how beneficial it actually is and how difficult implementation was. In this case, the decision makers are tapping into their professional network. Such communication can take place by picking up the phone or striking up a conversation at a trade conference, for example. And to be sure, the firm that introduced the innovation and that wishes to expedite its diffusion may proactively try to connect past adopters with prospective adopters. You may recall that in chapter 5, we discussed the notion of "referencing," which means touting past adopters' positive experiences to serve as a source of validation for future adopters. Referencing is a common practice in the world of B2B, and it makes sense: businesses like to make decisions based on sound analysis and by involving multiple people and hierarchies in the organization. Consequently, if a peer company took the time to vet the innovation and ultimately concluded it was worth the risks, that's a strong signal. This is why you will often see firms selling B2B innovations prominently listing their client base on their website and in other communication materials. There may even be nuanced social dynamics among business segments. For example, large research hospitals can serve as early validators of new medical procedures and equipment, acting as "influentials" to the many smaller and less cutting-edge hospitals that are of the "imitators" ilk.

Competition among businesses can play a huge "social" role as well. If a firm's competitive intelligence reveals that a rival has adopted a certain new technology or practice and as a result its strategic position and financials have been positively impacted, that can serve as a trigger to adopt as well. As more firms in the same market space opt for the innovation, there could actually arise a "social penalty" for lagging, in that not adopting the innovation can result in a competitive disadvantage of sorts. Note that organizations do not necessarily need to converse to be affected; observing may be enough. Several information sources on firms' adoption of innovations may be available in the B2B arena: they can appear in business publications, be discussed at industry conferences, and be mentioned by sales reps and account executives.

That said, it is true that many examples in marketing books and academic studies feature B2C products. This in part stems from the greater public availability of data for such products (relative to B2B contexts where firms sometimes try to keep their adoption decisions secret for strategic reasons) and from the fact that B2C examples are recognized by a larger audience. But don't let that fool you: diffusion models thrive in B2B situations. Furthermore, the customer management side of the equation is highly relevant as well.

I am ultimately interested in running the analysis for a (my) specific brand; should I start with assessing diffusion at the category level or go directly to the brand level?

In chapter 6 we presented several options for analyzing innovation diffusion at the brand level. You may recall that one approach is to start at the category level and assess the overall diffusion pattern of the innovation class without distinguishing how sales will be divvied between the various brands and, after that is established, move to a brand-level analysis by assigning market shares to each player. One can use a number of techniques to assess what share of new adopters each brand will likely garner in each period. If the researcher has knowledge of the brands that are or will be competing in the market, including their attributes and likely pricing, he or she can use the information in conjunction with customer research to predict market shares.

A popular method in this regard is conjoint analysis, which examines customers' reactions to various configurations of products and services in a category. In particular, various levels of the key attributes (including price and brand) are studied to learn about consumer preferences. Using the results, the probability that an individual will choose the profile of one competing alternative over others can be assessed. Aggregating the results across the study's respondents can help predict the market share for each alternative. It is a good idea to consult a professional market research firm if this approach is pursued. (See also the references and recommended reading section for literature on conjoint analysis.) It is worth noting that the expected market share of each alternative may change over time as competitive dynamics evolve. For instance, if one firm cuts the product's price or adds a desired feature into the product but the other firms do not, the former's share of demand is expected to increase at its rivals' expense.

The category-first approach should be used when one holds a strong belief, or obtains research on consumption patterns to suggest, that customers' decision-making process in the category will likely entail two stages—specifically, if prospective customers are expected to first attempt to figure out whether they even want to "dip into" this kind of innovation and only then make a determination of which specific brand is the most pertinent for them. For instance, consumers may first be interested in learning how much better LED televisions are in image quality and durability before they inquire about or delve into particular differences between the offerings of Sony, Toshiba, Samsung, and LG. In such cases, running an appropriate basic diffusion model at the category level makes sense. Furthermore, if WOM is instigated regardless of which brand a past adopter chose and is primarily geared toward hyping advantages that are common across brands, again, category-level diffusion analysis is warranted.

However, if one expects consumers to engage in a one-step process whereby the decision to adopt the innovation type (e.g., a smartphone) is linked directly to their interest in a specific brand (e.g., the iPhone), then it makes more sense to analyze things directly at the brand level. In addition, if the social forces driving adoption operate at the brand level—that is, past adopters influence prospective adopters to buy the same brand they have chosen—then, once again, brand-level diffusion analysis is warranted. And this is true even if some of the social influence spills over to help rivals in the category, or what we called cross-brand WOM effects. Lastly, if one expects competition between the firms introducing innovations in the same market space to be intense, such that they will compete for the very same potential adopters, and churn is likely (i.e., customers defecting from one brand to another), then again, applying models that directly account for diffusion at the brand level may be more appropriate.

The multitude of ways firms may interact with each other as their innovations diffuse leads to a number of modeling options. These range from letting each brand have its own set of diffusion parameters, including the pool from which it draws adopters, to models that incorporate much more connectivity between the brands, like a common pool of adopters, cross-brand WOM effects, and churn. All of these options, and in particular a comprehensive competitive diffusion model, are described in greater detail in chapter 6.

It is worth mentioning that much of what we know about the diffusion patterns of innovations is at the category level. This is largely because information on new product growth was predominantly available at this level of granularity. But that is changing: the abundance of information sources that are becoming available and the difficulty of keeping firm plans and performance metrics secret in the digital world we live in mean that we can expect more access to company-level data in the future. Consequently, more brand-level analyses will likely be conducted, and we can anticipate more insights emerging on this topic.

Can conducting diffusion analysis with data on the number of current users, which is often what firms report, introduce bias because some past adopters may have stopped using the innovation while others started? Can this issue be handled?

Yes and yes. This issue is particularly relevant for services where reported data on customer base growth are often based on the number of current users, reflecting the net change in customers in the period—that is, the difference between those that have newly adopted and those that have left due to attrition. The innovation equity framework we presented, however, relies on the number of new adopters in each period, so we need a way to move from the net change in current users to actual new adopters.

In chapter 6 we dealt with some of these issues in the context of a competitive scenario. We differentiated between two kinds of attritions—churn and disadoption—and presented a comprehensive approach to deal with such a distinction. If examining the simpler category-level setting is sufficient, then a more straightforward analysis is possible. We can employ the retention rate, which is used for the lifetime value calculation, for the analysis. For each period, we can calculate the number of new customers acquired (i.e., new adoptions) by applying the attrition rate to the number of users reported at the end of the previous period and adding the result to the net change in users between the two periods.

Consider a simple example. Assume that at the beginning of year 4, a firm has 100,000 users, and at the beginning of year 5, 120,000 users, and the annual retention rate is assessed at 90 percent. Based on this information, during year 4, the firm actually added 30,000 new adopters, as it presumably lost 10,000 prior customers due to attrition (which equals 1 − retention, or 10 percent in this case), for a net overall change in users of 20,000. It is the 30,000 adoption figure that should be used in year 4 for purposes of innovation equity assessments. A similar analysis should be done in all periods in order to adapt the data to the actual number of new customers acquired rather than the net change in customers.

While we are on the topic of the data available for diffusion analysis—for example, to estimate diffusion model parameters or to compare to a prelaunch diffusion forecast—we note that some caution may need to be exercised when using unit sales (as opposed to the explicit number of new customers added in each period). Specifically, recall that the various diffusion models are meant to capture the number of first-time or new adopters in each period (and perhaps reentry by those that had disadopted, if relevant). Hence, when the sales data include repeat or multiple purchases by the same individuals—either because the nature of the category is such that consumers buy products or services regularly after they have adopted, because some people wish to own more than one unit, or because of the need to replace products that break down—these sales should not be counted as reflecting new adoptions. In such cases, the data may need to "cleaned" by removing these types of sales. Alternatively, one can take the diffusion model forecast and convert it to a unit sales forecast by multiplying the number of customers that have adopted by a factor that reflects the average repeat or multiple-item purchase rate (and adding that to the unit sales expected from new adopters in the period).

When creating an innovation diffusion forecast, how do I figure out the long-run market potential parameter (m)?

Any sensible firm planning to launch an innovation must care about the "market potential" for its new offering. Indeed, future revenues, market share, and profitability will all hinge in some form or fashion upon this quantity. However, what this quantity refers to in practice tends to be somewhat vague because it is not always linked to a specific time horizon or is expressed in differing ways (revenues, units sold, addressable population—i.e., the set of people that meet some criteria for which the innovation is deemed most relevant or that can be easily reached).

In the context of the diffusion models presented here, the market potential quantity we are after is well defined, although we concede it may be challenging to determine its exact value ex ante prior to launch. As you may recall from chapter 1, we need to assess the expected number of people that will ever adopt the innovation in question. So bear in mind that we seek a number that will be realized at a future point in time and that is intended to capture the exhaustive set of people who will ever become customers of the product or service under study. Importantly, even if the good or service is one that the same person might buy or consume repeatedly, we would still count that as one adopter (as the diffusion models capture the first time an innovation is embraced).

So how do you obtain this quantity? From our experience, it involves a combination of pulling together various information sources and infusing managerial judgment. Let us elaborate. First, one could solicit the advice of analysts, industry experts, consultants, and the like to help scope out the types of customers that could be interested in the innovation at hand. Their experience from recently launched innovations in the category may further help refine the relevant segments that would ever consider adoption. Mapping out all possible use cases for the innovation is an important step in being able to identify all the potentially relevant adopter groups.

Once all customer segments have been identified, it is helpful to conduct a market survey with representative samples of these segments to assess what portion of them are likely to adopt and how that might depend on certain marketing mix variables—for example, price. Experience has shown that consumers tend to overstate their purchase intentions in surveys (e.g., the share indicating a "very high likelihood" of purchasing the innovation when it becomes available) relative to their actual behavior observed subsequently. The study's researchers should take that tendency into account when interpreting the findings. Methods for adjusting these stated intentions should be employed (some suggestions appear in the references and recommended reading section).

Another approach for gauging the long-run market potential is to benchmark it from other innovations for which diffusion data are readily available and for which the parameter m is known or can be reliably estimated. This method is often called "guessing by analogy" because you're essentially extrapolating from one innovation to another. The analogy can be drawn from past innovations/generations in the same market that are presumably related or from the very same innovation under study that was launched in another country earlier.

For example, the long-run number of VCR adopters in the United States could serve as a baseline figure for assessing the market potential of the DVD. But as explained in chapter 7, caution should be exercised. First, it is recommended to use the penetration level that the previous innovation attained (say among all US households) and adjust that number according to relevant demographic changes that transpired in the interim: the size of the population, average income, the penetration of enabling or complementary goods (e.g., computers, broadband, high-definition television sets), and so on. Second, it may be important to factor in greater awareness of the category as a whole as a result of previous generations paving the way to market acceptance. Third, if pertinent legislation or regulations have since been introduced—for example, healthcare reforms (such as the Affordable Care Act) or new requirements on vehicle fuel standards (known as CAFE)—it may affect certain innovation categories (like telemedicine and electric drive vehicles, respectively) and the populations they become relevant for. Such scenarios necessitate an adjustment of the long-run market potential relative to the benchmark.

When relying on the adoption level of the same innovation but from a different country or region—what is commonly referred to as an intercountry analogy—one again needs to exercise caution when extrapolating to the country of interest. Specifically, as explained in chapter 8, characteristics such as gross domestic product (GDP) per capita and technological readiness may vary across countries, and such differences can impact the diffusion model parameters. Therefore, adjustments may be required in drawing inferences from one country to another in the percentage of the population expected to adopt (known as the "penetration ceiling").

The market potential will also likely be a function of marketing effort undertaken by the firm(s) introducing the innovation. Companies can again use market research ahead of the launch to assess the effect of various marketing actions on the expected long-run market potential. In particular, price can considerably affect the set of people in the marketplace that consider the innovation. XM, for instance, ran a survey to examine how many people would be willing to sign up for the innovative radio service at various prices for the receivers and for the monthly subscription fee. As expected, the higher the price, the less "purchase intent" was stated.

Ultimately, management needs to decide which long-run market potential makes the most sense to use based on all the information it has. It is common to have two or three values under final consideration, each backed by the assumptions that led to it, and let managers with experience in the category weigh in on the final value to use. This is true for other diffusion model parameters as well, and we provide an example in the context of figuring out values for the adoption forces (p and q) as part of the response to a subsequent FAQ.

Suppose the market potential changes over time. Do I need to address this issue?

The long-run market potential used in the various diffusion models presented in the book should reflect the total number of people that will ever adopt the innovation, which means it can span an extensive duration.

Within this time frame, many things can change: the innovation itself may be augmented or made more reliable; variants may be introduced to cater to new segments; marketing actions taken well after the launch phase can make additional consumers aware; and the economic, political, or social conditions may not be the same. Therefore, de facto, the market potential rarely stays constant. If these changes are not too dramatic, to avoid complexity, it is common to use the same long-run market potential throughout the diffusion process (and if estimating a long-run market potential of another innovation based on data, to assume that m is constant during the entire estimation period).

Nevertheless, in some instances, this assumption is too strong, and modifications may be needed to the value of the long-run market potential over time. One scenario where this can occur is when the market potential for a new product depends on the diffusion of another product. For example, the market potential for an online video game will depend on the diffusion of the console. In such a case, the game title's market potential will be positively correlated with the cumulative number of console adopters. Hence if at some point the market potential for the console changes— for example, because of a drastic price cut (as was the case with Sony's PlayStation 3) or because of the inclusion of a new feature (as was the case with the Xbox 360 when the Kinect motion sensor was introduced as an add-on)—the market potential for the video game will likely change, even if there was no change to the game or to its price. Another scenario is when new competitors affect the long-run market potential by, for example, creating more consumer awareness and confidence in the innovation's value and encouraging more complementary producers to participate.

Lastly, as already noted, postlaunch changes in the marketing mix of the innovation under study may impact its long-run market potential. A dramatic increase or decrease in price, advertising, sales efforts, retailer support, or other marketing vehicles may alter the market potential beyond the firm's initial assumptions. Chapter 3 has dealt extensively with the effect of marketing mix variables on demand per the basic diffusion model, and the insights derived there can be used to think about how to assess a nonconstant long-run market potential.

On a practical note, when one wishes to allow the market potential pool to evolve, the diffusion analysis needs to be conducted in a flexible manner in order to generate as accurate a forecast as possible for the number of new adopters in each period. For example, the spreadsheet in which the forecast is performed can have distinct breakpoints where the cumulative adopters up to a point are taken as a given and the long-run market potential going forward is different than what it was assumed before.

When creating an innovation diffusion forecast, how do I figure out the adoption force parameters (p and q)?

Obtaining estimates for the expected values of the adoption forces p and q is typically more complicated than for the long-run market potential, mainly because the managerial intuition for the level of these variables— and executives' experience in dealing with them—is less extensive. The most common approach here is to rely on analogies from other innovations and, similar to the case of market potential, use either other innovations in the same market or the same innovation in other countries or regions for which data are already available. This approach was taken, for example, by Frank M. Bass (who you may recall was a diffusion modeling pioneer) and his team of researchers when forecasting in the early 1990s the likely penetration of satellite television. In that case, a set of past innovations relevant for drawing an analogy from was presented to the management of the new venture (DIRECTV), who decided on cable television as the closest one (over other analogies such as color television). Since by then the penetration of cable had already been under way for about a decade, its diffusion parameters, p and q, were easily estimated from available data using the basic diffusion model. By the way, for the long-run market potential (m), Bass and his colleagues used as a baseline the number of homes with televisions and then applied the results of a survey on purchase intent (correcting for response biases) to adjust that number, again presenting management with a few options for scaling back that baseline.

It is worth a reminder that, per chapter 7, if the innovation at hand is a new generation of an existing technology/category (such as a next-generation video game console or a next-generation heart stent), then a reasonable option is to use the adoption force parameters of the previous generation (provided it was not launched too long ago and that no major market changes have occurred).

There are two options for obtaining estimates of the adoption forces of past innovations in order to employ the guessing-by-analogy method. The first is to make use of already calculated estimates performed by scholars and practitioners. In the appendix, we list sample p and q values estimated for various innovations that entered the US market since 1980.

If you can't find a library of relevant innovations in which adoption force parameters are reported, another option is to do it yourself. This means identifying those innovations that seem highly relevant to draw an analogy from, obtain their actual diffusion data over some period, and empirically estimate diffusion parameters using the appropriate model. A common statistical estimation method to apply in this context is called "nonlinear least squares" and can be conducted in Excel using the Solver function. In essence, what you are trying to do is find parameter values that will make the diffusion model that uses these parameters come as close as possible to representing the trajectory of adoptions that took place in reality for the innovation (i.e., that best fit the actual data). In the book's companion website, we describe this estimation procedure and provide an Excel worksheet that enables you to plug in data to run it. As we explain there, you need to have a sufficient history of data on the analogous innovation to be able to estimate its parameters reliably. In particular, unit sales must have already peaked (i.e., passed the apex of the typical diffusion bell curve) in order to be able to estimate the long-run market potential. If, however, unit sales have not yet peaked, the market potential m should be determined based on external sources, as described in response to an earlier FAQ, and plugged into the statistical analysis as a given parameter. The adoption forces p and q can still be estimated in that case. In addition, when the data available are in the form of revenues, it is advisable to divide by the price charged to get the number of units sold in each time period. This is especially important if price changes considerably with time. Obviously, if any of this empirical analysis is too challenging to accomplish internally, you can always outsource the task to a third party such as a market research firm.

Note that if the forecast is prepared *after* the innovation in question has already been launched, and a few years have gone by (though the innovation is far from completely diffusing; otherwise, it's not really a forecast, is it?), one can use the proposed regression analysis on these data to get preliminary estimates for the p and q parameters of the innovation being analyzed. However, because of the limited nature of such an approach, it is recommended to combine the information on actual adoptions with the information obtained on other innovations to generate a robust forecast (triangulating from the various sources appropriately).

Increasingly, data are becoming available on the growth patterns of innovations, which allows performing the type of statistical analysis described above to determine parameter values. Prominent sources of data include market research reports, financial reporting by companies, blogs that cover a certain market, and industry groups that focus on certain categories of products and services. As described in chapter 8, Google Trends is a tool that might help in assessing p and q, particularly in cases where it is reasonable to assume that online searches serve as a good proxy for consumption.

What time period should be used in the diffusion analysis—annual, quarterly, or monthly?

In constructing a forecast using "off-the-shelf" parameter values of analogous innovations or when running statistical analyses on gathered data to obtain estimates, the issue of which time scale or time interval to use arises. The important thing is to maintain consistency. In particular, the diffusion parameters p and q represent the intensity of individual and social adoption forces in a *given time period*. If the unit of time you are interested in is a *year*, then all the analyses should be done in this time scale, and you need to make sure that the parameter values at your disposal and that you plan to plug into the forecast are yearly values. If you are interested in a quarterly interval, same story: make sure you are plugging in quarterly values (and so on for other time scales).

If you are wondering what to do if the parameter values at your disposal are based on data analyzed in one time scale of measurement but you wish to create a forecast with a different time scale, no need to worry: it turns out that a reasonable approximation for moving from one time unit of analysis to another is to apply a linear conversion rule. For example, diffusion model parameters that were obtained using annual data are about twelve times the value of parameters expressed monthly and four times those expressed quarterly (and a reciprocal conversion factor should be applied when going in the other direction).

Note that monthly data are typically "noisier" than annual data, which could affect estimation, whereas using annualized data tends to smooth things out. Users of monthly data should also beware of seasonality effects, where in some categories, demand is high in certain periods during the year (e.g., the November–December holiday season in the United States and Europe) and low at other times (e.g., summer). There are statistical methods that can be employed to "clean" the data analysis and account for seasonality in such cases, and it may be a good idea to consult experts if this is expected to present a problem.

Is the social adoption force (q) always positive? Can there be social influences that have a negative effect on the diffusion of an innovation?

In the basic diffusion model and its various extensions, the social adoption force (q) is associated with the likelihood that a potential customer will adopt as a function of a set of customers who have already adopted. The typical view is that this parameter should be nonnegative. Bear in mind, though, that a positive value for q does not mean that there is no negative WOM being spread by some people. It only means that, on average, the net effect of the social influences of all past adopters on potential new adopters is positive.

Notwithstanding, there are scenarios where possible negative social effects are worth taking into consideration. In particular, when multiple segments exist in the population, the dynamic interaction between segments could lead to asymmetric social effects. For example, if members of one segment are seen as "trendsetting," "cool," and "innovative" when they decide to adopt an innovation, this may have a positive social effect on members in other segments who wish to emulate these trendsetters and have some of the "coolness" rub off on them. However, once the trendsetters sense that the innovation is becoming common and no longer associated only with them, members of this group who have not yet adopted will be deterred, and many who have already purchased the innovation may disadopt/stop using it. This can be accommodated per the multisegment diffusion model presented in chapter 4 by modifying the model to allow the cross-segment social effect to be positive for one segment and negative for the other. Such social dynamics are common in luxury and fashion good contexts yet can also be observed in several consumer electronics markets.

Another scenario that can give rise to a negative social effect has to do with the dissatisfaction or disappointment that some customers may discover after adopting the innovation. As we have emphasized numerous times throughout, consumers make adoption decisions under uncertainty. This uncertainty can be about the purported benefits of the innovation or about the possible hassles and costs of making proper use of it. Since it may take time for customers to fully resolve these issues, initially, social effects might be positive (one sees or learns that others have recently adopted, and that induces him or her to buy as well). However, once customers begin to realize that on the whole they get net negative utility from consumption, they offer unfavorable reviews that lower the likelihood of future adoptions. Of course, if the negative WOM is strong enough, it might cause the innovation to flop before it achieves many sales, and the typical snowball effect that accompanies successful innovations will never materialize.

We know that some customers leave the firm or disadopt the innovation. What happens to their social effect?

We incorporated disadoption into the diffusion framework in the context of competition (chapter 6). We distinguished between attrition as a result of churn (switching to a rival brand) and attrition as a result of exiting the category (i.e., not using any brand offering the innovation); the latter type of attrition was called disadoption. However, one could observe disadoption even if one is analyzing the category as a whole or if there is only one relevant brand. Basically, you would have a disadoption force that decreases the accumulated base of adopters in each period. We provide the formal modeling details for this process in math box 9 in the appendix.

Recall that the cessation of revenue from a disadopting customer is already taken into account in the customer lifetime value (CLV) model through the attrition rate. So you may be wondering why it is important to explicitly incorporate disadoption into the basic diffusion model even without competition. The reason has to do with social influence, which is proportional to the product of the social adoption force parameter q *and* the number of people that exert social influence. If someone who disadopts no longer has a social effect on potential new adopters—for example, because he or she can no longer be seen using it, because it reduces the number of customers the firm can boast as "active," or because disadopters stop talking about the innovation—then we should not be including disadopters as part of the social effect going forward. Thus by accounting for disadoption in the diffusion model, we can ensure that only the set of currently active customers are relevant for the social effect. In fact, we gave some sense of this issue in chapter 3 in connection with why it might be important to increase customers' retention rate (see figure 3.3).

The social dynamics described in relation to this FAQ and the previous one can give rise to phenomena such as fads, whereby a very rapid spike in units sold takes place early on in the diffusion followed by an equally rapid decline in adoptions. In this case, one would expect the individual force of the trendsetters to be very high, the cross–social effect of the trendsetters on the imitators (or "wannabes") to be high and positive, yet the cross–social effect of the imitators on the remaining potential trendsetters to be negative. Moreover, as a greater percentage of the imitating segment adopts, there is likely to be a strong disadoption component among trendsetters who have already embraced the innovation (presumably because they want to dissociate themselves from the imitators). This will lead to a vicious cycle: after a while, fewer trendsetters will be current customers (i.e., active users that exert a positive social effect), and as a result, remaining potential imitators will have less of an incentive to adopt.

Alternatively, if one believes that disadopters continue to exert a positive social force—for example, if their disadoption was not due to any dissatisfaction with the innovation and they remain strong advocates for it—then one can continue to use the basic diffusion model, as only the direct loss of their revenues is relevant for innovation equity assessments (and is accounted for through the CLV model).

FAQs on Customer Lifetime Value/Customer Management Topics

In addition to the number of new customers that adopt in each period, provided courtesy of the various diffusion models, we need to assess the profitability of each customer as part of a monetary forecast. The fundamentals of assessing customer lifetime value (CLV) were discussed in chapter 2. As you may recall, four major inputs are needed: *per-period profit margins, retention rate, discount rate,* and *acquisition costs.* Below you will find some common queries that arise regarding the customer management side of the innovation equity framework.

You gave many examples of CLV analysis using a simple formula that was accurate for a long horizon. What if the analysis is being conducted over a shorter time frame?
The appeal of the short CLV formula (go back to chapter 2, expression 2.9, if you need a refresher) is that it is simple and approximates most time frames quite well. This is because the attrition rate used in the formula (which is one minus the retention rate) leads to the decreasing relevance of periods that are far into the future, so an "infinite horizon" produces a close enough approximation. For example, if the retention rate is 80 percent, then after five years, the chances that someone will still be a customer are less than one-third ($0.8^5 = 0.328$); coupled with the need to discount future revenues (for present valuation purposes), this results in the relative insignificance of years that are beyond five. Hence and though slightly overestimated, a five-year customer lifetime value can be reasonably assessed in most cases by using the simple infinite-horizon formula.

However, if the retention rate is high (say 95 percent) and/or the time horizon of interest is short (say three years), the simple formula is likely to be off. In such cases, one needs to resort to a period-by-period calculation of customer profitability and then sum up over the number of years desired (as shown in expression 2.8). Furthermore, if any of the CLV model inputs change from period to period, once again use of the simple infinite-horizon formula, which assumes that all the inputs are constant, will not yield a good approximation, thereby necessitating a period-by-period analysis.

A limited-horizon, period-by-period approach is definitely feasible and in fact was the basis for the analysis conducted in chapter 4 in connection with the pharmaceutical new drug launch. Yet to make this even more practical for you, an example using Excel is given in the book's companion website. In the example provided there, each period can have its own retention rate, per-period profit, and customer acquisition cost if desired. The worksheet, which you can easily customize to your own situation, calculates the expected profits from a customer in each period into the future, appropriately discounts each of these profits, and then totals the resulting present values to produce a limited-horizon customer lifetime valuation.

The Excel worksheet provided on our site allows exploring the difference between using the infinite-horizon formula and the period-by-period calculation. For instance, assuming a yearly retention rate of 80 percent and a discount rate of 12 percent, the seven-year limited-horizon CLV analysis is about 90 percent of that calculated by the infinite-horizon formula.

Managerial considerations often dictate the time horizon relevant for the customer profitability assessment. Generally speaking, firms often invest substantial funds and resources to develop innovations, which they anticipate recouping over an extended period of time. It is thus reasonable to consider the value they can capture from such innovations over a long horizon into the future. However, sometimes the firm wants to understand its financial position a few years down the road or may need to respond to impatient shareholders. In such cases, taking into account cash flows that will accrue beyond the horizon of interest will not be relevant. In these instances, the limited-horizon CLV analysis is more pertinent. Lastly, a limited-horizon CLV analysis is appropriate when there are considerable market uncertainties regarding the model inputs beyond a few years ahead. When more information becomes available and the uncertainty is resolved, one can resort to the longer-term projections.

How can I obtain reasonable estimates for the CLV parameters? What issues should I be aware of when formulating these estimates?

Per-period profit margins. At the core of a sound strategic plan for launching a new product or service is the business model proposed, which reflects how the company seeks to monetize the innovation it is introducing—in

other words, how it plans to make money. This effectively means laying
out the sources of revenue, whether they be from end users directly or
from other entities in the industry's value chain who stand to benefit from
the innovation and are willing to pay for access to it or to the end users (as
is the case with an ad-driven business model). It also means laying out the
costs expected to be incurred in generating the revenues. From the business model proposed, it should be possible to extract what the per-period
profit margins will be on average for each customer. As we have noted in
several places throughout, one should take into account not only profits
from the initial purchase but also subsequent expected profits from services, additional add-ons, or third-party payments. In some instances the
business model is consciously based on recurrent purchases, such as with
a new razor that is sold cheaply (perhaps even at a loss) only to charge
consumers a premium for the blades that they need to buy repeatedly or
with reasonably-priced printers and expensive ink/toner cartridges. Often, analysts and investors that cover the planned activities of companies
will publish due diligence reports on an upcoming launch and furnish details on expected revenues and costs, from which per-period profits can be
deduced.

One issue worth expanding upon is that of the type of costs to be included in the per-period profit margin, particularly the distinction between variable and fixed expenses. The former are typically associated
with costs incurred when serving each customer and can include unit-
manufacturing costs of any physical product supplied, direct labor costs of
service provision, or a targeted marketing promotion. Variable expenses
relate quite closely to the number of customers. The latter (fixed) expenses have to be incurred regardless of the size of the customer base—
for example, management overhead expenses or a mass communication
campaign. Although theoretically one could divide fixed expenses by the
size of the customer base in each period, this could unduly complicate the
analysis because the customer base is constantly changing over time. Thus
even if fixed costs remain the same in each period, their per-customer
level will change. It is therefore advisable to use only variable costs when
calculating the per-period profit margins as part of CLV analysis. This
is not to say you should ignore fixed costs; on the contrary, they can and
should be tallied and compared to the innovation equity calculated. This
comparison can aid in making go/no-go launch decisions, in trying to determine how many years it would take to recoup all the fixed expenses
(including upfront R&D outlays), in assessing the advisability of running

a marketing promotion, or in attempting to figure out if and when more funding will be necessary to continue operations.

Retention rate. To get a handle on a reasonable retention rate to use, an approach similar to the "guessing by analogy" of the diffusion model parameters is recommended. In particular, it is common practice to examine retention rates that have been reported through the years in the relevant category or rates that are currently observed in related categories. In some categories, such as wireless communications or Internet services, retention rates are published regularly. For others, assessments are often provided in market reports. Studies conducted by Bain & Company suggest that the average yearly retention rate across all industries is about 80 percent. However, retention rates can vary substantially across industries. Online and mobile software applications often exhibit much lower retention rates than 80 percent, for example.

Sometimes the firm has data on customers' purchases of other products and services when it aims to assess the likely retention rate of an innovation—for example, the percentage of these customers who purchased/subscribed in one period and continued to purchase/subscribe in the next period. In such cases, the firm can draw a reasonable inference from customer behavior in those domains to the domain of the innovation in question (assuming these customers are strong candidates for this innovation).

Bear in mind that the retention rate used in the CLV model, which dictates the value of the attrition rate, should be consistent with the attrition rate used in the diffusion modeling to capture disadoption and/or churn (if relevant), as they are manifestations of the same phenomenon. This is true when attrition is accounted for both in a competitive diffusion setting, as described in chapter 6, and in a noncompetitive diffusion setting, as described in connection with category-level disadoption in our response to an earlier FAQ (and formalized in math box 9 in the appendix).

When, on the other hand, attrition is not part of how the diffusion process is modeled but only part of how customer management is analyzed, one is essentially assuming that a customer who leaves is "lost for good"—that is, that customer will never readopt. Furthermore, in this case a customer that departs continues to be counted as part of the cumulative number of past adopters that have a social effect. This certainly simplifies the modeling and was the approach taken in the first few chapters of the book. This assumption is not implausible, but it could very well be that a customer who stops creating cash streams for the company ceases to contribute to the social force as well. There is no clear resolution on this matter, though the reason for disadoption may provide some clues. For example, if customers disadopt because their circumstances change such that they no longer need the innovation yet had a great experience with it when there was a need, they may continue to positively advocate for it. However, if the reason for disadoption was disappointment or discovery that the innovation's benefits are insufficient, then disadopters might cease to spread favorable WOM once they break their relationship with the firm.

Discount factor. As mentioned in chapter 2, the weighted average cost of capital (WACC) can be used as a good proxy for the discount rate to apply in order to bring future revenue streams to the present. The discount rate can vary by industry as well as over time. Several financial sources exist that provide discount rate values; we list a few in the references and recommended reading section. Historically, a discount rate between 10 percent and 15 percent per year for customer-related cash streams has been used in the United States, though it has certainly fallen below this number in recent years as a result of the global economic recession and the low interest rates set by the Federal Reserve in response.

Customer acquisition costs. Once again, your best bet to get an estimate of this variable prelaunch would be to examine the cost to acquire customers in the same category for past innovations or for recently launched innovations in related categories. Market research may help with understanding how effective various marketing communications will be and hence the level of effort or promotion that will be required to convert prospects into customers. One can update the estimates postlaunch as actual expenses are incurred. Although various acquisition elements often decline in cost after a while, competition may alter that dynamic and prevent acquisition costs from coming down materially as firms find themselves spending heavily to lure potential adopters by offering lavish incentives (as we saw with satellite radio).

Many business plans today present a "conversion funnel" that incorporates the share of potential customers who are expected to respond to certain marketing actions. Given the planned expenditures to convert along the funnel—for example, from awareness to consideration to purchase—one can then extract how much each customer effectively costs to acquire. And remember that even efforts that were expended on those who did not convert matter: they should be incorporated as part of the costs "expended" on those who have converted.

Lastly, note that when an expenditure cannot be tied directly to an acquired or prospective customer, then one should take the overall expenditure and divide it by the total number of customers who were acquired.

Often firms will simply take all their acquisition expenditures during the fiscal quarter or year and divide by the number of customers added in that time period to assess the effective acquisition cost per customer. Of course, this may ignore carry-over effects that the marketing effort may have, such as a mass media ad campaign that is still recalled by consumers months later when they are in the market to buy.

On a final note regarding this FAQ, as in the case of diffusion parameters, the time scale for the various CLV inputs has to be consistent across all parameters. For example, if a year is the temporal unit of analysis for the calculation, then the per-period profit margins, the retention rate, and the discount factor should all likewise be yearly.

Are some of the CLV parameters likely to change over time? If so, how?

We've already mentioned that the discount factor could change with time due to macroeconomic circumstances. The other CLV inputs could vary with time as well, in particular the per-period profit margin and the retention rate. We'll discuss them in turn.

With respect to changes in the per-period profit margin, studies conducted by Bain & Company, for example, suggest that the profitability of a customer typically goes up with the duration of their relationship with the firm. The reason for this upward trend in profitability is that with time, customers tend to buy more products from the firm, become less costly to serve, or are willing to pay more (often this means less need to offer discounts or to waive fees). Firms' greater familiarity with its customers, which comes with the passage of time, allows tailoring more complementary products and services to their liking, again allowing for extracting more customer value. However, this phenomenon may not occur in all industries, and the increase in customer profitability when witnessed is usually not linear in time.

Similarly, with respect to changes in the retention rate, extensive research in this area suggests that it, too, tends to go up with time. One possible explanation for this trend is that customers become more loyal to the firm and to the innovation; another is that inertia sets in as time goes by, resulting in *all* customers' tendency to develop a higher retention rate. However, another explanation could be at work: if there is heterogeneity among the customers acquired, so that some have a higher retention rate than others to begin with, what will happen over time is that those with the low retention rates will, on average, leave the firm well before those with the high retention rate. Therefore, a "natural selection" process will be at work: customers who are not as satisfied with the innovation (relative to its cost) or who have low switching costs may leave earlier. With time, customers who stay on tend to be those for whom there is a better fit with the new product or service, and hence the chance they will continue to the next period is higher. Consequently, when we examine a cohort of adopters, the retention rate in the first few periods will on average be lower than the retention rate of those remaining in later periods. It is not that they *become* more "loyal"; we are simply left with those who were more "loyal" to begin with.

Still, for simplicity, a fixed retention rate and constant per-period profit margin are often used when calculating the lifetime value of a customer. It is further common to plug in the average values observed (or expected) for these inputs over a reasonable time frame for all customers (at least at the segment level). That is certainly the approach we used in many of the examples presented in the book. Notwithstanding, it is possible to calculate customer lifetime value when these parameters change over time. This requires moving from the simple infinite-horizon formula to a period-by-period limited-horizon calculation. An Excel worksheet analysis supplied in our companion website, as mentioned in connection with a previous FAQ, can aid with this task.

FAQs on Merging the Diffusion and CLV Models, a.k.a. Innovation Equity

How should I think about the relevance of the innovation equity framework for different business models?
The innovation equity framework can be used for any type of business model the firm employs. Arguably, though, it is more pertinent when there are recurring forms of revenue during the customer's stay. As we have demonstrated throughout, when the innovation is a service, such as in the financial domain (a new type of investment product, credit account, mode of interaction with the bank) or in the entertainment arena (a cable television, satellite radio, or online streaming video subscription), the relevance is obvious given monthly or annual fees. But we have also given numerous examples for ongoing revenue streams from many product categories, such as a game console that generates royalties over time; an e-reader that makes money on a continued basis from the sale of e-books, apps, and even advertising; an electric vehicle that after the initial purchase yields additional earnings from offering extended warranties, certified service, and accessories and parts; and goods that are perishable or have a perishable

component and that entail repeated purchases (such as packaged food or razors). Cross-selling opportunities are also a revenue generator for many innovations.

The massive digitization of content and solutions in today's economy has boosted the relevance of recurring revenues and thus expected future earnings from customers. The abundance of digital freemium products, like Dropbox, is a testament to the fact that firms increasingly view the initial adoption decision as just the beginning of a long-term relationship with the customer. In fact, marketing thought leaders increasingly encourage managers to look at all products as "service *de facto*." All these developments feed nicely into the main messages of the book and the relevance of the innovation equity framework.

It is important to note that even if the bulk of revenues from a customer accrue at the time of adoption, as might be the case with certain durables such as a new refrigerator (though rumors have it that "smart" refrigerators are just around the corner, and who knows what "cool" recurring revenue streams they might bring!), the combined framework is still quite helpful. First, diffusion modeling remains indispensable for purposes of forecasting the customer acquisition pattern over time. Second, the revenues that accrue from each adoption in the future still need to be properly discounted to bring them to the present value. Third, and quite importantly, the various embellishments to the basic diffusion model have substantive consequences for the overall value of an innovation. For example, we have shown how to think about multiple segments and the implications for the timing of revenue accrual; the introduction of next generations can result in various effects, such as cannibalization and leapfrogging, that impact innovation equity as they alter how many people will adopt a given generation from a certain pool and when. And even though a customer might "pay his or her dues" upon adoption, if he or she ceases to use the innovation (i.e., disadopts), this can still affect future revenues because of the implications disadoption has for the social forces (as discussed in previous FAQs).

You explained in an earlier FAQ how negative social effects can doom an innovation. Are there other reasons for innovation failure that can be handled by the frameworks presented?
The desire to classify the performance of innovations as either "successes" or "failures" is quite natural—it makes thinking about their outcomes much simpler, and it tells you which innovations you should consider as

having exhibited "best practices" and therefore learn what was done correctly and emulate and which you should consider as reflecting "bad practices" and therefore learn what was done incorrectly and avoid. Reality is much more complex. Even if we go by a well-defined yardstick to measure performance, such as profitability or return on investment (ROI), then innovations will fall on a continuum, from utter flops (hefty financial losses) to modest losses to moderate gains to spectacular hits (huge financial profits)—and any level in between these four.

The innovation equity framework allows capturing this richness in possible outcomes. An innovation may achieve a robust cumulative penetration level, selling many units in a fairly short time frame, but because expected customer profitability is low, per the CLV analysis, the overall innovation equity is mediocre. This can be compared to ongoing fixed investments and any outstanding debt and may lead to a grim outlook. Conversely, the diffusion model parameters might suggest modest long-run potential and modest adoption forces yet predict healthy innovation equity because of extremely high expected customer profitability levels (a scenario not uncommon in B2B markets where, while adoption might be slow and limited in scope, each adopter generates substantial profits to the firm). Indeed, the substantial variance in the diffusion and CLV model parameters observed in practice suggests that innovations will fare differently from one another on a continuum of marketplace performances.

That said, you may still be wondering about how complete flops can be captured. Recall that in chapter 5, we discussed situations where innovations show promising success initially by penetrating segments that are of the early adopter, innovation-forward type but fall flat when it comes to penetrating mainstream segments. The likely cause for this outcome was the lack of a strong social connection between the segments. Furthermore, innovations that are assessed as having limited perceived benefits and/or high barriers to adoption—for example, when appraised as per the factors described in chapter 1 (relative advantage, complexity, trialability, compatibility, observability)—are expected to have weak adoption force parameters. This, in turn, will negatively impact innovation equity, possibly to the point where the company's cash burn on the innovation (development, launching, and future expenses) may not allow enough time to turn the corner on profits before funds run out, leading to the demise of the start-up or the termination of the innovation initiative. Furthermore, if a company ex ante underestimated any of the barriers, it may find itself in a situation of either having to considerably bolster the marketing outlay or "pull the plug" on the innovation; the latter option may be more sensible depending on the circumstances.

It is worth noting that the diffusion parameters available for using the analogous-innovations approach, such as those provided in the appendix, are based on nonfailures. This is virtually by definition, as these innovations endured sufficiently in the marketplace to provide enough data to estimate their diffusion parameters. This suggests that firms should carefully examine whether the innovation they are planning to develop and launch needs any parameter adjustments relative to the candidate analogs. It is not uncommon to characterize optimistic and pessimistic scenarios, articulate what would lead to one scenario versus the other, and propose parameter values that would correspond to each case (while using the analogous innovations as a baseline).

What happens if there is an unforeseen "shock" or if unexpected circumstances occur? Can these be incorporated?

Innovation equity figures should not be thought of as "one and done" but rather as evolving assessments. For example, as launch approaches and more information becomes available about customers' likely reactions, as the firm is more certain about the business model it will implement (e.g., pricing strategy, marketing activity), and as more clarity emerges on environmental conditions (competition, regulation, unemployment, GDP growth, etc.), a previously formulated innovation equity analysis may benefit from an update. One should adjust any of the parameters in the combined framework that may be affected.

Any innovation equity assessment, even one conducted under the utmost care and diligence, is subject to being impacted by unforeseen circumstances that occur well after launch. For example, XM Satellite Radio could not have predicted with certainty that Howard Stern would join Sirius, nor could they have anticipated the exact effects this would have (the details are described in chapter 6). In another example, medical device makers could not have easily foreseen that a few years after launching innovative drug-eluting heart stents, studies would emerge suggesting that their products increased the risk of fatal blood clots forming in patients (or predict how long concerns over this matter would persist). And not many companies (if any) that launched an innovation in the early 2000s projected the global recession that shook the economy later that decade. Of course, events that positively impact an innovation's fate can also occur, such as when the FDA eased regulations in 1997 on direct-to-consumer advertising, enabling pharmaceutical companies to market their new drugs much more effectively on television.

How should one account for these types of major events and dramatic changes in the environment? We separate our response into trying to deal with them *before* and *after* their occurrence. Undoubtedly, trying to predict various scenarios not under the firm's control is no small task; it has a "gazing into the crystal ball" feel to it. One option is to examine historic data and try to form a rough average probability estimate for major economic, competitive, and regulatory scenarios; propose how the parameter values (such as the adoption forces and per-period profit margins) would be impacted; and either generate multiple forecasts or go with some weighting of the various scenarios that might occur (taking, say, some average probability in each period that a negative or positive shock will take place and incorporating that).

As for accommodating a major event or shock after it has occurred, well that is a bit more straightforward. One must recognize the impact the event has on all the parameters of the framework, usually by either looking at how the data are trending as a result of the new circumstances or conducting quick market research to assess the implications and adjust the models (diffusion and CLV) accordingly. The revised innovation equity assessment should further take as a given what has already transpired with respect to customer adoption. Specifically, the current customer base should be part of the social adoption force, and the lifetime value of these acquired customers going forward should be included as part of total innovation equity. One also needs to assess whether the altered circumstances or major event will have a permanent or temporary effect on model parameters, with values potentially reverting back to previous levels after some time.

Most of the analysis presented in this book is based on aggregate-level data—for example, category-level yearly sales or retention rates. Especially in the case of digital products or products sold online, I may be able to analyze individual-level data on consumers. Is it worth the effort?

Indeed, the framework presented in this book for the most part relies on aggregate-level information, although the microfoundations that lead to it are based on how individuals are expected to behave with respect to innovation adoption and use. Particularly the diffusion models presented throughout are intended to provide the total number of adoptions expected in a period rather than the identities of specific individuals that will adopt, and when using the models to estimate the diffusion parameters of innovations that have already been launched, aggregated per-period unit sales data are used. For the CLV parameters, averages across customers were typically employed for the various elements, given that data are often available only at that level.

Even today, many companies have a difficult time getting finer level data for all the parameters of interest, especially when a large number of customers are involved. Furthermore, such highly granular "big data" can sometimes be prone to measurement error. Also recall that in order to assess the appropriate inputs to the innovation equity framework, we often have to rely on analogies from other products, industries, and sometimes countries. Obtaining such data is not a trivial task and often, at best, will be at an aggregate level.

Individual-level data on one's own customers can be of much value if it can be collected. This is particularly true for the CLV parameters. Individual-level data can help in better understanding and assessing the future retention rate, per-period profit margin, and acquisition costs. Such data may also lead to better identification of consumer segments and a more granular characterization of the profits that will be generated per customer acquired (rather than having to rely on a single average value).

Individual-level data can also help assess how best to influence the diffusion process through marketing intervention. For example, we discussed the possibility of seeding the market with new products to accelerate diffusion and how approaching opinion leaders can help in that regard. If one has individual-level data on social influence, such as the Klout score that firms can purchase on the online influence of their customer base (http://www.klout.com), it can aid in such targeting efforts. Data on which specific customers adopt new products relatively early or how certain customers react to marketing incentives over time, and understanding how these characteristics relate to lifetime value at the individual level, can definitely help fine-tune the innovation equity assessment.

Business literature increasingly refers to "customer engagement" as an important strategic objective. How is customer engagement related to the innovation equity framework presented here?
Customer engagement, a recent buzzword, refers to the extent of interaction a customer has with the company and its offerings or with other customers. Engaged customers are thought of as being highly involved with the brand and helping it flourish in the marketplace both directly and

indirectly. The engagement level of customers is expected to be reflected in their purchase behavior but does not stop there. Engaged customers typically spread positive word of mouth on the company's products, write positive reviews on social media, support fellow customers, and counter negative reactions instigated by others. Highly engaged customers are often active in online communities related to the product category or to the specific brand. They may also help the firm create new products by supplying ideas and providing feedback.

Customer engagement can affect innovation equity in several ways. Clearly it can affect the lifetime value of customers. Engaged customers may be willing to pay more and buy additional products, and their retention rate is often higher. Their activities and WOM in relation to the brand can increase other customers' retention rates and reduce acquisition costs (much like in the Dropbox example given in chapter 3, whereby a more engaged customer, who uses the service extensively, will likely send out more referrals to friends and colleagues to obtain additional space). The word of mouth and social media involvement of engaged customers can be taken into account in the diffusion model as well. They may increase the social force and accelerate the customer base growth of the innovation. It may even prove appropriate to use a multisegment diffusion model and distinguish between high versus low engaged customers.

While customer engagement is increasingly discussed in the business press, quantifying its monetary implications remains a mystery for many companies. The innovation equity framework presented here can provide a useful step in this regard, as it's a comprehensive framework that takes into account the various byproducts of customer engagement and translates them into a financial estimate. The framework can also be used for conducting what-if analyses on how various levels of customer engagement impact profitability. Future research will hopefully shed more light on how highly engaged customers differ from other customers in what they do and in how they affect others.

The Innovation Equity Checklist

At this point in the chapter, and the entire book for that matter, you might be feeling you have read enough, that you get it and it is now time to use what you have learned to perform some innovation equity assessments of your own. For your convenience, we provide below a set of steps that you should follow to accomplish this task. These five steps give you, in a nutshell, the key ingredients that go into preparing an innovation equity "dish." Subbullets highlight issues you should consider as you conduct each step. The checklist is intended to serve as a quick reference guide. Naturally, if you need more specifics on any of the steps or believe that your setting involves issues described in greater detail in a particular chapter, by all means refer back to any part of the book to enrich your assessment.

Steps 1 through 3 on the checklist are geared toward allowing you to "start your engine" and create an initial valuation of a new product or service, primarily for one that has not been introduced yet. Step 4 is all about making the most of your assessment and "kicking its tires" to understand the implications of modifying various assumptions. Step 5 instructs you on what to do postlaunch, when the "rubber has met the road," so to speak, and explains how to update your initial assessment with one that takes into account the realities that have materialized. In the event that you plan to carry out calculations, you will find in our companion site (http://www.InnovationEquityBook.com) an Excel worksheet that can help you implement the various steps, based on your context. So without further ado, we present the checklist:

1. Create a diffusion trajectory forecast for your innovation.
    *   Characterize the innovation you plan to value. Think about the most relevant category or market space it fits in. What are consumers currently doing to solve the problem or satisfy the needs that your innovation purports to solve/satisfy?
    *   Identify similar innovations that can help you in formulating the individual and social adoption forces for your innovation. You can use previously launched products/services or the same innovation that is already diffusing in other countries.
    *   Consider the extent of any differences between the analogous innovations you identified and your innovation and adapt these parameters to your context. Use criteria (such as those described in chapter 1) to think about how quickly your innovation is likely to be adopted compared to the other innovations. Remember to consider potential barriers to adoption: What might be missing for potential customers with your innovation? What will they have to do differently to integrate it into their work/life setting? Consider the role of word of mouth and other social effects (such as network effects) in influencing adoption.
    *   Assess your innovation's long-run market potential. Segment potential customers along dimensions that pertain to the likelihood of adoption: For

whom does the innovation deliver the greatest value and produce minimal barriers to adoption? For whom is the innovation a tough proposition to accept? Look at past relevant innovations' long-term cumulative penetration levels.

- Collect as much information as possible to fine-tune the diffusion parameters. Talk to experts outside of the organization and to experienced people within the firm. Get their perceptions on which analogous innovations are most pertinent and how they believe customers will react to the innovation considered. Conduct market research to evaluate various customer segments' receptivity to the innovation's characteristics and apply a multisegment approach to diffusion if appropriate (see chapter 4 for details). Adjust the input you get from the market research to reflect possible response biases, such as overstating purchase intent.

- Determine if you should try to forecast the brand's diffusion directly or if a category-level projection is most appropriate, depending on the expected nature of competition and customer behavior (one-stage or two-stage decision making). In each case, additional parameters may be needed (see chapter 6 for specifics).

- If you plan to launch the innovation in multiple countries or in a country for which you do not have direct analogies to refer to, establish how country characteristics may affect the speed and scale of adoption. Make any necessary adjustments to the parameters you have come up with from one country to the other and include cross-country effects if relevant (see chapter 8 for specifics).

2. Build a customer lifetime value projection for your innovation.
- Get clarity on the business model that will be implemented. Accordingly, evaluate the expected per-period profit margin from each customer for the innovation at hand. Make sure you take into account all possible sources of revenue from customers directly and from third parties (e.g., advertisers). Also, make sure you properly integrate all costs, such as manufacturing and service, and focus on the variable costs that need to be incurred to serve each customer.

- Come up with an appropriate retention rate. Study customer behavior with existing products and services in the same or in related categories, gauge attrition rates there, and adapt to your innovation. Depending on the specific diffusion model you use—competitive or category level—you may need to formulate an estimate of the churn rate as well.

- Figure out an appropriate discount factor to be used. Refer to external financial sources, which regularly publish relevant discount rates (such as the weighted average cost of capital). Try to pin down the rate most applicable to your industry setting and for your company specifically; consult with finance and accounting professionals in your organization as necessary.

- Calculate the lifetime value of a customer by using the infinite-horizon formula (per chapter 2) or by running a period-by-period analysis for the relevant limited horizon (using an Excel spreadsheet, for example).
- Think carefully about what would be required to most effectively and efficiently get a customer to adopt your innovation and switch from using existing alternatives (including the inertia of currently doing nothing). What inducements are needed to get him or her to take a risk on a new technology/ solution? Does your company have a plan for the marketing actions that will be undertaken at launch and beyond to acquire customers? What is the expected balance in the plan between targeted efforts (e.g., seeding the innovation among influential consumers) versus mass marketing efforts (e.g., television ads)? To get a sense of the costs associated with the plan, examine how much firms spend on similar marketing programs in this or a related category. Refer to industry studies that report marketing ROI metrics for various acquisition activities.
- Include both direct expenses per customer, such as subsidies and rebates, and broader marketing activity aimed at attracting new customers in order to obtain a final acquisition cost estimate per customer added (divide any broad acquisition expenses by the expected number of new adopters to translate them into a per-acquired customer basis). Subtract the acquisition costs from the lifetime value figure to obtain the prospective CLV estimate.
3. Perform an innovation equity assessment.
    - Combine the diffusion trajectory forecast with the lifetime value of a customer projection. Specifically, multiply the number of new adoptions expected in each period by the prospective lifetime value of a customer (PCLV).
    - Discount customer valuations expected in each future period to the present. The same discount factor applied in the CLV calculation should be employed in doing so.
    - Consolidate all expenses and investments that are fixed (excluding any that were already taken into account as part of acquisition efforts). Bring those expenses to a commensurate net present value using the discount factor.
    - Start examining the implications of your analysis. Compare the innovation equity assessed to the upfront costs of development. Will the costs be recouped? Are any ongoing fixed expenses a drag on reaching profitability in a reasonable time frame? How long will it take for the innovation to break even? Will extra funding likely be needed, and if so, when?

4. Run sensitivity analyses.
   - Examine your assumptions. Is it reasonable to expect that some of the parameters used in your innovation equity assessment will change with time? If so, by how much? What would be the best-case and worst-case levels for these parameters? In turn, what would optimistic versus pessimistic innovation equity assessments look like?
   - Ponder various future eventualities. What will happen to your innovation equity assessments if the economic conditions in the market change dramatically? How will negative or positive shocks matter?
   - Consider the advisability of taking specific actions postlaunch. What will be the impact of intensifying marketing activities? How will improvements to the product or customer service affect innovation equity?
   - Perform what-if analyses by manipulating the parameters of both the diffusion and CLV models to reflect various scenarios and interventions; assess the implications on innovation equity each time.

5. Revisit your innovation equity assessment postlaunch.
   - As data begin flowing in after launch, both on unit sales and on customer reactions, reassess the various components of the models. Are customer profit margins per period higher or lower than anticipated? Are acquisition efforts more or less effective than expected? Does initial customer behavior point to strong or weak loyalty? Do the adoption forces used in the prelaunch forecast appear to correspond to those from the postlaunch data?
   - Revise your prelaunch innovation equity assessment, based on the observed market realities, by redoing steps 1 through 3 with the updated parameter estimates.
   - Add the lifetime value of current (already acquired) customers to the revised innovation equity assessment going forward, as existing customers will continue to generate expected profits. Current customers should also be included in the set of past adopters relevant for exerting a social force.
   - Understand the implications of the revised innovation equity assessment by going through step 4 again; consider different what-if scenarios as appropriate.

And there you have it. Five straightforward steps to assess the value of an innovation and better manage it for commercial success. We encourage you to use these steps, and the many insights delivered throughout the book, to evaluate innovations your firm is contemplating developing, is poised to launch, or has already introduced. Or use the material to be in a better position to investigate how a new product or service you are curious about will fare over time. Whether it be driverless cars, drones for business and private use, smart watches (e.g., Apple Watch), or smart eye-wear (e.g., Google Glass), there's much to be gained by looking at these novelties through the innovation equity lens.

A Few Final Words

At the outset of the book, we invited you to embark on a journey with us to explore the vast repositories of knowledge and the treasure troves of experience that have accumulated on the topics of innovation diffusion and customer management, to join us in discovering the power of combining these two topics into one integrated framework. Well, it is now time to "return home" (or to the office, as might be the case) and put into practice what you've learned—to let the innovation equity framework work for you. How you fill in the "[Enter Quote Here]" line is now entirely up to you.

Appendix

Math and More

As demonstrated repeatedly in this book—and hopefully by now you have "bought" the argument—by combining the concepts of innovation diffusion and customer lifetime value, we can arrive at an innovation's equity—in other words, its monetary worth. In this appendix, we provide a few "extras" that should allow interested readers to delve deeper into various aspects of the framework.

Much of the material described in connection with the innovation equity framework—in particular, the various models and expressions that were presented throughout—can be conveyed formally through sets of equations. We begin the appendix by providing the mathematical representations that correspond to these models and expressions. In subsequent sections, we elaborate on and justify the set of parameters used in conjunction with the satellite radio example presented in the book and lastly include a table of adoption forces (p and q) for select innovations in the United States in the last three decades.

Mathematically Formalizing the Expressions

The theory and practice of innovation equity can be described mathematically by sets of equations that depict an innovation's diffusion process in a given market as well as the lifetime value of customers who adopt it. We provide those equations here and organize them in "math boxes." These math boxes were referred to in the various chapters of the book (and a math box's number corresponds to the chapter for which it is relevant).

Math Box 1: The Basic Diffusion Model (a.k.a. the Bass Model)
and Its "Epidemiological Origins"

Figure 1.2 provides us with a blueprint for how to construct a mathematical representation of the basic diffusion model. The model has several building blocks. First, let's specify those consumers who have adopted the innovation by a particular point in time as well as those who have not yet adopted (it is from this latter pool that new adoptions in the current period can originate). We will use the following notation:

- $N(t)$ is the total or *cumulative* number of consumers who have already adopted the innovation through period t.
- $N(t-1)$ is the cumulative number of adopters of the innovation by the end of the previous period (i.e., $t-1$) who can affect through social influence those who have not yet adopted in the current period (i.e., t).
- $n(t)$ is the number of *new* adopters *during* period t and can be expressed as

$$n(t) = N(t) - N(t-1).$$

Having defined these terms, we now move to the three key parameters of the model, usually labeled m, p, and q. The parameter m captures the long-run market potential for the innovation, representing the relevant population that will ever adopt. The two other parameters in the model, p and q, capture the individual and social forces that can drive adoption, respectively, as depicted in figure 1.2. Together, p and q specify how fast or slow the adoption of a new product is expected to proceed and what shape the diffusion curve will take.

In order to better understand the mechanisms behind the individual and social forces, also called *external* and *internal influences*, it is instructive to refer to models proposed in the field of epidemiology, which in fact served as the main inspiration for innovation diffusion modeling efforts. The simplest such epidemiology model is the susceptible-infected-removed (SIR) model. Consider an epidemic such as cholera in a given community. Since there is no known natural immunization against cholera, the entire population is susceptible to the disease. There are two ways to get infected: by an external source, usually contaminated water, and by coming into physical contact with a sick person. Once a person is infected, there are two ways to leave this group: die or recover. Under the first circumstance, the person is removed from the epidemic process, and under the latter, the person is *again* susceptible—as if he or she never got the disease in the first place, thus he or she is back in the susceptible group. Despite the age and simplicity of the SIR model, its variants are still used today to estimate and control outbreaks of diseases, such as varicella in schoolchildren in Medellin, Colombia, or avian influenza in the Netherlands.

The analogy to the diffusion of an innovation is clear: m, the long-run market potential for the innovation, corresponds to the entire population that is "susceptible to the disease"; $N(t-1)$, the cumulative number of adopters leading up to period t, corresponds to the number of those "infected"; hence, the remaining market potential that can adopt in period t is $m - N(t-1)$ and corresponds to those who are "healthy." A portion of the remaining untapped potential for the innovation adopts ("contracts the disease") in the current period due to independent, external influence, and its size is $p \cdot (m - N(t-1))$, where p corresponds to the susceptibility to contract the disease from external sources. The portion of the remaining untapped potential that adopts due to social, internal influence is a bit more intricate: If the cumulative number of adopters is $N(t)$, their proportion of all potential adopters in the relevant population is $N(t)/m$. Since the greater the proportion of the population that has already adopted, corresponding to the proportion of infected people, the more likely someone is to be affected by social interactions, corresponding to coming into contact with an infected person, we write $\dfrac{qN(t-1)}{m} \cdot (m - N(t-1))$ for the number of adoptions in the current period due to social influence, where q corresponds to the susceptibility to contracting the disease from internal sources. Note that in both routes to adoption, we count only newly "converted" individuals by multiplying the adoption forces (or susceptibility to each influence) by the number of those who have not yet adopted. This characterization is similar to how new adoptions might take place for a smartphone such as the iPhone: if two iPhone adopters meet, at most they might congratulate each other on their wisdom in having adopted the iPhone, but no new adoptions will come out of this meeting. For new adoptions to occur, at least one sick and one healthy individual need to meet and "exchange bacteria"; analogously, an iPhone user needs to meet a non-iPhone user and exchange information (visual, verbal, or both) for a new iPhone adoption to occur.

Combining the two adoption terms yields the following equation that captures the number of new adoptions in each period t, often called the Bass equation:

$$n(t) = \left(p + \frac{qN(t-1)}{m} \right) \cdot (m - N(t-1))$$

If each adopter buys exactly one unit, then these equations describe the sales growth of the innovation that follows an inverted U or bell shape, while the cumulative function has a classical S shape.

The Bass equation could also be applied to penetration instead of sales. To see the equivalence, define the following variables:

- $F(t) = N(t) / m$ is the cumulative penetration—that is, the fraction of consumers (out of the total market potential) who have already adopted the innovation through period t.
- $f(t) = n(t) / m$ is the fraction of *new* adopters (out of the total market potential) *during* period t and can be expressed as $f(t) = F(t) - F(t-1)$.

Dividing the equation for $n(t)$ by the market potential m yields the penetration level version of the Bass equation:

$$f(t) = (p + q \cdot F(t-1)) \cdot (1 - F(t-1))$$

Math Box 2: Customer Lifetime Value (CLV) Analysis and Innovation Equity Assessment

An innovation is introduced into the market, and T years after its launch, the firm wishes to calculate its value. The period or time unit of analysis we use is a year, and thus the retention rate, discount rate, and attrition rate are all expressed yearly. We will use the following notation:

- g—annual profit margin of a single customer
- r—annual retention rate
- i—cost of capital of the firm (annual discount rate)
- a—acquisition cost of a new customer

If a firm has a customer in this period, the probability of that customer still being with the firm in the next period is r; two periods from now that probability is r^2; and more generally, the probability of that customer still being with the firm t periods from now is r^t. Similarly, given n customers that are using the firm's new product or service today, nr^t will still be using it t periods from now.

It is straightforward to show that the expected number of periods a customer with a retention rate of r stays with the firm, also known as the average stay, is given by the following:

$$\text{average stay} = \frac{1}{1-r}$$

Thus if the retention rate is 0.8 or 80 percent, for example, the consumer on average stays with the firm $1 / (1 - 0.8) = 5$ years. A quick-and-dirty way to compute the lifetime value of a customer is to multiply his or her average stay by the gross profit margin that he or she brings in annually.

The value of $g / (1 - r)$ is of course an upper bound on a customer's lifetime value, since it does not take discounting into account. With discounting, it is straightforward to show the following:

$$\text{CLV} = \text{current customer lifetime value} = \frac{g}{1+i-r}$$

And by the same token, given that a is the acquisition cost, we have the following:

$$\text{PCLV} = \text{current prospective customer lifetime value} = \frac{g}{1+i-r} - a$$

As in the basic diffusion model, we define the following:

- $N(t)$ is the total or *cumulative* number of customers who have already adopted the innovation through period t.
- $n(t)$ is the number of *new* adopters *during* period t.

The diffusion process is expected to occur according to

$$n(t) = (p + q \cdot N(t-1)/m) \cdot (m - N(t-1)).$$

As we are performing the assessment T periods after the launch, we need to separate the calculation for current and future customers (note that the case of $T = 0$ coincides with an analysis conducted at launch with only future acquired customers). The lifetime value of current customers, who have already been acquired by period T, is given by $N(T) \cdot CLV$, and this quantity does not need to be discounted, as it is assessed in the current period T. The lifetime value of future customers expected to be acquired in year t $(t > T)$ is given by $n(t) \cdot PCLV$. To bring this quantity to the present value, we need to apply financial discounting appropriate for the number of periods into the future beyond period T—in other words, multiply it by $\frac{1}{(1+i)^{t-T-1}}$. Innovation equity is thus given by the following expression:

$$\text{Innovation equity at time } T = N(T) \cdot CLV + \sum_{t=T+1}^{\infty} \frac{n(t) \cdot PCLV}{(1+i)^{t-T-1}}$$

Math Box 4: The Multisegment Diffusion Model

The basic diffusion model with a single segment was presented in math box 1. The description there showed us how to formalize the diffusion process and incorporate its three main components: the individual force (p), the social force (q), and long-run market potential (m). Moving from the basic model to an expanded two-segment diffusion model is relatively straightforward. Once again, we will want to distinguish between consumers who have already adopted and those who have not yet adopted by a given point in time, except that now we also need to distinguish between adopters from one segment versus the other. So we will use similar notation as in math box 1 but attach subscripts to the variables in order to indicate those that belong to the first segment and those that belong to the second segment. When relating to the innovation-forward segment, we will use a subscript of 1, and when referring to the innovation-moderate, or mainstream segment, we will use a subscript of 2. Accordingly, we will employ the following notation:

- $N_1(t)$ is the total number of innovation-forward consumers who have already adopted the innovation through period t.
- $n_1(t)$ is the number of new adopters from the innovation-forward segment during period t and can be expressed as $n_1(t) = N_1(t) - N_1(t-1)$.
- $N_2(t)$ is the total number of innovation-moderate consumers who have already adopted the innovation through period t.
- $n_2(t)$ is the number of new adopters from the innovation-moderate segment during period t and can be expressed as $n_2(t) = N_2(t) - N_2(t-1)$.

We can write a diffusion model for each segment in the form of

$$n_1(t) = \left(p_1 + \frac{q_1 N_1(t-1)}{m_1} \right) \left(m_1 - N_1(t-1) \right)$$

$$n_2(t) = \left(p_2 + \frac{q_2 N_2(t-1)}{m_2} + \frac{q_{21} N_1(t-1)}{m_1} \right) \left(m_2 - N_2(t-1) \right)$$

As can be gleaned from these two equations, for segment 1, adoption is either an individual decision (through the impact of p_1) or a socially affected decision from other segment 1 adopters (through the impact of q_1)—exactly as in the basic diffusion model. But for segment 2 individuals, there is also the potential of being influenced by segment 1 adopters through the parameter q_{21}. If p_1 is very high compared to p_2, while q_{21} is very low compared to q_2, in essence, what will happen is that total adoptions of the innovation as a function of time $n_1(t) + n_2(t)$ will exhibit a rapid initial uptake (driven by segment 1) only to be followed by a dramatic dip in new adoptions until a critical mass of segment 2 adoptions take place so that the social force internal to that group can kick in. This pattern corresponds to the "saddle" phenomenon discussed in chapter 4.

Math Box 6: The Competitive Diffusion Model

The equation that governs the diffusion pattern of brands in a competitive market is best understood with the help of figure 6.3 (in chapter 6). We focus on the two-firm case and define the following variables and parameters:

- $N_1(t)$ is the *total* number of consumers who are users of brand 1 through period t.
- $n_1(t)$ is the number of *new* adopters of brand 1 during period t.
- $N_2(t)$ is the *total* number of consumers who are users of brand 2 through period t.
- $n_2(t)$ is the number of *new* adopters of brand 2 during period t.

Let the diffusion process parameters in the model, p_i and q_i, capture the individual and social adoption forces for brand i. The two firms draw customers from a common pool whose long-run potential is m. Word of mouth is exchanged between users and nonusers and occurs at the brand level but with possible cross-brand social effects q_{ij}, where the subscripts indicate the impact of brand j adopters on new adoptions for brand i. The churn and disadoption rates for firm i are denoted by c_i and d_i. The two equations that govern the evolution of the market for the two firms are given by the following (the time arguments t and $t-1$ are suppressed for convenience):

$$n_1 = \left(p_1 + \frac{q_1 N_1}{m} + \frac{q_{12} N_2}{m} \right)(m - N_1 - N_2) - c_1 N_1 + c_2 N_2 - d_1 N_1$$

$$n_2 = \left(p_2 + \frac{q_2 N_2}{m} + \frac{q_{21} N_1}{m} \right)(m - N_2 - N_1) - c_2 N_2 + c_1 N_1 - d_2 N_2$$

Looking at the leftmost parenthetical in the expression for n_1, the first term (p_1) represents the individual influence, much like in the basic diffusion process. The second and third terms in this parenthetical (functions of q_1 and q_{12}) represent the within-brand and cross-brand social effects, respectively. These forces prompt the available market potential who are currently not customers of either brand, $(m - N_1 - N_2)$, to adopt firm I (note that the available market potential includes individuals who have not yet adopted either brand as well as those that had but disadopted in the past). The next set of terms, $c_1 N_1$ and $c_2 N_2$, represent outgoing and incoming customers who churned to and from the competitor, respectively. The last term ($d_1 N_1$) captures the firm's customers who disadopt—that is, leave the category altogether. The equation for $n_1(t)$ can be used to compute the innovation equity of brand I at any time T by plugging it into the innovation equity expression given in math box 2 (and similarly for brand 2):

Innovation equity of brand 1 *at time* $T = N_1(T) \cdot CLV_1$

$$+ \sum_{t=T+1}^{\infty} \frac{n_1(t) \cdot PCLV_1}{(1+i)^{t-T-1}}$$

Where CLV_1 and $PCLV_1$ are customer lifetime value and prospective customer lifetime value of brand I, and i is the discount rate. Note that in general, each brand may have different CLV parameters. It is important to ensure that the attrition rate $(1-r)$ used in the CLV and PCLV expressions corresponds to the attrition rate in the expression for $n_1(t)$; therefore $c_1 + d_1 = 1 - r_1$.

Math Box 7: The Next-Generation Diffusion Model

Observe figure A.1, which replicates figure 7.4 with added notations that
will be used in this math box, and assume that at period t, there are two
innovation generations, denoted by 1 and 2, that operate in the market (and
that a third generation has not yet been launched). Define the following
variables:

- $N_1(t)$ is the *total* number of consumers who have adopted generation 1 through
  period t and are continued users of it (i.e., have not upgraded to generation 2).
- $n_1(t)$ is the number of *net new* adopters of generation 1 during period t.
- $N_2(t)$ is the *total* number of consumers who have adopted generation 2 through
  period t.
- $n_2(t)$ is the number of *new* adopters of generation 2 during period t.

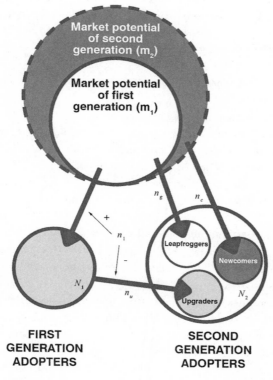

FIGURE A.1. Sources of demand for successive generations (with complete notations)

In the above notation, observe that in the case of generation 1's adoption, we need to account for the fact that some people who adopted that generation in the past upgrade to generation 2. In particular, in the case of $n_1(t)$, we look at the number of new adopters in each period but subtract those who upgrade to generation 2 (hence the word "net" in the definition); this is also reflected in the definition of $N_1(t)$ (hence the wording "and are continued users of it").

Following the entry of generation 2, the older generation continues to acquire customers from those remaining in the m_1 pool. However, some of the m_1 potential adopters may decide to *leapfrog*—that is, skip generation 1 and buy generation 2 instead. *Upgraders* to generation 2 are customers of generation 1 who switch to the newer generation, and *newcomers* are those adopters of generation 2 who originate from the expansion of the market potential from m_1 to m_2. Consequently, generation 2 acquires adopters from (1) users of generation 1 who decide to upgrade, (2) potential adopters of generation 1 who decide to leapfrog directly to generation 2, and (3) new adopters from the expanded market potential of size $m_2 - m_1$.

We have the following new definitions:

- $N_u(t)$ is the total number of *upgraders* from the first to the second generation through period t.
- $n_u(t)$ is the number of new *upgraders* during period t.
- $N_g(t)$ is the total number *leapfroggers*—that is, consumers in the market potential of generation 1 who adopt generation 2 through period t.
- $n_g(t)$ is the number of new *leapfroggers* during period t.
- $N_c(t)$ is the total number of *newcomers* who adopt generation 2 through period t.
- $n_c(t)$ is the number of new *newcomers* during period t.

Using this notation, the potential remaining pool of adopters for generation 1 at period t is $\left(m_1 - N_1 - N_u - N_g\right)$, while for generation 2, it is $\left(m_1 - N_1 - N_u - N_g\right)$ for leapfroggers, N_1 for upgraders, and $\left(m_2 - m_1 - N_c\right)$ for newcomers.

In the general case, each generation may be characterized by its own adoption force parameters (p and q). Importantly, each has a distinct set of existing adopters, N_1 and N_2, respectively, which exert the relevant (generation-specific) social force.

Thus we have the following equation for generation 1's net new adopters in period t:

$$n_1(t) = \left(p_1 + \frac{q_1 N_1(t-1)}{m_1} \right) \cdot \left(m_1 - N_1(t-1) - N_u(t-1) - N_g(t-1) \right) - n_u(t)$$

Note from this expression that while generation 1 enjoys an incoming flow from its remaining market potential, it suffers from an outflow of up-graders to generation 2.

For generation 2, we decompose new adoptions in period t into the three sources and then combine, as in the following set of equations (the time arguments t and $t-1$ are suppressed for convenience):

$$n_u = \left(p_2 + \frac{q_2 N_2}{m_2} \right) \cdot N_1$$

$$n_g = \left(p_2 + \frac{q_2 N_2}{m_2} \right) \cdot \left(m_1 - N_1 - N_u - N_g \right)$$

$$n_c = \left(p_2 + \frac{q_2 N_2}{m_2} \right) \cdot \left(m_2 - m_1 - N_c \right)$$

$$n_2 = n_u + n_g + n_c$$

For many successive product generations, we find that $p_1 \approx p_2$ and $q_1 \approx q_2$ as discussed in chapter 7. (Note also that, in general, the parameters p_2 and q_2 could differ for each source of demand; for simplicity, we have assumed they are equivalent.)

Math Box 8: The Global Diffusion Model

In order to understand and analyze the diffusion of innovations in multiple countries, one can extend the basic diffusion model to a case in which an innovation's growth in one country affects the same innovation's growth in other countries. While a worldwide model that includes the effects of many countries on each other can be very complicated to build and estimate, one can more tractably consider a model that takes into account the effects between two entities, where the entities can be two countries, one country and the "rest of the world," or some other region (e.g., "the rest of Western Europe").

For example, assume that we have two countries, country 1 and country 2, as follows:

- $N_1(t)$ is the *total* number of country 1 consumers who have adopted the innovation through period t.

- $n_1(t)$ is the number of *new* adopters in country 1 during period t.
- $N_2(t)$ is the *total* number of country 2 consumers who have adopted the innovation through period t.
- $n_2(t)$ is the number of *new* adopters in country 2 during period t.

We label the cross-country effect of the adopters in country 2 on potential adopters in country 1 as q_{12} and similarly for the cross-country effect of adopters in country 1 on potential adopters in country 2. The equations that govern the growth of the innovation in the two countries in period t are as follows:

$$n_1(t) = \left(p_1 + \frac{q_1 \cdot N_1(t-1)}{m_1} + \frac{q_{12} \cdot N_2(t-1)}{m_2} \right) \cdot \left(m_1 - N_1(t-1) \right)$$

$$n_2(t) = \left(p_2 + \frac{q_2 \cdot N_2(t-1)}{m_2} + \frac{q_{21} \cdot N_1(t-1)}{m_1} \right) \cdot \left(m_2 - N_2(t-1) \right)$$

The two equations can be used to assess how an innovation will diffuse in a country given its diffusion in another country. It is interesting in particular to understand how one can assess the cross-country parameters q_{12} and q_{21}. As explained in chapter 8, this effect can arise either from direct communications between citizens of the two countries (in which case geographical proximity and ease of travel can be especially important) or due to mere knowledge of the adoption level in the other country, which can serve as an indication for expected benefits from the innovation. In either case, it is highly conceivable that some countries have more effect on others; hence, the cross-country parameters will most likely not be equal.

The model above can also accommodate any *lead–lag* effects between two countries as discussed in chapter 8. The lead country's diffusion may begin earlier than the lag country's diffusion. In that case, the lead country will initially follow the basic diffusion model and have a set of cumulative adopters at the time the lag country's diffusion commences. At that point one switches to the above set of equations, taking care to use the lead country's already accumulated set of adopters, which continues to grow. Second, one should entertain the distinct possibility that the cross-country effects are not symmetric. If country 1 is the leader and country 2 is the laggard, then q_{21}, which captures how country 1 affects country 2, will probably be larger than q_{12}, which captures how country 2 affects country 1.

If sufficient time has elapsed, there will be enough adopters from the lead country to ignite a social influence process on the lag country. This cross-country effect will be particularly strong if q_{21} is indeed high as expected.

Thus once the population of the lag country begins to adopt, we may expect a rapid diffusion process.

Math Box 9: The Basic Diffusion Model with Disadopters

In this math box, we describe the category-level diffusion model when disadopters are explicitly taken into account as part of the basic diffusion process. This can also be thought of as a "single-brand" version of the model presented in math box 6; note that in this case though, we do not deal with churn, and therefore disadoption in effect captures all the attrition (and its value should generally coincide with the attrition rate used in the CLV analysis). Such a model will also allow us to account for the fact that disadopters no longer exert a social force.

As in a basic diffusion model, let the parameters p and q capture the individual and social adoption forces, respectively. The firm draws adopters from a market whose long-run potential is m. Let $N(t)$ denote the number of current customers (past adopters net those that have left due to disadoption), and let the parameter d denote the disadoption rate from the category. The equation that governs the evolution of *net new* adoptions in each period is as follows:

$$n(t) = \left(p + \frac{qN(t-1)}{m} \right) \cdot \left(m - N(t-1) \right) - d \cdot N(t-1)$$

The first term represents the number of new customers acquired due to the adoption forces from the untapped/available potential $(m - N)$, which includes those that have never adopted as well as those that have disadopted in the past. The second term counts the number of current customers who decide to disadopt the innovation in the current period. Thus $n(t)$ is the number of net new additions into the category (or single brand if there is no competition). Further note that the expression for $n(t)$ assumes that disadopters are thrown back into the pool of remaining potential adopters and may readopt in the future.

Derivation of XM and Sirius Parameter Estimates for the Prelaunch Forecast

In analyzing the satellite radio industry, we generally kept the parameter values for the innovation diffusion as well as the customer lifetime value

TABLE A.1 **XM Satellite Radio lifetime value parameters**

Annual retention rate	81 percent
Cost of capital	9.3 percent
Gross profit margins	$77
Acquisition costs	$95

models consistent across the two competitors and across chapters (except if otherwise noted explicitly). We did this knowing full well that these values, for such a relatively young industry, are constantly changing and that the questions we posed in different chapters correspond to different times in the product life cycle. Thus, for example, the subsidy issue was a prelaunch decision, while the dilemma of signing up Howard Stern arose a couple of years following Sirius's introduction. We kept these values constant for ease of following the logic and consistency across chapters. (And as noted in the various chapters, all these values as well as the forecasts themselves are based on our own assessments using various sources of publicly available information.)

For the innovation diffusion parameters (p and q), we have chosen values that are the average across three analogous products (CD players, automobile radios, and cellular phones) to come up with the (rounded) values of $p = 0.026$ and $q = 0.403$.

For the market potential, we relied on market research conducted by XM to come up with 24.8 and 31.5 million subscribers for a car radio receiver priced at $300 and $200, respectively (at a monthly subscription price of $12). For purposes of applying the basic diffusion model, the (rounded) midpoint of this range has served us as the market potential $m = 28$ million.

As we showed in chapter 2, these simple prelaunch estimates were quite reasonable at predicting the growth of the industry. Thus, for example, at the end of 2011, Sirius and XM Satellite Radio had 21.9 million subscribers, while the forecast based on these parameter values was 21.1 million. (We wish to note that throughout, we treated 2001 as the first full year postlaunch for forecasting purposes, even though XM's actual launch took place only in the third quarter of that year. This simplified the analysis and exposition and had little bearing on conclusions, and it avoided computing annual growth as between third quarters year to year. This approach also allowed capturing any pent-up demand that had possibly accumulated prior to the launch and materialized soon after.)

For the financial values needed to compute lifetime values, we mainly relied on a paper by Libai, Muller, and Peres (see the references and recommended reading section for the full citation) and complemented it when necessary with values taken from XM's and Sirius's 10-K forms. To emphasize again, the numbers were generally taken as constant across the years and across the two competitors (except when otherwise explicitly noted) for ease of explanation as well as consistency across chapters. These figures are as presented in table A.1, where a subscriber's lifetime value could easily be computed as $272, while the lifetime value of a prospect is $177.

Table of Adoption Force Parameters (p and q) for Select Innovations in the United States

The following is a list of diffusion parameters for thirty consumer electronics products in the United States that may serve as a basis for the analogy method described and used in various chapters.

TABLE A.2 **Adoption force parameters for select innovations in the United States**

	Start year	p	q
VCR decks	1974	0.0022	0.237
Aftermarket PC monitors	1980	0.0014	0.184
Computer printers	1980	0.0018	0.195
Cordless telephones	1980	0.0020	0.256
Personal word processors	1982	0.0328	0.211
Telephone answering devices	1982	0.0085	0.141
Analog handheld LCD monochrome television	1983	0.0323	0.134
Dedicated CD players	1983	0.0032	0.298
Analog projection television	1984	0.0037	0.400
Modems/broadband gateways	1984	0.0023	0.170
Standard wireless phones	1984	0.0006	0.305
Analog handheld LCD color television	1985	0.0147	0.157
Camcorders	1985	0.0095	0.143
Laserdisc players	1985	0.0178	0.533
LCD television	1985	0.0002	0.482
DBS satellite receivers	1986	0.0015	0.275
Portable CD equipment	1987	0.0076	0.330
Analog television combinations	1990	0.0115	0.373
Aftermarket remote controls	1991	0.0152	0.210
Digital cameras	1996	0.0058	0.394
DVD players/recorders	1997	0.0215	0.299
Family radio devices	1997	0.0398	0.282
Set-top Internet access devices	1997	0.1430	0.502
Digital television sets and displays	1998	0.0055	0.413

continues

	Start year	p	q
Digital projection television	1999	0.0396	0.637
Plasma DTV	1999	0.0075	0.492
Portable MP3 players/media players	1999	0.0101	0.486
Portable and transportable navigation	2000	0.0055	0.641
HDTV	2003	0.0261	0.376
VOIP adapters	2003	0.0449	0.604

Notes

Information Sources and Comments

In this section, we provide sources for various pieces of information and quotes that appeared in the book. These are organized by chapter under the heading "Facts and Quotes." In some instances, we felt it was appropriate to embellish on a certain point or communicate a finer explanation regarding an aspect that was presented; such items are again organized by chapter under the heading "Comments." Lastly, at the end of this Notes section, we comment on the sources used in constructing several of the tables and figures that are based on external information. All website addresses listed were checked for access between September 1 and 10, 2015.

Introduction

FACTS AND QUOTES

Time hailed Google Glass: *Time*, "Best Inventions of the Year 2012," October 21, 2012, http://techland.time.com/2012/11/01/best-inventions-of-the-year-2012/slide /google-glass/.

Fortune Magazine suggested that "it's poised to possibly revolutionize computing": J. P. Mangalindan, "5 Ways to Make Google Glass Better," *Fortune*, May 3, 2013, http://fortune.com/2013/05/03/5-ways-to-make-google-glass-better/.

A prominent tech blogger . . . went on record as saying, "I think this will be a product that will stand up for decades . . . a new genre.": John Koetsier, "Google Glass Could Be Worth $3.3b in Just 4 Years," *Venture Beat*, September 4, 2013, http://venturebeat.com/2013/09/04/google-glass-could-worth-3-3b-in-just-4 -years/.

Businessweek cited critics who called it a "Segway for your face": Brad Stone, "Inside the Moonshot Factory," *Bloomberg Businessweek*, May 22, 2013, http:// www.bloomberg.com/bw/articles/2013-05-22/inside-googles-secret-lab.

The editor-in-chief of . . . *The Verge* . . . asking, "Who would want to wear this thing in public?": Joshua Topolsky, "I Used Google Glass: The Future, but with Monthly Updates," *The Verge*, February 22, 2013, http://www.theverge.com /2013/2/22/4013406/i-used-google-glass-its-the-future-with-monthly-updates.

Jack Dorsey . . . said [about Glass] "I think it's an amazing technology . . . can't imagine my mom wearing them": Brian X. Chen, "Jack Dorsey Talks Square and Wearable Devices," *New York Times*, April 29, 2013.

These responses caused the blog's author . . . to conclude . . . with the question: "If they build it, will people wear it?": Nick Bilton, "Big Question for Wearable Computing: Is It Ready for Consumers?," *New York Times*, May 31, 2013, http://bits.blogs.nytimes.com/2013/05/31/is-wearable-computing-ready-for -mainstream-consumers/.

Google . . . its total R&D budget rose 79 percent, to $6.8 billion, in the two years following X's establishment: Brad Stone, "Inside Google's Secret Lab," *Bloomberg Businessweek*, May 22, 2013, http://www.bloomberg.com/bw/articles/2013 -05-22/inside-googles-secret-lab.

Generating considerable buzz by unveiling the concept at prominent electronics and fashion shows: *Marketing Land*, September 9, 2012, http://marketingland .com/google-glass-glasses-used-to-record-dvp-fashion-show-20993; Glass Almanac, "The History of Google Glass," http://glassalmanac.com/history-google -glass/.

The program's promotional material stated that Google was looking for "bold, creative individuals": "Seeking Glass Explorers," Google Glass Google Plus post, February 20, 2013, https://plus.google.com/+GoogleGlass/posts/N95x6 MCS7hD.

One developer created a program he called "Winky," . . . take a photo with the wink of an eye: Addy Dugdale, "Winky App Lets You Take a Photo on Google Glass in the Blink of an Eye," *Fast Company*, May 2, 2013, http://www.fast company.com/3009173/most-innovative-companies-2013/winky-app-lets-you -take-a-photo-on-google-glass-in-the-blink.

In early 2015, Google abruptly announced that it was ending its Explorer program: "We're Graduating from Google[x] Labs," Google Glass Google Plus post, January 15, 2015, https://plus.google.com/+GoogleGlass/posts/9uiwXY42tvc.

The company would now put a dedicated team . . . overseen by several technology heavyweights: Kevin Oliver, "Google Glass 2: Everything You Need to Know," *TechRadar*, August 11, 2015, http://www.techradar.com/us/news/wearables/google -glass-2-release-date-price-features-1300484.

Predictions ranging from only 1 million units sold to 9.4 million: IHS, "Spurred by Google Glass, IHS Forecasts Nearly 10 Million Smart Glasses to Ship from 2012 to 2016," April 24, 2013, http://press.ihs.com/press-release/design-supply-chain /spurred-google-glass-ihs-forecasts-nearly-10-million-smart-glasses.

One firm predicted more than 21 million units of Glass sold in the third year: Tony Danova, "BI Intelligence Forecast: Google Glass Will Become a Mainstream

Product and Sell Millions by 2016," *Business Insider*, December 31, 2013, http://
www.businessinsider.com/google-glass-sales-projections-2013-11.

Survey after survey found senior managers . . . expressing dissatisfaction when comparing their expected financial returns from R&D: For example, Boston Consulting Group, "Innovation 2005," BCG Senior Management Survey, https://
www.bcg.com/documents/file14520.pdf; Boston Consulting Group, "Innovation 2010: A Return to Prominence—and the Emergence of a New World Order," April 2010, https://www.bcg.com/documents/file42620.pdf.

R&D spending globally has practically doubled over the past decade: National
Science Foundation, Science and Engineering Indicators 2014, http://www.nsf
.gov/statistics/seind14/index.cfm/chapter-4/c4s2.htm.

COMMENTS

1. Google CEO and cofounder Larry Page . . . Sergei Brin, Google cofounder
and director of its Special Projects Group: In August 2015, Google announced
plans to reorganize its various interests. As part of the corporate restructuring, a
new holding company was created, called Alphabet, which would house a number
of subsidiaries (or a "collection of companies" as Larry Page put it). Each subsidiary would have its own CEO and report to Alphabet. Larry Page would be
the CEO of Alphabet and Sergei Brin its president. In the new structure, Google
would become the umbrella company in charge of the Internet-related products
(Android, Search, YouTube, Maps, Apps, etc.) and its CEO would be Sundar Pi-
chai. Google X would also operate as a separate subsidiary and would be run by
Brin. See Larry Page, "G is for Google," Google Official Blog, August 10, 2015,
https://googleblog.blogspot.com/2015/08/google-alphabet.html; Heather Kelly, "Meet
Google Alphabet—Google's new parent company," *CNNMoney*, August 11, 2015,
http://money.cnn.com/2015/08/10/technology/alphabet-google.

Chapter 1: The Basic Diffusion Pattern of an Innovation

FACTS AND QUOTES

"I wish developing great products was as easy as writing a check": Jim Dalrymple,
"Jobs Addresses Backdating, Environment at Shareholder Meeting," *Macworld*,
May 10, 2007, http://www.macworld.com/article/1057843/shareholder.html.

Segway . . . was introduced with much fanfare . . . on the ABC News program
Good Morning America: "'IT' Unveiled: A Self-Balancing Scooter," *ABC News*,
December 3, 2001, http://abcnews.go.com/GMA/story?id=126341.

Touted the Segway as a breakthrough . . . "bigger than the Internet, and more important than the PC": John Heilemann, "Reinventing the Wheel," *Time*, December 2, 2001, http://content.time.com/time/business/article/0,8599,186660
-1,00.html; Mark Gimein, "Reinventing the Wheel, Slowly," *Businessweek*, September 11, 2006, http://www.bloomberg.com/bw/stories/2006-09-10/reinventing
-the-wheel-slowly.

Segway Inc. the fastest company in history to reach $1 billion in sales: John Heile-
mann, "Reinventing the Wheel," *Time*, December 2, 2001, http://content.time
.com/time/business/article/0,8599,186660-1,00.html.

More than 100,000 Segways had been sold by the end of 2011: "Segway Celebrates
10th Anniversary," *New Hampshire Union Leader*, January 24, 2012, http://www
.unionleader.com/apps/pbcs.dll/article?AID=/20120125/NEWS02/701259985.

When introducing the Segway, Kamen declared that it "will be to the car what
the car was to the horse and buggy": John Heilemann, "Reinventing the
Wheel," *Time*, December 2, 2001, http://content.time.com/time/business/article
/0,8599,186660,00.html.

The national US average being about 2 vehicles per household: Michael Sivak,
"Has Motorization Peaked?," University of Michigan Transportation Research
Institute, UMTRI-2015-10, March 2015, http://deepblue.lib.umich.edu/bitstream
/handle/2027.42/110979/103186.pdf.

Three million devices were sold just 80 days after the official release date: Associated Press, "Number of iPads Sold by Apple by Quarter," *Yahoo! Finance,* October 23, 2012, http://finance.yahoo.com/news/number-ipads-sold-apple-quarter
-201153619.html.

Steve Jobs declaring . . . "this is a truly magical product": John D. Sutter and Doug
Gross, "Apple Unveils the 'Magical' iPad," *CNN*, January 28, 2010, http://www
.cnn.com/2010/TECH/01/27/apple.tablet/.

Initial reviews came back suggesting the iPad was "like a bigger iPhone": Yukari
Iwatani Kane, "First-Day Sales of Apple's iPad Fall Short of Sky-High Hopes,"
Wall Street Journal, April 6, 2010, http://www.wsj.com/articles/SB10001424052
702304017404575165621713345324.

Steve Jobs . . . "[The iPad] will be the most important thing I have done": Michael
Arrington, "Overheard: Steve Jobs Says Apple Tablet 'Will Be the Most Important Thing I've Ever Done,'" *Techcrunch*, January 24, 2010, http://techcrunch
.com/2010/01/24/steve-jobs-tablet-most-important/.

Steve Jobs . . . admitted at one point that work on developing it actually started
before . . . the iPhone: Michael J. Miller, "Apple's Jobs: iPad Plans Began before iPhone," *PCMag*, June 1, 2010, http://www.pcmag.com/article2/0,2817,
2364498,00.asp.

Apple's CEO . . . : "A lot of folks in this tablet market are rushing in and they
are thinking of this as the new PC": Alexei Oreskovic, "Apple's Steve Jobs Unveils New iPad with a Clenched Fist and Jabs Aplenty," *Reuters,* March 3, 2011,
http://blogs.reuters.com/mediafile/2011/03/03/apples-steve-jobs-unveils-new
-ipad-with-a-clenched-fist-and-jabs-aplenty/.

[The Segway] was initially distributed through Amazon.com: "Amazon.com Begins Selling Segway Human Transporter," *Wall Street Journal*, November, 18,
2002, http://www.wsj.com/articles/SB1037631947739311148.

The first such service was launched by XM Satellite Radio in the fall of 2001, followed shortly by Sirius in the winter of 2002: David B. Godes and Elie Ofek,

"XM Satellite Radio (B)," Harvard Business School Case 504065, 2004; "The History of Satellite Radio," SatelliteRadioUSA, http://satelliteradiousa.com /satellite_radio_history.html.

A national telephone survey it commissioned . . . more than 6,000 surveys were completed: David B. Godes and Elie Ofek, "XM Satellite Radio (A)," Harvard Business School Case 504009, 2003.

COMMENTS

1. Far exceeding the predictions of many industry analysts: Examples of experts underestimating the iPad's sales trajectory prior to the launch include market research firm iSuppli, which estimated only 7.1 million iPads would sell by the end of 2010, and guests on Fox News's *Strategy Room* whose estimates ranged from 3 to 9 million units. The actual number was about 14.5 million units; Erick Schonfeld, "Nobody Predicted the iPad's Growth. Nobody," *Techcrunch*, January 19, 2011, http://techcrunch.com/2011/01/19/nobody-predicted-ipad-growth/; Dan Nystedt, "iSuppli Raises iPad Sales Forecast after Apple's Strong Q3," *PCWorld*, July 20, 2010, http://www.pcworld.com/article/201548/article.html.

2. A formal version of the basic diffusion model is presented in math box 1 in the appendix: In math box 1, we describe parallels between innovation diffusion modeling and disease-spread modeling in the field of epidemiology. A good reference on the latter is O. Diekmann and J. A. P. Heesterbeek, *Mathematical Epidemiology of Infectious Diseases: Model Building, Analysis and Interpretation* (West Sussex: Wiley, 2000).

Chapter 2: The Whole Is Bigger than the Sum of Its (Diffusion and Customer Lifetime Value) Parts

FACTS AND QUOTES

"The purpose of a business is to create a customer": Peter F. Drucker, *The Practice of Management* (New York: HarperBusiness, 1993; first published 1954). See also Jack Trout, "Peter Drucker on Marketing," *Forbes*, July 3, 2006, http:// www.forbes.com/2006/06/30/jack-trout-on-marketing-cx_jt_0703drucker .html.

Asking whether the billions of dollars . . . would ever be recovered: most sources suggest that XM Satellite Radio had raised over $1 Billion prior to its launch: see, for example, Simon Romero, "XM Satellite Radio Completes Its Financing," *New York Times*, July 10, 2000.

Humphrey Bogart's famous line . . . "I think this is the beginning of a beautiful friendship": *Casablanca*, directed by Michael Curtiz (Warner Bros., 1943).

Consider an owner of . . . the Kindle Fire, who buys 5 e-books and downloads 3 paid apps per quarter: These figures are consistent with, for example, Eric Savitz, "Amazon Kindle Fire: More Profitable Than Expected?," *Forbes*, January 18, 2012, http://www.forbes.com/sites/ericsavitz/2012/01/18/amazon-kindle -fire-more-profitable-than-expected/.

A recent analysis (January 2013) by New York University researchers: Aswath Damodaran, "Damodaran Online," Department of Finance, New York University
Stern School of Business, http://pages.stern.nyu.edu/~adamodar/.

1. For each period, we can express the expected cash flow from the customer
in present value terms: In calculating present values for purposes of assessing the
CLV of a customer, as in expressions 2.6 and 2.7, the timing of profit margin accrual
to the firm affects the level of discounting required. We wanted to bring all future
customer margins to the *beginning* of the current period and further assumed that
profit margins were earned at the *end* of each period. Hence, and denoting the
discount factor by d, the period 1 profit margin was discounted by d (to bring it
to the beginning of period 1), the period 2 profit margin by d^2, the period 3 profit
margin by d^3, and so on (with the period N profit margin discounted by d^N). This
approach meant that in calculating innovation equity, we had to discount the CLV
of customers acquired in period N by $d^{(N-1)}$. For example, for a customer acquired
in period 2, his or her CLV was already expressed in present value terms for the
beginning of period 2, and thus only discounting by d is needed to bring his or her
CLV to the beginning of period 1. Similarly, only discounting by d^2 is needed for
customers acquired in period 3, and so on.

2. To account for discounting when the time horizon is "infinite": The CLV formula derived in expression 2.9 is sensitive to the assumptions on when per-period
profits accrue (beginning or end of the period) and on when customer attrition
takes place (beginning or end of the period). For example, were we to assume that
per-period profit margins are earned at the beginning of the period, then we would
need to multiply the formula in expression 2.9 by a factor of (1 + cost of capital)—
in other words, by the discount factor. Alternatively, if we assumed that attrition
occurs at the beginning of each period (including the first period), then we would
need to multiply the formula in expression 2.9 by the retention rate. Interested
readers are referred to Ofek Elie, "Customer Profitability and Lifetime Value"
(2002), Harvard Business School Note 503019, specifically additional comment *e*
on page 7.

Chapter 3: Don't Just Stand There: Do Something!
Growing Innovation Equity through Marketing Actions

"Innovation is like a plant that needs constant attention": Opening statement by
Florian Fichtl at Sixth National Innovation Forum Science, Technology and
Innovation: Policies for Growth in the Next Decade, March 1, 2010, http://www
.arcfund.net/arcartShow.php?id=15051.
The idea for Dropbox . . . came to Houston in late 2006 . . . a bus from Boston to
New York City: Victoria Barret, "Dropbox," *Forbes*, October 19, 2011, http://

www.forbes.com/forbes/2011/1107/best-companies-11-drew-houston-steve -jobs-ferdowsi-dropbox-barret.html; see also Thomas R. Eisenmann, Michael Pao, and Lauren Barley, "Dropbox: 'It Just Works,'" Harvard Business School Case 811065, 2011.

Industry analysts . . . each PS3 cost more than $800 to make in early production batches: Tuan Nguyen, "PS3 Costs Sony $800?," *Daily Tech*, February 19, 2006, http://www.dailytech.com/PS3+Costs+Sony+800/article871.htm.

Pfizer . . . with ads that told men . . . to "join the millions" . . . asked their physician about Viagra: For example, see Pfizer ad in *Popular Science*, December 2001, 11; also Herzog Dagmar, *Sex in Crisis: The New Sexual Revolution and the Future of American Politics* (Basic Books, 2008).

As Chevrolet did in 2013 in ads . . . the Volt, as receiving the highest customer satisfaction scores: "Chevrolet Volt Tops Consumer Reports' Owner-Satisfaction Survey for Second Straight Year," *Consumer Reports*, November 29, 2012, http://pressroom.consumerreports.org/pressroom/2012/11/my-entry-6.html; Anthony Facceda, "Chevy Volt Owners Are Most Satisfied, Says Consumer Reports," *TorqueNews*, November, 29, 2012, http://www.torquenews.com/1081 /chevy-volt-owners-are-most-satisfied-says-consumer-reports.

Market research revealed that a far greater number . . . willing to consider satellite radio when receivers were priced at $200: David B. Godes and Elie Ofek, "XM Satellite Radio (A)," Exhibit 9, Harvard Business School Case 504009, 2003.

XM implemented similar subsidies early on: David B. Godes and Elie Ofek, "XM Satellite Radio (C): The Next Generation of Radio Receivers," Harvard Business School Case 505015, 2004.

Between 2012 and 2014 more than two-thirds of new smartphone apps . . . were offered free: "Paid vs. Free Apps in the App Store vs. Google Play," SourceBits, July 16, 2014, http://sourcebits.com/app-development-design-blog/paid-vs-free -apps-app-store-vs-google-play/; and "Distribution of Free and Paid Android Apps in the Google Play Store from 2009 to 2015," Statista, http://www.statista .com/statistics/266211/distribution-of-free-and-paid-android-apps/.

Close to 1 billion [Facebook] daily active users as of early 2015: "Number of Daily Active Facebook Users Worldwide as of 2nd Quarter 2015 (in Millions)," Statista, 2015, http://www.statista.com.ezp-prod1.hul.harvard.edu/statistics/346167 /facebook-global-dau/.

Wired magazine reported that of the 50 highest-grossing apps . . . only three did not support in-app purchases: Ryan Rigney, "iOS Game Developers Must Choose: Sell Digital Currency or Lose Money," *Wired*, September, 26, 2012, http://www.wired.com/2012/09/life-after-disc-digital-coins/.

In 2014 eMarketer indicated that 92 percent of free apps offered in-app purchase opportunities: Based on Melania Calinescu, "Unveiling the Secrets behind App Store Category Dynamics," *Distimo*, March 27, 2014.

For each new account referral, you get 500MB of additional storage: "How Do I Earn Bonus Space for Referring Friends to Dropbox?," Dropbox, https://www.dropbox.com/en/help/54.

Based on industry estimates, we will take Dropbox's share of the nascent category to be 24 percent: Eric Newcomer and Dina Bass, "Dropbox Is Struggling and Competitors Are Catching Up," *Bloomberg Businessweek*, June 24, 2015, http://www.bloomberg.com/news/articles/2015-06-24/dropbox-is-struggling-and-competitors-are-catching-up.

Dropbox had 4 million users in January 2010 . . . 100 million in November 2012 . . . and 400 million by June of 2015: "Number of Registered Dropbox Users from April 2011 to June 2015," Statista, http://www.statista.com/statistics/261820/number-of-registered-dropbox-users/.

You can at most refer 32 friends and obtain an additional 16GB of storage: Dropbox website, Help Center section, https://www.dropbox.com/en/help/200; Casey Chan, "Dropbox Will Give You 32GB of Free Storage for Referring Friends," *Gizmodo*, April 4, 2012, http://gizmodo.com/5899011/dropbox-will-give-you-16gb-of-free-storage-for-referring-friends.

The percentage . . . who convert to become premium paying customers . . . about 1 percent on the conservative side and 1.5 percent on the more aggressive side: Derived from Mark Rogowsky, "Dropbox Is Doing Great, but Maybe Not as Great as We Believed," *Forbes Tech*, November 19, 2013, http://www.forbes.com/sites/markrogowsky/2013/11/19/dropbox-makes-hundreds-of-millions-so-why-is-it-only-asking-for-an-8b-price/; Thales Teixeira and Elizabeth Watkins, "Freemium Pricing at Dropbox," Harvard Business School Case 514053, 2013.

Dropbox's premium service for individuals . . . offers 1TB . . . of extra space for $10 per month: Mark Rogowsky, "Storage Wars: Dropbox Offers More Bytes for Less, but Everyone Wants to Sell You a Bit of the Cloud," *Forbes*, August 28, 2014, http://www.forbes.com/sites/markrogowsky/2014/08/28/storage-wars-dropbox-joins-the-terabyte-race-but-apple-microsoft-google-all-want-to-file-your-digital-bits/.

Drew Houston . . . "It is hard to master freemium products. . . . If you think of your free user cost as your marketing budget . . . things make more sense.": Thomas R. Eisenmann, Michael Pao, and Lauren Barley, "Dropbox: 'It Just Works,'" Harvard Business School Case 811065, 2011.

At the time of the launch, XM had only set up 800 such repeaters in 75 cities: Justin Martin, "Radio Heads XM Radio CEO Hugh Panero Has Built the Biggest Satellite Radio Service in America. Now He Must Figure Out How to Make His Company Profitable," *CNN Money*, February 1, 2004, http://money.cnn.com/magazines/fsb/fsb_archive/2004/02/01/360665/index.htm.

COMMENTS

1. It can use the basic diffusion model with the baseline parameters: The basic diffusion model parameters used in the video game example are approximately

based on estimated parameters from previous video game console generations; see, for example, Vijay Mahajan, Eitan Muller, and Yoram Wind, ed., *New-Product Diffusion Models* (Springer, 2000).

2. If Sony considers dropping the price by more than 10 percent: Sony changed the memory capacity and cut the price of the PS3 models it offered every so often. For example, it initially launched 20GB and 60GB versions (at $499 and $599, respectively); it discontinued these versions in April and October 2007, respectively. It introduced an 80GB version (at $599) in August and a 40GB version (at $499) in November of that year. The 40GB version was later dropped, and a 160GB version was introduced (at $499) in November 2008; in fall 2012, 250GB and 500GB versions were introduced (at $269 and $299, respectively). As for price cuts, the 60GB was cut by $100 (prior to being discontinued); the 80Gb version saw three price cuts, each by $100 (so by August 2009, it was selling for $299); and the price of the 160GB version was dropped to $399 (August 2009).

3. The Big Bang Theory: This show is an American sitcom airing on the television channel CBS. The show is set in Pasadena, California, and is about two fictional Caltech physicists who live across the hall from an attractive blonde waitress and aspiring actress. As of fall 2015, the show was in its ninth season.

4. An indirect though much cheaper way is to offer manufacturers a subsidy: The distribution chain calculations related to the radio subsidy are straightforward. If the manufacturer seeks a 33 percent margin on a device that costs $135 to make, then it needs to calculate the price P_m to charge retailers such that $(P_m - 135) / P_m = 0.33$, from which we can deduce that the manufacturer would sell to retailers at $P_m = 202. Then retailers use a similar formula for the retail price P_r to charge consumers, with the cost for them being $202: $(P_r - 202) / P_r = 0.33$, from which we can extract that $P_r = 302, which we have rounded to $300. Similarly, applying the same distribution margin calculation but using a manufacturer effective cost of $90 due to the $45 subsidy, we obtain $(P_m - 90) / P_m = 0.33$, from which we can see that the manufacturer would sell to retailers at $P_m = 134. Then for retailers, $(P_r - 134) / P_r = 0.33$, from which we can extract $P_r = 200.

5. The free sign-up Dropbox offers (on its consumer version): In addition to the consumer service described and analyzed in this chapter, of which only the Pro version was paid for, Dropbox also targeted organizations with its Dropbox Business. This service was entirely paid for and provided administrative controls and auditing to IT departments while allowing users the option to create separate cloud containers for their work and personal documents (each user received 1TB of storage). As of fall 2015, the Business version was priced at $15 per user per month (there was a 17 percent discount for a full year commitment); the minimum number of users per organization signing up was five.

6. The company also gives you another way out of the capacity crunch: Aside from referrals, Dropbox offered a few other ways for members to marginally increase storage capacity for free. These included connecting one's Facebook or Twitter account to Dropbox and linking Dropbox with one's Mailbox account.

7. The conversion rate would be 1.25 percent: Some reports pegged the consumer conversion rate from free to paid Dropbox usage at above 2 percent and as high as 4 percent. We used the more conservative estimates based on sources (listed in the references and recommended reading section) that tried to back out the conversion rate from annual revenue and total number of registered users.

8. The cost to Dropbox of hosting an average paying customer: Dropbox's hosting cost was taken to be $20–$30 a year. This was based on the cost per giga-byte of storage, which was around $0.03 per month in mid-2015 on Amazon Web Services (Joab Jackson, "Price War! Amazon Cuts Cloud Costs to Counter Google," *Computerland*, March 26, 2014, and as seen at https://aws.amazon.com /s3/pricing/) and on a conservative estimate of about 70GB effective storage used a month per subscriber.

Chapter 4: Foreseeing Bumps and Potholes along the Diffusion Road
FACTS AND QUOTES

"I could tell you my adventures" . . . said Alice a little timidly, "but it's no use go-ing back to yesterday . . .": Lewis Carroll, *Alice's Adventures in Wonderland* (Boston: Lothrop Publishing Company, 1898), 84.

HEV sales in the US: . . . from under 10,000 units sold in 2000 to about 352,000 units sold in 2007; . . . about 266,000 in 2011(with all-electrics and plug-ins . . . less than 17,500 units); . . . in 2012, sales of HEVs topped 430,000 units: Data compiled from the Electric Drive Transportation Association (EDTA), http:// electricdrive.org/index.php?ht=d/sp/i/20952/pid/20952; yet another source, in close agreement with these data patterns is "Table 1-19: Sales of Hybrid Vehicles in the United States," US Department of Transportation, Fuels Data Center, http://www.rita.dot.gov/bts/sites/rita.dot.gov.bts/files/publications/national _transportation_statistics/html/table_01_19.html.

Annual number of new passenger vehicle sales in the US averaging 12 million: Jeff Bennett, "U.S. Auto Sales Finish Year Strong," *Wall Street Journal,* Janu-ary 5, 2012, http://www.wsj.com/articles/SB1000142405297020351360457714040852581080.

A study involving . . . 19 developed countries . . . a clear saddle pattern in about 45 percent of the innovation-country pairs . . . after 30 percent of the long-run market potential . . . drop was nearly 30 percent: Jacob Goldenberg, Barak Libai, and Eitan Muller, "Riding the Saddle: How Cross-market Communica-tion Can Create a Major Slump in Sales," *Journal of Marketing* 66, no. 2 (2002): 1–17.

In 2001, the *Economist* listed seven consumer electronics innovations that had a profound commercial impact: "Gadget Wars," *Economist,* March 8, 2001, http:// www.economist.com/node/529105.

As one prominent Northeast car dealer put it: Quoted in Elie Ofek and Polly

Ribatt, "'Plugging In' the Consumer: The Adoption of Electrically Powered Vehicles in the U.S.," Harvard Business School Case 510076, 2010.

Chapter 5: Jumpstarting Stalled Adoption: Getting the Mainstream to Take the Plunge

FACTS AND QUOTES

Geoffrey Moore and Dean Kamen quotes, "It's like Gulliver and the Lilliputians . . ." and "the Segway 'is a product destined to live in the chasm forever'" and "Although technology moves very quickly, people's mindset changes very slowly": Kher Unmesh, "The Segway Riddle," *Time*, August 14, 2006, 48, http://content.time.com/time/magazine/article/0,9171,1226171,00.html.

A leading analyst . . . "We haven't issued forecasts for the industry in two years . . . E-books were a dumb idea": David Card, as quoted in "Mystery of E-books: Who Reads Them?," *USA Today*, May 8, 2002, http://usatoday30.usatoday.com/tech/2002/05/08/ebooks.htm; Bootie Cosgrove-Mather, "E-book Story Fails to Unfold," *CBS News*, May 14, 2002, http://www.cbsnews.com/news/e-book-story-fails-to-unfold/.

"Maintenance unease" . . . option to request a "Tesla Ranger" . . . until your original was delivered back: Daniel Sparks, "My First-Hand Experience with Tesla Motors, Inc.'s Ninja-Like Service," *Motley Fool*, September 27, 2004, http://www.fool.com/investing/general/2014/09/27/my-first-hand-experience-with-tesla-motors-incs-ni.aspx; "Service Answers," Tesla, http://my.teslamotors.com/service/faq.

Tesla Model S information and Musk quote: . . . sleek exterior design . . . impressive performance numbers . . . touch screen . . . battery allows for driving more than 200 miles . . . Supercharger stations throughout the US . . . recharge . . . in about 20 minutes . . . also piloted swap stations in California . . . Tesla's financing program . . . sell it back to the company . . . stores in high-end malls . . . 'There are people that take a lot of convincing' . . . First electric car to win *Motor Trend*'s Car of the Year . . . highest car rating ever by *Consumer Reports* . . . Tesla also announced . . . the Model X . . . and a more affordable sedan: Ashlee Vance, "Why Everybody Loves Tesla," *Bloomberg Businessweek*, July 18, 2013, http://www.bloomberg.com/bw/articles/2013-07-18/the-tesla-electric-cars-creators-chase-their-iphone-moment.

As one prominent car review website, Edmunds, glowingly described: "Full Expert Review: 2013 Tesla Model S," Edmunds.com, http://www.edmunds.com/tesla/model-s/2013/?tab-id=reviews-tab#overview-pod-anchor; Mo Abusham, "Exclusive—Driving the 2013 Tesla Premium Electric Cars with Hand Controls from Better Life Mobility," *Better Life Mobility Center*, October 21, 2013, https://www.betterlifemobility.com/About-Us/Blog/Exclusive-Driving-the-2013-Tesla-Premium-Electric-Cars-with-Hand-Controls-from-Better-Life-Mobility-VIDEO.

Model S sales during its first full year . . . a pace of almost 22,500 cars sold globally in 2013 . . . (about 32,000 . . . globally in 2014): Data compiled from Jerry
Hirsch, "Tesla Motors Ends Year with Higher Sales but Still a Big Loss,"
Los Angeles Times, February 19, 2014, http://www.latimes.com/business/la-fi
-hy-fourth-quarter-loss-telsa-20140219-story.html; Angelo Young, "Tesla Motors (TSLA) Sales 2015: Did Investors Misread the Q1 Numbers? 2015 Model
S Deliveries Include Cars Sold In 2014," *International Business Times*, April 7,
2015, http://www.ibtimes.com/tesla-motors-tsla-sales-2015-did-investors-misread
-q1-numbers-2015-model-s-deliveries-1873189; *Wikipedia*, s.v. "Tesla Model S,"
https://en.wikipedia.org/wiki/Tesla_Model_S.

Tesla Motor's stock price climbed by more than 900 percent: "Tesla Motors, Inc.
Historical Stock Prices," Nasdaq, http://www.nasdaq.com/symbol/tsla/historical.

Agassi . . . made *Time's* list of 100 "people who most affect our world": Alan Salz-
man, "The 2009 Time 100," *Time,* April 30, 2009, http://content.time.com/time
/specials/packages/article/0,28804,1894410_1893209_1893476,00.html.

An impressive visitor center was built near Tel Aviv: Ron Friedman, "Better
Place's Electric Vehicles Land in Israel," *Jerusalem Post*, February 8, 2010,
http://www.jpost.com/Health-and-Sci-Tech/Science-And-Environment/Better
-Places-electric-vehicles-land-in-Israel.

The seeds of Better Place were sown at the 2006 World Economic Forum . . . Shai
Agassi, a high-ranking SAP executive . . . Agassi had lined up $200 million in
funding . . . commitment of a car maker . . . garnered support from key Israeli
politicians . . . exempting EVs from sales and import taxes . . . Gasoline prices
in Israel and Denmark: Elie Ofek and Alison B. Wagonfeld, "Speeding Ahead
to a Better Place," Harvard Business School Case 512056, 2012.

Demand was extremely sluggish. Fewer than 1,500 cars were sold . . . In October
of 2012, Agassi resigned as CEO . . . His replacement . . . was fired within
months. The next CEO . . . didn't last more than a few months . . . company
filed for bankruptcy in May 2013 . . . more than $800 million of investment:
Isabel Kershner, "Israeli Venture Meant to Serve Electric Cars Is Ending Its
Run," *New York Times*, May 26, 2013, http://www.nytimes.com/2013/05/27
/business/global/israeli-electric-car-company-files-for-liquidation.html?_r=1.

As one security company executive put it, there is a "multiplier effect" . . . results
in annual savings of $50,000–$60,000 in personnel expenses: Tom Dorgan, as
quoted in " 'Non-conventional Security," *Security Magazine*, September 1, 2007,
http://www.securitymagazine.com/articles/78614-non-conventional-security-1;
Joel Griffin, "More on Retail Parking Lot Security," *Security InfoWatch*, December 15, 2011, http://www.securityinfowatch.com/blog/10533747/more-on-retail
-parking-lot-security; Segway Patrol, http://www.segway.co.nz/patrol/security/.

Segway developed a three-wheeled version: Jacob Kastrenakes, "Segway Just Started a Three-Wheeled Vehicle War," *The Verge*, May 21, 2014, http://www.the
verge.com/2014/5/21/5739420/segway-introduces-three-wheeled-law-enforce
ment-vehicle.

A recent Frost & Sullivan report . . . more than a hundred and fifty new models . . . by 2020: "One- to Three-Wheeled Micro-Mobility Models Complement Four-Wheeled OEMs Strategy, Says Frost & Sullivan," Frost & Sullivan press release, July 16, 2012.

Much cheaper "hoverboards . . . perhaps even representing . . . extension to Segways (though some early versions seem to have safety issues . . .)": Sarah Mitroff, "Before You Even Think of Buying a Hoverboard, Read This," *Cnet*, December 18, 2015, http://www.cnet.com/how-to/buy-a-hoverboard/; Alex Kantrowitz, "Everything You Need to Know about the Hoverboard Craze," *BuzzFeed News*, August 27, 2015, http://www.buzzfeed.com/alexkantrowitz/a-crash-course -in-hoverboards#.aezanZZJK.

Summit Strategic Investments . . . acquired the company in 2013, announcing plans to grow: "Ninebot Limited and Segway Inc. Complete Strategic Combination," Segway Inc. press release, February 23, 2013, http://www.segway.com /about-segway/media-center/.

COMMENTS

1. Summit Strategic Investments . . . announcing plans to grow and expand in the years to come: On April 15, 2015, Segway announced that it had entered into a "strategic combination" with Ninebot, a Chinese start-up that made similar personal electric transportation products. After the transaction, Segway became a wholly owned subsidiary of Ninebot, though both companies would continue to operate under their existing brand names. See Segway Inc., "Ninebot Limited and Segway Inc. Complete Strategic Combination," press release, April 15, 2015; Paul Mozur, "Segway Finds Some Respect and a Buyer in China," *New York Times*, April 15, 2015.

Chapter 6: Survival in the Presence of a Rival: Valuing Innovations at the Brand Level

FACTS AND QUOTES

"Whether it's Google or Apple or free software . . . fantastic competitors and it keeps us on our toes": "Apple v. Microsoft: What Steve Jobs and Bill Gates Really Think of Each Other," *Telegraph*, February 11, 2010, http://www .telegraph.co.uk/technology/7213848/Apple-v-Microsoft-What-Steve-Jobs-and -Bill-Gates-really-think-of-each-other.html.

XM . . . $100 million marketing campaign . . . ads featuring such artists as Snoop Dogg . . . and David Bowie "falling from the sky": "XM Satellite Plans to Start Satellite Radio Broadcasts," *Wall Street Journal*, July 24, 2001, http://www.wsj .com/articles/SB996020698305437753; David B. Godes and Elie Ofek, "XM Satellite Radio (B)," Harvard Business School Case 504065, 2004.

The launch date . . . had to be pushed out . . . XM was able to garner more than 30,000 adopters within a few short months: Renae Merle, "XM Satellite Radio Draws 30,000 Subscribers," *Washington Post,* January 8, 2002, http://www

.washingtonpost.com/archive/business/2002/01/08/xm-satellite-radio-draws
-30000-subscribers/4140b251-e9c2-4ac3-b3d8-7821ba2335d1/.

Hugh Panero, to declare . . . "Will people pay for radio? . . . 'Yes.'": Yolanda
Cuesta, "Satellite Radio Wants You to Turn On, Tune In and Pay Up," *Sacra-
mento Business Journal*, January 13, 2002, http://www.bizjournals.com/sacramento
/stories/2002/01/14/focus3.html?page=all.

XM launched . . . price of $9.99 per month . . . Sirius . . . at $12.95 . . . all its music
channels were commercial free . . . two to four minutes of ads . . . on many of
XM's music channels: Gail Kachadourian, "Future of Satellite Radio Is Still
Up in the Air," *Automotive News*, October 8, 2001, http://www.autonews.com
/article/20011008/SEO/110080708/future-of-satellite-radio-is-still-up-in-the
-air; see also Godes and Ofek, "XM Satellite Radio (C)."

XM announced . . . it too would cut all ads from its music channels: Justin Martin, "Radio Heads XM Radio CEO Hugh Panero Has Built the Biggest Satellite Radio Service in America. Now He Must Figure Out How to Make
His Company Profitable," *CNN Money*, February 1, 2004, http://money.cnn
.com/magazines/fsb/fsb_archive/2004/02/01/360665/.

In spring 2005, XM raised its subscription price . . . to $12.95: Seth Sutel, "XM
Raises Satellite Radio Prices," *USA Today*, February 28, 2005, http://usa
today30.usatoday.com/money/media/2005-02-28-xm_x.htm.

Sirius . . . rights to the NBA and NFL, while XM locked down MLB and
NASCAR . . . Bob Dylan and Oprah Winfrey: Todd Leopold, "New Tricks
for Old Broadcast Medium," *CNN*, July 20, 2006, http://www.cnn.com/2006
/SHOWBIZ/Music/07/20/radio/index.html; Christina Lagorio, "Oprah Signs
with XM Radio," *CBS News*, February 9, 2006, http://www.cbsnews.com/news
/oprah-signs-with-xm-radio/.

Howard Stern was known as a 'shock jock' . . . outspoken and controversial
style: Jill Serjeant, "Howard Stern Pledges to Stir Up *America's Got Talent*,"
Reuters, December 15, 2011, http://www.reuters.com/article/us-howardstern
-gottalent-idUSTRE7BE18Y20111215; "'Shock Jock' Howard Stern Promises
to Tone Down Act for 'Got Talent,'" *Washington Magazine*, May 11, 2012,
http://www.washington-magazine.com/shock-jock-howard-stern-promises-to
-tone-down-act-for-got-talent.html.

Stern's shift to satellite radio . . . a "watershed event" by Sirius's CEO: Krysten
Crawford, "Howard Stern Jumps to Satellite," *CNN Money*, October 6, 2004,
http://money.cnn.com/2004/10/06/news/newsmakers/stern_sirius/.

Sirius agreed to pay Stern $500 million over 5 years . . . as well as stock incentives
after he joined: Sarah McBride and Joe Flint, "Radio's Howard Stern Leaps
to Satellite in $500 Million Deal," *Wall Street Journal*, October 7, 2004, http://
www.wsj.com/articles/SB109706646880937838.

A Verizon Wireless spokesperson . . . "I would have to think that a rising tide lifts
all ships": Hiawatha Bray, "Hello? iPhone? Competition Calling. As Apple

Cranks up for Debut, Makers of Rival Multifeature Devices Look to Hitch a Ride," *Boston Globe*, June 14, 2007, http://www.boston.com/business/globe /articles/2007/06/14/hello_iphone_competition_calling/; see also Barak Libai, Eitan Muller, and Renana Peres, "The Diffusion of Services," *Journal of Marketing Research* 46, no. 1 (2009): 163–75.

For a full decade . . . the Swedish . . . market was a monopoly . . . In 1992, the market was opened up . . . Tele2's entry coincided with the advent of GSM . . . TeliaSonera . . . management considered downsizing and layoffs: See Libai, Muller, and Peres, "The Diffusion of Services," 163–75; report from meeting of Nordic director generals on November 7, 2005, "Competition and Regulation in the Nordic Mobile Markets," 33, https://www.pts.se/upload/Documents/SE /Competition_regulation_nordic_mobile_markets_sept06.pdf.

Sony called its format Betamax, while JVC's . . . VHS . . . The two formats were "incompatible": "Chapter2 Sony Goes to Battle for Its Favorite Child," Sony, http://www.sony.net/SonyInfo/CorporateInfo/History/SonyHistory/2-02.html.

By the late 1980s . . . VHS's share in the United States climbed to about 90 percent. In 1988 . . . Sony practically conceded defeat when it brought to market its own VHS devices: Alex Pham and Jon Healey, "Format Wars, Episode II: The DVD," *Los Angeles Times*, June 26, 2005, http://articles.latimes.com/2005 /jun/26/business/fi-dvdwar26/2; Priya Ganapati, "June 4, 1977: VHS Comes to America," *Wired*, April 6, 2010, http://www.wired.com/2010/06/0604vhs-ces/; Janice Castro, "Goodbye Beta: Sony will make VHS players," *Time*, January 25, 1988, http://content.time.com/time/magazine/article/0,9171,966523,00.html; Matt Haig, *Brand Failures, The Truth About the 100 Biggest Branding Mistakes of All Time* (London: Kogan Page, 2013); *Wikipedia*, s.v. "Videotape Format War," https://en.wikipedia.org/wiki/Videotape_format_war.

The main contenders were Toshiba, with its HD-DVD format, and Sony, with its Blu-ray format: Sarah McBride and Phred Dvorak, "Toshiba Says Four Studios Back Its HD-DVD Format," *Wall Street Journal*, November 29, 2004, http:// www.wsj.com/articles/SB110172194995385468.

Sony decided to incorporate a Blu-ray player into . . . the PlayStation 3, which was launched in November 2006: Chris Morris, "PlayStation 3 Prices: $499 and $599," *CNN Money*, May 9, 2005, http://money.cnn.com/2006/05/08/technology /ps3_pricing/.

A PS3 . . . was in many cases cheaper . . . than many stand-alone Blu-ray or HD DVD models: Edward C. Baig, "PlayStation 3's a Lot of Fun, and a Lot of Money," *USA Today*, November 11, 2006, http://usatoday30.usatoday.com /tech/columnist/edwardbaig/2006-11-15-ps3_x.htm.

Once Warner Bros. . . . declared that it would support Blu-ray only . . . US retailers such as Wal-Mart and Best Buy dropped HD-DVDs: Franklin Paul, "Wal-Mart Picks Blu-ray in HD DVD Disaster," *Reuters*, February 15, 2008, http:// www.reuters.com/article/2008/02/15/us-walmart-dvd-idUSWEN397220080215.

In February 2008, Toshiba waved the white flag . . . no longer manufacture HD DVD devices: Toshiba, "Toshiba Announces Discontinuation of HD DVD Businesses," press release, February 19, 2008, https://www.toshiba.co.jp/about /press/2008_02/pr1903.htm; David Katzmaier, "It's Official: Toshiba Announces HD DVD Surrender," *CNET*, February 22, 2008, http://www.cnet.com/news /its-official-toshiba-announces-hd-dvd-surrender/.

Apple's iOS and Google's Android platforms . . . (the two standards held more than 90 percent share): Ben Geier, "Basically Nobody Uses Anything Other than iPhone or Android," *Fortune*, February 24, 2015, http://fortune.com/2015 /02/24/iphone-android-smartphones/; Microsoft, HP, and Ford seeding examples: see Barak Libai, Eitan Muller, and Renana Peres, "Decomposing the Value of Word-of-Mouth Seeding Programs: Acceleration vs. Expansion," *Journal of Marketing Research* 46, no. 2 (2013): 161–76.

Microsoft hosted thousands of "parties" . . . to help introduce Windows 7 . . . estimated that 7 million people were likely eventually reached: Sara Zucker, "Branded Parties Move into Private Homes," *Brandchannel*, February 3, 2010, http://brandchannel.com/2010/02/03/branded-parties-move-into-private-homes/.

In 2008, HP provided 31 leading US bloggers . . . new Dragon HDX laptop . . . the results . . . HP observed an immediate 85 percent bump in Dragon sales and a 15 percent increase in traffic to its site: "Enter the Dragon," *Chief Marketer*, October 1, 2008, http://www.chiefmarketer.com/enter-the-dragon/.

In 2009, Ford gave 100 influencers a new Ford Fiesta . . . The campaign gained 6.2 million YouTube views, 750,000 Flickr views and 40 million Twitter impressions . . . over 6,000 preordered the car: David Vinjamuri, "Ford Remixes the Fiesta Movement for 2014," *Forbes*, February 19, 2013, http://www.forbes .com/sites/davidvinjamuri/2013/02/19/ford-revives-the-fiesta-movement-to-launch -the-2014-fiesta/.

Market reports by firms such as the Keller Fay Group suggest that the majority of . . . social influence still occurs offline: Ed Keller and Brad Fay, *The Face-to-Face Book: Why Real Relationships Rule in a Digital Marketplace* (New York: Free Press, 2012).

Homophily. Several studies have shown a positive correlation between the revenue one person generates and the revenue generated by others: Michael Haenlein and Barak Libai, "Targeting Revenue Leaders for a New Product," *Journal of Marketing* 77, no. 3 (2013): 65–80.

The ten movies that made the 2014 list were downloaded illegally over 270 million times . . . the top ten movies that made the list the year before only reached about 75 million: Kirsten Acuna, "The 10 Most Pirated Movies of the Year," *Business Insider*, December 28, 2014, http://www.businessinsider.com/most -pirated-movies-2014-2014-12; Kirsten Acuna, "The Most Pirated Movies of 2013," *Business Insider*, January 2, 2014, http://www.businessinsider.com/most -pirated-movies-2013-2014-1.

The director of HBO's *Game of Thrones*, David Petrarca . . . shows like *Game of Thrones* "thrive on the cultural buzz . . . That's how they survive.": Ernesto Van der Sar, "Piracy Doesn't Hurt Game of Thrones, Director Says," *Torrent-Freak*, February 27, 2013, https://torrentfreak.com/piracy-doesnt-hurt-game -of-thrones-director-says-130227/.

The CEO of Rovio, publisher of *Angry Birds*, remarked, "Piracy may not be a bad thing. . . . It can get us more business at the end of the day": Stuart Dredge, "Angry Birds Boss: 'Piracy May Not Be a Bad Thing: It Can Get Us More Business,'" *Guardian*, January 30, 2012, http://www.theguardian.com /technology/appsblog/2012/jan/30/angry-birds-music-midem.

FCC . . . stricter stance . . . trigger . . . Super Bowl XXXVIII in February 2004: Marin Cogan, "In the Beginning, There Was a Nipple," *ESPN The Magazine*, January 28, 2014, http://espn.go.com/espn/feature/story/_/id/10333439/wardrobe -malfunction-beginning-there-was-nipple; Marlow Stern, "Super Bowl's 'Nipple-gate' Fiasco 10 Years Later: The Pop Diva, the Boob, and the Outrage," *The Daily Beast*, February 1, 2014, http://www.thedailybeast.com/articles/2014/02 /01/super-bowl-s-nipplegate-fiasco-10-years-later-the-pop-diva-the-boob-and -the-outrage.html; *Wikipedia*, s.v. "Howard Stern," https://en.wikipedia.org/wiki /Howard_Stern.

As Timberlake sang . . . "I'm gonna have you naked by the end of this song," he pulled off part of Jackson's costume . . . CBS . . . claimed that the incident was not intentional: Brian Dakss, "Janet's Bared Breast a PR Stunt?," *CBS News*, February 2, 2004, http://www.cbsnews.com/news/janets-bared-breast-a-pr-stunt/.

FCC ended up fining Viacom . . . $550,000: Lloyd Vries, "CBS Dealt Record Fine over Janet," *CBS News*, July 1, 2004, http://www.cbsnews.com/news/cbs -dealt-record-fine-over-janet/.

Clear Channel Communications . . . pull the *Howard Stern Show* . . . from all its stations: Reuters, "Clear Channel Pulls Howard Stern Show off Radio," *USA Today*, February 25, 2004, http://usatoday30.usatoday.com/life/people/2004-02 -25-stern-off_x.htm.

"The Super Bowl did us in," remarked Stern . . . adding that it made him feel "dead inside" . . . obligated . . . producing the show at Infinity . . . end of 2005: Krysten Crawford, "Howard Stern Jumps to Satellite," *CNN Money*, October 6, 2004, http://money.cnn.com/2004/10/06/news/newsmakers/stern_sirius/; Howard Kurz, "Stern on Satellite: A Bruised Flower, Blossoming Anew," *Washington Post*, December 11, 2005, http://www.washingtonpost.com/wp-dyn /content/article/2005/12/10/AR2005121001432.html.

Stern's 5-year deal with Sirius . . . The first . . . annual budget of $100 million . . . The second . . . stock incentives based on the number of subscribers Sirius would acquire: "SiriusXM and Howard Stern in a Contract 'Dance,'" *CNN Money*, March 11, 2015, http://money.cnn.com/2015/03/11/media/howard-stern -sirius-xm-contract-speculation/.

Stern giving television interviews . . . that satellite radio was "the next big thing" . . . ranted relentlessly about broadcast radio's stifling environment . . . Infinity Broadcasting even suspended him: Krysten Crawford, "Howard Stern Jumps to Satellite," *CNN Money*, October 6, 2004, http://money.cnn.com/2004 /10/06/news/newsmakers/stern_sirius/; Joe Flint, "Stern's Move to Satellite Radio Is Critical to Sirius and Infinity," *Wall Street Journal*, November 9, 2005, http://www.wsj.com/articles/SB113139827961890370.

Hugh Panero . . . declaring that "Howard Stern has raised awareness of the entire satellite category.": Eric A. Taub, "With Stern on Board, Satellite Radio Is Approaching a Secure Orbit," *New York Times*, December 19, 2005, http://www .nytimes.com/2005/12/19/business/media/with-stern-on-board-satellite-radio -is-approaching-a-secure-orbit.html.

At Sirius . . . Programming costs escalated from roughly $63 million in 2004 to $236 million in 2007; and 2006 . . . Stern's stock option payouts causing the programming costs to exceed the $520 million mark . . . At XM . . . net losses exceeded $640 million, while at Sirius net losses were well above $550 million: Annual reports and SEC filings by both companies, in particular Sirius Satellite Radio Inc. Form 10-K for years 2004, 2005, 2006, and 2007 and XM Satellite Radio Inc. Form 10-K for years 2004, 2005, 2006, and 2007; these can be found at http://investor.siriusxm.com/investor-overview/default.aspx#reports-tab2; http:// www.sec.gov/Archives/edgar/data/1091530/000119312508041106/d10k.htm; http://www.sec.gov/Archives/edgar/data/1091530/000119312507044379/d10k.htm.

In 2007, details began surfacing of what a proposed "merger of equals" between the two companies would look like: David Ellis and Paul R. La Monica, "XM, Sirius Announce Merger," *CNN Money*, February 20, 2007, http://money.cnn .com/2007/02/19/news/companies/xm_sirius/.

When the FCC issued . . . licenses . . . it stipulated that: "One licensee will not be permitted to acquire control of the other remaining one": David Lieberman, "How Sirius-XM Merger Would Cut Companies' Costs Still Unclear," *USA Today*, February 20, 2007, http://usatoday30.usatoday.com/money/media/2007 -02-19-xm-sirius-talks_x.htm.

Karmazin and his XM counterpart . . . were now also facing competition from other forms of digital and mobile entertainment . . . by merging they would actually offer customers better value: Sarah McBride, Dennis K. Berman, and Amy Schatz, "Sirius and XM Agree to Merge, Despite Hurdles," *Wall Street Journal*, February 20, 2007, http://www.wsj.com/articles/SB117190978981912915.

After a lengthy, 57-week review process, the Justice Department . . . approved the merger. The FCC took another 17 weeks . . . approved the merger under a few conditions: Olga Kharif, "The FCC Approves the XM-Sirius Merger," *Bloomberg Businessweek*, July 25, 2008, http://www.bloomberg.com/bw/stories/2008 -07-25/the-fcc-approves-the-xm-sirius-mergerbusinessweek-business-news -stock-market-and-financial-advice.

XM stock ceased trading on July 28, 2008 . . . Programming was merged in November . . . receivers to play both Sirius and XM audio . . . within a few months: Rick Aristotle, "The Sirius XM Merger Finally Matters," *The Motley Fool*, January 8, 2009, http://www.fool.com/investing/general/2009/01/08/the-sirius-xm -merger-finally-matters.aspx; *Wikipedia*, s.v. "Sirius XM Holdings," https://en .wikipedia.org/wiki/Sirius_XM_Holdings; "XM and Sirius Channels Merge at Long Last," *Engadget*, November 12, 2008, http://www.engadget.com/2008/11/12 /xm-and-sirius-channels-merge-at-long-last/; "Sirius XM Rolls Out Interoperable MiRGE Satellite Radio," *Engadget*, January 8, 2009, http://www.engadget.com /2009/01/08/sirius-xm-rolls-out-interoperable-mirge-satellite-radio/.

Analysts estimated . . . after the merger, any original content deals were negotiated at much lower rates: J. P. Mangalindan, "What Howard Stern's $400 Million Sirius Contract Means to the Street," *Fortune*, December 9, 2010, http://archive .fortune.com/2010/12/09/news/companies/Sirius-Stern-400-million.fortune /index.htm.

Acquisition costs per subscriber declined to $64 that year: Sirius XM Holdings Inc. Form 10-K (Annual Report), filed February 25, 2010, for the period ending December 31, 2009, http://investor.siriusxm.com/investor-overview/default.aspx #reports-tab2.

Liberty Media Corporation . . . stepped in with the necessary funds: Cecilia King, "Liberty Extends $530 Million Loan to Bail Out Sirius XM," *Washington Post*, February 18, 2009, http://www.washingtonpost.com/wp-dyn/content /article/2009/02/17/AR2009021700928.html.

SiriusXM and Howard Stern negotiated a 5-year extension that would last into 2015: Ben Sisario, "Putting Rumors to Rest, Howard Stern Renews His Sirius XM Contract," *New York Times*, December 9, 2010, http://www.nytimes .com/2010/12/10/business/media/10stern.html.

Stern filed a $300+ million lawsuit . . . The judge sided with SiriusXM and dismissed the claim. Stern appealed and lost again: Joseph Ax, "Howard Stern Loses Appeal in Lawsuit vs Sirius XM over Pay," *Reuters*, April 11, 2013, http:// www.reuters.com/article/2013/04/11/entertainment-us-sirius-howardstern-laws -idUSBRE93A0YX2013041.

In mid-2011 . . . SiriusXM quickly exercised its right and increased the monthly fee to $14.49: Liana B. Baker, "Sirius XM Raises Prices, Shares Gain," *Reuters*, September 14, 2011, http://www.reuters.com/article/2011/09/14/us-siriusxm-id USTRE78D63B20110914.

Attrition continued to hover around 1.8–1.9 percent a month and subscriber acquisition costs continued to steadily drop to $50 by 2013: Sirius XM Holdings Inc. Form 10-K, filed February 4, 2014, for the period ending December 31, 2013, http://investor.siriusxm.com/investor-overview/default.aspx#reports-tab2.

Another modest subscription price increase (50¢ a month) was implemented in early 2014: Liana B. Baker, "Update 2-Sirius XM Raises Prices; Sees 2014

Results below Forecasts," *Reuters*, October 24, 2013, http://www.reuters.com
/article/2013/10/24/siriusxm-results-idUSL1N0IE0EV20131024.

Stern's contract was renewed for an additional five years: Ben Sisario, "Howard
Stern and SiriusXM Sign New Deal for 5 Years," *New York Times*, December 15, 2015, http://www.nytimes.com/2015/12/16/business/media/howard-stern
-and-siriusxm-reach-new-deal.html.

COMMENTS

1. In 1992 . . . the market was opened up to competition: When the Swedish
mobile telephony market was opened for competition in 1992, another firm entered the market (Nordic Tel, later changing its name to Europolitan, which was
subsequently acquired by Vodafone and later became part of the Telenor Group).
We focused on Tele2's entry as it was clearly the most competitive and garnered
much more market share in the period studied.

2. The result is a net innovation equity increase of close to $700 million: In
assessing the innovation equity of the "Stern effect," as indicated, we assumed that
Sirius incurred minimal acquisition costs on Stern-generated customers. If this assumption is not true, we would need to subtract the relevant acquisition costs from
the CLV estimates (prior to discounting and multiplying by the net additional subscribers). For example, in the extreme event that acquisition costs are the same for
Stern-generated customers as for all other acquired customers, the innovation equity decreases by about $325 million, negatively impacting the overall ROI of signing
Stern.

3. The companies further argued that by merging, they would actually offer
customers better value: Prior to the merger between XM and Sirius, interested
consumers had to purchase two separate hardware devices and pay two separate
subscription fees to enjoy the content on each of the services.

4. XM stock ceased trading . . . and SiriusXM became the name of the new company: Formally, Sirius "acquired XM by merger," with XM stocks being converted
to Sirius stocks. The merged company was listed as Sirius XM Holdings.

5. The judge sided with SiriusXM and dismissed the claim: In the first contract
between Sirius and Howard Stern, there was an explicit clause stipulating that, in
the event of a merger between Sirius and XM, Stern would be entitled to a one-
time fee of $25 million. The judge in the case saw that clause as indicative that the
parties never intended to treat XM's added subscribers in the compensation calculation; Eriq Gardner, "Howard Stern Attempts to Revive $300 Million Lawsuit
against Sirius XM Radio," *Hollywood Reporter*, April, 27, 2012, http://www.holly
woodreporter.com/thr-esq/howard-stern-sirius-radio-lawsuit-317497.

6. The company predicted . . . the value of the service justified the new price:
After the price hikes in mid-2011, the ARPU for SiriusXM climbed to $12 and
then to $12.23 in the subsequent two years. After the price hike in 2014, the ARPU
climbed to $12.38; Sirius XM Holdings Form 10-K, filed February 5, 2015, for the

period ending December 31, 2014, http://www.getfilings.com/sec-filings/150205 /SIRIUS-XM-HOLDINGS-INC_10-K/.

7. Play out adoption dynamics according to the diffusion model: Given that the two companies have merged, cross-brand WOM effects and churn are no longer relevant. In this case, and assuming a desire to still capture the possibility of attrition through disadoption, one can use a modified version of the competitive diffusion model that is presented in math box 9 in the appendix.

Chapter 7: Leaping Ahead to Valuing the Next Generation

FACTS AND QUOTES

"Forecasting is very difficult, especially about the future": This quote and variants of it have often been attributed to Mark Twain—for example, Jay B. Abrams, *Quantitative Business Valuation: A Mathematical Approach for Today's Professionals*, 2nd ed. (Hoboken, NJ: Wiley, 2010). We note that this quote has also been attributed to other notable people, such as Niels Bohr and Yogi Berra.

The advent of the phonograph in 1877: *Encyclopaedia Britannica Online*, s.v. "Phonograph," http://www.britannica.com/technology/phonograph.

By 1998 . . . The first MP3 players were launched into the marketplace: Daniel Ionescu, "Evolution of the MP3 Player," *PCWorld*, October 29, 2009, http://www.pcworld.com/article/174725/evolution_of_the_mp3_player.html.

The first Walkman appeared in Japan in 1979 . . . owes its genesis to pressure from Sony's chairman: Meaghan Haire, "A Brief History of the Walkman," *Time*, July 1, 2009, http://content.time.com/time/nation/article/0,8599,1907884,00 .html.

In the classic film *Out of Africa* . . . Denys Finch Hatton (played by Robert Redford) operating a gramophone: "Look, they finally made a machine that's really useful!" he says: *Out of Africa*, directed by Sydney Pollack (Universal Pictures, 1985).

By the mid-1910s, the gramophone disc (at 78 RPM) won the war: David L. Morton, *Sound Recording: The Life Story of a Technology* (Baltimore, MD: John Hopkins University Press, 2006); *Wikipedia*, s.v. "Gramophone Record," https://en.wikipedia.org/wiki/Gramophone_record; *Wikipedia*, s.v. "Sound Recording and Reproduction," https://en.wikipedia.org/wiki/Sound_recording_and _reproduction.

Portable CD players in the early 1980s and MP3 players . . . in the late 1990s: "Music Players in the Pre-iPod Era," Retro Junk, http://www.retrojunk.com /article/show/3889/music-players-in-the-preipod-era.

A UK analyst on the sales of DVD . . . : "This level has been achieved in eight years, substantially quicker than the 20 years it took VCRs . . .": Jane Bainbridge, "Sector Insight: DVD Players—Confusion Slows Sales," *Marketing Magazine*,

August 22, 2007, http://www.marketingmagazine.co.uk/article/732921/sector
-insight-dvd-players—confusion-slows-sales.

There are now eight distinct video game console generations, beginning with the
Atari 2600 . . . to the PS4, Xbox One, and Wii U: Elie Ofek, "Home Video
Games: Generation Seven," Harvard Business School Note 505072, 2005; Wi-
boon Kittilaksanawong and Gary Gillet, "Nintendo Wii U: Lessons Learned
for New Strategic Directions," Ivey Publishing Case W14682, 2015.

In Denmark, the first mobile telephony generation . . . was introduced in 1982; the
second generation . . . commenced in 1992; and the third generation . . . was
introduced in 2003: "Competition and Regulation in the Nordic Mobile Markets," report from meeting of Nordic director generals on November 7, 2005,
https://www.pts.se/upload/Documents/SE/Competition_regulation_nordic
_mobile_markets_sept06.pdf.

Vista operating system, which was released . . . five years after the previous generation . . . Vista was somewhat poorly received . . . Microsoft released . . . Windows 7 . . . in 2009: John Markoff, "Microsoft Introduces Windows 7, Ending
Vista Brand," *New York Times*, October 28, 2008, http://www.nytimes.com/2008
/10/29/technology/business-computing/29soft.html?_r=0.

Windows 8 . . . was launched in late 2012. The successor . . . is called Windows 10
and not 9: Darren Allen, "Microsoft Reveals the Reason Why There Was No
Windows 9," *IT ProPortal*, July 5, 2015, http://www.itproportal.com/2015/05/07
/microsoft-reveals-the-reason-why-there-was-no-windows-9/.

Per-game royalty (about 15 percent for games costing around $50–$60): "The
Economics of Game Publishing," *IGN*, May 5, 2006, http://www.ign.com
/articles/2006/05/06/the-economics-of-game-publishing; Rachel Rosmarin, "Why
Gears of War Costs $60," *Forbes*, December 19, 2006, http://www.forbes.com
/2006/12/19/ps3-xbox360-costs-tech-cx_rr_game06_1219expensivegames_slide
.html.

IBM general purpose computers (also known as "mainframes"): *Wikipedia*, s.v.
"IBM Mainframe," https://en.wikipedia.org/wiki/IBM_mainframe; Montgomery Phister, *Data Processing Technology and Economics* (Santa Monica Publishing, 1976, supplement 1979).

"History doesn't repeat itself, but it does rhyme": This quote and variants of it
have often been attributed to Mark Twain—for example, Ian Cowie, " 'History
Does Not Repeat Itself, but It Often Rhymes, as Mark Twain Noted,' " *Telegraph*, March 20, 2009, http://www.telegraph.co.uk/finance/personalfinance
/comment/iancowie/5018093/History-does-not-repeat-itself-but-it-often
-rhymes-as-Mark-Twain-noted.html.

COMMENTS

1. These "lost" revenues: In the years under consideration, IBM sold as well as
rented its mainframe systems. The mix of sales to rentals was roughly 25 percent

to 75 percent, respectively. Consequently, even though there were some leapfroggers, in practice the effect of a fraction of them not buying twice from the firm was not substantial. To simplify our illustration of the introduction timing dilemma, we assumed that all IBM systems were rentals (and converted the 25 percent of purchases into annual fees appropriately).

Chapter 8: Innovation Equity Makes the World Go 'Round

FACTS AND QUOTES

"It has been said that arguing against globalization is like arguing against the laws of gravity": Kofi Annan, "Secretary-General Kofi Annan's Opening Address to the Fifty-third Annual DPI/NGO Conference," August 28, 2000, http://www.un.org/dpi/ngosection/annualconfs/53/sg-address.html.

The first-generation iPhone . . . was released in only a handful of countries . . . The second-generation iPhone 3G . . . reached . . . more than 80 countries, by most counts: Chuck Jones, "Analysis of iPhone Launch Countries, Timing and First Weekend Sales," *Forbes*, September 5, 2013, http://www.forbes.com/sites/chuckjones/2013/09/05/analysis-of-iphone-launch-countries-timing-and-first-weekend-sales/; *Wikipedia*, s.v. "History of the iPhone," https://en.wikipedia.org/wiki/History_of_the_iPhone.

In a recent study, 19 percent of US respondents . . . "friends or family" as the primary source of information . . . in Brazil (4 percent), China (8 percent) and Italy (6 percent): Todd A. Mooradian and K. Scott Swan, "Personality-and-Culture: The Case of National Extraversion and Word-of-Mouth," *Journal of Business Research*, 59, no. 6 (2006): 778–85.

The Big Mac Index, published by the *Economist* . . . the Big Mac was found to cost 63 percent more . . . in the US than in China: "The Big Mac Index: Global Exchange Rates to Go," *Economist*, July 16, 2015, http://www.economist.com/content/big-mac-index.

Subscribers in European countries . . . were reported to have used fewer services on their smartphones than did consumers in the US, China, Brazil, and Japan: Chris Burns, "GfK Group Finds One in Five iPhone Owners Would Rather Change Banks than Smartphones," *Slash Gear*, November 25, 2011, http://www.slashgear.com/one-in-five-iphone-owners-would-rather-change-banks-than-smartphones-25198045/.

Research . . . by Nokia . . . found that customer retention is high in emerging markets yet much lower in mature and developed markets: Nokia Siemens Networks Corporation, "How to Generate Customer Loyalty in Mobile Markets," product code B301-00419-B-200906-1-EN Indivisual, March 2009, http://networks.nokia.com/system/files/document/AR_Mobile_A4_0107.pdf.

The satellite radio services of Sirius and XM were extended in late 2005 to Canada . . . In 2011, the FCC . . . allowed SiriusXM . . . to set up repeaters in

Hawaii and Alaska: "Sirius, XM Take Rivalry to Canada," *CNN Money*, June 17, 2005, http://money.cnn.com/2005/06/17/technology/sirius_xm/; Herbert A. Sample, "FCC Says Sirius Radio Can Broadcast in Hawaii," Boston.com, January 19, 2011, http://www.boston.com/business/technology/articles/2011/01/19/fcc_says _sirius_radio_can_broadcast_in_hawaii/.

WorldSpace was a Washington, DC–based firm founded by an Ethiopian-born lawyer . . . began transmitting signals in October of 1999 in Africa: George Leopold, "Worldspace Switches on Digital Radio Service," *EETimes,* October 13, 1999, http://www.eetimes.com/document.asp?doc_id=1229982.

The company went public in mid-2005 . . . and entry into European markets was on the horizon . . . The stock closed on its first day . . . at a price of $22.36, by October of 2008 . . . WorldSpace had to file for bankruptcy . . . The total number of subscribers WorldSpace had amassed . . . was less than 200,000: David S. Hilzenrath, "Satellite Radio IPO Carries a Disclosure," *Washington Post*, August 5, 2005, http://www.washingtonpost.com/wp-dyn/content/article/2005/08/04/AR 2005080401969.html; Eric Morath, "WorldSpace Files for Bankruptcy, Listing $2.12 Billion in Debt," *Wall Street Journal*, October 17, 2008, http://www.wsj.com /articles/SB122428124284945981; *Wikipedia*, s.v. "1Worldspace," https://en.wiki pedia.org/wiki/1worldspace.

In places like India, the basic subscription was priced at . . . $3 per month. The radio receivers had to be heavily subsidized . . . acquisition costs were high . . . investment and funding of over $2.5 billion had poured into WorldSpace: Nihkil Pahwa, "Worldspace Bankrupt and on the Block: What Happened & What They Were Waiting For," *Medianama*, http://www.medianama.com/2008/10/223-world space-bankrupt-and-on-the-block-what-happened-what-they-were-waiting-for/.

Solaris Mobile . . . suggested in 2013 that their technology could be used to provide a pan-European digital radio platform: Solaris Mobile (now EchoStar Mobile), "Solaris Mobile Launches EUR Radio," press release, September 9, 2011, http://echostarmobile.com/media/press-releases/solaris_mobile_launches_eur _radio; suggested applications by EchoStar Mobile, "Digital Satellite Radio for Europe," http://echostarmobile.com/services/applications.

The first-generation iPhone was first released in the US, and it then took more than 4 months before . . . UK, Germany, and France . . . followed by Austria and Ireland some 4 months later: *Wikipedia*, s.v. "iPhone," https://en.wikipedia .org/wiki/IPhone.

Apple followed a similar rollout . . . for the 3G model . . . The first wave . . . in Asian and Latin American countries . . . Eastern European countries and India . . . Middle Eastern countries . . . had to wait until early 2009 . . . China . . . welcomed into the iPhone family late in 2009 . . . An exclusive agreement, as was the case in the US with AT&T . . . Apple typically benefited . . . AT&T had to fork over roughly $10 a month: Apple, "Apple Introduces the New iPhone 3G," press release, June 9, 2008, http://www.apple.com /pr/library/2008/06/09Apple-Introduces-the-New-iPhone-3G.html; Philip Elmer-

DeWitt, "iPhone 3G: Now Serving 660 Million Potential Customers," *Fortune*, August 22, 2008, http://fortune.com/2008/08/22/iphone-3g-now-serving -660-million-potential-customers/; Olga Kharif, "Apple iPhone's China Problem," *Bloomberg Business*, November 3, 2009, http://www.businessweek.com /the_thread/techbeat/archives/2009/11/apple_iphones_c.html; Peter Cohan, "How Steve Jobs Got ATT to Share Revenue," *Forbes*, August 16, 2013, http://www .forbes.com/sites/petercohan/2013/08/16/how-steve-jobs-got-att-to-share-revenue/; *Wikipedia*, s.v. "History of the iPhone," https://en.wikipedia.org/wiki/History _of_the_iPhone; AppleInsider staff, "Apple Preparing to Launch iPhone in 29 More Countries," *AppleInsider*, http://appleinsider.com/articles/08/09/23/apple _preparing_to_launch_iphone_in_29_more_countries.

In countries where subsidies were not provided, like India, the iPhone 3G's $700+ price tag was prohibitive: "iPhone in India: Has Apple Dialed the Wrong Number?," *Knowledge@Wharton*, September 4, 2008, http://knowledge.wharton .upenn.edu/article/iphone-in-india-has-apple-dialed-the-wrong-number/.

Media coverage, with some hailing the device as "the Jesus phone": "Where Would Jesus Queue?," *Economist*, July 5, 2007, http://www.economist.com /node/9443542; Iain Mackenzie, "Speculation That Apple May Launch Touchscreen 'iSlate,'" *BBC Newsbeat*, http://www.bbc.co.uk/newsbeat/article/10005038 /speculation-that-apple-may-launch-touchscreen-islate.

Apple was estimated to have spent nearly $650 million on advertising the iPhone in the US between 2007 and 2011: Dan Rowinski, "4 Real Secrets We've Learned So Far About Apple," *readwrite*, Aug 7, 2012, http://readwrite.com/2012/08/07 /4-real-secrets-weve-learned-so-far-about-apple.

Apples falling from a tree . . . the inspiration for Sir Isaac Newton's . . . law of universal gravitation: Steve Connor, "The Core of Truth behind Sir Isaac Newton's Apple," *Independent*, January 18, 2010, http://www.independent.co .uk/news/science/the-core-of-truth-behind-sir-isaac-newtons-apple-1870915 .html.

COMMENTS

1. These ratios can be used to adjust the per-period customer profit margins: In calculating the per-period profit margins for the various countries in the European satellite radio example, we extrapolated from the relative average price levels in each country. While this is likely to be a reasonable approximation for customer revenues, the per-period cost to serve a customer might be commensurately different in each country (and in fact drive the relative price variations to a certain extent). If this is the case, the adjustment from the US values would likely be smaller. Again, we stress that our calculations were primarily meant for illustration purposes.

2. Figure 8.1 shows how Google searches for the popular social media application Facebook evolved . . . a leveling-off phase, and a decline that starts in 2013: We speculate that the "abrupt" spike in searches for the term "Facebook" in early

2012 (as seen in figure 8.1) was due, at least in part, to the initial public offering of the company in May 2012.

Chapter 9: Making the Framework "Work" for You

FACTS AND QUOTES

Studies conducted by Bain & Company . . . suggest that the profitability of a customer typically goes up with the duration of their relationship: Frederick F. Reichheld and Thomas Teal, *The Loyalty Effect: The Hidden Force behind Growth, Profits, and Lasting Value* (Harvard Business Review Press, 1996).

With respect to changes in the retention rate . . . tends to go up with time: V. Kumar and Werner J. Reinartz, *Customer Relationship Management: Concept, Strategy, and Tools* (Springer, 2012).

Marketing thought leaders . . . products as "service *de facto*": Stephen L. Vargo and Robert F. Lusch, "Evolving to a New Dominant Logic for Marketing," *Journal of Marketing* 68, no. 1 (2004): 1–17.

Medical device makers could not have easily foreseen . . . studies would emerge suggesting that their products increased the risk of fatal blood clots: Elie Ofek, "Examining the Adoption of Drug-Eluting Stents," Harvard Business School Case 509028, 2008.

FDA eased regulations in 1997 on direct-to-consumer advertising: John E. Calfee, Randolph Stempski, and Clifford Winston, "Direct-to-Consumer Advertising and the Demand for Cholesterol-Reducing Drugs," Brookings, June 2003, http://www.brookings.edu/research/articles/2003/06/consumerdrugs-winston.

The Klout score that firms can purchase on the online influence of their customer base: Mark Schaefer, *Return on Influence: The Revolutionary Power of Klout, Social Scoring, and Influence Marketing* (McGraw-Hill Education, 2012).

COMMENTS ON TABLES AND FIGURES BASED ON EXTERNAL INFORMATION

Customer base sizes and CLV-related data for XM Satellite Radio, Sirius (and later SiriusXM), and other publically held companies such as T-Mobile, Capital One, AT&T, Mobistar, Belgacom, SK Telecom, and E*Trade were compiled by the authors from the companies' publicly disclosed financial reports (10-Q and 10-K reports of the appropriate years).

WACC data were compiled by Aswath Damodaran of the Department of Finance at New York University Stern School of Business (Damodaran Online, http://pages.stern.nyu.edu/~adamodar/).

All consumer electronics data (such as portable CD players, personal computers, and MP3 players used in various figures in chapters 4 and 7) were compiled from information made available by the Consumer Electronic Association, except for the iPhone data used in figure 1.1, which were compiled by Statista (http://www.statista.com/statistics/263401/global-apple-iphone-sales-since-3rd-quarter-2007/).

Information in connection with Sirius forecasted subscribers (internal estimates), per table 6.5, was based on One Twelve Inc. and Don Buchwald complaint filing to the Supreme Court of the State of New York, Summons Index No. 6507 62/2011, March 22, 2011, and on Osborne ("A Deeper Look at the Howard Stern Lawsuit," *Sirius Buzz,* April 18, 2012, http://siriusbuzz.com/a-depper-look-at-the-stern-lawsuit.php).

International wireless service subscriber data were compiled in part from the World Cellular Information Service (WCIS).

Tie Ratio data for table 7.3 and other home video game console sales data in chapter 7 were compiled from VGChartz (http://www.vgchartz.com/).

Growth and CLV data for IBM mainframe systems-in-use—for example, in figure 7.5—were compiled by Montgomery Phister (*Data Processing Technology and Economics*, Santa Monica Publishing Co., 1976, and Supplement 1979).

Diffusion and CLV data for broadband and satellite radio in tables 8.1, 8.4, and 8.5 were compiled by the authors based on publicly available OECD records.

Figure 8.1 and table 8.7 were based on entering "Facebook" on Google Trends (https://www.google.com/trends/) in July 2015.

References and Recommended Reading

For each chapter, we provide a list of relevant references. Many of these references constitute the main source for the concepts, theories, studies, and findings that were covered in the respective chapters. Some of the references are suggestions intended for those readers interested in gaining a deeper understanding of a particular topic matter. (Under each chapter, references are listed alphabetically.)

Chapter 1: The Basic Diffusion Pattern of an Innovation

Bass, Frank M. (1969) "A New Product Growth Model for Consumer Durables," *Management Science* 15, 215–27.

Bass, Frank M. (2004) "Comment on 'A New Product Growth Model for Consumer Durables,'" *Management Science* 50 (22), 1833–40.

Gourville, John T. (2006) "Eager Sellers and Stony Buyers: Understanding the Psychology of New-Product Adoption," *Harvard Business Review*, June.

Lilien, Gary L., Arvind Rangaswamy, and Christophe Van den Bulte (2000) "Diffusion Models: Managerial Applications and Software," in *New-Product Diffusion Models*, edited by Vijay Mahajan, Eitan Muller, and Yoram Wind. New York: Springer.

Mahajan, Vijay, Eitan Muller, and Yoram Wind (2000) "New-Product Diffusion Models: From Theory to Practice," in *New-Product Diffusion Models*, edited by Vijay Mahajan, Eitan Muller, and Yoram Wind. New York: Springer.

Muller, Eitan (2013) "Innovation Diffusion," in *The History of Marketing Science*, edited by Russell Winer and Scott Neslin. Boston: New Publishers.

Ofek, Elie (2009) "Forecasting the Adoption of a New Product," Harvard Business School Note 505062.

Rogers, Everett M. (2003) *Diffusion of Innovations*, 5th ed. New York: Free Press.

Chapter 2: The Whole Is Bigger than the Sum of Its (Diffusion and Customer Lifetime Value) Parts

Bejou, David, Timothy L. Keningham, and Lerzan Aksoy (2013) *Customer Lifetime Value: Reshaping the Way We Manage to Maximize Profits*. Routledge.

Blattberg, Robert C., Byung-Do Kim, and Scott A. Neslin (2008) *Database Marketing: Analyzing and Managing Customers*. Springer.

Godes, David B., and Elie Ofek (2003) "XM Satellite Radio (A)," Harvard Business School Case 504009.

Gupta, Sunil, and Donald Lehmann (2005) *Managing Customers as Investments: The Strategic Value of Customers in the Long Run*. Wharton School Publishing.

Kumar, V. (2008) *Managing Customers for Profit: Strategies to Increase Profits and Build Loyalty*. Wharton School Publishing.

McGovern, Gail (2003) "Virgin Mobile USA: Pricing for the Very First Time," Harvard Business School Case 504028.

Ofek, Elie (2002) "Customer Profitability and Lifetime Value," Harvard Business School Note 503019.

Ofek, Elie (2014) "Customer Lifetime Value (CLV) vs. Customer Lifetime Return on Investment (CLROI)," Harvard Business School Note 515049.

Chapter 3: Don't Just Stand There: Do Something! Growing Innovation Equity through Marketing Actions

Eisenmann, Thomas R., Michael Pao, and Lauren Barley (2011) "Dropbox: It Just Works!," Harvard Business School Case 811065.

Fader, Peter S. (2011) *Customer Centricity*. Wharton Digital Press.

Harvard Business School Press (2009) "The Right Customers: Acquisition, Retention, and Development," in *Harvard Business Essentials: Marketer's Toolkit*.

Hogan, John E., Katherine N. Lemon, and Barak Libai (2003) "What Is the True Value of a Lost Customer?," *Journal of Service Research* 5 (3), 196–208.

Keller, Kevin L., and Philip Kotler (2011) *Marketing Management*, 14th ed. Upper Saddle River, NJ: Pearson Prentice Hall.

Krishnan, Trichy V., and Dipak C. Jain (2006) "Optimal Dynamic Advertising Policy for New Products," *Management Science* 52 (12), 1957–69.

Kumar, V., and Werner J. Reinartz (2012) *Customer Relationship Management: Concept, Strategy, and Tools*. Springer.

Kumar, V., and Denish Shah (2015) *Handbook of Research on Customer Equity in Marketing*. Elgar.

Lee, Clarence, Vineet Kumar, and Sunil Gupta (2015) "Designing Freemium: A Model of Consumer Usage, Upgrade, and Referral Dynamics," Yale University Working Paper.

Rogers, Everett M. (2003) *Diffusion of Innovations*, 5th ed. New York: Free Press.

Teixeira, Thales, and Elizabeth Watkins (2013) "Freemium Pricing at Dropbox," Harvard Business School Case 514053.

Van den Bulte, Christophe, and Gary Lilien (2001) "Medical Innovation Revisited: Social Contagion versus Marketing Effort," *American Journal of Sociology* 106 (5), 1409–35.

Watts, Duncan J., and Steve Hasker (2006) "Marketing in an Unpredictable World," *Harvard Business Review*, September.

Chapter 4: Foreseeing Bumps and Potholes along the Diffusion Road

Berger, Jonah, and Chip Heath (2008) "Who Drives Divergence? Identity Signaling, Outgroup Dissimilarity, and the Abandonment of Cultural Tastes," *Journal of Personality and Social Psychology* 95 (3), 593–607.

Chandrasekaran, Deepa, and Gerard J. Tellis (2011) "Getting a Grip on the Saddle: Chasms or Cycles?," *Journal of Marketing* 75 (4), 21–34.

Goldenberg, Jacob, Barak Libai, and Eitan Muller (2002) "Riding the Saddle: How Cross-market Communication Can Create a Major Slump in Sales," *Journal of Marketing* 66 (2), 1–17.

Golder, Peter N., and Gerard J. Tellis (2004) "Growing, Growing, Gone: Cascades, Diffusion, and Turning Points in the Product Life Cycle," *Marketing Science* 23 (2), 207–18.

Van den Bulte, Christophe, and Yogeh V. Joshi (2007) "New Product Diffusion with Influentials and Imitators," *Marketing Science* 26 (3), 400–21.

Chapter 5: Jumpstarting Stalled Adoption: Getting the Mainstream to Take the Plunge

Choi, Jay Pil (1997) "Herd Behavior, the 'Penguin Effect,' and the Suppression of Informational Diffusion: An Analysis of Informational Externalities and Payoff Interdependency," *RAND Journal of Economics* 28 (3), 407–25.

Farell, Joseph, and Garth Saloner (1987) "Competition, Compatibility and Standards: The Economics of Horses, Penguins and Lemmings," in *Product Standardization and Competitive Strategy*, edited by H. Landis Gabel. Amsterdam: Elsevier Science Publishers.

Mahajan, Vijay, and Eitan Muller (1998) "When Is It Worthwhile Targeting the Majority Instead of the Innovators in a New Product Launch?," *Journal of Marketing Research* (35), 488–95.

Moore, Geoffrey A. (2004) *Inside the Tornado: Strategies for Developing, Leveraging and Surviving Hypergrowth Markets*. New York: HarperCollins.

Moore, Geoffrey A. (2014) *Crossing the Chasm: Marketing and Selling Disruptive Products to Mainstream Consumers*. New York: HarperCollins.

Chapter 6: Survival in the Presence of a Rival: Valuing Innovations at the Brand Level

Berger, Jonah (2013) *Contagious: Why Things Catch On*. New York: Simon & Schuster.

Godes, David B., and Elie Ofek (2004) "XM Satellite Radio (B)," Harvard Business School Case 504065.

Godes, David B., and Elie Ofek (2004) "XM Satellite Radio (C): The Next Generation of Radio Receivers," Harvard Business School Case 505015.

Goldenberg, Jacob, Barak Libai, and Eitan Muller (2010) "The Chilling Effect of Network Externalities," *International Journal of Research in Marketing* 27 (1), 4–15.

Haenlein, Michael, and Barak Libai (2013) "Targeting Revenue Leaders for a New Product," *Journal of Marketing* 77 (3), 65–80.

Hinz, Oliver, Bernd Skiera, Christian Barrot, and Jan U. Becker (2011) "Seeding Strategies for Viral Marketing: An Empirical Comparison," *Journal of Marketing* 75 (3), 55–71.

Krishnan, Trichy V., and Demetrios Vakratsas (2012) "The Multiple Roles of Interpersonal Communication in New Product Growth," *International Journal of Research in Marketing* 29 (3), 292–305.

Libai, Barak, Eitan Muller, and Renana Peres (2005) "The Role of Seeding in Multi-market Entry," *International Journal of Research in Marketing* 22 (4), 375–93.

Libai, Barak, Eitan Muller, and Renana Peres (2009) "The Diffusion of Services," *Journal of Marketing Research* 46 (1), 163–75.

Libai, Barak, Eitan Muller, and Renana Peres (2009) "The Effect of Within-Brand and Cross-brand Communication on Competitive Growth," *Journal of Marketing* 73 (1), 19–34.

Libai, Barak, Eitan Muller, and Renana Peres (2013) "Decomposing the Value of Word-of-Mouth Seeding Programs: Acceleration vs. Expansion," *Journal of Marketing Research* 46 (2), 161–76.

Lovett, Mitchell, Renana Peres, and Ron Shachar (2013) "On Brands and Word of Mouth," *Journal of Marketing Research* 50 (4), 427–44.

Madden, Gary, Grant Coble-Neal, and Brian Dalzell (2004) "A Dynamic Model of Mobile Telephony Subscription Incorporating a Network Effect," *Telecommunications Policy* 28, 133–44.

Peres, Renana, and Christophe Van den Bulte (2014) "When to Take or Forgo New Product Exclusivity: Balancing Protection from Competition against Word-of-Mouth Spillover," *Journal of Marketing* 78 (2), 83–100.

Scaglione, Miriam, Emanuele Giovannetti, and Mohsen Hamoudia (2015) "The Diffusion of Mobile Social Networking: Exploring Adoption Externalities in Four G7 Countries," *International Journal of Forecasting* 31 (4), 1159–70.

Chapter 7: Leaping Ahead to Valuing the Next Generation

Bertini, Marco, John T. Gourville, and Elie Ofek (2011) "The Best Way to Name Your Product 2.0," *Harvard Business Review* 89 (5), 36.

Mahajan, Vijay, and Eitan Muller (1996) "Timing, Diffusion, and Substitution of Successive Generations of Technological Innovations: The IBM Mainframe Case," *Technological Forecasting and Social Change* 51 (2), 109–32.

Norton, John A., and Frank M. Bass (1987) "A Diffusion Theory Model of Adoption and Substitution for Successive Generations of High-Technology Products," *Management Science* 33 (9), 1069–86.

Norton, John A., and Frank M. Bass (1992) "Evolution of Technological Generations: The Law of Capture," *Sloan Management Review* 33 (2), 66–77.

Oreg, Shaul, and Jacob Goldenberg (2015) *Resistance to Innovation: Its Sources and Manifestations*. University of Chicago Press.

Phister, Montgomery (1979) *Data Processing, Technology and Economics*. Santa Monica Publishing.

Shi, Xiaohui, Kiran Fernandes, and Pattarin Chumnumpan (2014) "Diffusion of Multi-generational High-Technology Products," *Technovation* 34, 162–76.

Stremersch, Stefan, Eitan Muller, and Renana Peres (2010) "Does New Product Growth Accelerate across Technology Generations?," *Marketing Letters* 21 (2), 103–20.

Van den Bulte, Christophe (2000) "New Product Diffusion Acceleration: Measurement and Analysis," *Marketing Science* 19 (4), 366–80.

Van den Bulte, Christophe (2002) "Want to Know How Diffusion Speed Varies across Countries and Products? Try Using a Bass Model," *PDMA Visions* 26, 12–15.

Van den Bulte, Christophe (2004) "Multigeneration Innovation Diffusion and Intergeneration Time: A Cautionary Note," *Journal of the Academy of Marketing Science* 32, 357–60.

Van den Bulte, Christophe, and Stefan Stremersch (2004) "Social Contagion and Income Heterogeneity in New Product Diffusion: A Meta-analytic Test," *Marketing Science* 23, 530–44.

Chapter 8: Innovation Equity Makes the World Go 'Round

Agarwal, James, Naresh K. Malhotra, and Ruth N. Bolton (2010) "A Cross-national and Cross-cultural Approach to Global Market Segmentation: An Application Using Consumers' Perceived Service Quality," *Journal of International Marketing* 18 (3), 18–40.

Beise, Marian (2004) "Lead Markets: Country-Specific Drivers of the Global Diffusion of Innovations," *Research Policy* 33 (6), 997–1018.

Cavusgil, Tamer S., and Erin Cavusgil (2012) "Reflections on International Marketing: Destructive Regeneration and Multinational Firms," *Journal of the Academy of Marketing Science* 40 (2), 202–17.

Dekimpe, Marnik G., Philip M. Parker, and Miklos Sarvary (1998) "Staged Estimation of International Diffusion Models: An Application to Global Cellular

Telephone Adoption," *Technological Forecasting and Social Change* 57 (1), 105–32.

Dekimpe, Marnik G., Philip M. Parker, and Miklos Sarvary (2000) "Globalization: Modeling Technology Adoption Timing across Countries," *Technological Forecasting and Social Change* 63 (1), 25–42.

Dekimpe, Marnik G., Philip M. Parker, and Miklos Sarvary (2000) "Multimarket and Global Diffusion," in *New-Product Diffusion Models*, edited by Vijay Mahajan, Eitan Muller, and Yoram Wind. New York: Springer.

Friedmand, Thomas L. (2005) *The World Is Flat: A Brief History of the Twenty-First Century*. New York: Farrar, Straus and Giroux.

Gelper, Sarah, and Stefan Stremersch (2014) "Variable Selection in International Diffusion Models," *International Journal of Research in Marketing* 31 (4), 356–67.

Golder, Peter N., and Gerard J. Tellis (1997) "Will It Ever Fly? Modeling the Takeoff of Really New Consumer Durables," *Marketing Science* 16 (3), 256–70.

Griffith, David A., Goksel Yalcinkaya, and Gaia Rubera (2014) "Country-Level Performance of New Experience Products in a Global Rollout: The Moderating Effects of Economic Wealth and National Culture," *Journal of International Marketing* 22 (4), 1–20.

Hofstede, Geert (2003) *Culture's Consequences: Comparing Values, Behaviors, Institutions and Organizations across Nations*, 2nd ed. Thousand Oaks, CA: Sage.

Kotabe, Masaaki, and Kristiaan Helsen (2009) *The Sage Handbook of International Marketing*. Thousand Oaks, CA: Sage.

Krishnan, Trichy V., and A. T. Suman (2009) "International Diffusion of New Products," in *The Sage Handbook of International Marketing*, edited by Masaaki Kotabe and Kristiaan Helsen, 325–45. Thousand Oaks, CA: Sage.

Levitt, Theodore (1983) "The Globalization of Markets," *Harvard Business Review* 61 (3), 92–102.

Meade, Nigel, and Towhidul Islam (2015) "Firm-Level Innovation Diffusion of 3G Mobile Connections in International Context," *International Journal of Forecasting* 31 (4), 1138–52.

Morgeson, Forrest V., Pratyush Nidhi Sharma, and G. Tomas M. Hult (2015) "Cross-national Differences in Consumer Satisfaction: Mobile Services in Emerging and Developed Markets," *Journal of International Marketing* 23 (2), 1–24.

Patterson, Paul G., and Tasman Smith (2003) "A Cross-cultural Study of Switching Barriers and Propensity to Stay with Service Providers," *Journal of Retailing* 79 (2), 107–20.

Stremersch, Stefan, and Gerard J. Tellis (2004) "Understanding and Managing International Growth of New Products," *International Journal of Research in Marketing* 21 (4), 421–38.

Talukdar, Debabrata, K. Sudhir, and Andrew Ainslie (2002) "Investigating New Product Diffusion across Products and Countries," *Marketing Science* 21 (2), 97–114.

Tellis, Gerard J., Stefan Stremersch, and Eden Yin (2003) "The International Takeoff of New Products: The Role of Economics, Culture, and Country Innovativeness," *Marketing Science* 22 (2), 188–208.

Turk, Tomaž, and Peter Trkman (2012) "Bass Model Estimates for Broadband Diffusion in European Countries," *Technological Forecasting and Social Change* 79 (1), 85–96.

Van Everdingen, Yvonne, Dennis Fok, and Stefan Stremersch (2009) "Modeling Global Spill-Over of New Product Takeoff," *Journal of Marketing Research* 46 (5), 637–52.

Yogev, Guy (2012) *The Diffusion of Free Products: How Freemium Revenue Model Changes the Strategy and Growth of New Digital Products.* Saarbrücken, Lap Lambert Academic Publishing.

Chapter 9: Making the Framework "Work" for You

Bass, Frank M., Kent Gordon, Teresa L. Ferguson, and Mary Lou Githens (2001) "DIRECTV: Forecasting Diffusion of a New Technology Prior to Product Launch," *Interfaces* 31 (3), S82–S93.

Bayus, Barry L. (1993) "High-Definition Television: Assessing Demand Forecasts for a Next Generation Consumer Durable," *Management Science* 39 (11), 1319–33.

Blattberg, Robert C., Byung-Do Kim, and Scott A. Neslin (2008) *Database Marketing: Analyzing and Managing Customers.* New York: Springer.

Damodaran, Aswath, "Damodaran Online," Department of Finance at New York University Stern School of Business, http://pages.stern.nyu.edu/~adamodar/.

Dolan, Robert J. (1990) "Conjoint Analysis: A Manager's Guide," Harvard Business School Note 590059.

Goodwin, Paul, Sheik Meeran, and Karima Dyussekeneva (2014) "The Challenges of Pre-launch Forecasting of Adoption Time Series for New Durable Products," *International Journal of Forecasting* 30 (4), 1082–97.

Gupta, Sunil, Donald Lehmann, and Jennifer Ames Stuart (2004) "Valuing Customers," *Journal of Marketing Research* 41 (91), 7–18.

Jacobs, Michael T., and Anil Shivdasani (2012) "Do You Know Your Cost of Capital?," *Harvard Business Review*, July–August, https://hbr.org/2012/07/do-you-know-your-cost-of-capital (link for calculating the weighted average cost of capital: http://forio.com/simulate/hbr/cost-of-capital/simulation/).

Jamieson, Linda F., and Frank M. Bass (1989) "Adjusting Stated Intention Measures to Predict Trial Purchase of New Products: A Comparison of Models and Methods," *Journal of Marketing Research* 26, 336–45.

Kim, Taegu, Jungsik Hong, and Hoonyoung Koo (2013) "Forecasting Diffusion of Innovative Technology at Pre-launch: A Survey-Based Method," *Industrial Management & Data Systems* 113 (6), 800–816.

Lee, Jongsu, Chul-Yong Lee, and Kichun Sky Lee (2012) "Forecasting Demand for a Newly Introduced Product Using Reservation Price Data and Bayesian Updating," *Technological Forecasting and Social Change* 79 (7), 1280–91.

Lilien, Gary L., and Arvind Rangaswamy (2004) *Marketing Engineering*, 2nd ed. Victoria, BC: Trafford Publishing.

Morwitz, Vicki (2014) "Consumers' Purchase Intentions and Their Behavior," *Foundations & Trends in Marketing* 7 (3), 185–89.

Muller, Eitan, Renana Peres, and Vijay Mahajan (2009) *Innovation Diffusion and New Product Growth*. Cambridge, MA: Marketing Science Institute.

Ofek, Elie, and Olivier Toubia (2014) "Conjoint Analysis: A Do It Yourself Guide," Harvard Business School Note 515024.

Orme, Bryan K. (2010) *Getting Started with Conjoint Analysis: Strategies for Product Design and Pricing Research,* 2nd ed. Madison, WI: Research Publishers.

Putsis, William P., Jr. (1996) "Temporal Aggregation in Diffusion Models of First-Time Purchase: Does Choice of Frequency Matter?," *Technological Forecasting and Social Change* 51 (3), 265–79.

Thomas, Robert J. (1985) "Estimating Market Growth for New Products: An Analogical Diffusion Model Approach," *Journal of Product Innovation Management* 2, 45–55.

Acknowledgments

Completing the *Innovation Equity* journey would not have been possible without the generous assistance and unrelenting support of numerous individuals. They include our many amazing coauthors who were kind enough to work with us on the academic papers and case studies that form the backbone for this book; colleagues who were unselfish with their time in discussing various aspects of innovation, marketing, and customer management at conferences and seminars and over countless lunches; research assistants who tirelessly toiled on various analyses; doctoral students who asked tough questions that allowed us to constantly evolve and refine our thinking; and managers and MBA students to whom we presented our ideas and who challenged us to better tie our work to business reality.

While we cannot mention all of these individuals here by name, we do want to thank a few people in particular whose inspiration and wisdom have undoubtedly shaped our view of what innovation equity is and how best to communicate it: Gil Appel, David Godes, Jacob Goldenberg, Michael Haenlein, Renana Peres, Ron Shachar, Vijay Mahajan, and Peter Wickersham.

We would further like to acknowledge Danielle Levy and Miriam Erez, whose research assistance and suggestions on early drafts of the book is greatly appreciated, and to express our sincere gratitude to the folks at the University of Chicago Press: David Pervin (a former editor who believed in the potential of the book early on), Joe Jackson (who continued to strongly believe in it), and Jillian Tsui and Jenni Fry (who helped move things along at the final stages of publication).

Lastly, warm and very special thanks go out to our families: Michal Pe'er, Danna, and Talia Ofek; Yonah, Yavin, Itai, and Assaf Muller; and Hila, Ya'ara, and Omer Libai. They accompanied us throughout this incredible experience, from start to finish, during ups and downs, offering their unwavering encouragement and heartfelt advice.

Index